## Wards of Lower Manhattan, 1863

# THE ARMIES OF THE STREETS

# THE
# ARMIES
# OF THE
# STREETS

*The New York City Draft Riots of 1863*

ADRIAN COOK

THE UNIVERSITY PRESS OF KENTUCKY

ISBN: 0–8131–1298–2

Library of Congress Catalog Card Number: 73–80463

Copyright © 1974 by The University Press of Kentucky

A statewide cooperative scholarly publishing agency serving Berea College, Centre College of Kentucky, Eastern Kentucky University, Georgetown College, Kentucky Historical Society, Kentucky State University, Morehead State University, Murray State University, Northern Kentucky State College, Transylvania University, University of Kentucky, University of Louisville, and Western Kentucky University.

*Editorial and Sales Offices:* Lexington, Kentucky 40506

88274

*To My Mother*

# Contents

# *Acknowledgments*

Since much of this book reads like a blood-and-thunder penny dreadful, academic readers may be reassured to find evidence of scholarly sobriety in the appendixes. I hope, however, that the material in the latter part of the book will find a more practical use. The great objection to using police and court records in building up a statistical profile of a mob is, of course, that in most disorders one cannot be certain whether or not the authorities were obliging enough to arrest a representative sample of rioters. This objection applies less to the Draft Riots records than to those of any other civil disturbance known to me. Very few people were detained until the very end of the Draft Riots, and there was usually solid and convincing evidence against those arrested afterwards. Consequently, the list supplied here consists of people who really were hard-core rioters, not just those who were unusually foolhardy or slow in running away. I hope that anyone concerned with the study of riots, political scientists and sociologists as well as historians, will find the appendixes useful.

Researching this topic was not an easy matter, and I would like to express my sincere gratitude to all the many people who helped me. Above all, I would like to thank Professor Leo Hershkowitz of Queens College, who generously shared his unrivaled knowledge of the New York City archives with me. Without his aid, it would have been impossible to write this book. I am also especially indebted to Professor Willie Lee Rose, Professor John William

Ward, Professor H. C. Allen, Professor Ibby Nathans, Professor James P. Shenton, Mr. Arthur Breton and Mr. Tom Dunnings of the New York Historical Society, and to the staff of the Old Military Records Division at the National Archives.

Two fellowships from the American Council of Learned Societies made it possible for me to do the research, and Mr. Richard W. Downar, director of the A.C.L.S. American Studies Program, and his assistant Miss Ruth Craven, smoothed my path. Another generous fellowship from the Institute for Research in the Humanities, University of Wisconsin, Madison, enabled me to tackle the writing without financial worries. Professor E. David Cronon, the director of the Institute, his two charming and able secretaries, and the other Fellows provided an ideal environment in which to work, and the long-suffering staff at the University of Wisconsin and State Historical Society of Wisconsin libraries always dealt efficiently with my importunate demands. To all, my thanks.

Finally, I should also express my sense of gratitude to the professor under whom I received the bulk of my graduate training some years ago, David Herbert Donald, then of Johns Hopkins University.

# *Proem*

*When the Civil War began, loss of the lucrative southern trade caused massive unemployment in the industrial cities of the North. The unemployed began to organize vast demonstrations, which turned into riots. The police and the militia put down the initial troubles with heavy loss of life, but the situation grew worse. With the northern forces suffering military defeat and the northern government floundering in financial difficulties, the number of unemployed rose and the price of food spiraled. The city of New York broke into open rebellion. Thousands of rioters raided the gun stores and plundered the liquor shops. The police were helpless, and the militia could do no more than protect themselves. Four thousand federal troops were sent in to confront 30,000 rioters. A thousand of the regulars were veterans, and they fought well, but were overwhelmed by superior numbers. Most of them were killed, fighting to the last. The rest of the troops were recent recruits, many from New York itself, and they had no stomach for the fight. First singly, then in twos and threes, and finally in whole units, they deserted and joined the rioters.*

*As night fell on that day of disorder, all opposition ceased. Banks were broken open and their vaults robbed. Churches were looted. The avenues were filled with terrified refugees, struggling to escape the mob. Hundreds of dollars were offered for any kind of conveyance out of danger. Drunk and gorged with plunder, the mob set the city on fire. A high wind whipped the flames into a hurricane of fire, and when morning came New York was a blackened, charred ruin. Riots in other towns forced the northern government to give up the idea of conquering the South and ask for a truce.*

Or so the Virginia fire-eater Edmund Ruffin predicted in his *Anticipations of the Future to Serve as Lessons for the Present Time*, written in 1860 to urge the South to seize independence. For a few bloody summer days in 1863, when New York City was gripped by the Draft Riots, it seemed as though Ruffin might be a true prophet.

# THE CITY
# IN 1863

*What apparent cause of any riots may be,
the real one is want of happiness.*

—TOM PAINE

# 1

## *Packed and Pestilential Town*

COMING THROUGH the Narrows at dawn, the traveler on a vessel bound for New York saw a view of astounding beauty and grandeur. On both sides of the channel, white mansions stood among green trees and lawns. In the distance, the city rose against the bay and the sky, the spires of the churches and the masts of anchored ships standing out in the clear light of early morning.[1]

Once ashore, the traveler found little beauty in a city racked by the problems of explosive growth. Between 1820 and 1860, the population had increased sevenfold, from 123,706 to 813,662. Stimulated by the Erie Canal, the railroads west, and cheap transportation across the Atlantic by packet and steamship, the orderly Knickerbocker port that Hamilton and Livingston had known became "a huge semi-barbarous metropolis, one-half as luxurious and artistic as Paris, and the other half as savage as Cairo or Constantinople." After 1820, more than 70 percent of all immigrants who came to America landed at New York, and many remained to seek homes and jobs in the city. By 1860 New York had 383,717 citizens of foreign birth, including 203,740 Irish and 119,984 Germans.[2]

As the population and commerce of the city grew, the tide of construction raced up Manhattan Island. When City Hall was built in 1812, the front and sides were faced with marble, but the brownstone rear was left unadorned, since everyone assumed that it would be decades before there was any building to the north of

Chambers Street. But by 1860 the city was built up to Forty-second Street, and here and there a few isolated rows of houses dotted the vacant lots to the north. The upper and middle classes were in the vanguard of the movement out of the older parts of town. In the 1850s, the phrase "above Bleecker" was a synonym for wealth and elegance, and in 1858 the fashionable Brick Church moved from Beekman Street in the Second Ward to the corner of Fifth Avenue and Thirty-seventh Street, "on the top of Murray Hill, in the most aristocratic quarter of the city." The great houses of the wealthy businessmen and bankers lined Fifth Avenue down as far as Fourteenth Street. Stuyvesant Square, Gramercy Park, and Madison Square were only slightly less desirable neighborhoods. Some of the well-to-do still lived in Greenwich Village, especially on Washington Square, where Commodore Vanderbilt had a town house, and some blocks of the principal crosstown streets—Fourteenth, Twenty-third, and Thirty-fourth—were the home of the prosperous and successful.[3]

As the wealthy moved uptown, the stores, hotels, and restaurants that catered to them followed. In the late 1840s and early 1850s, the center of retail trade moved from its first location, around Broadway and Pearl Street, up to the streets where Broadway met City Hall Park. A second center developed on the East Side, on Cherry and Catherine streets, catering to the affluent and respectable inhabitants of the Seventh Ward and of downtown Brooklyn, who could cross the East River by the Catherine ferry. But by 1860 the stores were moving again. In August 1859 Lord and Taylor abandoned Catherine Street and opened an imposing marble building on the corner of Grand and Chrystie streets. Nearby was Edward H. Ridley and Sons, a large establishment noted for its notions and millinery. Arnold and Constable had a store on Canal Street, just west of Broadway, and in April 1862 Lorenzo Delmonico moved his famous restaurant to Fifth Avenue and Fourteenth Street. The city's largest dry-goods merchant, A. T. Stewart, moved his retail store up Broadway from the corner of Chambers Street to the corner of Tenth Street in 1862, and many others followed his lead.[4]

Slaughterhouses, breweries, warehouses, lumberyards, sawmills, and limekilns clustered along the waterfront in the newer West

Side wards, but most of New York's burgeoning industry and commerce was concentrated in the lower part of the city.[5] For the most part, it was true that

> From Eighth Street down, the men are earning it,
> From Eighth Street up, the women are spending it.
> That is the manner of this great town,
> From Eighth Street up and Eighth Street down[6]

Wholesale provision merchants were located on Broad, Water, and Front streets, and the tobacco market was also on Water Street. The Cotton Exchange was on Pearl Street, jewelers and watchmakers were found on Maiden Lane, and the leather merchants carried on their trade in the area known as "the Swamp," bounded by Frankfort, William, Beekman, and Cliff streets. The city's shipyards were strung out along a mile of the East River waterfront from Thirteenth Street, around the bulge of Lower Manhattan to just below Corlear's Hook, and the foundries, machine shops, and ironworks that supplied the yards were bunched around them. Further down the East Side was "the great workshop of the city," the Second Ward, which contained 19 percent of all the factories in New York and produced 18 percent of the value of all manufactured goods.[7]

Because most of the city's industry was collected in the lower wards, most of the population also crowded into the same area. In 1860, 58 percent of the city's population, 468,549 people, were crammed into the fifteen downtown wards, which covered less than 9 percent of Manhattan Island. Four small wards on the East Side, the Sixth, Eleventh, Thirteenth, and Fourteenth, had 147,264 people. There were several reasons why so many of the city's poor people chose to live near the industrial areas. The casual day laborer and the immigrant found more opportunities to obtain work there; housewives could take in work at home to supplement their husbands' wages; workers who lived near their jobs could save money on carfare. Despite all the advantages of living in the central city, by mid-century conditions there were so bad that the better-paid, skilled workers were moving out. The population of the upper wards rose from 113,344 to 337,109 between 1850 and 1860. But there, the safety valve jammed. The movement north could not go on; in 1870 the number of people who lived south of Fourteenth Street had risen to 497,294–28,745 more than had lived there in 1860.[8]

The inadequacies of New York's transportation system and the physical configuration of Manhattan halted the city's expansion. North of Fiftieth Street, the island was a real estate developer's nightmare, an area of jagged rock outcrops and ravines, crags and hollows that would be impossibly expensive to grade, level, and fill for streets and buildings. Until the 1870s, when the steam shovel made it possible to level the rocky terrain at a reasonable cost, and when the creation of Central Park and Riverside Drive made the area attractive, it remained a semi-wilderness.[9] The flatlands of Harlem and the villages of southern Westchester County offered more promising opportunities for suburban development, but the deplorable transportation facilities of the 1860s discouraged all but a few from moving there.

Omnibuses, called "stages," served only the built-up areas, and only two of the streetcar lines ventured very far up the island: the Third Avenue line, which ran as far as Harlem Bridge at 130th Street, and the Eighth Avenue cars, which ended at 125th Street. Drawn by horses, they were both excruciatingly slow, taking over two hours to cover the eight miles of their route. The cars were filthy; the matting on the floor was used as a spittoon; and there was no ventilation. People might be carrying anything from dirty washing to sole leather. In this fetid, mephitic atmosphere, the passengers were packed like herrings in a barrel. The cars had seats for twenty-four people and enough standing room for six or eight more, but they often carried fifty, and some conductors boasted of squeezing seventy passengers into these "hog-pens on wheels."[10]

The railroads to Morrisania, Fordham, Yonkers, and the other villages of southern Westchester were faster than the cars: a railroad traveler could reach Ossining in the time a streetcar rider took to go from City Hall to 100th Street. The conditions of travel were better, too: after Commodore Vanderbilt took over the New York and Harlem Railroad in the late 1850s, accidents were fewer, the roadbed and rolling stock were improved, and the "rotten cars and wheezy old engines that could not make schedule time" disappeared.[11]

But neither Vanderbilt nor the managements of the other two commuter railroads, the New Haven and the Hudson River, realized the vast possibilities of speculative building in Westchester and Fairfield counties. Any railroad corporation offering a combination of middle-class housing and cheap commutation fares to the city might well have multiplied even Vanderbilt's fortune. As it was, the fares and infrequency of service did not encourage people to live in the suburbs.[12]

Those who did travel daily to the city could reach the upper wards quickly enough, but getting downtown was another matter. As the city grew, it became intolerably dangerous and inconvenient to have locomotives running through the streets. In 1844 the Common Council banned steam engines from below Thirty-second Street. Ten years later, the council ordered that they should not go below Forty-second Street, but this law was not enforced until 1858. When the trains reached the limit set by the council, the locomotives were taken off, horses were hitched up to the passenger cars, and they were drawn through the streets to the depots, encountering all the traffic and delays that made the streetcars and the stages so slow.[13]

The technology of the early 1860s was not equal to bridging the Hudson or the East rivers, and ferries provided the only access to the suburban areas nearest New York's business districts. The Staten Island ferry cost too much—the fare was 12½ cents—and took too long for most people. The Jersey Shore was much nearer, but it was difficult to travel from the marshy, low-lying coastal areas up into the pleasant highlands. Brooklyn, in contrast, was nearby, the ferries took only ten minutes to cross the East River, the fare was only two cents, and it was easy to get from the downtown section to the residential areas. Half an hour after leaving Manhattan, a traveler could be two miles from the ferry landings. Such advantages made Brooklyn "the City of Homes" for thousands of New Yorkers.[14]

Travel to Brooklyn was not without its tribulations. The ferries were pleasant enough in summer, but in winter they were frequently delayed by fog and freezing weather. Forcing its way through sheets and floes of ice, a boat might take hours to make the short trip across the East River. In their haste to complete the crossing and pick up more passengers, the crews took dangerous risks that sometimes ended tragically. In November 1858 a man was killed and a woman critically injured when the ferry *Niagara*, racing to beat the *Nebraska* into Peck Slip, collided with a merchant ship. In February 1863 the *Nebraska* collided in the fog with another ferry, the *Seneca*, and catastrophe was barely averted as the rapidly sinking ship was towed to shore just in time to save the passengers from being thrown into the icy river.[15] The ferries were more crowded every year, and by the early 1860s it was plain that they were approaching their full capacity. In May 1863 Mayor George Opdyke of New York condemned a proposal to charter another Brooklyn ferry, pointing out that allowing more boats to ply the East River would create a grave danger of collision and that new ferries would only take up dock space badly needed for ships in the overseas trade.[16]

The obvious answer to New York's transportation problem was some kind of rapid-transit system, and during the 1850s proposals were offered for both elevated and underground railroads.[17] Both were open to serious objections. An elevated system would block highways, turn streets into dark and dismal passages, and fill the air with noise, steam, and sparks. On the other hand, passengers emerged half-asphyxiated and covered in soot from the airless tunnels of the world's first subway, the London Metropolitan Railway, which was opened in January 1863. Only three miles long, it had taken ten years to build at a cost of $1,670,000 a mile;[18] the difficulties and expense would obviously be compounded when digging through Manhattan rock, instead of London clay. The debate dragged on, complicated by opposition from the streetcar and stage owners and by political meddling, and it was not until the early 1870s that the decision was taken to adopt Charles T. Harvey's elevated railroad as New York's system of rapid transit.[19]

Until then, the city remained fearfully congested. Better transportation would not, of course, have helped the average Irish or German laborer, who had no skills to sell and who lived constantly on the edge of penury, earning perhaps a dollar a day when he was employed. Such a workingman could not afford five or ten cents for carfare; he had to stay within walking distance of his job. But the skilled artisans, or the middle classes, would have welcomed cheap rapid-transit facilities out of the city, and their departure would have eased New York's chronic shortage of decent housing.

The immigrants who swarmed into the city found it impossible to rent adequate living quarters. Instead, they were packed into slums that rivaled the rookeries of London in squalor and filth. Speculators bought up the old Knickerbocker mansions and merchants' town houses and divided the drawing rooms and halls into tiny compartments. Commercial buildings, too, were partitioned into hundreds of small cubicles to create "human beehives" like the infamous Old Brewery in the Sixth Ward or the Old Match Factory at the corner of Forsyth and Stanton streets, where a hundred families lived. Shacks were set in garden plots and backyards, and cellars were converted into apartments.[20]

Finally, there were the real tenements, huge barracks built specifically to house large numbers of people in the smallest possible space. On a lot twenty-five feet by one hundred, two buildings were put up, one in the front, the other in the rear. Between the two houses there was an open space, filled by rows of stalls which were used as lavatories. The houses were usually seven or eight stories high; through the middle of each ran a hall three or four feet wide. On each side of the hall were the dark hutches optimistically termed "suites of apartments." These consisted of two rooms. One, eight feet by ten and seven feet high, was the common room, where all the cooking and washing was done. Quite often, it was used as a workroom, too, if the tenant was a tailor or a shoemaker who ran his own business or took in work. The other room, seven feet by eight, was used for sleeping. There were six or eight suites of apartments on every floor of the building, and it was by no means unusual for a family to take in lodgers or for two, three, or even four families to occupy the same apartment.[21]

In 1856 a select committee of the New York State Assembly was appointed to investigate the tenement house problem in the city, and they made a tour of inspection, trying to see all kinds of tenements, from the best to the worst. At 16 Washington Street, a decrepit old three-story place, the ground floor was used as a stable. The building was on its last legs; the rickety floors trembled under the tread, and the mortar had vanished from some of the walls, leaving only smoke-blackened lathing, through which moisture was constantly oozing. The roof leaked so much that the top floor was flooded every time it rained. Behind this building was another three-story house, nearly as dilapidated as the first. Altogether, seventy people lived in the two houses, paying from two to six dollars a month in the front, and from six to eight dollars in the rear. In one of the front rooms, measuring six feet by ten, a widow lived with her five children. The landlord said he leased the two buildings from the owner, an Irishwoman who lived nearby in Pearl Street, for $1,456 a year, including taxes.

Further down Washington Street, at Number 97, there was another decrepit three-story building. The cellar, two upper floors, and garret were divided into rooms; the first floor was used as a sailors' lodging house and was fitted up with bunks. Under the leaking roof, in a space so low that they could not stand up, three families lived. One of them, a woman and her child, paid three dollars a month for their part of the garret. She had been forced to sell her bed to pay the rent and then slept on the floor.

In Mulberry Street, the committee inspected a huge wooden barracks converted from an old Baptist church. The eighty-five apartments housed 310 people. In the damp, chill cellar rooms, five feet two inches below street level, the rent was $3.00 a month. Apartments on the fifth floor, divided from each other by pine boards, cost $4.50 a month.

The black mud in the entrance to 17 Baxter Street was two inches deep, and the locality was the worst slum in the city, the infamous Five Points, once described by the well-known journalist George G. Foster as "the great central ulcer of wretchedness—the very rotting skeleton of civilization."[22] The basement of the house was a barroom and dance hall, with a couple of beds for lodgers. They paid from sixpence to a shilling[23] for a night and slept three to a bed, men and women together indiscriminately. On the upper floors, seventy-five people lived in twelve dark, dank, ill-ventilated apartments, for which they paid four dollars a month. In the rear was a collection of wooden hovels, each containing four dismal rooms rented at three dollars a month. The inhabitants made a living by growing spearmint on the roofs and selling it to hotels and bars, which, as the committee remarked, might taint a fashionable cocktail with the malaria and filth of the Five Points.

Also in the Five Points was the pesthole known as Cow Bay, where the committee toured a four-story brick house in Mission Place. In one room, measuring ten feet by twelve, there were six people: two Irishmen, two women, a young boy, and a Negro, all dressed in tattered clothes and filthy. Three other people, they said, also lived there. The furniture comprised one bed, one chair, and an old table. A few coals in a furnace warmed the room. The rooms in the back of the house opened directly on to a blank wall, so no light ever penetrated them. There was no ventilation; the floors were covered with dirt and dust inches thick, and a dank green slime covered the walls. The rent was six shillings a week for the front rooms and five for the back. The committee's guide, the superintendent of sanitary inspection, offered to show the members through other tenements as bad as the one they had just seen, but said there were none worse. The legislators, however, replied they had seen enough and beat a hasty retreat.

Among the buildings specifically designed as tenement houses that were inspected by the committee was a four-story structure at 6-7 Hester Street, where the apartments cost from $5.00 to $6.50 a month. "It was evident," the committee reported, "that no thoughts of providing comfort, or preserving health, had entered in the plan of construction; and it was quite as apparent that, in the business of letting, no rule was followed but to secure the occupancy of every part of the building. The place literally swarmed with human life, but life of so abject and squalid a character as to scarcely merit the name." Sluttish women, filthy, half-naked children, and roughs with black eyes and scarred faces made up the population. There was no ventilation, hardly any drainage, and a nauseating odor filled the air.

A much better building was 88 and 90 Willet Street: built of brick, six stories high, well-lit and well-ventilated, with gas and water piped into every apartment. The rooms were larger than usual, and every story had a balcony where the children could play and washing could be hung. The apartments rented for four, six, or nine dollars a month. Twenty-six families numbering 123 people lived here.[24] Few tenants were so lucky.

Even the best tenements stood in filthy, reeking slum neighborhoods. In the late summer of 1863 the parents of Samuel Gompers, just arrived from England, went to live in a tenement on the corner of Houston and Attorney streets in the Eleventh Ward. Across the street was one of the area's many slaughterhouses. The cries of the animals and the stench of death filled the air so that the boy could not eat meat for months, even after his family moved away from this area, which was known as the "Place of Blood."[25] More than two and a half million animals a year were killed in New York's 176 slaughterhouses, which were mostly in tenement districts. Many of them had poor connections with the sewers or discharged waste into sewers running against the grade, which were constantly getting clogged up and overflowing. The blood and putrefying offal filled the gutters, and it was common to see children daubing their faces with blood or sailing paper boats on pools of gore.

The various places making use of the slaughterhouse by-products were just as bad in blighting neighborhoods. Dozens of barrels of putrid offal, waiting to be cleaned and used as sausage skins, stood outside butchers' shops. Hide houses kept malodorous green hides hanging for days, and fat and bone-boiling yards filled the air with rank and sickening smells. Equally offensive were the stables of the city. Loads of stable manure were collected together on vacant lots and left to molder into compost.

On the East Side, the neighborhood around the great gashouse on Fourteenth Street was a pesthole. Every day, chimneys belched ammoniacal gas, sulfureted and carbureted hydrogen into the atmosphere. On East Third Street and Sheriff Street were a couple of infamous rookeries called "Cottage Row" and "Rag Pickers' Paradise," inhabited by German chiffoniers. Their yards, doors, and passageways were filled with long washing lines of drying rags and baskets of bones which made the area all around a stinking plague spot.[26]

For the landlord, a tenement house was an immensely profitable venture. Calculated by the square foot, the poor paid more for living space in their sordid rookeries than millionaires spent for an equal amount of room on Fifth Avenue. Rooms in the most squalid hovels cost just as much as the apartments in a few model tenements built by philanthropists.[27] Owners could spend nothing on the maintenance of their buildings, make no repairs at all, and yet, so great was the housing shortage, they could still be sure of full occupancy. Money invested in tenements showed an annual return of between 25 and 100 percent. Middle-class housing, in contrast, yielded only 10 to 25 percent interest, and residences for the wealthy only 5 to 10 percent.[28]

Despite their poverty, the inhabitants of the tenements were scrupulous about paying their rent on time. A witness told the Select Committee that "the poor must and do pay the rent. It is the first thing they think of and many, as I have myself witnessed, deny themselves the necessaries of life, that their scanty earnings may suffice to keep a roof above their heads, and this, because they know they are liable, at any moment, to be turned into the street, perhaps, with the loss of their scanty effects. The poor dare not be otherwise than punctual with the rent, even though their children go unshod through the snows, their hearths be destitute of fuel and their clothes be ticketed to the pawnbroker. The rent, sir, must be, and in nine cases out of ten, is met."[29] Landlords were allowed to seize most of a tenant's property and sell it to make up his arrears of rent, and some tenement owners maintained blacklists of evicted tenants, who consequently found it difficult to rent new quarters.[30]

Those too poor to pay the rent of a tenement room might sleep in the cellar lodging houses of the Five Points and the waterfront. These dark, damp, rat-infested breeding grounds for malaria and cholera sold sleeping places for five to ten cents a night to a clientele described in a police report as "drunken wretches, male and female beggars, rag-pickers of the poorest sort, sneak thieves, juvenile pimps [and] ragged and drunken prostitutes."[31]

Alternatively, some of the poor moved out to the fringe of the city and settled on the rocky highlands in the middle of Manhattan Island. Here they lived as squatters, paying no rent or taxes, dwelling in a picturesque squalor that closely resembled the Irish small holdings they had left. The *Journal of Commerce* estimated that there were as many as 20,000 of these squatters living in shanties that perched precariously on the edge of crags or huddled in the scrubby hollows of the desolate wasteland, on whose edge the partially built walls of the new Saint Patrick's Cathedral stood, covered in vines and surrounded by weeds, like a symbol of the half-finished state of the area.[32] Around the shanties, made of turf and wood scavenged from packing cases, with a battered stovepipe or a bit of old drain for a chimney, pigs, dogs, fowls, geese, goats, and children wandered through the manure, muck, and garbage. Some of these squatters worked as laborers, but most eked out a living as ragpickers.[33] Charles Loring Brace, a leading figure in New York's charities, remembered one Irishwoman who lived in a shanty village called Dutch Hill, on the rocks above First Avenue, between Thirty-ninth and Fortieth streets. "All the odds and ends of a great city seemed piled up in her home," he wrote, "bones, broken dishes, rags, bits of furniture, cinders, old tin, useless lamps, decaying vegetables, ribbons, cloths, legless chairs and carrion, all mixed together and heaped up nearly to the ceiling, leaving hardly room for a bed on the floor where the woman and her two children slept."

All the squatters suffered terribly from rheumatism, and in the winter they might awake to find their bedclothes covered with snow.[34] Even so, they were probably healthier than the tenement dwellers. Despite its healthy situation, built on rock and washed by the Hudson River and the sea, New York in the 1860s had the highest death rate of any city in the civilized world. In London, the number of deaths yearly was 1 to every 45 of its population, in Liverpool, 1 to 44. The figure in Boston was 1 to 41, and in Philadelphia, 1 to 50. In 1863 in New York 25,196 people died, a death rate of 1 to 35. Contemporary physicians estimated that two-thirds of these mortalities could have been avoided by better sanitation.

The wards containing the greatest concentration of tenement houses had the highest death rates, while Murray Hill's mortality figures compared favorably with those of country towns. The Fifteenth Ward, Greenwich Village, had hardly any tenements, and its death rate was 1 to 60. The figures for the Fourth and Sixth wards, in contrast, were 1 to 25 and 1 to 24. Some tenements in those wards had death rates as high as 1 to 19.

Disease roared through the congested tenement districts of New York, which had a greater density of population than anywhere outside Asia. In the East End of London, the rate of population in the 1860s touched 175,816 inhabitants per square mile. In 1864 people were jammed into the tenements of New York's Fourth Ward at the rate of 290,000 per square mile.[35] Moreover, things were getting worse. As industry expanded, more and more space was needed for factories and warehouses, and the population of the downtown wards was being pushed into even smaller areas.

The food of the poor was poisonous and tainted. Adulteration was common: sand in the sugar, red lead in the pepper, Prussian blue in the tea, and sawdust and street sweepings in the coffee. Worst of all was the milk, the product of spavined old cows confined in dirty, dark stalls in the back streets of New York, Brooklyn, and Williamsburg. "Broken horns," wrote a reporter who visited one of these stables, "bleared eyes, loose skins, projecting ribs, worn hoofs, running sores, offensive ulcers and rotting tails were there in profusion." These cows were fed on swill, the residue of grain left from the distillation of whiskey. The whitish fluid they yielded, improved in appearance by liberal admixture of starch, plaster of paris, chalk, and magnesia, was sold as "Pure Orange County Milk."[36]

Over large parts of New York, sanitation was nonexistent. At the start of the 1860s, two-thirds of the city was without sewers. Many of the tenements did not even have cesspits. Their privies were emptied at lengthy intervals; in the meantime, they poisoned the water supply, for few of the tenements were supplied with the piped Croton, and the poor had to use well water. In several neighborhoods, like Thompson and Wooster streets in the Eighth Ward, the slops and waste ran through a trough to the gutter or were thrown out of doors or windows into the alleys and entries. "It seemed questionable," wrote a sanitary inspector, after visiting some buildings in the Seventh Ward, "whether the alley was intended as an entrance-way to a rear house, or a sewage-ditch for slops, water, garbage, human excrements, and urine."[37]

Where sewers did exist, they were often inadequate, dilapidated, or badly constructed. The sewer in East Twenty-fourth Street, between Madison and Fourth avenues, had a descending grade of only four inches in seven hundred feet, which was equivalent to stagnation. In many instances, the sewers actually ran uphill. In Madison Avenue, between Thirty-third and Thirty-second streets, the sewer rose against the grade eleven inches in two hundred feet; in Thirty-third Street, it rose against the grade eight inches in two hundred feet; in Thirty-fourth Street, between Fifth and Mad-

ison avenues, it rose two feet in two hundred and fifty. Not surprisingly, the sewers were often choked with filth. One of the main
drains, the Canal Street sewer, was so poorly designed that high
tides flooded it and made the privies and cesspools connected with
it overflow. None of the sewage was treated; it was simply poured
raw into the North and East rivers, surrounding lower Manhattan
with a belt of pollution. The tides could not carry all the waste
away, and deposits of excrement built up around the docks and
piers of the waterfront.[38]

Besides the seepage from privies, the streets of the city were foul
with horse dung and garbage. Dead cats and dead dogs, cabbage
leaves and rotten potatoes, oyster shells, broken bottles, old boots
and shoes, bits of smashed crockery–every kind of trash was
thrown into the streets and left to rot. Some houses had ash-boxes
in front of them, but collection was so slow and unreliable they
were usually full to overflowing. In June 1863 the *Commercial
Advertiser* complained that ash-boxes in the lower wards had not
been emptied for ten days. The stench from them, it added, "is
strongly suggestive of an epidemic." The contractors to whom the
city authorities delegated the task of keeping New York clean
habitually collected their money and did no more about it. The
city streets were choked with snow and slush in the winter, filled
with dust and dirt in the summer, and turned into muddy quag-
mires whenever it rained. Nearly 50,000 cartloads of dirt were
removed from the streets during one of the intermittent campaigns
to clean up the city. When a new machine for street cleaning was
demonstrated in April 1857, the filth in Mulberry Street was found
to be three feet deep. Some streets had not been swept since the
September before.[39]

To add to the other horrors of life in the slums, many of the
tenements were firetraps. Built four, five, and six stories high, they
had only one staircase, running directly from top to bottom of the
building. A fire on the lower floors quickly spread to the staircase,
following the ascending column of heated air, and this left the
people on the upper floors the choice of jumping from the windows
or being burned alive in the building. Fire escapes were unknown
in the tenement districts, although the danger of conflagration was
great. Many tenement dwellers used highly inflammable camphene

to light their apartments and children were often left alone for hours while their mother and father were at work.[40]

All the squalor and disease of the tenement districts was only a stone's throw from the homes of the wealthy. Because New York had fashionable streets and squares, rather than one distinct fashionable area like London's Mayfair, poverty and riches were close neighbors. Mansions and fever nests, town houses and slaughterhouses stood side by side. Even on Murray Hill, the rich were annoyed by goats belonging to the squatters of Dutch Hill, and the prosperous lawyer George Templeton Strong, who lived in Gramercy Park, worried about the danger of typhoid from the tenements on the other side of Third Avenue. Such contrasts of wealth and want, affluence and suffering led one traveler to call New York, Paris with a touch of the backwoods, and another to compare the city to a savage whose resplendent trinkets, war paint, and chromatic blanket only half covered his dirty body.[41]

*It may seem strange that none of our political writers on the English Constitution should take notice of any more than three Estates, namely, Kings, Lords and Commons; all entirely passing by in silence that very large and powerful body which form the fourth estate in this community, and have been long dignified and distinguished by the name of the Mob. . . . There are two sorts of person of whom this fourth estate do yet stand in some awe, and whom consequentially they have in great abhorrence. These are a justice of the peace and a soldier. To these two, it is entirely owing that they have not long since rooted all the other orders out of the Commonwealth.*

—HENRY FIELDING

# 2

## *The Reasons for Riot*

Riot was endemic in the social process of mid-nineteenth-century New York. Between 1834 and 1874 there were sixteen major civil disturbances[1] and innumerable minor disorders. Every summer weekend brought some kind of outburst. On Sunday, June 21, 1835, for example, there was one riot in Grand Street and another in Chatham Street. A third melee broke out in Pearl Street in the evening. "In this city," wrote the *Herald* on May 24, "we have had since the opening of the spring, probably six or seven riots—besides hotel rows and a few personal attacks."[2] On Sunday, July 31, 1864, a brawl in a lager-beer saloon at Tenth Avenue and Twenty-seventh Street turned into a battle with the police, in which one man was killed and six were arrested. On Saturday night, July 10, 1870, gangs of young drunks celebrating payday started three fights in the uptown Nineteenth and Twenty-second wards. Two began in bars when the roisterers ordered drinks and then refused to pay; the third erupted when some toughs attacked a party of Germans. The night's fun left one man dead and two critically injured.[3]

Elections and holidays—the Fourth of July, New Year's, or Saint Patrick's Day—were frequently accompanied by a riot. "Early in the afternoon," reported the *Journal of Commerce* about the elections of 1858, "the fighting spirit broke out in several of the wards —parties having become stimulated by bad rum and the election excitement." Mayor Daniel Tiemann personally led a platoon of police to put down an affray in the Sixth Ward, which "originated among a party of rowdies and was speedily swollen to large proportions by crowds of the 'fancy,' who rushed in from the neighboring streets. Clubs and stones were freely used and several Dead Rabbits mixed in with the 'muss,' armed with guns and pistols, which they fired into the crowd at random." There was a particularly exciting contest in the First Ward between Daniel Sickles and Hiram Walbridge. Late in the afternoon, some Walbridge partisans heard that a number of soldiers were coming over from Governor's Island to vote for Sickles, and they swarmed down to the wharf to stop them from landing. The troops, taking note of the reception committee from the deck of their steamer and being outnumbered and unarmed, concluded that discretion was the better part of valor. They asked the captain to land them somewhere else, and he took them to the Hamilton ferry in Brooklyn. Four of the more determined soldiers decided to take the ferry over to New York and vote. A force of police, again headed by Mayor Tiemann, escorted them as far as Greenwich Street, where the polling place was situated, but there a solid mass of Walbridge supporters blocked the way, in the hope of keeping the soldiers out until the polls closed at sunset, only a few minutes away. The police charged into the crowd repeatedly, but could not break through, and the doors of the polling place were closed amidst the exultant cheers of the victorious Walbridge faction.[4]

Labor disputes often led to violence, especially during the hard times of the 1830s and 1850s. Practically no employer was willing to recognize and bargain with a trade union, and the poorly organized unions often had to use threats and force to make workers join a strike or to frighten off strike-breakers. In February 1836 the stevedores demanded an increase in wages. The employers agreed, but would not guarantee that the increase would be maintained for at least a year, and the men went out on strike. On Tuesday the twenty-third, large groups of stevedores roamed the waterfront, beating men who were still at work and finally attacking laborers who were busy cleaning away the debris of the great fire of 1835, which had destroyed forty blocks of the commercial district. Several ships loaded cannon and prepared to resist boarders. The city watch battled the strikers, and the mayor ordered the National Guard to parade through the streets and make ready for action. These measures restored peace, but a short time later twenty journeymen tailors who had organized a strike were sent to jail for conspiracy, and the watch had to break up violent demonstrations protesting "the hellish appetites of the Aristocracy." Another tailor's strike in the summer of 1850 caused a series of melees, including the mobbing of a priest who was distributing work to the tailors in his parish, and culminating in the storming of a clothing store on August 5. The police intervened, and two strikers were killed.[5]

New York City did not escape the wave of anti-abolitionist riots that swept the North in the early 1830s. In July 1834 a Negro church was burned and the homes of many blacks attacked. New York's leading abolitionist, Lewis Tappan, had his house ransacked and his furniture burned, and two clergymen prominently identified with the movement had their churches and houses attacked.[6]

New York's blacks themselves sometimes rioted. On April 12, 1837, a crowd of Negroes rescued a runaway slave who was claimed by a Baltimore physician, beat his escort, and roughed up the judge who was hearing the case. The slave was recaptured later, but another attempt was made to free him on April 20.[7]

Thanks to the courage of Archbishop John Hughes and to the greater proportion of immigrants in its population, New York City did not suffer as badly from the Know-Nothing fury as Philadelphia or Baltimore. Samuel G. Moses, a lieutenant of the militant Protestant street preacher John S. Orr, the "Angel Gabriel," caused several free fights by his speeches, and one fracas, on June 4, 1854, grew so serious that the militia had to be called out to restore order. In 1854 the Papal Nuncio had to be smuggled out of the city to avoid a threatening mob. But such events were exceptional; Know-Nothing violence in New York usually took the form of clashes between the gangs of toughs that all political parties recruited, such as the famous brawl in the Stanwix Hall saloon in which Lew Baker shot "Butcher Bill" Poole.[8]

There were communal troubles, some caused by the collision of different ethnic groups, some brought about by rivalries transferred from the Old World: Catholic Irish and Orangemen repeatedly clashed. In 1836 Connaught and Ulster men fought over the allocation of jobs clearing the ruins left by the previous year's great fire. In 1842 the bitter political dispute over state aid to parochial schools caused an outbreak of violence in which Orangemen attacked old Saint Patrick's Cathedral and the bishop's house.[9]

In 1870–1871 this ancient hatred led to one of New York's bloodiest riots. On the twelfth of July 1870 the Orange lodges of New York and Brooklyn celebrated the anniversary of the Battle of the Boyne by marching up Eighth Avenue, with bands playing and flags flying, as far as Elm Park at Ninetieth Street, where they planned to hold a grand picnic. A number of Catholics followed the procession, shouting threats and insults. At the park, they enlisted the help of the laborers working on the roads around the area, and about a thousand Catholics stormed the Orangemen's festivities. In half an hour, the police arrived and broke up the mob, but not before three people were killed and seventeen injured.[10]

As the time for the celebration approached the next year, rumors were rife that the Catholics meant to attack the Orangemen's march. Archbishop William McCloskey ordered his clergy to speak out against any such violence, but the reports of Catholics buying guns and preparing for trouble became so alarming that the superintendent of police, James Kelso, and Mayor Oakey Hall banned the Orange demonstration. A howl of protest went up not only from the Orangemen but also from the city's upper and middle classes, who had long nourished a hearty dislike of "Papistical Paddy." The *Times* called the ban "as flagrant an instance of party subservience as has ever been exhibited, even under this corrupt municipal government." Mayor Hall, the press and public charged, was thinking solely of preserving his popularity with the Catholic voters. "Everybody knows," wrote George Templeton Strong, "that if a St. Patrick's Day procession had been threatened with lawless violence and attack, it would have been protected by the whole power of the country." Kelso, said the *Herald*, "has permitted a lawless few to overawe the Police of a great City, and dragged the magnanimity of the Metropolis into the dust." The *Tribune* declared that "the greatest city of the Republic is on its knees to a few thousand disorderly foreigners."[11]

So intense was the public revulsion that Governor John T. Hoffman, who had presidential ambitions, resolved to step in. The Orange procession, he proclaimed, would be allowed after all and would be given the full protection of the city and state authorities. Twelve regiments of the National Guard were called out, the police massed along the route of the march, and the city held its breath, waiting for the expected explosion.

The procession set off down Eighth Avenue from the corner of Twenty-ninth Street at 2:30 P.M. on the twelfth, a brass band playing "The Red, White, and Blue." Surrounded by police and troops were 160 grim Orangemen, the Seventh Regiment leading the way, the Eighty-fourth and the Sixth on the flanks, and the Ninth guarding the rear. The sidewalks were jammed, the windows of houses along the avenue were black with protruding heads, and people were even perched on rooftops.

The procession had not gone half a block before a shot was fired from a window, and bricks and stones began to fly about the heads of the marchers. At Twenty-fifth Street, an old boot and a tin kettle were hurled into the midst of the Orangemen; other missiles followed, and one hit the Orange Grand Marshal. A detachment of police, swinging their nightsticks, rushed the crowd. At Twenty-fourth Street, the rain of paving stones and bricks became a hail; a private of the Eighty-fourth was hit by a bullet, and the infuriated troops, without any orders, leveled their rifles and fired into the densely packed mob. The Sixth and the Ninth took up the shooting and poured more volleys into the panic-stricken crowd. Screams and groans, curses and cries for help filled the air as people scrambled to escape, trampling the fallen under their feet. In a moment, only the dead, dying, and wounded were left, and the firing stopped. The sidewalk was red with blood.

The band had stopped playing at the sound of the shooting, but now it struck up a lively quickstep, and the procession moved off. It was not attacked again. Three soldiers, all members of the Ninth, were killed, and seven others were wounded. One policeman was shot in the face, and another in the arm. Twenty-two police were injured, two seriously, and two Orangemen were hurt. Forty-one of the crowd were killed and fifty-six wounded.[12]

This death toll gave the Orangeman's Day Riots of 1871 the un-

enviable distinction of being one of the three worst disturbances of
New York's riot years. The Draft Riots, of course, were the worst
of all; the other civil disorder with a heavy casualty list was the
Astor Place Riot of 1849. This belonged to a type of disturbance
which occurred repeatedly in New York City: the theater riot
caused by an English actor insulting the United States.

Several times during the 1830s, aggressive American national-
ism was the cause of battered or fearful transatlantic thespians
hastily decamping. In 1831 there were three nights of riots at the
Park Theatre after Joshua R. Anderson was said to have "abused
the Yankees" and "indulged in conversation at the Table of one
of our Hotels in remarks derogatory to the country." [13]

The anti-abolitionist riots of July 1834 began when some of the
mob went to the Bowery Theatre to wreck the benefit of George P.
Farren, who had made himself obnoxious by publicly proclaim-
ing, "Damn the Yankees, they are a damn set of jackasses, and fit
to be gulled." His appearance on stage was greeted by shouts of
"Down with the Englishman! down with the British b————!" [14]

In October, Charles Mathews was accused of staging an anti-
American play in London. On this occasion, trouble was averted.
Mathews publicly denied the charge, expressed his respect and
affection for the Americans, and finally promised to present "A
Trip to America" in New York, so that people could judge for
themselves. He did so, and the play was universally pronounced
innocuous; Philip Hone thought that it was also "excessively
stupid." [15]

Two years later, the tenor Joseph Wood was not so fortunate.
On this occasion, there was no allegation that he had insulted
America or the Americans, but a strong element of anglophobia
was clearly present in the affair. Wood had been asked to sing at
the benefit for one of his divas, Mrs. Conduit (who was also English), and had refused in insulting language. The drama critic of
the *New York Courier and Enquirer*, Dr. Hart, heard of this and
wrote an article attacking Wood for his discourtesy and ingrat-
itude. A night or two later, the powerfully built Wood confronted
Hart in the lobby of the Park Theatre and spat in his face. The
little old man struck Wood, who knocked him down. The pugna-
cious, dueling editor of the *Courier and Enquirer*, James Watson

Webb, immediately declared that Wood should never appear again before an American audience and appealed to the populace to drive him out. The next time the tenor appeared, the mob stormed the stage, and Wood had to flee for his life. Shortly afterwards, he returned to England.[16]

The mob in the Astor Place Riot was acting in a venerable tradition. This particular clash was caused by the rivalry between two celebrated tragedians, the Englishman William C. Macready and the American Edwin Forrest. In 1845 Forrest had become convinced that Macready was using his influence to stop him from obtaining new plays and engagements. He retaliated by leading an Edinburgh audience in hissing Macready's Hamlet, and from then on the two were at daggers drawn. Macready, making an American tour in 1848–1849, was harassed by Forrest's admirers in Philadelphia, and on May 7, 1849, a performance of *Macbeth* in New York had to be abandoned partway through, due to a constant barrage of rotten eggs, vegetables, coins, old shoes, and chairs, accompanied by groans, hisses, and shouts: "Three groans for the English bulldog!" "Huzza for native talent!" Further downtown, Forrest was also playing Macbeth, and the entire house rose, cheering, at the lines: "What rhubarb, senna, or what purgative drug/ Would scour these English hence?"

Macready was ready to give in and actually booked passage for home. Not until he received a letter signed by forty-seven of New York's leading citizens, including Washington Irving and Herman Melville, assuring him "that the good sense and respect for order prevailing in this community will sustain you" did Macready agree to stay and give another performance, on Thursday the tenth.

Early in the morning of that day, handbills were posted throughout the city:

WORKINGMEN

SHALL

AMERICANS OR ENGLISH RULE

IN THIS CITY?

The crew of the English steamer has threatened all Americans who shall dare to express their opinion this night at the English Aristocratic Opera House!! We advocate no violence, but a free expression of opinion to all public men!

WORKINGMEN! FREEMEN!!
STAND BY YOUR
LAWFUL RIGHTS

American Committee

Mayor Caleb Woodhull called out the Seventh Regiment and some troops of horse and light artillery, and the chief of police, George W. Matsell, stationed 325 men in the Astor Place Opera House and the streets around. The house was full, and an enormous crowd gathered outside. As soon as Macready came on, the audience erupted in boos, groans, and hisses, and though the play proceeded, not a word could be heard. Outside, the crowd grew restive. They began to hurl stones at the building and then tried to break in. The police were forced to retreat inside the theater and called for the military.

With some difficulty, the soldiers cleared the street to the north of the theater (East Eighth Street), but they could make no headway against the mob in Astor Place itself. Under a rain of paving stones, they were forced back against the theater doors, and their commander told the sheriff and the recorder he must have permission to fire. Both the officials addressed the mob, warning them to disperse or be shot, but the tumult was so great that very few heard them, and no one moved. The sheriff then authorized the troops to fire, but ordered them to aim their first volley over the rioters' heads. At the sound of gunfire the mob surged back, but someone shrieked that the troops were firing blanks, and the rioters "commenced wresting the muskets from the soldiers' hands, and pelting stones as large as your double fist like a shower of hail." The soldiers fired again, directly into the mob this time, and marched across Astor Place, firing volleys and driving the rioters before them.

Macready was taken to a friend's house. At four o'clock that morning, he was driven in a carriage to New Rochelle, where he took the early morning train for Boston. From there, he sailed for England. A mass meeting to protest the action of the soldiers sparked another mob on the night of the eleventh, but troops and police were out in force and had little trouble dispersing the crowd. In all, thirty-one people were killed in the battle of Astor Place; twenty-two lost their lives on the tenth, and nine more died of their wounds; forty-eight civilians and from fifty to seventy police and soldiers were hurt.[17]

Many reasons can be adduced to explain why mid-nineteenth-century New York City was so racked by riots. Some of the disturbances of the 1830s proceeded from an older European tradition of civil disorder, in which the mob was in a symbiotic relationship with the authorities. Rioters acted as a loyal opposition in a society that had not yet developed institutions of political opposition and battled the king's evil councillors or unscrupulous merchants or landowners who were trying to oppress the poor. The Flour Riots of 1837, caused by unemployed and starving workmen attacking the warehouses of flour dealers whom they believed to be charging exorbitant prices, closely resembled the "natural justice" riots so common in Europe in earlier centuries.[18]

In a society so open and uncontrolled by any traditional restraints as mid-nineteenth-century America, it was natural for people to take the law into their own hands. This explains incidents such as the 1853 resurrection riot in which 3,000 people sacked an apothecary's shop owned by a surgeon, after a rumor spread that human bones had been found in the cellar; the tearing up of the Harlem Railroad track in Centre Street when the cars ran over a little girl in May 1843; or the trouble caused in 1844 when the authorities tried to banish pigs from the downtown streets.[19]

The new intensity of political conflict that began in the 1830s and continued throughout the years of sectional antagonism naturally led to violence and disorder. "The election for Mayor and charter officers," wrote Philip Hone in April 1834, "commenced this day with a degree of spirit and zeal in both parties never before witnessed." In 1840 he noted, "The greatest excitement prevails. Men's minds are wrought up to a pitch of frenzy, and like tinder a spark of opposition sets them on fire. . . . Riot and violence stalk unchecked through the streets."[20]

Besides this, violence was an everyday thing in mid-nineteenth-century America. As late as the 1840s, the state of New Jersey branded convicted persons on the cheek and gave them public floggings. In 1844 a young girl, convicted of petty theft, received 210 lashes. The state of Delaware held public floggings into the 1870s. In 1842 two prizefighters met at Hastings-on-Hudson and battled for 119 rounds, until one of them dropped dead. Violent crime abounded. The *New York Herald* declared that "a man can only ensure his safety in the best parts of the city by making armories of his pockets."[21]

For most workers, life was drab, conditions hard, and drink the greatest comfort; it is not surprising that the outlet of violence was frequently used. Some of the vignettes of the Report on Tenement Houses give vivid glimpses of conditions in New York's lower depths. The committee saw one room, twelve by twelve, which was home for twenty people of both sexes and all ages, who lived by collecting dung from the streets and selling it at four cents a basket. The only furniture in the room was two beds. Another room was inhabited by a man, a woman, two girls, and a boy; they lived by allowing prostitutes to bring their clients to the room and pocketing part of the proceeds. A third place was warmed only by a tin pail of lighted charcoal placed in the center of the floor. Over this, a blind man huddled, while three or four men and women quarreled and bickered around him. In one corner lay the body of a woman who had died the day before. Her children slept nearby on a pile of rags.[22]

Most of New York's unskilled laborers lived permanently on the edge of destitution. Children of six or eight had to be sent out to work to supplement the family income, by sweeping the crossings, selling apples or hot corn, hawking newspapers and matches, begging, perhaps stealing. "No one," wrote George Templeton Strong, "can walk the length of Broadway without meeting some hideous troop of ragged girls, from twelve years old down, brutalized already almost beyond redemption by premature vice, clad in the filthy refuse of the rag pickers' collections, obscene of speech, the stamp of childhood gone from their faces, hurrying along with harsh laughter and foulness on their lips that some of them have learned by rote, yet too young to understand it; with thief written in their cunning eyes and whore on their depraved faces." Some of these pauper children, especially boys, would cut loose from their families altogether and lead an outcast life, sleeping in alleys and coal-boxes and living from hand to mouth.[23]

No class of New York's wage earners was so exploited and degraded as the 24,000 women workers. In November 1863 girl sewers in the hair cloth industry were paid $2.50 a week. Burnishers got $2.50 or $3.50; umbrella sewers who worked from 6 A.M. to midnight earned $3.00 or $4.00, but the employers deducted the cost of needle and thread from this. A seamstress who worked from 7 A.M. to 9 P.M. received seventeen cents a day. It was impossible to live on such wages, and these women had to turn to prostitution and crime to survive.[24] In such a society, people were soon brutalized. Violence was a release, entertainment, a way of expression, and a form of adaptive behavior.

Riot was an integral part of the activities of the slum gangs and the volunteer fire companies, the native forms of association of the poor. The gangs, based on ethnic, communal, or local groups, were characteristically made up of young men between sixteen and thirty. Most of them were employed, and though many were simply unskilled laborers, it was by no means uncommon to find gang members who were skilled artisans or tradesmen. The gangs were not usually criminal, and they did not, as a rule, use guns or knives, preferring instead to rely on bare knuckles and brute strength. Their main concern was fighting other gangs or the police, and a famous gang might be able to turn out over a thousand members, ready for battle.

The gangs were linked in an unholy trinity with political parties and volunteer fire companies. The Bowery Boys, for example, had Know-Nothing sympathies, while the Dead Rabbits were affiliated with the Democrats of Tammany Hall and the Empire Club. Tom Walsh, the leader of the Dead Rabbits, was foreman of Engine Company Number 21. Many Bowery Boys were members of Hose Company Number 14. William M. Tweed launched into politics after he became foreman of Americus Engine Company Number 6 and made the emblem of "Big Six," the Bengal tiger, his personal trademark.[25]

The journalist Junius H. Browne wrote that a fire in New York caused "much more clamor and excitement than a change of Government in Mexico or the South American Republics. When the alarm was sounded, the town was turned upside down. A wild mob rushed through the streets with the engines, bellowing through their trumpets, hallooing at the top of their voices to the terror and danger of all quiet citizens. A fire . . . was little less than a riot."

The firemen and their runners, boys who hung about the engine houses and followed the companies when they went into action, cared much more about winning a race with another company than putting out the fire. Hose companies whose pumps could not throw a stream high enough to put out a blaze would wait until the building burned down to their level, rather than give way to another company. Dwellings and stores near a fire were often broken open and ransacked, and it was charged that some "fire laddies" would start conflagrations themselves to keep busy when there were no alarms.

Battles between rival companies were regular occurrences. The 1863 minute book of the Fire Commissioners, for example, shows that on February 23, Hook and Ladder Company Number 18 attacked Engine Company Number 26. On March 9 Hose Companies Number 9 and Number 50 slugged it out, and on June 1 Hook and Ladder Company Number 4 took on both Hose Company Number 1 and Hook and Ladder Company Number 3. In the winter of 1864–1865, five policemen were shot while trying to separate skirmishing firemen. One conflict in Broadway left a dozen men wounded. Five companies had to be disbanded, four of them for shooting at each other with pistols. Another beat a member of a rival company into insensibility and kicked his face in, disfiguring him for life. In 1843 Black Joke Engine Company Number 33 fortified their engine house with a howitzer to guard against raids by other companies.[26]

Even the Roman Catholic Church condoned the use of violence. During the Know-Nothing frenzy, Bishop John Hughes declared that "if a single Catholic church was burned in New York, the city would become a second Moscow." In April and May 1844, when the nativists were at the height of their power, Hughes rallied thousands of armed Catholics to guard the churches and published a special edition of his newspaper, the *Freeman's Journal*, warning his parishioners "to keep peace as long as possible, but to defend their property at all costs."[27]

The Irish, New York's largest ethnic group, had a tradition of political violence. Repressive British rule in Ireland caused the Irish peasantry to view government as a hated abstraction. They saw rick-burning, cattle-maiming, and terrorism as the only method of asserting their rights. Between the failure of Daniel O'Connell's attempt to work for change within the British parliamentary system and the rise of Parnell, there was no alternative to violence.[28]

The sabbatarianism so prevalent in mid-nineteenth-century America caused a great deal of the urban disorder. The Protestant clergy effectively stopped all music, dancing, and entertainment on Sundays. There were no parks (Central Park was not completed until after the Civil War) and virtually no public transportation on Sundays. A scheme to run Sunday excursion trains to the country at reduced fares was killed by sabbatarian enthusiasts in 1840, and the New York and Harlem Railroad's decision in 1863 to run thirteen excursion trains every Sunday was bitterly criticized by the Protestant churches and by suburbanites who objected to the invasion of "the rowdies of the Sixth Ward or the Seventeenth." But until then, the only weekend diversions available to working-class New Yorkers were the Elysian Fields, a pleasure garden in Hoboken, and a couple of steamboats running trips on the East River. Not surprisingly, people spent their Sundays drinking at the corner groggeries and getting into brawls.[29]

New York City's authorities had neither the will nor the ability to control this pervasive violence. The city government did not command respect. The division of function and power among city, county, and state governments made it almost impossible to get anything done. And the universal corruption and venality of New York politics encouraged a cynical disrespect for the law.

"A clock without a pendulum, a hive of bees without a queen, a chicken with its head cut off," wrote the *Journal of Commerce*, were appropriate similes for the state of New York's municipal government in the 1860s. The mayor was elected for a one-year term, which gave him just enough time to learn his duties before he had to face a campaign for reelection. The only real power he enjoyed was the veto, and even that could be overridden by a two-thirds vote of the Common Council. The mayor could not disburse any city money or order a prosecution; those powers belonged to the comptroller and the corporation counsel. Both those officials were elected directly. The mayor's powers of patronage extended only to the appointment of four clerks, two marshals, an inspector of vessels, an interpreter, a messenger, seven clerks of courts, and a couple of other minor officials. In contrast, the comptroller had eighty-seven appointments in his gift, and through these offices he controlled 500 more places. True, the mayor could nominate men to be city chamberlain, city treasurer, street commissioner, city inspector, and commissioners of the Croton Water Board, but the Board of Aldermen had to approve his selections. In practice, the aldermen indicated who they wanted named and held up all other business until they got their way. The mayor could not dismiss these officials without the concurrence of the aldermen, but the aldermen could discharge them without the agreement of the mayor. And these officials themselves could freely fire subordinates.

The mayor of New York had no control over the city's finances, taxation, police, education, or health. The state legislature was constantly meddling in city affairs and creating commissions, picked by the governor, to handle city matters. There was the Central Park Commission, the Quarantine Commission, the Commissioners of Emigration, and the Pilot Commission. The Comptroller named the Commissioners of Public Charities, and the New York County Board of Supervisors controlled the city's finances. This was not a system of checks and balances, but a structure in which authority was so diffused that no one could ever be held responsible.

Twenty quarreling officials balkanized the city. Two different sets of officers, the police sanitary squad and the city inspector's health wardens, were paid for doing precisely the same job, and neither did it properly. The streets were controlled by three different bureaucracies, each completely independent of the other. The Fire Department was an autonomous power; a board chosen by the aldermen provided the water supply the firemen relied upon, but the two never consulted together.[30]

The upper classes of New York were thoroughly uninterested in city politics and left men like Fernando Wood to win by default. If, occasionally, the commercial middle classes did bestir themselves to take some part in local politics, they chose dense, unimaginative creatures like William F. Havemeyer or George Opdyke for their leaders, men with nothing more to offer as a solution for the city's ills than a sterile formula of reform and retrenchment.[31]

The New York city government was fabulously corrupt. Nominations were openly sold; one mayoral candidate in the late 1850s paid $10,000 for the privilege of being his party's standard-bearer. The primaries, which were supposed to be open to all members of the party, were controlled by the district leaders, who used their bruisers and shoulder-hitters to keep out anyone whose vote they did not own. "Fancy men, Bowery boys, and the scum of New York," said the *Herald*, "decide who shall be the candidates for the suffrages of the citizens." Party splits regularly produced battles between the rowdies of different factions, as they competed for the privilege of stuffing the ballot boxes. Some factional leaders who were more astute than others avoided this and concentrated on bribing the primary election inspector appointed by the party's General Committee to count their opponents out, irrespective of the number of votes cast.[32]

With the nominations settled, the work of stealing the general election began. Ballot boxes were stuffed; aliens were naturalized by the dozen; seamen from ships anchored in the harbor were brought in. Votes were bought, repeaters sent around, and inhabitants of Brooklyn "colonized" in New York City. In the weeks before Election Day, the slightest bump or hole in a road was used as an excuse to hire new workmen, who all voted as the street commissioner directed. Just before the 1863 mayoral election, the city inspector Francis I. A. Boole (himself a candidate) hired 250 new men. One hundred and fifty were fired immediately afterwards, having served their purpose. Election inspectors and canvassers were bribed to alter totals and change votes. Gangs of roughs were sent out by the parties to try and fill up the polling places, with instructions to let no one through except those who intended to vote right.[33]

All this cost a candidate dearly, but once elected, he could concentrate on recouping his fortunes. Everything to do with the city government had a price on it. As early as 1851 the Common Council had earned the title of "the Forty Thieves." In 1855 a grand jury indicted the street commissioner Joseph E. Ebling for malfeasance. Ebling had promised to award a city contract to Smith, Sickel and Company if he could keep all proceeds over $150,000.

Because of Ebling's influence, the company was awarded a temporary contract, but there proved to be no honor among thieves. Instead of a bid of $175,000, as Ebling expected, for the permanent contract, Smith, Sickel and Company put in one of $144,000. The disconsolate Ebling took his revenge by awarding the contract to a firm that had bid nearly twice as much. As usual with New York city government scandals, the wheels of justice ground to a halt after the indictment; no one was ever brought to trial.

An investigation of the Department of Repairs in 1856 disclosed that the city glazier was a butcher and the city carpenter a hotelkeeper. The man hired to clean out the city wells was a doctor's apprentice. Oddly enough, these amateurs valued their services highly. The *Herald* obtained bids on a number of jobs from several tradesmen and then compared them with the prices charged by the department's workmen:

| *Jobs* | *Prices Demanded by Respectable Mechanics* | *Price Paid* |
|---|---|---|
| Tinning the 22nd Ward Police Station House | $28.81 | $220.81 |
| Repairs to Franklin Market | $64.60 | $236.81 |
| Repairing the roof at Engine House No. 29 | $45.14 | $247.50 |
| Repairing the roof at Jefferson Market | $106.78 | $302.50 |
| Repairing the roof at the 8th Ward Station House | $46.90 | $134.18 |
| Repairs at Engine House No. 38 | $17.19 | $263.20 |
| Repairs at Hook and Ladder House No. 54 | $161.60 | $285.27 |
| Repairs at Clinton Market | $72.50 | $246.75 |

The city pump maker never obtained less than 350 percent profit on the items he supplied, and when this did not satisfy him, he repaired pumps where no one could find them. The commissioner of repairs knew nothing about his duties, having never read the acts of the legislature concerning them. The plumber knew nothing about the cost of lead pipes; the tinman knew nothing about the price of tinning a roof; and the department's clerks were utterly ignorant of its business.

In 1860 the city inspector's department was in the limelight again. Daniel E. Delavan was accused of forcing his employees to kick back part of their pay. The money was used for bribing members of the state legislature to vote against the bill setting up a Metropolitan Health District, which would take over Delavan's duties. In 1864 it was revealed that jobs in the department were being sold for $150 or $200 each and that teachers in the public schools had to pay for their appointments. One teacher had paid $75 to get a position worth $300 a year.[34]

Many concluded that the city was so corrupt it had lost the power of self-government. Unfortunately, the state legislature was every bit as venal as the city government; George Templeton Strong called it a "legislative cloaca" and a "Sanhedrin of rascality." As a warden of Trinity Church, Strong was sent to Albany in 1857 to lobby against a bill that would restrict Trinity's freedom to dispose of its immense wealth. He failed, but reported that "$1,000 in bribery would have secured us the majority report, and nine votes in the House."[35] Corruptionists who could not succeed in the city turned to Albany, like the syndicate that sponsored a bill chartering them to build a railroad through Broadway. This would have wrecked the city's finest street, tangled traffic, and sent property values plummeting, but the bill's most objectionable feature was that it gave away free a franchise for which others had offered $5 or $6 million. Yet the bill passed the legislature and was only stopped by the governor's veto.[36]

The administration of justice in New York was a public disgrace. Popular election and short terms of office made the judges and district attorneys mere creatures of powerful politicians. No criminal with the slightest political connections had to fear punishment. Scarcely one-third of the people arrested in New York were presented to a grand jury for indictment. When A. Oakey Hall was New York County District Attorney in 1857, it was said that from 1,500 to 2,000 indictments were being held in his office. If a case did come to trial, political influence could once again be brought to bear on the judge or the jury could easily be suborned.

Few people wanted to waste time on jury duty, and most of the wealthy and respectable classes of the city who could not claim exemption by serving in the militia either paid the fines for non-attendance or used their influence to have their names removed from the jury list. Consequently, most jurors were poor, ignorant, and easily bribed. Alternatively, the court officers could be persuaded to place a personal or political friend of the accused on the jury. In 1858 a man called Cancemi was on trial for killing a policeman, when one of the witnesses told the court that the counsel for the defense had offered him $3,000 to disappear and that one of the jurors had urged him to accept the offer.[37]

An 1859 double murder case provided an eloquent illustration of the difficulties of securing justice in New York City. Some members of a gang who had long terrorized the Duane Street area went on a drunken spree and invaded an assignation house kept by a German. He forced them outside and was shot dead by one of the gang, called James Glass. A stevedore from Brooklyn who was passing by stopped to see what the trouble was, and another of the gang, James Loftus, knocked him down. James Glass went up to him, put the revolver to his heart, and fired, killing him instantly. Loftus and James Glass were arrested, together with Glass's brother John and a man called James Higgins who had been with them at the time of the murders. Another man called Patrick Quinlan, who had hidden the gun that was used in the killings, was also arrested. All five were indicted on two counts of murder each.

The gang to which they belonged had been extensively used to carry primaries throughout the city, and intense political pressure was brought to bear on the district attorney, Nelson J. Waterbury, to drop the matter. Waterbury, however, held firm, possibly recalling that his predecessor, Oakey Hall, had been driven from office by public indignation over his lackadaisical prosecution of a sensational murder case.[38] The prosecution was no easy matter. The people living in Duane Street were all frightened into silence, and there was very little evidence on which to build a case. Waterbury brought John Glass to trial first, hoping that his defense would furnish enough evidence to convict his brother. But the defense attorney, James R. Whiting, was obsessed with saving James Glass and called no witnesses at all. John Glass was convicted of first-degree manslaughter and sentenced to twenty years. Next, Waterbury tried the same tactic on Higgins, but he, too, refused to implicate James Glass, and he, too, was convicted.

The two convictions had their effect, however; both Loftus and Quinlan turned state's evidence. James Glass, realizing that their testimony would give the district attorney a strong case, offered to plead guilty to murder, but neither Waterbury nor the judge in the case would agree. Glass, they believed, should hang, but a man's life could not be taken upon his own confession. Later, the counsel for the defense offered a plea of guilty to first-degree manslaughter, but Waterbury again refused and put Glass on trial. After ninety-two hours of deliberation, the jury reported that they were hopelessly deadlocked, eleven for a verdict of guilty and one for not guilty, and the judge declared a mistrial. Waterbury later charged that the lone dissenter had been seen exchanging signals with one of the defense attorneys.

Glass was brought to trial again, and this time a perjured defense was offered. Several rowdies appeared to swear that they had been to see a play called *Putnam* at the Broadway Theatre on the night in question, that they had witnessed the murders when they were coming away from the theater, and that Glass was not the killer. Once again, the trial ended in a hung jury, eight for a verdict of guilty to four for not guilty. Eleven of the jurors would have agreed to a verdict of guilty of manslaughter, but one held out for a murder conviction, and there was nothing for it but to declare a mistrial.

Afterwards, Waterbury offered to accept a plea of guilty to a first-degree manslaughter charge, but the defense, seeing a chance of escaping altogether, refused. At the third trial, Waterbury managed to destroy the defense case by showing that *Putnam* had ended at 9 P.M. and the murders did not take place until 11 P.M. He sensed, though, that the jury did not want to send a man to the gallows on the evidence of the two informers Loftus and Quinlan. In his summation, Waterbury asked only for a verdict of guilty to first-degree manslaughter, and this time the jury agreed. Glass was sentenced to life imprisonment. Under such circumstances few could disagree with the murderer Jack Reynolds's scornful remark that "hanging in New York is played out."[39]

Even if a criminal were convicted, he stood an excellent chance of being pardoned. John Glass was set free in 1863. Politicians were constantly badgering the governor for remission of the sentences of their constituents, and many occupants of the gubernatorial chair were by no means averse to gaining easy popularity by the exercise of clemency. Horatio Seymour and Myron Clark were especially fond of the pardoning power. Leaving office in 1857, Governor Clark crowned his career by freeing fourteen people convicted of capital crimes and commuting the sentences of five more. "A man," summed up the *New York Herald*, "must in fact be very friendless and very unlucky indeed if he serves out his time in prison in the State of New York." Surveying Governor Morgan's pardons, the *Herald* called for the power to be taken away from the executive and vested in a special court.[40] Given the state of criminal justice in New York, a witness who could not provide surety for his appearance in court and who had to be kept in the House of Detention of Witnesses might well spend as much time in custody as the criminal.[41]

The weakness, venality, and popular ill-repute of the other agencies of social control placed an extra heavy burden on the police and the militia, a burden that they were by no means fit to bear. Due to their English heritage, Americans initially distrusted and disliked the police. English "Revolution principles" emphasized that popular liberty could be preserved only by carefully limiting the power of government. During the Gordon Riots, Charles James Fox said in the House of Commons that he would "much rather be governed by a mob than a standing army." Suggestions of a paid police force made by Shelburne and the younger Pitt were greeted with horror; the only police Englishmen were familiar with were the gendarmes and political spies of France and Austria, and most believed that the establishment of a police force in England would be the first step toward despotism. Peel's Metropolitan Police, founded in 1829 after it had become evident that crime in London was utterly out of hand, met tremendous public hostility. When a "peeler" was killed during a riot in 1833, twelve good men and true ruled it justifiable homicide, and delighted citizens presented each juror with a silver loving cup.

In a few years' time, the vast improvement in public order

achieved by the Metropolitan Police brought them the respect of the British upper and middle classes.[42] No American police department, certainly not the New York force, ever succeeded in duplicating this feat.[43] After their initial suspicion and mistrust wore off, the respectable classes of New York regarded their policemen with a mixture of contempt and amusement.[44]

From the start in 1844, the New York Police Department was riddled with political favoritism, inefficiency, and graft. Officers were appointed by local ward politicians and had to seek reappointment every year. When political control of a ward changed hands, the policemen were changed, too. They wore no uniform, only a star-shaped badge which was easy to conceal or remove if they wanted to shirk duty. For years, there were far too few men to control such a large and rapidly growing city. They were given no training; once a policeman was appointed, he was immediately sent out to patrol the streets. There were no standards of education, age, or health. In March 1847 a police surgeon listed fifty men, all of them receiving full pay, as physically unfit for duty. Groggeries, gambling houses, and brothels quickly nullified the police threat to their existence through political influence or bribery. A lucrative "skinning" business was developed at the Tombs prison by the police, the jailers, and some shyster lawyers. The only attorney a prisoner was allowed to see was one whom the police and the jailers recommended; in return, they received 40 percent of the lawyer's fees.

Police commanders found it difficult, sometimes impossible, to impose discipline on their men. During 1847, when the force numbered 800 men, 242 were brought up for departmental trial on disciplinary charges, and twenty-two more were charged, but resigned before their cases could be decided. Fifty-nine of those charged were suspended for various lengths of time. Drunkenness, neglect of duty, abusive language to a superior, and disobedience of orders were the most common charges. Surveying the force, the *Herald* called the New York police "as lazy a set of fellows as ever broke bread," spending their time "lounging at grocery corners, reading a newspaper or chatting on politics to some familiar acquaintances."[45]

Improvement came slowly. In 1849 the term of appointment

was lengthened from one year to four; in 1853 policemen were granted tenure during good behavior. An influential pamphlet by James W. Gerard, *London and New York—Their Crimes and Police*, played a large part in bringing about this change, as well as some others. The police were at last compelled to wear uniforms,[46] and from 1853 on the force was controlled and appointed by a commission made up of the mayor, the city judge, and the recorder. After 1854 a physical examination was required for all recruits, and they had to demonstrate that they were literate. In 1855 a sergeant major was brought in to drill the men and instruct them in the proper use of the club. A telegraph system was put into operation, linking the various station houses with the chief of police's office.[47]

Many reformers attributed the political impartiality and incorruptibility of the London police to the fact that the commissioner was appointed by the home secretary and was free from local interference. Applying the principle to New York, they suggested that control of the police should be taken away from the city authorities and entrusted to the governor. A bill to this effect was first introduced into the state legislature in 1851, but was not passed until 1857, after Mayor Fernando Wood had demonstrated how far the politicizing of the police could go.

Under the law of 1853, the recorder and the city judge were supposed to sit with the mayor as a Board of Police Commissioners. In fact, they took little interest in their duties, and the mayor gradually assumed sole control. When Wood, one of the first great machine politicians, became mayor in 1854, he was quick to exploit the opportunities of this situation. Appointments and promotions went only to men known to be loyal to him. "There is no incentive to promotion," the New York County District Attorney testified in 1857. "On the contrary, captains are taken from citizens and placed over lieutenants and sergeants of ten years' experience." Before the election of 1856, large numbers of policemen were furloughed to electioneer for Wood, and every member of the force was made to contribute to the mayor's campaign fund. One officer who was foolhardy enough to refuse was kept on duty for twenty-four consecutive hours. On election day, the police assiduously looked the other way while Mayor Wood's supporters beat up their opponents and then proceeded to vote early and often.[48]

It was estimated that control of the police was worth fifteen thousand votes to Wood,[49] and alarm at the prospect of the force becoming simply another political gang supplied a number of the votes that passed the Metropolitan Police bill in the state legislature on April 15, 1857. This set up a Board of Police Commissioners responsible for the preservation of the public peace and health and for conducting elections in the counties of New York, Kings, Westchester, and Richmond. Mayor Wood declared that the act was unconstitutional and refused to obey it. For a time, New York had two police forces, the new Metropolitans and Wood's Municipals, and criminals arrested by one might be liberated by the other. Ultimately, the courts upheld the legality of the Metropolitan Police bill and Wood capitulated, but not before the Metropolitans had made an attempt to storm City Hall, which Wood had garrisoned with 500 Municipals. The outnumbered Metropolitans were routed, and the Seventh Regiment had to intervene to end this police riot.[50]

All this dealt a staggering blow to the slim prestige and authority the police had painfully built up. Two days after Wood's surrender, the Bowery Boys and the Dead Rabbits celebrated the Fourth of July with the bloodiest battle in the history of the gangs. When a squad of Metropolitans marched into the Sixth Ward to restore order, they ran into a couple of hundred Dead Rabbits, who made short work of them. Only the arrival of a crowd of Bowery Boys enabled the police to break off the engagement and ignominiously retreat to headquarters. Fighting continued the next day, and two regiments of militia were needed to restore order. Twelve people were killed, including two policemen; forty-one were injured.[51]

Worse was to come. Due to disagreements among the commissioners, it took a year to bring the new Metropolitan force up to full strength. In the interim, inadequate police protection and economic depression caused crime and disorder to spiral. The Democrats kept up a constant drumfire of criticism, and when they gained control of the legislature in the autumn of 1857, an investigating committee was set up which reported "that the Metropolitan Police was organized less with regard to its public duties than to its efficiency as a political machine" for achieving Republican victory. The new force, the report continued, "included in its numbers a large proportion of worthless and dishonest men, more fitted in their character and by their antecedents to be the accessories of crime than to trace out its hiding places and arrest and expose it."[52] A first-class scandal erupted when it was revealed that appointments to the force were being sold and that officers had been forced to contribute part of their pay to buy a $17,000 house for Commissioner Nye. The first two general superintendents of the new force both resigned in disgust,[53] charging that the commissioners were usurping their powers and reducing them to the level of clerks. The seven commissioners constantly squabbled among themselves, especially in 1857–1858 and 1860, when Fernando Wood sat on the board.[54]

After 1860, things improved. A new police law reduced the unwieldy seven-men Board of Commissioners to three, and the mayors of New York and Brooklyn lost their right to seats on the board. An able and energetic new general superintendent, John A. Kennedy, was appointed, and he was able to establish a harmonious working relationship with Thomas C. Acton, who emerged as the strongest personality on the new Board of Commissioners. Together, they succeeded in raising the force to a level of efficiency never previously attained. Between 1860 and 1870, the New York Police Department was more efficient than at any other time in the nineteenth century, with the possible exception of Theodore Roosevelt's term as a police commissioner in 1895–1897.[55] With 1,452 patrolmen available for duty in New York City by 1863, the force had at last reached a size that was reasonably adequate for the duties it had to perform.[56]

There were still defects in the system, however. Commissioner James Bowen still meddled with the drill of the force; there were still attempts at political interference from Albany. Sixteen years of corruption, inefficiency, and political intervention could not be easily overcome. In 1863 and 1864 the rampant wartime inflation shrank the value of the patrolman's salary, and most policemen who had any kind of skill or training left the force to seek better wages. New recruits were generally unskilled laborers, inferior in intelligence and character to those who resigned.[57]

The hours a patrolman was expected to spend on duty were sometimes unnecessarily long or awkwardly arranged and did not encourage men to join or remain on the force. One patrolman of the Fifteenth Precinct reported that his squad came off duty at 6 A.M. in the morning on New Year's Day 1863. At 9 A.M., they had to assemble for roll call; at 1 P.M. for dinner; at 3 P.M. for another roll call; and at 3:40 P.M. for supper. At 5 P.M. they were on duty again, having snatched what sleep they could in the few hours between calls. Two meals were served in four hours while they were off duty, but they had nothing to eat for sixteen hours after they went back on patrol. Even on ordinary duty, they had to consume three meals in nine hours, and then go without eating for fifteen hours.[58]

Complaints that only Republicans were accepted to be Metropolitan policemen ceased after 1859. Many of the Municipal police were allowed to rejoin the force; and a check of those New Yorkers giving their occupation as "policeman" in the 1860 federal census reveals that 309 were born in Ireland, and eighty-four in Germany.[59]

A sizeable minority of immigrants on the force did not make the police any more acceptable or trustworthy to the poor immigrants who made up most of New York's population.[60] Command of the police was still vested in representatives of the Protestant mercantile and industrial oligarchy and the Republican party. Many of the laws regulating social behavior which were passed by the state legislature, with its heavy overrepresentation of rural upstate areas, were simply not understood, much less accepted, by the immigrants. The Germans could see no reason why they should not listen to a band in a beer garden on Sundays, as they did at home, just as the Irishman could see no reason why he should not relax in a bar after a hard day's work. The immigrants found all their entertainments, from prizefighting to gambling a few cents with a policy dealer, were illegal. The Metropolitans were like a colonial police force, trying to enforce laws unsupported by the local system of social control.[61]

To be sure, many of the laws were never enforced against any establishment that could afford a bribe or that was protected by political influence. But this only reinforced the impression that the police were the agents of the rich and the enemies of the poor. Prostitutes soliciting on the shilling side of Broadway or on the Bowery found themselves taken up and sent to "the Island,"[62] but the large brothels and assignation houses rarely suffered even the formality of a raid. Beggars, street traders, newsboys selling papers on Sundays, and tramps were all arrested, but gambling houses and the "swell mob" seemed to be left undisturbed. No one could believe that the police were the impartial enforcers of the law. They behaved more like an army of occupation, and since they totally lacked moral authority, they had to use either the threat or reality of force to compel obedience or respect. Their presence in an area increased the probability of an eruption of violence rather than diminishing it.[63]

Despite the appalling frequency of disorders in the streets from the 1840s to the 1870s, the New York police never established a riot squad. No one even seems to have thought of using mounted police in riot control.[64] The London Metropolitan Police had gradually developed great skill in handling mobs, as they demonstrated in their highly effective management of the Chartists in 1848, but no one tried to apply their methods to New York's troubles.[65] The only type of riot control the New York police ever used was direct attack on the mob, with a vigorous use of the club.

Such strong-arm tactics could even create a riot where none existed. On Sunday, July 12, 1857, two Germans got into a fight on the corner of Third Street and Avenue B, and a crowd gathered to watch. One of the contestants was quickly placed *hors de combat*, but as he was led away, two Metropolitans came up and ordered the crowd to disperse. One man refused, saying he had a right to stand where he liked, and one of the policemen clubbed him, chased him down the street, and clubbed him again. The crowd became threatening, and the policemen retreated amidst their jeers. Probably there would have been no further trouble and the crowd would have broken up and gone home if Sergeant Lockwood of the Seventeenth Precinct had not decided to assert his authority. Lockwood was on Second Avenue with a detail of seven men, guarding streetcar conductors after a rash of robberies. When he heard the patrolmen's report, he gathered his men and marched them down Fourth Street into *Kleindeutschland*. They were set upon and driven back to Second Avenue under a shower of stones and brickbats, and Lockwood sent to the precinct commander, Captain Hartt, for reinforcements. Hartt mustered thirty-five men, took them down to Fourth Street to join the others, and led them against the mob. They clubbed and beat their way through the crowds of people, the stones flying thick and fast. At Avenue A some of the police drew their pistols and began firing. A man called John Muller was shot dead. The crowds scattered, but for the remainder of the night the police continued to roam the streets, clubbing anyone they found out of doors. Several days of unrest followed, as New York's Germans protested what they considered wanton murder by the police.[66]

Several times during New York City's riot years, the police and the civil authorities found that the disorders were beyond their control and had to call out the National Guard. During the late 1830s and early 1840s, the universal militia system which enrolled every able-bodied man between eighteen and forty-five fell into disuse, and most people commuted their militia duty for a sum of money. The only regiments left were made up of volunteers, and though enthusiastic, they were seldom well-officered, -trained, or -equipped. With the exception of the Seventh Regiment, whose crack reputation was upheld by the efficient Civil War service of many of its former members, New York's volunteer militia was merely a fashionable diversion for the affluent youth of the city.[67]

Even the officers of the Seventh had no sophisticated ideas of riot control. In 1857 Colonel Abram Duryee, the Seventh's commander, stated his maxims for putting down mobs. Troops, he said, should not be called in until the police had clearly lost control of the situation. Unless authorized to fire, they should not be brought into view of the mob, nor used to perform police duty, for this would weaken their moral authority: "Temporizing with a mob should be carefully avoided; for any indication of timidity and weakness on the part of the troops, gives confidence to the timid and wavering, who are thus led to join in the popular tumult." If one man in a crowd broke the law, then the whole crowd was involved, and if one rioter attacked the troops, they would be justified in firing on the entire mob.

Officers, continued Duryee, should be familiar with the public buildings and houses which they might have to protect. Troops should never be taken into action without a good supply of ammunition, at least forty rounds of ball cartridge apiece. "When necessary to act, do so with promptness, energy and courage; for insurrection or rioting should be quickly checked in its incipient stages. . . . All unlawful assemblies are without subordination or unity of action; therefore, any movement of troops not anticipated by the mob produces terror and dismay. . . . When ordered to fire, aim at point blank range; do not fire high; if you do you will waste ammunition." In a disturbed area, the troops ought to be formed the width of the street, allowing enough room for the companies to move to the rear after firing, reload, and move forward again. This would protect the flanks and sweep the crowd through the streets. A mountain howitzer would be invaluable in street fighting. "Artillery gives great confidence to troops; it bears a relative and important support to infantry, and is an effectual antidote to the most infuriated mob. . . . Never charge bayonets upon a mob. One bullet will command more respect than a hundred bayonets." A commander should find out precisely what the position of a mob was, and he should then pick the precise point to deliver a decisive blow.[68] Any riot suppressed in this way would be a bloody affair indeed.

# THE DAYS
# OF THE RIOT

*In America conscription is unknown and men are induced to enlist by bounties. The notions and habits of the people of the United States are so opposed to compulsory recruitment that I do not think it can ever be sanctioned by their laws.*

—ALEXIS DE TOCQUEVILLE

# 3

## *The Fuse and the Powder*

N EW YORK in the third summer of the war seemed little different from peacetime. Fifth Avenue and the dollar side of Broadway were deserted by fashionable promenaders as the wealthy left for Newport, Cape May, or Saratoga. Along the Bowery, the crowded beer gardens and theaters were filled with the sounds and sights of the *Vaterland*. The Jewish clothing stores, with goods hung outside, still stood in ranks along Chatham Street, and the pedestrian found coattails and pantaloon-legs flapping about his face like low branches in a wood. Only the large number of men in the streets wearing army blue, the barrack hospitals in City Hall Park, and the placards outside the newspaper offices on Nassau Street bore witness to the fighting going on two hundred miles to the South.[1]

The previous winter, the Union cause had reached its lowest ebb. "Our general conviction," wrote George Templeton Strong, "is that the national cause is fast going to destruction–that we are without leaders and on the verge of bankruptcy."[2] The fearful slaughter at Fredericksburg, the failure of General Grant's advance on Vicksburg, and the depredations of the C.S.S. *Alabama* at sea convinced many that the North had lost the war. In the spring, yet another Union general failed against Lee in Virginia, and Admiral Du Pont's assault on Charleston was repulsed with heavy loss.

The arrest and banishment of Clement L. Vallandigham caused a storm of protest and raised opposition to Lincoln's restriction of civil liberties to a new intensity. Arrests without trial, the suspension of habeas corpus, the suppression of newspapers, and "the horrors of the abolition Bastilles" were denounced across the country, and Lincoln was described as "a weak imitation of the besotted tyrant Nero."[3]

The Emancipation Proclamation was ridiculed as a pope's bull against the comet, liberating slaves where federal authority could not reach and keeping them in bondage where it did extend. Governor Horatio Seymour of New York, delivering his inaugural at Albany, called it "clearly impolitic, unjust and unconstitutional, and . . . calculated to create so many barriers to the restoration of the Union."[4] Democratic and conservative opinion (including a fair proportion of Republicans) feared that the Proclamation would only bolster southern fighting spirit by demonstrating that the federal government was in the hands of abolitionists and that there could be no reunion with the North on such terms. The Proclamation was denounced as an incitement to servile insurrection; the *New York Herald* feared that the European powers might use a slave uprising as a pretext to intervene in the war "on the plea of humanity." Lincoln, the paper concluded, was "steering among the breakers of a perilous coast."[5]

Inflation was rampant, and wages failed to keep up with rocketing prices. By July 1863 retail prices had risen 43 percent since 1860, while wages had only gone up 12 percent. The northern worker found his standard of living drastically lowered, and a rash of strikes broke out. In New York City everyone from longshoremen to barbers, from tailors to leatherworkers, from shipwrights to journeymen coopers, demanded higher wages.[6]

Against this background of defeat and unrest, the Lincoln administration proposed the first federal conscription bill in the nation's history. All male American citizens between the ages of twenty and forty-five were ordered by this bill to be enrolled in two classes. The first comprised single men between twenty and forty-five and married men from twenty to thirty-five; the second included married men between thirty-five and forty-five. The second class was not to be called up until all the men in the first class had been drafted or exempted. Exemption was granted for a number of reasons—mental or physical disability, or proof that a drafted man was the sole support of aged or widowed parents or of orphaned children. A draftee could also escape service by providing a substitute or by paying a three-hundred-dollar commutation fee. The draft machinery was entrusted to a provost marshal general, responsible to the secretary of war, who would appoint provost marshals to arrange the draft in each congressional district.

There is no question that the bill was needed. The old system of reliance on volunteer enlistments simply could not supply the number of men the army needed. General apathy had cut down the flow of volunteers, and desertion had become a "formidable and widespread evil." But conscription was such a radical departure from the long American tradition of voluntarism and distrust of standing armies and centralized power ran so deep in the American mind that it inevitably aroused strong opposition.[7] Congressman Chilton A. White of Ohio declared that the bill rode roughshod over the rights of the states and created one of the largest standing armies known in the history of the world. "I would not give a rush," he announced, "for the reserved rights of the States or the boasted liberties of the people if this power is granted to the United States. . . . I fear me, sir, that this is a part and parcel of a grand scheme for the overthrow of the Union and for the purpose of building upon its ruins a new government based on new ideas—the idea of territorial unity and consolidated power. . . . Arm the Chief Magistrate with this power—and what becomes of the State Legislatures? What becomes of the local judicial tribunals? What becomes of State constitutions and State laws?"[8]

"It will be seen," commented *Frank Leslie's Illustrated Newspaper*, "that this law converts the Republic into one grand military dictatorship." The *Freeman's Journal* called the act "a palpable and perilous infraction of the Constitution." The draft, it was charged, conferred despotic powers on that "deluded and almost delirious fanatic," Abraham Lincoln, and made him "as absolute a monarch as the Autocrat of all the Russias." Even some newspapers sympathetic to the administration were uneasy about such an aggrandizement of federal power. The *New York Sunday Mercury* came to the conclusion that "the Government has not shown such a capacity for effectively using the means at its command as to justify this infringement of State rights."[9]

Criticism of the clause allowing commutation of $300 or substitution was particularly fierce. Many Republican congressmen were not happy about this provision and joined the Democrats in an attempt to remove it from the bill; it failed by a vote of 67 to 87.[10] Senator Edgar Cowan of Pennsylvania explained that the commutation fee would prevent the price of substitutes from rising to astronomical heights,[11] and the provost marshal general, Colonel James B. Fry, later argued that the clause gave an advantage to the poor. Since the payment of $300 exempted a man only from the current draft and left him liable to be called again in the future, there would be more rich men on future draft lists. Therefore, the chances of a poor man's name being drawn would be correspondingly diminished.[12] But this was no consolation to the laborer to whom $300 was nearly a year's wages. This clause brought charges that the Lincoln administration was waging a rich man's war and a poor man's fight all too convincing, and it was bitterly resented. "We're coming, Father Abraham," ran a parody of a popular recruiting song printed in the *New York Copperhead*: "three hundred thousand more./We leave our homes and firesides with bleeding hearts and sore,/Since poverty has been our crime, we bow to the decree;/We are the poor who have no wealth to purchase liberty."[13]

Attempts to enforce the draft caused violent resistance in many places. In Holmes County, Ohio, there was a minor insurrection, and 370 troops and a company of artillery were needed to disperse the resisters.[14] In Indiana, one enrolling officer was murdered in Rush County, and another one was killed in Sullivan County.[15] In Milwaukee, draft officials were "assaulted by Irish mobs, and knocked down in the performance of their duties, compelling them to flee for their lives."[16] There was bitter opposition to conscription in the mining regions of Pennsylvania, and there was trouble in Missouri, Maryland, Delaware, and Kentucky.[17]

Similar difficulties might have been anticipated in New York City, where peace sentiment was strong and indignation high over the government's abrogation of civil liberties. On June 3, a "Monster Peace Convention," organized by former Mayor Fernando Wood, attracted 30,000 people and even the Republican *Times* had to admit that it was "in many respects, a decided success."

In his speech, Wood declared that popular enthusiasm for the war was vanishing and that the draft would not succeed in filling up the army's empty ranks. "Republicans who have grown up with the idea of personal freedom and right to political opinions and action," he asserted, "cannot be so suddenly changed as to become willing instruments of power, and be used effectually against their own convictions of policy and right." The Convention ended by calling for a cease-fire and negotiations for national reconciliation.[18]

On the Fourth of July, Governor Seymour spoke at a meeting at the Academy of Music. Seymour was a strong Union man, as he had just proved by the vigorous measures he had taken to hurry the New York militia regiments down to meet Lee's invasion of Pennsylvania, but he was also a firm Jeffersonian Democrat with a passion for civil liberties. In his speech, he called for the North to unite and help the war effort. But, he said, this could never be achieved while the Republicans were trampling on individual rights. The administration pleaded the necessity of strong action to obtain victory, but, said Seymour in words that would come back to haunt him, "Remember this, that the bloody, and treasonable, and revolutionary, doctrine of public necessity can be proclaimed by a mob as well as by a Government." Pointing to the dangers of military dictatorship, Seymour called on his audience to maintain and defend the principles of the Declaration of Independence and the Constitution. The federal government, he said, should be obeyed as long as it did not clearly transgress its constitutional powers. People must do their duty. But they must also insist that the government do its duty: uphold states' rights, freedom of the press, and the independence of the judiciary.

Seymour's companion on the platform, his cousin, former Governor T. H. Seymour of Connecticut, called for a compromise peace. He argued that states could not be compelled to remain in the Union by force of arms. A military victory might be attained, but this would not restore the Union. An army of occupation numbering not less than 500,000 men would be needed to hold the South down, and freedom would be crushed. The country really needed reconciliation of North and South and reunion.[19]

Yet New York City accepted the advent of conscription with

surprising calm. There was one incident in which Captain Joel T. Erhardt, provost marshal of the Fourth District, had to beat a hurried retreat before a belligerent gang of laborers at the corner of Liberty Street and Broadway, and in the lower wards of the city the enrolling officers found that people were inclined to give false names.[20] The draft was certainly not popular in New York, but there seemed to be no violent disposition to resist it.

The news of Vicksburg and Gettysburg, and the real possibility (until the night of the thirteenth of July) that Lee's whole army might yet be cornered and cut to pieces, raised spirits and encouraged hopes that the war might soon be over. In this atmosphere, nearly everyone agreed that "the lot in the impending draft will fall noiselessly as the snowflake." Even the *Daily News*, the most rabidly anti-administration paper in the city, was talking only of bringing a court case to test the constitutionality of the conscription law or of asking the Common Council to vote enough money to pay the commutation fees for drafted New Yorkers.[21]

The New York militia regiments were not yet back from Pennsylvania, and the discipline and authority of the police were suffering from Governor Seymour's attempt to remove the commissioners, who were all Republicans. It was taken for granted that new Democratic commissioners would replace many of the sergeants and captains, and some disgruntled officers began to disobey departmental rules and regulations, feeling confident that they would not be called to account for it.[22] But, under the circumstances, the provost marshal general's bureau was fully justified in ordering a start to the draft in New York City in the second week of July.

Colonel Robert Nugent, who headed the Bureau's staff in New York City and Long Island, did take the precaution of leaving the lower wards of the city until last. If there was to be any trouble, it would surely erupt in the Five Points and Corlear's Hook, and any resistance there would be much less likely after a successful drawing in the uptown wards. Consequently, Nugent set Saturday, July 11, as the day to begin drawing names in the Ninth District, which consisted of Manhattan above Fortieth Street. The Eighth District, which comprised the Eighteenth, Twentieth, and Twenty-first wards, would start drafting on July 13.[23]

Early on the morning of the eleventh, a large crowd gathered outside the Ninth District headquarters at 677 Third Avenue, on the corner of Forty-sixth Street, in that melancholy, half-urban, half-rural area of vacant lots and isolated buildings on the edge of the city. Superintendent Kennedy was on hand, with a large force of police posted nearby. An informer had passed a story that there was a plot to seize the Thirty-fifth Street Arsenal and resist the draft, so a sergeant and fifteen men were put on guard there. At nine o'clock, the doors of the office were opened, and Provost Marshal Charles E. Jenkins, standing on a table, read his orders to begin the draft. Slips of paper, bearing the names of all the men who had been enrolled, were put into a large hollow wheel mounted on a stand. One of the enrolling clerks was blindfolded, and a handle was attached to the wheel. It was turned, the clerk pulled out a slip, and the name of the first man drafted in New York City was called out: "William Jones, 49th Street near Tenth Avenue." A low murmur rose from the crowd. As the day wore on, people became more jocular and shouts of "How are you, Brady?" "How are you, Jones?" "Goodbye, Patrick!" "Goodbye, James!" greeted the announcement of each new name. By four o'clock, 1,236 names had been drawn. The office was closed, and the crowd quietly dispersed.[24]

A *Herald* reporter, visiting the Irish bars in the Twentieth Ward on Sunday, heard much grumbling about the draft and many threats to oppose it. Men relaxing over their whiskey threatened "black eyes and bloody noses" and complained that "poor men are to give up their lives and let rich men pay $300 in order to stay at home." In a drinking place on East Broadway, a man who had served as a captain in the army during the 1850s declared that "he would sooner blow his own brains out than shoulder the musket in defence of an abolition administration," and everyone there cheered.[25] But all this was mere bravado. If indignation over the draft had been going to spark any spontaneous riot, trouble would have begun after the bars closed on Saturday night, or, possibly, Sunday night. When Superintendent Kennedy went home on Saturday evening, he said that "the Rubicon was passed and all would go well."[26] There is no doubt that he would have been proved right, if only the Ninth District authorities had not had the bad luck to draw the names of several members of Black Joke Engine Company Number 33, including John Masterson, brother of the company's foreman, that day.[27]

One of the privileges of the volunteer firemen was exemption from militia duty, and the fire laddies considered that they should be exempt from the draft, too.[28] Over the weekend, they decided to attack the Ninth District office when it opened on Monday morning. They would treat the draft officials to a "muss," break the wheel, burn the lists, and destroy all evidence that the army had ever claimed the men of the Black Joke.[29] News of what the fire laddies intended spread among the laborers and workmen of the Nineteenth and Twenty-first wards, and many of them resolved to go and see the fun. When the engineer in charge of constructing the Croton Reservoir in Central Park arrived to start the day's work on Monday morning, he found that only half of his employees had turned up.[30]

Excitement grew through the hours between seven and ten o'clock. The Second and Third Avenue cars were stopped. A group of men marched through the Nineteenth Ward, headed by someone beating a copper pan like a gong, calling workers out of factories and workshops.[31] James L. Jackson, the owner of an iron works at 167 East Twenty-Eighth Street, was in the yard at ten o'clock that morning when one of his men beckoned him to come into the shop. He went in and found about a hundred men and boys outside the door, yelling and shouting. He told them they could not come in, but agreed to speak to their leaders. Five of the crowd came into the lobby way of his office, headed by Thomas Fitzsimmons, a carman who lived just down the street at 120 East Twenty-eighth Street. They said they wanted the shop to close for the day. "They stated that their only object was to make a big show to resist the draft. They said they had no other motive than to have the men join them to put down the draft."[32] Jackson agreed to close his works, and the crowd marched off to Franklin's Forge on First Avenue.

Superintendent Kennedy, of course, had anticipated no trouble that morning and had merely assigned a sergeant and twelve men to the Ninth District office to keep order among the expected crowd of spectators. But just after nine o'clock, Captain G. T. Porter, commander of the Nineteenth Precinct police, became worried as he received reports of the commotion in the streets and the groups of workmen making their way toward the drafting place. He sent a message to the Central Office: "The laborers have all suspended work, and are gathering with crowbars and other missiles in different parts of this and the 22nd Precinct, to make a grand demonstration at 677, Third Avenue." When he received a message from Provost Marshal Jenkins asking for all the men he could spare, Porter sent to the Seventeenth, Twenty-first, and Twenty-second precincts for help, and took a dozen more men of his own command down to the draft office.

There was an eerie atmosphere of expectancy around the office. The streets were crowded with people talking about the draft and its iniquity, yet no one made a move to resist it. When all the reinforcements arrived, Porter had sixty policemen to protect the office, and Jenkins felt confident enough to start the drawing. Fifty-six names had been called out, when shouts of "They are coming!" were heard and a Black Joke hose cart laden with large stones pulled up outside the office.[33] There was a pistol shot, a storm of stones crashed through the windows, and the toughs of the Black Joke charged in. Captain Porter and his men held off the attackers long enough for the draft officials to cram all their papers and records into the safe and escape out of the back door. Then the police, too, retreated. To the accompaniment of shouts of "Bully for the draft?" "How are you, Old Abe?" and "We'll hang Horace Greeley on a sour apple tree," the triumphant fire laddies smashed everything in sight, splashed turpentine on the floor, and set the place ablaze.[34]

The house in which the draft office had been opened was one of a row of four. Policemen hustled the inhabitants of the other houses down the backstairs as the flames spread, telling them to leave everything behind and save their lives. A deputy provost marshal, Edward S. Vanderpoel, tried to persuade the men of the Black Joke to put out the fire, saying that all the equipment of the draft office had been destroyed and that innocent women and children might be hurt if the houses were burned down. He was promptly clubbed to the ground, and so was Officer John Cook, a policeman who tried to protect him.

Now that the watching crowd had seen the draft office wrecked and the police put to flight, their natural tendency to violence and riot, their hostility to authority, and their dislike of the draft erupted. Some of them broke into the burning houses and carried off furniture and clothing. One man tried to save his belongings by throwing them out of the window. There was a crockery store in the third house of the row, and the crackle of the flames mingled with the crash of breaking china as the mob broke in and tore down the shelves.[35]

Perhaps to cut the authorities' communications, perhaps to block the tracks of the Third Avenue horse-cars, some of the rioters began to cut down the telegraph poles along the avenue. Fortunately, James Crowley, superintendent of the police telegraph system, happened to be on the scene. He was on his way to report for duty at police headquarters at 300 Mulberry Street and, finding no cars running, had decided to walk. Coming upon the felled poles, he took in the situation, gathered up the wires, and wound them around a lamppost to ground them and secure operation. To the threatening inquiries about what the devil he thought he was doing, Crowley cheerfully replied that he was "only getting the wire out of your way, boys." Due to his courageous action, the police special wire was kept open, and communications between the Central Office and the uptown precincts were preserved for several hours more. As soon as he had finished gathering the wires, Crowley rushed off to the Twenty-first Precinct police station on Thirty-fifth Street to call for help.

At police headquarters downtown, Superintendent Kennedy had been disturbed by the news that many of the laborers in Central Park had not reported for work.[36] He sent out a general order: "To all precincts in New York and Brooklyn: Call in your reserves. Platoon and hold them at the station house subject to further orders." Then, leaving instructions to send reinforcements to the two draft offices, Kennedy set off uptown in his buggy to see what was going on there. It would have been far better if he had stayed at headquarters.

Seeing the crowds around the Ninth District office, Kennedy left his buggy several blocks away and walked up Lexington Avenue with his driver, Officer Mellen D. Murphy and William H.

Kimball, a clerk at headquarters. The superintendent was in civilian clothes, but a former policeman called Francis Cusick recognized him. "Let's go in, boys!" he howled. "Stick together and we can lick all the damn police in the city. Here comes the son of a bitch Kennedy! Let's finish him!" Rushing up to Kennedy, he struck him a tremendous blow with his club and laid him senseless on the sidewalk. Turning to Murphy, Cusick brought his club down on the back of the officer's head. "You son of a bitch," shouted Cusick, tearing Murphy's uniform off, "now I've got you and I'll finish you."[37] He beat and kicked Murphy into insensibility, while other rioters thrashed Kimball. Kennedy came to and made a dash to escape, but he was overtaken in a vacant lot and battered bloody.

John Eagan, a minor Tammany politician who was in the mob, convinced them that Kennedy was dead, and leaving him sprawled in the dirt, the rioters went off in search of fresh amusement.[38] Kimball, the first to regain consciousness, commandeered a passing dray. With the help of Murphy and Officer William McTaggart, a member of the Sanitary Squad who had been observing the mob,[39] he loaded the prostrate Kennedy onto it and drove back to headquarters. They arrived there just as the president of the Board of Commissioners, Thomas C. Acton, was coming out. Kennedy had been beaten so badly that Acton did not recognize him. Gesturing toward the apparently drunken wreck on the dray, he told an officer, "Lock him up! Lock him up!"

Like Superintendent Kennedy, Colonel Nugent had heard that there seemed to be some trouble in the Nineteenth Ward. The only troops he had available were seventy men of the Invalid Corps, the regiment of veterans who had been wounded or disabled and were fit only for light guard duty. Nugent divided the Invalids into three groups. He kept one detachment at the Park Barracks and sent another to the Thirty-fifth Street Arsenal, near the Eighth District draft office. The third squad, thirty-two strong, he ordered to the Ninth District office.

They left the barracks at 10:30 A.M. and piled onto a Third Avenue horse-car. On the way uptown, they were jeered, groaned at, and hissed by groups of people on the sidewalk, and the further they traveled, the thicker and more menacing the crowds became.

The draft office was already on fire, and a few blocks away from it, the officer in command, Lieutenant Reed, told his men to get off the car, form a line across the avenue, and advance. They marched a couple of blocks, and then at Forty-third Street the mob attacked in a rain of paving stones. A hundred fresh, battle-ready troops might have ended the riot at that moment, with a couple of volleys, but the Invalids could not withstand the charge of the rioters, who were already flushed and exultant from their victory over the police. They got off a few shots, and then the whole detachment broke and ran.[40]

Some of the soldiers escaped with nothing more than a few bruises, but one man, Private Robert Proctor, was never seen again and was posted "missing, believed killed."[41] Private John McKinna was found lying in the street at the corner of Sixth Avenue and Fifty-first Street, his skull fractured. He was taken to Bellevue Hospital, where he died a few hours later. Private John Allcock was cornered by some rioters in East Fortieth Street. They took away his musket, knocked him down, kicked and beat him, and broke his left arm. They left him bleeding on the sidewalk, and a man called Thomas Maguire and a couple of others carried him into Maguire's store. In a moment, two of the rioters came into the store, clubbed Allcock again for good measure, and left. Maguire feared further attacks, and he carried Allcock down into the cellar and covered him with hay. Maguire called a doctor and sent a message to the Twenty-first Precinct police station, but it was three o'clock before two officers reached the house in a carriage and took Allcock to Bellevue Hospital.[42]

At eleven o'clock, Captain Porter, who had made his way back to the Nineteenth Precinct station, telegraphed police headquarters: "The marshal's office on Third Avenue is burning down. The police is of no avail." A tall, well-dressed man called John U. Andrews, a shyster lawyer from Isle of Wight County, Virginia, who had been in New York since 1859, harangued the rioters from the roof of a shanty opposite the burning buildings.[43]

He commenced by saying that he wished that he had stentorian lungs that he might make himself heard, which, however, he had no hope of doing beyond a very narrow space; but he wished most devoutly that there was a reporter present who might carry his words to the clique at

Washington, who had caused all this trouble to the country, and especially to the city of New York, which had sent more men to the war and had given more money to sustain it than was recorded on the history of the world. He had told them lately at a meeting in the Cooper Institute, that Lincoln, this Nero, this Caligula, this despot, meant by this Conscription Bill to let the rich man go and earn more money by shoddy contracts and have the poor man dragged from his family and sent to the war to fight for the negro and not to restore the Union. Why was this conscription now attempted? Had they been more free with their lives or their money in the Revolutionary War of their fathers? Had they given more freely in the war with Great Britain in 1812? Did men ever fight more bravely in any battles in the world, than they fought throughout the conflict with the South? And now the Abolition Administration wanted a conscription. He was not against a fair conscription, but he was against a conscription that exempted the rich man and sent the poor man to fight and leave his wife and children starve at home. Resist the draft, he continued. Organize to resist it! Appoint your leader; and, if necessary, I will become your leader.[44]

The speaker had been frequently interrupted by thunderous cheers and shouts of "That's the talk" and "To hell with old Abe," and at the end of his address he was carried off shoulder-high.

The alarm bell was sounded when the buildings were set on fire, and several fire companies were quickly on the ground. Many of the men sympathized with the Black Joke, but some were willing to do their duty and put out the blaze. The rioters held them back, and they were helpless. Finally, John Decker, chief engineer of the Fire Department, arrived, and after several failures, succeeded in getting the crowd to listen to him.[45] Shouting, he said:

Fellow citizens, I stand here before you to appeal to your commonsense. I will not say a word at present as to the rights of your cause. About the Draft you doubtless feel you are right. There is no mistake, it is a hard thing for a man to have to leave his home and go soldiering if he did not wish to go; but I can't argue that question now. You probably feel that you are right in what you have done. You came here to do a certain thing. You have done it. Now you ought to be satisfied. All the United States property is destroyed, and I now appeal to your common-sense to let us, as firemen, go to work and save the property of innocent men. The men whose houses are now burning are innocent. They have nothing to do with the Draft. They know nothing of it. They are hard-working men like yourselves. Now I ask you, will you let us go to work and put out this fire?

Alderman Peter Masterson, brother of the Black Joke's foreman, supported the fire chief, telling the crowd that he was in favor of burning the draft office but was against destroying the property of a poor man who would not get a cent of the insurance on it if it was destroyed.[46] The crowd gave a cheer and made way for Decker and his men. They dragged their engines into position, but before they could begin pumping, some of the rioters who had been on Forty-second Street fighting the police reinforcements which were beginning to arrive, rushed back and drove the firefighters away. After ten or fifteen minutes, they drifted off, and Decker and his firemen were able to regain possession of their machines. But by then it was one o'clock and the row of houses was almost burned to the ground. Despite their best efforts, the loyal firemen were only able to save part of the last building.

By that time, many members of the mob had fanned out across the East Side of the city. Some invaded Central Park and forced the rest of the laborers there to join them.[47] Others began going from one saloon to another, demanding money and free drinks, and wrecking the place if they were refused. "I keep a lagerbeer saloon," testified Christian Kochne of 791 Third Avenue. "I was on the inside of the door; a man jumped in with a large carving knife; five more came in a few minutes after; the first one staid in; one of them said he wanted $5 from me; I opened the drawer and took a handful of five and ten cents pieces, and laid them on the counter; one of them got on the counter and held a knife over me; they then took the money out of the drawer. . . . I think there was about $25." Then the intruders broke all the tumblers and bottles, overturned the tables, and smashed the windows. More telegraph poles were cut down on First Avenue. A spirit of vandalism appeared. Valentine Kase was driving his employer's horse and wagon up Second Avenue, taking some clothes to be washed. At Thirty-sixth Street, he was attacked by a group of rioters, who overturned the wagon, stole the clothes, and beat Kase so badly he almost completely lost his hearing.[48]

The weather was hot and humid—the kind of day, as George G.

Foster remarked, that "makes you feel as if you had washed yourself in molasses and water."[49] No one wanted to stay indoors in such weather, and the streets were full of people. The failure of the authorities to respond faster, the ridiculously easy victories over the police, and the Invalids encouraged many who might have remained mere spectators to join the mob. As news of the rioting spread, stores and businesses closed their doors, and their employees joined the crowd of curious onlookers (and potential rioters) in the streets.[50]

At police headquarters, all was confusion. Kennedy's prolonged absence left the force leaderless, and as late as 11:30 A.M., downtown precincts were telegraphing to ask "Is there a riot uptown?" The reserve sections of eleven precincts were ordered to the scene of the disorders, but coming from different areas of the city, they arrived at different times. If a common rendezvous had been fixed and a commander ordered to take charge of the united force, they might have been successful. As it was, the mob routed the various small detachments one by one.[51]

Sergeant Robert A. "Fighting Mac" McCredie and fourteen men from the Fifteenth Precinct joined thirty officers from the Twenty-eighth at Forty-third Street, and the combined force made a charge on the mob which was brilliantly successful at first. The rioters were sent hurtling back almost to Forty-sixth Street. But the force of police was too small to exploit its advantage or even to hold the ground it had won. The mob rallied and counterattacked, and the outnumbered police were overwhelmed. They fled, every man trying to save himself, with the population of the area throwing everything from stones to crockery at them. Those who could made their way back to their station houses, but some were not so lucky. Officer John M. Bennett was knocked senseless, stripped of his clothes, and left for dead in the street. Eventually, he was taken to Saint Luke's Hospital at Fifth Avenue and Fifty-fifth Street, where the staff also thought him dead and put him in the mortuary for several hours, until someone noticed he was still breathing. Officer William H. Travis was caught and pummeled senseless. Rioters jumped up and down on his prostrate body, broke his jaw, knocked his teeth out, and left him lying naked in the gutter. Another policeman, N. G. Phillips, was clubbed and stabbed before he made his escape across the empty lots and reached the Thirty-first Precinct station house on Eighty-sixth Street. McCredie himself took refuge in the house of a German family, who hid him under a mattress, while the mob ransacked the premises for him.

Another platoon of the Fifteenth Precinct, numbering eighteen men, had been sent to reinforce McCredie, but by the time they arrived, he and his men were defeated and scattered. The platoon held together in the face of the mob's assaults and made an orderly retreat, though one man was so badly beaten that he had to be sent to the station house in a wagon, and another officer collapsed after they had reached safety. Two stragglers from this platoon, who reported at the precinct after it had left and went up Third Avenue to join it, were caught by the mob and soundly thrashed.

Captain Porter and the police who had been chased from the draft office at the outset of the riot tried to battle their way back down Third Avenue, after they were reinforced by a few more officers, but once again they failed. Under the attacks of the mob, they faltered, and Captain Porter gave the order to withdraw. Immediately, discipline snapped. Every man took to his heels and ran for his life. By ones and twos, they wandered back to the Nineteenth Precinct station, where Porter ordered some of them to change into civilian clothes and sent them out to rescue the injured. A section from the Eighteenth Precinct, coming up from the South to join Porter, ran into a crowd of rioters first and was driven back. Twenty-five men from the Thirteenth had the same experience and could get no further than Thirty-fifth Street.

Half an hour after Porter's defeat, Sergeant Frederick Ellison and thirteen men of the Eighth Precinct ran into the mob at Forty-second Street. Ellison ordered a charge and picked a rioter brandishing a musket as his target. He grabbed the weapon, but a brick knocked it from his grasp, and he drew his revolver and began to fire. The men of his little command had to fall back, and Ellison barricaded himself in a store. Some of the rioters went around to the back of the building, climbed the fence, and took him by surprise. He was dragged out and paraded up and down the street, the mob clubbing him and pelting him with stones. At that moment, two platoons from the Ninth Precinct and ten more officers of the Eighth arrived and made a desperate charge to rescue Ellison. They succeeded, but found themselves surrounded, and they had to fight their way back down the avenue step by step.[52]

One of Ellison's detachment, Patrolman John T. Van Buren, received a broken leg in the fight. He never recovered his health, and on November 7, he died. Another of the injured, Sergeant S. B. Smith of the Ninth Precinct, was separated from the main body of police in the confusion of battle and was discovered that evening lying in the baggage car of a train stopped on Fourth Avenue. Three policemen, one of them badly injured, hid in a house on the corner of Lexington Avenue and Forty-first Street. The owner, a man called George Barker, told them it was not safe for them to stay there and supplied some old clothes for the two who were still on their feet. About one o'clock, they slipped out, made their way to the nearest station house, and sent a carriage for the injured officer. This attracted the attention of some rioters, who began to throw stones at the house, but Barker was able to persuade them to go away. As soon as they had gone, he sent his family to a friend's house; a wise precaution, for just after two o'clock, another crowd of rioters came along. Barker went out to speak to them; they knocked him down and rushed into the house, where they ate up his dinner, stole some clothes, and broke the windows. Officer John H. McCarty was caught in Forty-third Street and beaten by the mob, who dislocated his shoulder and tossed him into the area of a house. The owner, Carrie Cornell, brought him in and hid him in the woodshed. In a little while, the rioters came back and, not finding McCarty in the area, broke down the doors of the house and began to search for him. Miss Cornell told them "he had been taken away," and at last they left. She went out to seek a doctor, but not one would risk coming. At last, she went to the Twenty-ninth Precinct station, where the captain sent out some men in plain clothes to bring McCarty in.[53]

With the police out of the way, the mob seized the opportunity for looting. While some despoiled the Croton Cottage restaurant on Fifth Avenue, others invaded the Palace Park House, a hotel on Fortieth Street, and helped themselves to champagne, sherry, brandy, bourbon, port, gin, rum, and 1,700 cigars.[54]

The New Haven trains running down Fourth Avenue were

stoned. The frightened passengers took cover on the floor of the coaches or jumped off. A little later, the track was torn up for several blocks above Forty-second Street. The former city editor of the *New York Times*, a man named Howard, was recognized standing opposite the smoldering ruins of the Ninth District office. "Here's a damned abolitionist!" someone yelled. "Let's hang him!" "He's a *Tribune* man! Hang the son of a bitch!" Howard promptly decamped, but he was chased and stoned before he finally got away.

Just before three o'clock, a rumor spread that a house on Lexington Avenue belonged to the provost marshal. As the story spread, it was embellished, and Horace Greeley and Colonel Nugent were named as the owners. None of this was true, though a policeman who was being mobbed had rung the bell and tried to get in. The owner was out, and his family and servant girls were too scared to help the officer.[55] But the stories were believed, and with a shout the mob rushed toward the place. George Templeton Strong was a spectator. He wrote:

Every brute in the drove was pure Keltic-hod-carrier or loafer. They were unarmed. A few carried pieces of fence-paling and the like. They turned off West into Forty-fifth Street and gradually collected in front of two three-storey dwelling houses on Lexington Avenue, just below that street, that stand alone together on a nearly vacant block. . . . The mob was in no hurry; they had no need to be; there was no one to molest them or make them afraid. The beastly ruffians were masters of the situation and of the city. After a while sporadic paving-stones began to fly at the windows, ladies and children emerged from the rear, and had a rather hard scramble over a high board fence, and then scudded off across the open, Heaven knows whither. Then men and small boys appeared at rear windows and began smashing the sashes and the blinds and shied out light articles, such as books and crockery, and dropped chairs and mirrors into the back yard; the rear fence was demolished and loafers were seen marching off with portable articles of furniture. And at last a light smoke began to float out of the windows, and I came away.

The house was left a blackened shell.[56]

By this time, the authorities were at last pulling themselves together. Just after noon, Commissioner Acton had taken over command of the police. He put his colleague Commissioner John G. Bergen in control of the Brooklyn and Staten Island precincts and took Manhattan Island as his own responsibility. Acton's first step was to order all the police in the city to concentrate at the Central Office. It was three o'clock before any sizable force could be collected, and in the meantime the mob was running amok, with no opposition from the police. The disorders were still confined to the uptown wards, and ideally it would have been preferable for Acton to have fixed his headquarters somewhere nearer the riot area, perhaps at the Twenty-ninth Precinct station in East Twenty-ninth Street. But the inadequacies of the police telegraph system meant that the precincts could not communicate with each other, only with the Central Office. Under these circumstances, Acton was probably right to stay at Central, and in any case, the riot was soon to assume citywide proportions.

Mayor George Opdyke had begun firing off telegrams and messages as soon as he had heard of the disturbances on Third Avenue, but he could obtain little help. A storm had brought telegraph lines down and washed away railroad tracks in Maryland, and only a trickle of information about the riots reached Washington. Secretary of War Stanton, like everyone else in the federal capital, was slow to realize the gravity of the situation in New York and did nothing for twenty-four hours. Governor Seymour had gone to spend a long weekend with his sister-in-law in New Jersey. On Monday morning, they went to Long Branch, and the frantic telegrams sent to Seymour at the address he had given in New Brunswick did not reach him.[57] General John E. Wool, commander of the army's Department of the East, had only the Invalids and the garrisons of the harbor forts on hand. The former were not fit for combat, and the harbor garrisons had been reduced to a skeleton force when the orders came to send every available man to Pennsylvania. Less than four hundred federal troops could be collected for service in the city. The commander of the state militia, General Charles W. Sandford, was no better off. He thought that he could scrape up six hundred men at most. Opdyke and Wool began telegraphing everyone they could think of for help: Admiral Paulding, the commander of the Brooklyn Navy Yard; the superintendent of West Point; the federal commander in Newark; and the governors of New Jersey, Connecticut, Massachusetts, and Rhode Island. Sandford and Wool placed announcements in all the newspapers asking ex-soldiers to volunteer their services; a call was made for special policemen; and Opdyke issued a proclamation ordering the rioters to desist and warning that "all necessary measures will be taken to preserve the peace of the city, to enforce the laws, and to put down rioters at all hazards."[58]

A special meeting of the Board of Aldermen was called, but a quorum could not be mustered. Alderman Farley, whose district took in the Third Avenue and Forty-sixth Street neighborhood, urged that as a way of calming the population, the Corporation Counsel should be ordered to challenge the constitutionality of the draft act in the courts. Other aldermen were ready with a scheme to issue $3,750,000 worth of bonds and use the proceeds to buy drafted men out of the army by paying their $300 commutation fee.

Immediately after the burning of the Ninth District office, some of the mob shouted "To the Armory! To the Armory!" and at 12:15 P.M. a message was received at the Central Office saying: "There is danger of the mob attacking the Armory corner of 21st Street and Second Avenue. There is about five hundred stand of arms in it." This armory was really a rifle factory which supplied arms to both the United States and Russian governments. The upper floor was used as a drill room by some militia regiments, and this gave the building its name. The factory was operated by Opdyke's son-in-law, George W. Farlee, and the mayor had invested heavily in the concern. About 6,000 rifles were in the factory, although only 1,000 of them were ready for use. Even more worrisome, from the point of view of the authorities, was that there were over 3,000 carbines and muskets stored in the Union Steam Works, one block above the armory. Apart from the muskets taken from the Invalids, the rioters possessed very few firearms. Many of them had pulled down the fences around the vacant lots on Lexington Avenue to make clubs.[59] What the mob might do if it secured a large supply of guns did not bear thinking about.

Acton had only one detachment of men to send to the armory, but they were the thirty-four members of the Broadway Squad, the strapping six-footers whose usual assignment was to unsnarl the traffic and help pedestrians across the city's most congested street.

They were the only policemen most visitors to New York City ever saw, and their magnificent physiques and smart appearance had won the Metropolitan force a fine reputation. Acton hurried them off to the Eighteenth Precinct station house on East Twenty-second Street, and the commander there, Captain John Cameron, sent them to garrison the armory. Nothing could be done to protect the Union Steam Works, but fortunately the mob did not seem to know of the guns stored there.

The rioters were already too numerous in the neighborhood for the Broadway Squad to march to the armory in a body, and they had to reach their post by ones and twos, slipping through the streets as inconspicuously as possible. Some of the police assured the cashier at the armory "that they could hold the building with their clubs against any mob in New York," and for a while they made good their boast. Ellen Leonard, a young girl from upstate who was staying with her brother on East Nineteenth Street saw First Avenue crowded "with thousands of infuriated creatures, yelling, screaming and swearing in the most frantic manner; while crowds of women, equally ferocious, were leaning from every door and window, swinging aprons and handkerchiefs, and cheering and urging them onward. The rush and roar grew every moment more terrific. Up came fresh hordes faster and more furious; bare-headed men, with red, swollen faces, brandishing sticks and clubs, or carrying heavy poles and beams; and boys, women and children hurrying on and joining with them in this mad chase up the avenue like a company of raging fiends." [60]

For a time, the mob did nothing but hurl stones and curses at the armory. Just before half-past two, they tried unsuccessfully to set fire to the building, and this was followed by an attempt to storm the main entrance. The doors were splintered and smashed open with an improvised battering ram, but the police used their revolvers, several rioters were shot, and the rest were beaten off. The crowds around the armory increased, the paving stones flew thick and fast, and fresh attacks were mounted and repulsed. Sergeant Burdick, who was in command of the Broadway Squad, sent to Captain Cameron at the Eighteenth Precinct for reinforcements. [61] Cameron replied that he had none to send, and fearful of another attempt to set the building ablaze, he ordered Burdick to evacuate the armory. There is no doubt that this order was a mistake and that Cameron grossly overestimated the danger. J. W. Keane, the superintendent of the factory, and five of his men were still on the premises and would have joined in the defense. Plenty of carbines and a thousand rounds of ammunition were available to supplement the policemen's revolvers. Finally, a strong force of police was already fighting its way up Second Avenue.

Without making any attempt to destroy the ammunition or render the guns useless, Burdick obeyed Cameron's order. He and his men obviously could not leave by the main entrance. Instead, they squeezed through a twenty-four by eighteen inch window in the blacksmith shop, at the back of the factory, climbed down a drainpipe, and made their way over garden fences and through back ways to the Eighteenth Precinct station. Keane dispatched a desperate message to Captain Cameron, asking him to send some men, but the reply came back that there were none available. There was nothing for Keane and his men to do but leave.[62]

A few minutes later, just after four o'clock, the mob burst in and began carrying off the carbines. Now that the armory was taken, numbers of the rioters turned to looting the houses round about. Their sport was soon interrupted: at 4:50 P.M. the police reinforcements reached Twentieth Street, and the mob set the armory on fire, although a number of their fellows were still on the upper floor. The building burned like a torch, and those trapped inside were forced to jump from the upstairs windows to save themselves. The police fought their way past the armory down to the Eighteenth Precinct station, and the mob in that locality scattered for the time being. Altogether, thirteen people lost their lives at the battle of the armory: two were shot, eight (one of them twelve years of age) died of burns, and two were killed jumping from the windows of the upper floors of the building. Four more were seriously injured in the fight: one was seriously burned, one sustained head injuries when he was clubbed, and two were shot.[63]

At the same hour, on the other side of town, the Eighth District draft office was in flames. The drawing had begun at the office, on the corner of West Twenty-ninth Street and Broadway, that morning. Everything had gone on in perfect quiet until 11:30 A.M., when the provost marshal, Captain B. F. Manierre, heard of the attack on the Ninth District office and decided to close up. Taking all his enrollment sheets and ballots to the Twenty-ninth Precinct police station, Manierre went home.[64]

The district remained tranquil until four o'clock in the afternoon, when Patrick Merry, an Irish cellar-digger who lived in West Twenty-eighth Street, led a crowd of two or three hundred men and boys down Broadway to a marble yard opposite Number 1180. Merry ordered the men there to stop working and join the crowd, and then went across the street to the foundry shop of Newman, Onderdonk and Capron and did the same there. Out in the street again, he stopped one stage, tried to stop a second, and then sent one of his men up to another crowd gathered on the corner of Thirty-second Street and Broadway. The second crowd came rushing down the street, joined Merry's followers, and together they smashed open the door of the draft office. In no time the place was wrecked and the mob turned its attention to the other stores in the block.

One by one, they were entered and sacked. Many of the goods were thrown into the street. Gold watches, brooches, and bracelets from the jeweler's store gleamed and flashed as the looters examined their spoils and showed them to the spectators in the street. Richard Murphy, the owner of a grocery on the opposite side of the street, saved his property by offering the rioters free whiskey. They drank nineteen gallons altogether, but Murphy was luckier than Thomas Thornton, who owned a saloon at 1178 Broadway. The mob broke in, drank all the liquor in the bar, carried off the kegs and demijohns full of alcohol, and robbed him of $200.[65]

After plundering the stores, the mob turned to the apartments over them. A lady named Sarah Safford, who tried to save her belongings, was thrown over the banisters. Another woman, who begged the rioters not to steal her mother's watch because of its sentimental value, was told that she could save her life, and that was all. Mrs. Frances A. Taylor, who lived at 1184 Broadway, was talking to a neighbor just before the attack began. "She said she thought the mob would come, and hoped they would come; she thought that they had no right to draft." She waved a handkerchief from her window to welcome the rioters, but they turned her out of her apartment, and she lost everything.[66]

About 4:55 P.M. someone set fire to the awning of one of the stores and then went inside and put a light to a gas pipe. Those upstairs looting the apartments began to set fires, too, and before long all eleven buildings on the block that fronted on Broadway were ablaze.[67] One man who had some furniture and paintings stored at Number 1184 rushed over as soon as he heard that the building was burning and implored the mob to save his property. "Throw him in the fire!" bellowed a jovial rioter. But they only stole his gold watch and chain and let him off with a beating.[68]

That afternoon, the rioting had spread all over the city. Early on, an English immigrant called Thomas Sutherland turned up at the Allaire Iron Works, where he was employed as a boiler-maker, at the head of an unruly crowd. He ordered all the men there to stop work and join him and marched on throughout the Ninth Ward, stopping at other factories and foundries and calling on the workers to turn out. He ended up at the great Novelty Iron Works on Fourteenth Street, where, apparently deciding that he had collected enough followers, he led them uptown to join the mob which had just finished burning the houses on Lexington Avenue. Another rumor had spread through the crowd: there were papers belonging to the provost marshal in Allerton's Washington Drove Yard Hotel (also known as the Bull's Head) at Forty-third Street and Madison Avenue. They swept toward the hotel and rushed inside. Papers, furniture, and bedding were sent cascading out of the windows. A couple of barrels of liquor were rolled out into the street, the heads knocked in, and the drink dipped out with tins, pans, kettles, buckets—anything that came to hand.[69] At 4:35 P.M. the first tongues of flame came licking out of the windows. The mostly wooden building was soon a heap of ashes and cinders amidst some low, blackened brick walls.

Other members of the uptown mob had been ranging along Fifth Avenue. One nervous home owner put up a huge sign reading OPPOSITION TO THE DRAFT outside his house, hoping it would save his property from the torch.[70] Rioters flooded into the grounds of Columbia College at Forty-ninth Street and knocked on the door of Professor John Torrey's house, demanding to know what the college buildings were used for and whether a Republican lived there. The name of President Charles King struck a spark of recognition; he was a Republican, and giving a cheer for Jeff Davis, they prepared to burn King's house. A couple of Catholic priests dissuaded them and got them to leave.[71] Policemen had been seen taking injured officers into Saint Luke's Hospital, and "a huge, hatless and coatless laborer, his shirt sleeves rolled up to the armpits and bare-breasted, red with liquor and rage," burst into the main hall, roaring, "Turn out, turn out by six o'clock, or we'll burn ye in your beds." Dr. William A. Muhlenberg, the founder and head of Saint Luke's, was worried enough to make preparations for evacuating women and children in case of an attack and sent a messenger to General Wool asking for protection. Wool replied that he had no troops to spare for guard duty, but would send help if the hospital was attacked. This was none too reassuring, and Muhlenberg and his staff nervously scanned the avenue for signs of an advancing mob.[72]

Further down Fifth Avenue, Mayor Opdyke's house was a natural target for the rioters. Captain Manierre, the Eighth District provost marshal, lived nearby and as soon as he got home from the draft office, he organized a party of neighbors to defend the house. The first group of rioters that came along was addressed by Manierre and Judge George G. Barnard. Manierre urged them to go home. Barnard, who was later to attain infamy for his dealings with Jay Gould and Jim Fisk, denounced the draft as an unconstitutional act, as an act of despotism. The administration had gone too far; they had imposed upon the people. Tremendous cheering greeted this statement. But, Barnard said, he wanted to call attention to the fact that they still had law. The courts would protect them in the exercise of all their just and legal rights. The only way to resist the draft was by bringing it before the courts. He promised that he would issue a writ of habeas corpus for any drafted man who applied to him. The Republicans, he agreed, had brought on the war. But that was no reason for opponents of the Republicans to commit acts of violence that would be used in arguments against them. He hoped, for the honor of their city, that its people would not destroy the residence of their legally elected chief officer. Persuaded either by the speeches or by the sight of rifle-barrels protruding from the windows of the Opdyke mansion, the rioters quietly went away. A force of police arrived a little later and had no trouble scaring off a second crowd of roughs.

At 4:45 P.M. the Twentieth Precinct telegraphed the Central Office: "A very large mob now going down Fifth Avenue to attack *Tribune* office." Commissioner Acton had about two hundred men in reserve at Central, and he decided to intercept this mob on its way downtown. Daniel Carpenter, the senior inspector of the department, was put in command. Carpenter rose to the occasion, declaring, "I'll go, and I won't come back unless I come back victorious."[73] While receiving his orders from Acton, Carpenter asked what to do with any prisoners. "Prisoners?" shrieked the anxious commissioner. "Don't take any! Kill! Kill! Kill! Put down the mob. Don't bring a prisoner in till the mob is put down."

The men of Carpenter's force were drawn up in the street outside police headquarters, and the Inspector addressed them in the spirit of Acton's instructions. "Men!" he barked. "We are to meet and put down a mob. We are to take no prisoners. We must strike quick and strike hard." Carpenter marched his men up Broadway as far as Bleecker Street, where he drew them up in line across the road. The mob, two or three hundred strong, "a crowd of ill-dressed and ill-favored men and boys, each carrying a long stick or piece of board, and one or two of them a rusty musket" soon approached.[74] It was headed by one man carrying an American flag and another with a sign reading "No Draft." "By the right flank!" bellowed Carpenter. "Company front! Double quick! Charge!" For once, the police and the mob were roughly equal in numbers, and the officers' charge struck the ranks of the mob with irresistible force. The rioters struggled for a few moments and then fled, with the police pursuing and clubbing them. Two of the mob burst through the window of a store in their frenzy to escape. Broadway was littered with stunned and disabled rioters from Bond Street to Union Square, and the police, who marched back to headquarters exultantly singing "The Red, White and Blue," had won their first victory.[75]

*Let but law lift its hand from them for a season, or let the
civilizing influences of American life fail to reach them, and if the
opportunity offered, we should see an explosion from this
class which might leave this city in ashes and blood.*

—CHARLES LORING BRACE
*The Dangerous Classes of New York*[1]

# 4

## *Black Pogrom and the Old Whitecoat*

LIEUTENANT COLONEL Arthur Fremantle of the Coldstream Guards, who had been attached to Lee's army as an observer, had just come through the lines and was staying in New York while waiting for a passage home. Sauntering through the streets that Monday afternoon, he was astonished to see a crowd chasing a Negro, with cries of "Down with the bloody nigger!" "Kill all niggers!" He related: "Never having been in New York before, and being totally ignorant of the state of feeling with regard to negroes, I inquired of a by-stander what the negro had done that they should want to kill him? He replied civilly enough – 'Oh, sir they hate them here [because] they are the innocent cause of all these troubles.' "[2]

Animosity toward Negroes appeared several times during that afternoon. Blacks were pulled off streetcars downtown and beaten, and the rioters who had burned the Eighth District draft office turned to looting the houses of blacks in the West Thirties afterwards.[3]

A mob began to gather outside the Colored Orphan Asylum at Fifth Avenue and Forty-third Street before four o'clock. The 237 children who lived there, all under twelve years of age, were hurried out the back door, with the mob's yells of "Burn the niggers' nest" and "Down with the niggers" ringing in their ears. They were taken to the Twentieth Precinct station, the bigger children carrying the smaller ones on their backs. A few short moments after they had left, the rioters broke down the front door. The orphanage was pillaged. Men smashed pianos and carried off carpets, maps, stools, chairs, dishes, and a couple of hundred iron bedsteads. Fifth Avenue was strewn with books and papers. Clothing and furniture were pitched out of the windows. A ten-year-old girl named Jane Barry, who was standing on the sidewalk watching the scene, was hit by a bureau and killed instantly.[4]

Fires were set, and the building was soon in flames. Chief Engineer Decker, who had heard what was going on, arrived and forced his way into the building. Single-handed, he began trying to put out the fire, but he was knocked down twice and finally dragged outside. Decker found ten volunteer firemen on Fifth Avenue and led them inside again. Though they put out several blazes on the first two floors, the flames had too great a hold on the upper stories for the building to be saved.[5] Once again, Decker was pushed out into the street, and his men with him. The chief engineer appealed to the rioters to do nothing so disgraceful to humanity as to burn a benevolent institution which had only good for its object. It would, he declared, be a lasting disgrace to them and to the city of New York. But the mob only grew more infuriated with Decker himself, and his firemen had to protect him. A couple of volunteer companies had brought their engines around, and they began to pump water. The rioters promptly cut their hose and damaged the hydrants, sending great jets of water spurting into the air. Finally, the firemen gave up and pulled their machines away.[6]

New York's Negroes were especially vulnerable to attack, since they did not live in a separate quarter. Numbers of blacks were to be found in every ward of the city. It is true that there were some streets that were generally recognized as Negro areas: Roosevelt, Dover, James, Oak, and Water streets in the Fourth Ward; Baxter, Pell, and Park streets in the Sixth; Sullivan, Thompson, York, and Lispenard streets on the southern edge of Greenwich Village, and some blocks along Sixth Avenue in the West Twenties and Thirties. But even these black sections were still small enough for a white mob to penetrate without feeling that they might be confronted by an overwhelming number of blacks or trapped far from a white neighborhood.[7]

Crowds of white men gathered in the Negro streets of the Fourth and Sixth wards and Greenwich Village about four o'clock and started to attack the houses and beat the inhabitants. Emanuel McConkey, a ship's cook who had served as a steward on the government transport *Cadwallader* and who had cooked for the Thirty-first Massachusetts in garrison at Fortress Monroe, was staying at a sailor's boardinghouse in Roosevelt Street on that day. He later testified:

When the mob came to the house, they burst open the door; there were sixty or seventy who came in; I was in the front part of the house on Chambers street; they burst in on the Roosevelt street side; they ran up stairs and I saw them gathering up clothes, which had been washed, on the porch; then they went to the upper story, and threw out the bedsteads and beds into the street; then they went down into the basement and plundered it; I was looking at them all the time through a place in the door, where the lock had been broken off . . . then they set fire to the house; they burnt the stairs and some of the wood-part; I could not see what they did to my things which were in the main street; I left the house and went out on Chambers street, when they beat me [showed the marks on his face].

Somehow McConkey got away, and at 8:45 that night he staggered into the Forty-second Precinct station house across the river in Brooklyn, "very much bruised and badly cut, so that he could scarcely move." McConkey later said that he could remember nothing of what happened from 5 P.M. Monday until 4 P.M. the next day.[8]

McConkey's landlord, Henry Beverly, had also hidden himself when the rioters attacked, but he managed to get away safely. When he next saw his house "everything was gone and the house partially burnt, the partitions torn down and doors and steps gone." Another owner of a colored sailors' boardinghouse, John Brown of 74 Roosevelt Street, was caught in the street, robbed, and stripped of his clothes. Fighting off his assailants, he ran through the streets stark naked and reached the ferry. In Brooklyn a man gave him a pair of pants to wear. William Green, a boardinghouse runner who had rented the basement of Number 74 to open a saloon six months before, suffered the same kind of humil-

iation. "They stripped me naked," he recalled, ". . . they had a rope
to hang me, and a man saved me." A few doors down Roosevelt
Street, the rioters sacked the home of a black family, piled all their
belongings up on the opposite side of the street, and made a bonfire of them. Several Negroes were badly injured when they were
trapped in burning buildings and had to jump from upstairs windows to save themselves.[9]

William P. Powell, a former member of the Executive Committee of the American Anti-Slavery Society, was running the Globe
Hotel in Dover Street at this time. His son was a surgeon in the
army, and Powell himself had just received a commission in the
navy. About seven o'clock, boys began throwing stones at the hotel
windows, and a quarter of an hour later some young men turned
up and broke in. While they were carrying off the furniture and
smashing the dishes, Powell, his family, and boarders retreated to
the roof. The Jewish family who lived next door agreed to take
Powell's crippled daughter in and gave him a rope. With this and
a clothes line that ran a hundred feet across the rooftops, he rigged
up a bo'sun's chair and transported all his party to a housetop
some way off. They climbed down into the garden, hid in a friend's
cellar until 11 P.M., and then went to the police station. Powell
and his family still did not feel particularly safe and decided to go
and stay with some friends in New Bedford, Massachusetts. The
following night, the police escorted them to the New Haven boat,
and they thankfully said goodbye to the riot-torn city.[10]

All over town, Negroes were being attacked and their houses
looted. A white man watched the wrecking of Mrs. Maria Prince's
boardinghouse in Sullivan Street:

Enoch W. Jacques, sworn: I live at No. 64 Sullivan Street; lived there
since 1829; between ten and eleven o'clock there came up a crowd of
boys and young men; they dug up paving stones, and went to work and
battered the house; then they went away; then, about two hours and a
half after that, a party of men came along (about six or seven men and
fifteen or twenty young men and boys); they went to work and dug up
paving stones, and slam-banged at the house, and broke in the windows
and doors, and went into and took possession of the house; then they
struck a light; and went through and ransacked the house. I was sitting
on my stoop right opposite all the time, when I heard the glasses being

broken and I saw them lug out goods–bedquilts, petticoats and sheets, as near as I could judge, also dresses. They took a little of everything; then they went away and came again; I went through the house the next day, and saw that it had been sacked from top to bottom.[11]

Only one section of the police had been left in the Fourth Precinct, and though they rescued a number of Negroes, they were simply too few to break up the mob. At 6:50 P.M. the Fourth telegraphed the Central Office: "Great excitement in this ward. Only a section of men here. Ask inspector if they can't remain. Much needed. Station house being stoned. Muskets in use." Help was sent, and at 7:30 P.M. Central asked the Fourth: "How are things in your ward?" "Riotous condition" was the terse reply. A quarter of an hour later, the Fourth reported, "The rioters are attacking colored boarding houses, robbing them and setting them on fire. I have not force enough to prevent it." Shortly afterwards, the wires were cut, and the next news, at 8:25 P.M., came from the Twenty-sixth Precinct station at City Hall: "The Fourth wants help real bad." By nine o'clock, the telegraph had been repaired, and the Fourth told headquarters: "Things awful bad here. Inspector D. C. [Carpenter] here with big force, but excitement increases. Two colored men brought in almost dead." Carpenter's force pacified the area, and the whole squad from the Eleventh Precinct was left on guard. At 10:30 P.M. they had a hard fight at the corner of Roosevelt and Batavia streets, where the rioters had made a bonfire of furniture too heavy to carry away. Under a bombardment of bricks from the rooftops, the men of the Eleventh charged and succeeded in clearing the area.

Elsewhere, more protection was available. Negroes pulled off streetcars and stages around City Hall were quickly delivered from danger. Officers of the Sixth Precinct intervened when Negroes' houses in Baxter and Pell streets were attacked and repulsed an attempt to mob the Negro waiters at Crook's restaurant in Chatham Street. Rioters sometimes got what they wanted, in spite of the police. Some officers arrived just as William Pasel's boarding-house in Park Street was being attacked. They drove off the rioters, took Pasel to the station, and left a policeman on watch outside the house. But when Pasel returned at three o'clock on Tuesday afternoon, he found that the rioters had broken in through the back and had stripped the place bare. They had been so quiet about it that the guard at the front door had not heard a sound.[12]

Several times during the evening's rioting, the crowds of whites showed an inclination to enforce sexual morality by terror. Boardinghouses that rented rooms to black prostitutes were attacked, and so were bars and dancehalls where they congregated.[13]

Many Negroes were slow to realize the danger they were in and were attacked as they were going home from work in the evening. About six o'clock, three Negroes were walking down Varick Street in the Eighth Ward, carrying their dinner kettles. As they passed Boylan's liquor store on the corner of Charlton Street, John Nicholson, an Irish bricklayer who lived a few doors away, and two other men sailed out and attacked them. Two of the Negroes took to their heels and got away, but the third was closely pursued by Nicholson and his companions. Soon, other whites joined in the chase. "Kill the nigger!" "Kill the black son of a bitch!" came the cries. Several times, the whites overtook the Negro and kicked and beat him, but each time he fended them off and began running again. Turning into Clarkson Street, the terrified black pulled out a pistol, fired, and wounded Nicholson. This gave him enough time to make good his escape, but another Negro, named William Jones, happened to be walking down Clarkson Street. He had come out to buy a loaf of bread and was on his way home. The furious whites seized Jones and hanged him from the nearest tree. A fire was kindled underneath the body, and the whites stood around it and watched as the flames burned the dead man's clothes and charred his flesh.[14]

An Irishman called Patrick Oatis who had once been a policeman, but who was now working as a bricklayer, was roaming Seventh Avenue looking for trouble. He attacked one Negro, who beat him off and got away. Soon after, another black called Henry Johnson, who lived in West Thirtieth Street, came along, and Oatis grappled with him. They fell down, and Oatis bit Johnson on the cheek and bit part of his left ear off before he was able to escape.[15]

Nancy and Jeremiah Robinson, a Negro couple who lived in the Fourth Ward, decided to try and escape across the East River to

Brooklyn. The rioters, as the Robinsons knew, demonstrated a certain savage chivalry. Only black men were beaten or killed; black women were usually not molested. Relying on this, Robinson dressed up in some of his wife's clothes, and the two of them set out for the Grand Street ferry with a woman friend. But the hood that Robinson wore failed to conceal his beard, and he was spotted by some rioters at the corner of Madison and Catharine streets. The two women escaped and reached Brooklyn safely; but Robinson was set upon and beaten to death. His body was thrown into the river.[16]

Peter Heuston, a Mohawk Indian who had served in a New York volunteer regiment during the Mexican War and who now worked as a whitewasher, was caught by some rioters at the corner of Chambers and Oak streets. Taking him for a Negro, they gave him a merciless beating. Heuston spent the night in hiding, and at six the next morning, he staggered into the Seventh Precinct station house. He was taken to Bellevue Hospital, where he died on July 27. The coroner's jury found that his death was caused by "congestion of the liver, accelerated by blows received at the hands of the mob."[17]

Beginning on Monday evening, large numbers of Negroes went into hiding or fled from their homes.[18] Many left the city altogether and went to Long Island, New Jersey, or the upper part of Manhattan Island. There, they either found temporary quarters in Negro settlements like Weeksville,[19] or camped out in the woods along the Harlem River, and in Queens County, or on the Elysian Fields in Hoboken. Others went to the police station houses. At the height of the riot, there were over seven hundred Negroes in the Central Office. Only one precinct, the Twenty-ninth, refused to take in the refugees, and the sergeant in command there was charged with dereliction of duty by the commissioners after the riot.[20]

The safety of the station houses was often more illusory than real. At a critical time on Wednesday, when it seemed that the Central Office might be attacked, Commissioner Acton had only ten exhausted patrolmen in the building. As soon as the children from the Colored Orphan Asylum arrived at the Twentieth Precinct station, Captain Walling and his men were called to Central, leaving only a sergeant, two doormen, and a few partially disabled patrolmen who were on the sick list to guard the orphans.[21] Fortunately, the mob had no way of knowing how weakly garrisoned most of the station houses were. There were one or two close calls. On Monday a mob gathered outside the Second Precinct station, where there were several dozen Negroes, and only a sergeant and a patrolman to defend them. The sergeant held the rioters off with his revolver until some of the force returned. Later that night, eight officers armed only with their revolvers and a couple of empty muskets scared off some rioters who gathered in front of the Fourth Precinct station.

During the late afternoon and evening, help arrived for the hard-pressed police. Federal troops from the forts in the harbor were brought to Manhattan, and militia detachments that, for one reason or another, had not been sent to Pennsylvania were collected and armed. Numbers of veterans and soldiers who were on leave or on recruiting duty volunteered their services. Admiral Paulding, the commander of the Brooklyn Navy Yard, sent over some marines and three howitzers.[22]

Many of these troops were used ineffectively. Some were not used at all. The commander of the state militia in the city, Major General Charles W. Sandford, had led the First Division for twenty-seven years and was more of a bureaucrat than a soldier.[23] He was obsessed with the defense of the state arsenals in the city and seemed determined to preserve them from harm at all costs, though the rest of New York City suffer the fate of Carthage.[24]

That Monday, Sandford had at his disposal two troops of cavalry, which had been acting as an honor guard at the funeral of Brigadier General Samuel K. Zook, who had been killed at Gettysburg. He also had the Tenth Regiment of the New York National Guard, which was made up of raw recruits and had not been thought ready for service before. The Tenth was scheduled to set off for Maryland that Monday morning. Sandford took control of these troops and distributed them among the various arsenals.[25] He ordered three companies of the Tenth to the arsenal in Central Park and another three hundred men, with a battery of three six-pounders, to the arsenal at White and Elm streets. The rest of the Tenth Regiment, with the cavalry, went to the Thirty-fifth Street

Arsenal. Later, several units of federal troops were put under Sandford's command, and they, too, went to the Thirty-fifth Street Arsenal. And there, except for a very few forays, they stayed. They did not even patrol the districts immediately around the arsenals. The Eighth District draft office was only seven blocks from the Thirty-fifth Street Arsenal and the White Street building was near the Negro streets of Greenwich Village. The office was burned, and the Negroes were attacked; and Sandford's troops did not lift a finger.

After what happened to the Invalids at Third Avenue and Forty-third Street, there was some justification for Sandford's decision to use the newly recruited Tenth for garrison duty, although the mobs rarely contained more than two hundred fighting men, and a large force—even one made up of green troops—would probably have been able to handle them. There is no such excuse for Sandford's misuse of the federal troops and the cavalry, which was particularly badly needed.

General John E. Wool, commander of the federal troops, had served in the army for forty-one years and had distinguished himself in both the War of 1812 and the Mexican War. But his battles had all been fought. Seventy-five years old and infirm, he was not fit for service in 1863. Captain Walter Franklin of the Twelfth United States Infantry reported to Wool late Monday night. "A section of battery," he wrote, "had just arrived from Fort Hamilton, with no one but a volunteer quartermaster in charge. The general did not seem to know what to do with it." Franklin made a suggestion, but "the room at this time was filled with gentlemen, and the general seemed to be very much confused; it was a long time before the attempts made by several of his staff to make him understand this were successful. Finally he issued the order. . . . General Wool seemed, during all the time I was there, very much confused and worn out, and I should judge unable to perform any duty."[26] Except for a few hours on Monday, Wool confined himself during the riots to a purely ceremonial function as the ranking federal general in the city.

Luckily, there was a general of skill and energy available for command during the riots, Brevet Brigadier General Harvey Brown. A West Pointer, Brown had entered the army in 1818 and served gallantly in the Seminole War and in the Mexican campaigns of both Scott and Taylor. In 1861 Brown had been sent to Fort Pickens, the federal stronghold in Pensacola Bay, where he commanded for over a year, repulsing a Confederate attempt to capture the island. Suffering from the climate, he returned home to New Jersey to recuperate, and in early 1863, he was put in charge of the federal forts in New York Harbor.

Brown first heard of the riots about two o'clock, when Wool's order to send troops to the city reached Fort Hamilton. Brown was astonished to find that Wool had asked for only eighty men. He ordered all the troops in the harbor forts to be ready to move at a moment's notice and then took the boat for the city, where he offered his services to General Wool. They were badly needed, for Wool's inadequacy was plain to all. Lieutenant McElrath, who had brought a detachment from Fort Hamilton, asked Wool's adjutant general, Major Christensen, what was going on. "Good God, McElrath," exclaimed Christensen, "this is the one spot in New York where the least is known of what is taking place!"[27]

Wool put Brown in command of all the federal troops in the city and directed him to report to Sandford. Brown, showing a sensible disregard for service prejudices and rank, did what Sandford should have done. He established his headquarters at the Police Central Office and cooperated closely with Commissioner Acton. It did not take Brown long to find out that Sandford was less concerned about the mobs than he was about safeguarding the arsenals. Brown started to ignore Sandford in disposing the federal troops; Sandford complained to Wool, and the latter, who had a long-standing dislike of Brown, reiterated that the militia general was in command.[28]

At nine o'clock that night, General Brown stormed into Wool's headquarters at the Saint Nicholas Hotel on Fifth Avenue, blasted Sandford and his defensive mentality, and demanded that the federal troops should be placed under his independent command. Wool refused, relieved Brown, and put Colonel Nugent in his place, under Sandford's orders. Early the next morning, Brown reappeared. At the urging of Mayor Opdyke and the prominent Republican George W. Blunt, he said he had been wrong and asked to be reinstated. Wool agreed, and Brown went back to police headquarters, where, fortunately for the city, he blithely ignored Sandford for the rest of the riot. Little harm had been done by his temporary absence from command, since General Sandford (unlike Commissioner Acton, who did not rest or change his clothes from Monday to Friday) left the Thirty-fifth Street Arsenal before midnight and went home to bed.[29]

At 8:35 P.M. the Central Office received a message from the Thirteenth Precinct: "The mob has fired Duffy's place, No. 429 Grand Street." This was the Fifth District draft office. No one was there, and all the provost marshal's books and papers had been taken to Fort Columbus in the harbor earlier. Several stores in the vicinity were also attacked by the mob, and for the first time, the people of the neighborhood joined together to try and protect their property. Such vigilante groups were to appear all over the city during the next few days.[30]

During the evening, reports of trouble poured in from other parts of the city. At 10:25 P.M. the Tenth Precinct, in the East Side bulge of Manhattan, telegraphed: "Send some men forthwith." "What is up?" asked Central. "A crowd is here," replied the Tenth, "and are going to destroy this station." Help was sent, and the throng was dispersed. Nearly all the First Precinct police had been called to the Central Office, but at 7 P.M. a telegram came from the section left in the station: "Tell Captain Warlow there is a riot in this ward." The men of the First, with the Twenty-sixth Precinct force and a few officers from the Fourth to help them, had to go back to their home district. Two sergeants who went ahead of the main body were badly beaten in New Street when they intervened to protect a Negro, but when the others arrived, they made short work of the assailants. There was soon another task for them: as soon as they reached the station house, Central telegraphed: "Leave a few men and take the rest to the *Tribune* office."

All the Republican newspapers of the city were apprehensive about attacks by the mob. The *Evening Post* and the *Times* armed their staff with rifles and barricaded their buildings. Henry J. Raymond, the editor of the *Times*, had used his influence to obtain three Gatling guns from the army. They were brought out and two were set up in the *Times* building's north windows, ready to sweep the streets. Raymond manned one and the millionaire speculator Leonard Jerome, a leading *Times* shareholder, took the other. The third gun was put on the roof.

Across Printing House Square at the *Tribune*, the pacifistic Horace Greeley forbade any preparations for defense, although a crowd was outside yelling "Down with the *Tribune!*" "Down with the old white coat what thinks a naygar as good as an Irishman!" The managing editor, Sydney Howard Gay, loudly objected: "This is not a riot, but a revolution." "It looks like it," replied Greeley. "It is just what I have expected, and I have no doubt they will hang *me*; but I want no arms brought into the building. We must rely upon the authorities, and submit to our fate, if no help comes from them." With this, Greeley went off to dinner with Theodore Tilton, the editor of the *Independent*.[31]

A short time later, James Parton and J. R. Gilmore arrived and decided on their own responsibility to arm the *Tribune* staff. Gilmore went to see General Wool and got an order on the ordnance officer at Governor's Island for a hundred muskets and some ammunition. But before he could get back to the *Tribune* with the arms, the mob attacked.

Several times during the afternoon, crowds had gathered in Printing House Square and drifted away again. They read the bulletins posted outside the newspaper offices about the riot uptown, cheered those that proclaimed the rioters triumphant, gave groans for the editors of Republican papers, and chased a few Negroes. A small force of police kept things from getting any worse.

At half-past twelve, James H. Whitten, a barber at Christadoro's hairdressing shop in the Astor Hotel, spoke to a knot of people in the square. He called for cheers for General McClellan and the *Caucasian*, a Peace Democrat paper, and groans for the *Tribune* and the *Times*. He challenged Horace Greeley to show himself, shouting that Greeley was a goddamned scoundrel and a damned abolitionist and swearing he would cut the editor's heart out. Whitten led his audience in chasing a policeman across City Hall Park and later talked to a Park Row merchant named William A. Hall, assuring him that the "*Times* and *Tribune* would have to come down, and they would have the life of Greeley."

At 1:30 P.M. Whitten went back to work, where he was well

known for his pro-Confederate views. "Before the battle of Gettysburg . . . [he] has said he hoped he would have the pleasure of
seeing Davis and shaving him inside of two months; he stated a
battle would soon be fought, the result of which would be the loss
of Washington, and the settlement of the war." While at work,
Whitten spoke to Abel A. Clark, the head waiter at the hotel, trying
to persuade him to lead all the waiters into the streets to join the
mob. "Whitten came to me," testified Clark, "and seemed to be well
posted in the movements of the mob told me what would be done
and said the mob would be the dominant party. He said to me you
don't go to enforce the draft you are one of those who do not want
to pay $300. I remarked at the time to persons near me that Henry
was blowing."

Whitten finished work at 7:30 P.M. and immediately returned
to Printing House Square, where he found a large crowd hurling
imprecations at the *Tribune* building. A man called George W.
Burrows threw a stone, and this was the signal for a barrage of
stones and bricks. Hearing the tinkle of breaking glass, James
Parton who had been standing on the edge of the crowd, rushed
into the police station at City Hall. Five men, he told the handful
of officers there, could stop the mischief if they acted now. In ten
minutes, a hundred men would not be able to control the mob. The
police at City Hall knew that reinforcements were on the way, but
what Parton said made sense. There were only six officers in the
station; one was left to telegraph the Central Office, and the other
five went across the square and took up their position on the sidewalk in front of the *Tribune* building.

The mob stopped throwing stones and fell back. But no more
police appeared, and none of the five drew his revolver. The rioters
regained their courage, surged forward, and swept the police out
of the way. Burrows kicked in the front door, and the rioters,
Whitten in the lead, stormed inside. Desks and counters were
overturned and piled together, camphene thrown on, a torch
applied.

At that moment, the police from the First, Fourth, and Twenty-
sixth precincts came in sight, marching down Nassau Street. With
a shout, they charged and drove the mob before them across the
square—right into the arms of two hundred policemen coming

down Broadway, led by Inspector Carpenter. The *Tribune* office emptied as if by magic, and the paper's employees rushed downstairs and beat out the flames. The two forces of police swept up Centre Street and through City Hall Park, driving the mob before them into the dark and narrow side streets.

Gilmore arrived with the muskets a little later (though the ammunition supplied proved to be the wrong caliber), and Raymond sent sixteen *Times* employees armed with rifles to help guard the *Tribune*. One hundred men of Carpenter's force were from the Brooklyn precincts, and they were ordered back across the river to make sure the riots did not spread to the "City of Homes." The rest were sent to break up the crowds attacking Negroes and their homes in the Fourth and Sixth wards. A few minutes before eleven o'clock, they returned to City Hall. Almost at once, word was flashed that another mob was coming down Broadway to attack the *Tribune*. Carpenter divided his force and placed his men in the deep shadows on either side of Broadway, near the east gate of the park. The rioters walked unsuspectingly into the ambush, and when Carpenter gave the word "Up, boys, and at 'em," the surprise was complete. The bewildered rioters ran like jackrabbits before the clubs of the police. At the same time, officers from the Twenty-sixth Precinct scattered a crowd that was gathering in Frankfort Street, and the *Tribune* was safe again.[32]

About six o'clock that evening, a mob appeared in the village of Yorkville. Their first target was the house of a leading Republican, New York City's postmaster, Abram Wakeman. Wakeman himself was downtown at that time, planning the defense of the Post Office. His family were warned of their danger, and his wife and brother tried to save part of his library by hiding books under bushes in the garden. The sight of a crowd coming down Eighty-sixth Street brandishing axes and clubs convinced them it was time to leave. The mob battered in the front door and pillaged the house from top to bottom. Furniture too heavy to carry away was chopped to pieces and set afire. The house was burned down, and even the trees and shrubs in the garden were uprooted or trampled into the ground.[33]

Next, the rioters moved on to wreck Colonel Nugent's apartment on the upper floors of a building at 156 East Eighty-sixth

Street. They broke into a store and stole some money and a few odd items of merchandise–tobacco, cigars, crackers, flour, cheese, and a pair of boots–but a man who rented the rooms over the store persuaded them not to burn the place. Finally, the rioters drifted along to the Twenty-third Precinct police station. They found it empty, all but one doorman; the officers had been called away to Central, and the mob set the building on fire.[34]

On East Nineteenth Street, Ellen Leonard watched the population of the Eighteenth Ward celebrating the day's victories. A huge bonfire was kindled in the center of the street, and men and boys danced around it with wild howls. "Bring out Horace Greeley" was one of the shouts that the watching girl caught. Professor John Torrey, making a cautious reconnaissance down Fifth Avenue, found a group of rioters threatening to burn the "large and superb mansion" owned by Dr. Ward, and the whole Ward family begging them not to, as "they were all Breckinridge Democrats and opposed to the draft." One of the leading rowdies told Torrey that they would burn the whole city before they were through and added that Wall Street would be their target the next day. Torrey, who was head of the United States Assay Office in the financial district, mentally resolved to offer them a warm reception.[35]

On First Avenue, some rioters dealt with "a d--d Republican" named Theodore Keeler, who kept a feedstore. They demanded the keys of the store from him, on pain of death. He gave them up and left while the mob took his stock of oats, cornmeal, hay, straw, and feed out in the street and burned it. They were careful not to hurt anyone else's property and refrained from burning Keeler's store, since it was in the middle of the block.[36]

Numbers of the well-to-do who had stayed in the city during the summer tried to leave under cover of darkness. They discovered it was not easy. Hack-drivers, when they could be found, demanded $100 or more for risking the journey to Westchester County. One man who had been spending the weekend with the Mitchell family on West Forty-second Street was anxious to get home to New England. He went to a livery stable and offered $25 to be taken beyond the Harlem River to a place where he could catch a train. The drivers laughed at him. He increased his offer to $50, $75, $100. A coachman finally agreed, but insisted on cash in advance.

Once a hack was found and paid for, travelers still had to get past the crowds of rioters on the avenues, who would demand money to let them pass or would rob them of all they had. An hour after he had left for the livery stable, the Mitchells' guest reappeared, "in a state of violent indignation, but rather uncommunicative as to the whereabouts of his watch and chain and pocketbook."[37]

Alderman Jacob M. Long was driving his wagon along Fifth Avenue when he was accosted by a laborer and volunteer fireman named Richard Lynch, "a tall young man with a great deal of hair and not much head."

He said "Hold up Colonel Long, give me a couple of dollars, or else, by Jesus, I'll upset your waggon!" I said "This is all wrong for a fire laddie to do this kind of business." He then said "Give us a couple of dollars, anyhow, I want to get something to drink." I gave him two dollars to get out of the clutches of those fellows–they were gathering around my wagon pretty thick. When I put my hand in my pocket to pull out the money . . . Lynch said "Give us a couple of dollars, or else I'll scratch your waggon." There were a dozen of these men getting around the wagon at the time . . . I thought they looked very furious and was very glad to get out of it for two dollars."[38]

A little later, about 9:45, Lynch and five or six of his friends robbed three people in Third Avenue: one man was relieved of his watch and $95, the second of $105, and the third, his silver watch and chain. Then Lynch and his gang wandered uptown until they met another group of rioters who were throwing stones at the Magdalen Asylum, a home for former prostitutes, at Fifth Avenue and Eighty-eighth Street. Thinking it was a hotel, they battered down the gate and front door and crowded inside, dancing and singing. They threw the furniture about, told the girls they were free to leave, and shouted that they were going to burn the place.

The girls persuaded the intruders to go away, but a couple of hours later, some came back. "Yelling and shouting, they broke in the front door," testified the superintendent, Cyrus Offer, "entered the building and pulled the girls about. I appealed to them and told them our place was for the protection of poor women several of the crowd raised clubs and threatened to strike me. My wife asked them why they attacked our place, and some of the mob answered that they were going to 'burn the building the same as they had Wakeman's house.' " Once again, the girls persuaded the rowdies to leave, though this time they stole a box containing $48 in cash and a gold pen and pencil case.[39]

Some other members of the mob that had burned Wakeman's house were busy elsewhere. Some windows were broken on Eighty-sixth Street; a couple of grocery stores were ransacked and set afire. Between four and five o'clock in the morning, a tavern called the Ivy Green, on the corner of Fifth Avenue and Ninety-second Street, was set on fire and burned down. A woman called Ellen Cavanaugh later testified that this had been planned earlier: "I was coming from Mr. Wakeman's house the night it was on fire; there were ten persons in front of me, and they swore they would set fire to the Ivy Green; this was at half-past ten o'clock."[40]

Many ordinary criminals took advantage of the breakdown in law and order to ply their trade with unusual ease, free of the fear of the police. A pickpocket called Charles Smith robbed a man in Spring Street and took a pocket purse containing $3,273.82 in Treasury notes and checks. He was later caught only because he confided in a loose-tongued Bowery prostitute. Other people who were usually law-abiding were tempted to take advantage of the confusion and dislocation caused by the riots. A man who had been honorably discharged after two years' service with the Fourth New York Volunteers was caught six weeks later trying to steal a watch and chain from someone in City Hall Park. Any Negro was fair game. A maid on the Providence, Rhode Island, boat named Ellen Washington was walking down to Pier Thirty-three to go aboard when two men came up and told her that if she did not give them her carpetbag they would beat her. She did not dare resist.[41]

Some people, knowing the police were occupied, used the time of the riots to pay off old grudges. A contractor who had built some stone stoops in East Forty-ninth Street had failed to pay his men. On Monday night, three or four of them went out with a stone hammer and broke all the steps on one of the stoops.[42]

At eleven o'clock, a heavy shower of rain sent people scurrying home, which cut down the number of incidents that night. After one unsuccessful attempt, a party of one hundred police finally reached Clarkson Street after midnight and cut down the body of William Jones. Inspector James Leonard, who had relieved Carpenter at City Hall, had to send some men to patrol York and Leonard streets to deter attacks on Negro dwellings, and about two o'clock, police were needed to disperse a mob that had broken into a provision store in Greenwich Street. Toward dawn, Leonard was warned that rioters meant to burn Fulton Market and seize Fulton ferry to repel any troops that might be sent over from the Brooklyn Navy Yard. The inspector dispatched a force which broke up the gathering crowd and removed the danger. In the village of Harlem, a gang of rioters plundered the Washington Hall hotel about three o'clock and then went and set fire to a large plan-ingmill on 129th Street. The blaze spread to five adjoining buildings. All were destroyed.[43] A little later, the rioters tried to set on fire the railroad bridge over Harlem River, but the rain-soaked timbers were too wet to burn.

Despite the rain, property-holders and Republicans spent some anxious hours that night. Professor John Torrey packed up all his most valuable possessions and was ready to leave his home at a moment's notice. Alfred Goldsborough Jones, the managing director of the Sixth Avenue horse-car lines, had most of the cars taken up to the vicinity of Central Park and the horses put in vacant lots on the corner of Broadway and Forty-third Street, out of harm's way. The Sixth Avenue depot was right behind the Colored Orphan Asylum, whose soot-encrusted ruins were still smoldering, and Jones had been told that the depot, too, would be destroyed. Captain Joel B. Erhardt, provost marshal of the Fourth District, shut himself up in his office at 271 Broadway. He rented forty muskets, improvised some homemade cartridges, and handed them out to his enrolling officers, who kept watch all night.[44]

George Templeton Strong joined with John Jay, Professor Wolcott Gibbs, and James Wadsworth in sending a telegram to President Lincoln: "Our city having given her militia at your call is at the mercy of a mob which assembled this morning to resist the draft and are now spreading fire and outrage—several buildings in different wards are in flames and the *Times* and *Tribune* offices are at this moment threatened. New York looks to you for instant help in troops and an officer to command them and to declare martial law. Telegraph wires cut in all directions." Then Strong went home to Gramercy Park, reflecting that Jefferson Davis seemed to be master of New York and thankful that his wife and children were away in the country.[45]

Others had different thoughts about the riot and different hopes for the morrow. About six o'clock Monday evening, Officer William McTaggart of the police sanitary squad paid a call on Thomas White, who owned a slaughterhouse off West Thirty-ninth Street, and found him talking to a man called John Piper:

When I went in Mr. White was giving him money Piper after getting the money invited me and the men in the street to drink with him. I consented having an object in it on our return to White's office Piper wanted to communicate something and asked Mr. White if I was reliable. White said I was. Piper then said he had been drafted and that all the G.D. drafted men would have to turn out and resist the draft he said he had been in the riot that day and that he had come over to inform his friends what they were going to do and that he would see that his friends would be protected and that he would let Mr. White know from ½ hour to an hour before the mob came so that they should not burn him out. That they were going to burn Allerton's hotel Bartlett's slaughter house, as he was a mean G.D.S. of B. and Spring and Jameson's slaughter house. . . . Piper also said we or they have been and burnt Allerton's Hotel on the other side of town we have been in a fight over there he then said "Tommy" meaning Mr. White "they shan't harm you."

Piper began to damn a man called Henry Alvorn,[46] "who they called Sow Henry from his being a dealer in hogs that he had informed on the rioters that they were going to burn out Spring and Jameson's and Bartlett's slaughterhouse and the G.D. Dutch son of a bitch he would put a ball through him before the next night at six o'clock and this threat he frequently repeated during all this conversation." Besides informing on the rioter's plans, "Sow Henry" had also prevented the burning of a Negro's home that day. The next day Albohm was shot and wounded as he was crossing Ninth Avenue. He lingered for weeks and died in the middle of August.[47]

*There is more law in the end of a policeman's nightstick than in a decision of the Supreme Court.*

—CAPTAIN ALEXANDER S. WILLIAMS[1]

# 5

## Clubs Are Trumps

Wʜɪʟᴇ sᴛᴀʀs still glittered in the summer sky, the rain ended. This guaranteed that there would be more rioting. A steady downpour would have discouraged all but the most violent and determined. But Tuesday was another sweltering hot day, and the weather brought crowds into the streets.

At six o'clock that morning, a schoolboy named Edward Ray was standing at the corner of Leroy and Washington streets in the Ninth Ward. William Williams, a Negro seaman from the government transport *Belvidere*, which was anchored at the foot of Leroy Street, came up and asked the boy where he could find a grocery store. As Ray was giving him directions, a man called Edward Canfield came out of a liquor store and asked Williams what he wanted. He answered, and without a word Canfield hit him, knocked him down, and jumped on him. A few men and boys gathered round to watch. Canfield stepped back, leaned on someone's shoulder, and leisurely kicked at the Negro's eyes. Another seaman from the *Belvidere*, William Butney, a white man, came down the street and tried to stab Williams with a knife. James Lamb, an Irish laborer who lived at 135 Leroy Street threw some stones at Williams and then picked up a heavy flagstone and smashed it down on his chest. With cheers and shouts for "vengeance on every nigger in New York," the group broke up. Canfield shambled off down Clarkson Street shouting "nigger! nigger! nigger!" and drunkenly warning "not to put any niggers to work."

A couple of onlookers, horrified at the brutality of the attack, had rushed over to the Twenty-eighth Precinct police station on Greenwich Street and reported what was happening. Expecting a fight, Captain John S. Dickson took a section of men and went to Leroy Street. But the area was quiet; the bleeding Negro was put on a cart and taken to the New York Hospital, where he died two hours later.[2]

All day long, the attacks on Negroes continued. Mobs stormed and ransacked houses belonging to blacks and sent the occupants fleeing for their lives. "I saw the brickbats coming through the window," testified Mrs. Anna Maria Dickerson, who lived at 9 York Street. "The mob came in, and I went out of the back window of the house." Mrs. Hester Scott lived at 3 Mechanics' Alley. "In the house there were hundreds [of rioters]," she recalled, "I escaped from the roof of the house; they threw stones and broke the window; I was lowered from the top of the house by sheets into the yard adjoining Mr. Hecker's stable; we tied the sheets together, attached them to the roof, and we got down on the sheets; one little girl, 10 years of age, was let down; my husband lowered me and then my little girl; and then my husband came down . . . the house is a four-story one."[3] At the Infirmary for Indigent Women and Children, the creation of the pioneer woman physician Dr. Elizabeth Blackwell, the white patients demanded, unsuccessfully, that the Negro women in the hospital be expelled, lest their presence provoke the rioters.[4]

C. L. de Rendanni, a merchant from Bassa County, Liberia, who was in town to promote a black emigration scheme, was caught and beaten while returning from the New York State Colonization Society's offices. There were many ships from the British West Indies in port, and after an attack on a vessel from Nassau that was anchored near Fulton ferry, their masters became concerned for the safety of their black crewmen. The nearest British warship was at Annapolis, and the British consul general appealed to Admiral Reymond of the French frigate *Guerriere*. He agreed to protect the black sailors and took two hundred of them on board his ship. Before the riot ended, one hundred more blacks from the West Indies took refuge in the British consulate.[5]

The wealthy *rentier* Philip Lydig had gone to the country for the summer, leaving his black servant to look after his house at 34 Laight Street, and she took in fifteen Negroes who were driven from their homes in York Street.[6] Several dozen blacks sheltered in the Church of the Transfiguration on East Twenty-ninth Street.[7] They filled the parish library, the choristers' robing room, the room over the chantry, the Sunday school, and overflowed into the church itself. Rioters threatened the church several times, but the rector, Dr. George H. Houghton, managed to persuade them to leave. Another fugitive was hidden in the home of the Reverend A. H. Burlingham, minister of the South Baptist Church, until he could be smuggled out over the roofs.[8]

Elizabeth Roberts, born in Santo Domingo, occupied a basement room in Hamilton Street and made a living by whitewashing and cleaning houses. She asked a white boardinghouse keeper she knew to hide her, but the woman refused and sent her home.

About eleven o'clock the boys came a-cursing; I went to a butcher; he told me that I had better stay at home; the mob came in the afternoon with three axes; they split the door open; I saw them coming in the door; I went up stairs; the people in the house put me in the necessary and locked me up; they called for the "black bitch"; I stayed there till four o'clock in the afternoon; the rioters found me there, and ordered me out; I went out to Mrs. Johnston's, and at night I was carried to the Seventh Ward station house in a carriage; I saw, from the necessary, the women, taking my things out from the cellar where I lived.[9]

When the white employees of William J. and J. S. Peck's brick-yard on the Hudson at Thirtieth Street arrived at Tuesday morning, they found John R. Adkins, a Negro who worked there, hiding in the stable. He had been driven from his home in West Twenty-sixth Street the previous night. Knowing that rioters were in force at Eleventh Avenue and Twenty-ninth Street nearby, the whites urged Adkins to escape and put him in a yawl which he rowed across to the Jersey Shore. A man named John J. Sturtevant was at the Canal Street ferry about noon talking to the ferrymaster, when there was a great shouting in Washington Street and a Negro came tearing down toward the ferry, pursued by a screaming crowd of men, women, and boys. "Come this way!" yelled Sturtevant. The Negro rushed onto the ferry, the master slammed the gates shut and cast off, and the boat pulled away. "We brought the poor fellow to Hoboken," recalled Sturtevant, "he said he would be safe if he could get to Paterson, he had no money, I went around and got some dollars from the passengers, gave them to him and sent him to the Erie Depot and safety." [10]

The few Negroes who had not fled from their homes were forced to skulk through the streets like hunted animals to get to the food stores. A *Herald* reporter saw black women stealing carefully through alleys, peering fearfully round the corners of buildings to see if the streets were safe, and then running at full pelt to the nearest grocery. Most storekeepers preferred to take the food to the Negroes, since it was dangerous to have blacks on their premises, even for a few moments.

The police were far too hard-pressed to provide much protection. Early in the day, Commissioner Acton began to receive reports of trouble brewing. "A large mob is collecting on Second Avenue and 34th Street," the Twenty-first Precinct telegraphed at 8:30 A.M., "and threatening to burn all property in that vicinity." A few seconds later, the Seventh sent word that "Everything is quiet, but the mob is congregating in the vicinity of South Street." "A large crowd had collected about the Hook," reported the Tenth Precinct at 9:05 A.M. "They were last seen going down Jackson Street."

The most alarming news came from the upper East Side wards. "Is everything all right?" Acton asked the Twenty-first Precinct at 9:15 A.M. "No," came the answer. "Far from it. The mob burned one or two buildings on Second Avenue and 34th Street." Acton decided to send a force to the area at once. Three hundred police took the Third Avenue cars uptown, with Inspector Carpenter in command.

A couple of blocks away from the trouble spot, the police got out, crossed over to Second Avenue and marched forward. Between Thirty-fourth and Thirty-fifth streets, a cascade of bricks, stones, tin kettles, and chunks of wood, and a ferocious yell, revealed that they had walked into a trap. The rioters were all around them—in the houses, on the rooftops, up and down the avenue. The police ranks quaked and wavered, several men fell, and for a moment it seemed as if another rout was in the making. But in another moment, the officers recovered and charged straight ahead. Breaking through the mob, they turned, re-formed, and charged back again, chasing the rioters down the avenue and into the houses. A porterhouse on the corner of Thirty-fourth Street was the rioters' stronghold, but the police forced an entrance and clubbed the inmates from room to room and up the stairs. As the officers were grappling with their enemies in the corridors and on the roof-tops, 150 men from the Eleventh New York Volunteers,[11] com-manded by Colonel Henry O'Brien, arrived, with a couple of six-pounders. The mob was advancing again up the avenue, and O'Brien decided to frighten them off. The troops were ordered to fire over the heads of the rioters, and the guns were loaded with blanks. When the word was given, the crash of musketry and the dense smoke did its work; the rioters dived for cover and fled. But the gunfire, aimed high, hit two small children who were standing at upper-story windows watching the fighting. One, John Mulhare, aged eight, was wounded; the other, a two-year-old girl called Ellen Kirk, died. One hundred and fifteen federal troops, under Captain Walter S. Franklin, joined O'Brien and Carpenter a few minutes later. This made a formidable body of men, and the remnants of the mob melted away. The district was quiet as the forces of law and order marched off.[12]

Thirteen blocks down the avenue, a reprise of the previous day's struggle for the armory was in full swing. That morning some of the rioters had discovered that there were over 3,000 carbines stored in the Union Steam Works at Second Avenue and Twenty-second Street. A few minutes before ten o'clock, they broke in and began to distribute the guns. Francis Cusick, the ex-policeman who had led the attack on Superintendent Kennedy the day before, was a leader in the affair.[13] Acton hurriedly assembled another two hundred men and sent them off, under the command of Inspector George W. Dilks. A rapid march brought them to the scene of the trouble, and the fiercest battle of the riots began. The mob fought Dilks and his men every inch of the way. Repeated charges and vigorous clubbing cleared the street at last, and the police turned to the Steam Works. In hand-to-hand fighting, they beat the rioters back and secured the factory. Dilks unwisely decided to leave most of the carbines in the Works, with a small garrison to guard them.

As a result, two more battles had to be fought before the guns were secure. It would have been far better if Dilks had tried to commandeer a wagon or a cart to carry all the weapons away. As it was, every man took a carbine, and Dilks and his battered force returned to headquarters.

At the same hour—ten o'clock—as the battles in Thirty-fifth Street, 130 federal troops from Forts Lafayette, Hamilton, and Richmond, who had been sent on patrol toward Corlear's Hook were confronted by a mob in Pitt Street waving crude signs reading NO DRAFT. Lieutenant Wood, the commander of the detachment, stepped forward and ordered the crowd to disperse. Instead, they surged forward, brandishing clubs and throwing stones. Wood gave the order to fire. Too late, the mob realized the soldiers were in deadly earnest. They began to scatter, but the volley caught twelve of them: eight were killed on the spot or died of their wounds, and four more were wounded.[14] A bayonet charge helped the rest of the fleeing rioters on their way. Wood reassembled his men, swung around the corner into Grand Street, and saw another gang of rowdies at the head of Division Street. Once again, he halted his detachment, walked ahead, and warned the crowd that if they did not disperse, his troops would fire. This time, some of the rioters fell back, and Wood seized his momentary advantage. Ordering a bayonet charge, he led his men forward and put the mob to flight. The only casualty among the soldiers was Wood himself, who fell and sprained his ankle on the march back to police headquarters.[15]

Wood did not know it, but his men were badly needed in the area immediately to the north and east of his line of march. The Thirteenth Precinct police were frantically telegraphing for help, and soon the Seventeenth was reporting that a crowd on Fourteenth Street was threatening to storm the Delamater Iron Works. Early in the morning, General Sandford had ordered all the troops in the city to concentrate at the Thirty-fifth Street Arsenal. There was no telegraphic communication between the arsenal and police headquarters, but Sandford was not interested in cooperating with the police. Acton's appeals to him for troops to deal with the deteriorating situation on the far East Side of town were fruitless. General Brown had decided that the best way to deal with Sandford was to ignore him, and he boldly announced that the order to concentrate at the Thirty-fifth Street Arsenal did not apply to federal troops, only to militia. From then on, the police and the federal soldiery assumed the burden of putting down the riots, leaving Sandford to his favorite occupation of assuring all and sundry that the arsenal was safe.

Acton ordered the Seventh Precinct to find Lieutenant Wood's force and ask him to take it to the Thirteenth, but they failed to locate it. When Captain Franklin's company returned to the Central Office, Brown and Acton were able to organize a pincer movement. Franklin and his men, with a party of police, were sent to Grand Street, and a company of marines from the Brooklyn Navy Yard were ordered to the Eleventh Precinct. Franklin's force marched to the East River and back, finding everything quiet, though as soon as they had gone, some rioters returned and sacked a large gun store in Grand Street. The marines found the Eleventh Precinct tranquil enough, but when they tried to turn south to Union Market, they ran into a tenacious and determined mob. Though they opened fire, they could make no headway, and at last they had to retreat. "The Marines have left us and gave away," the Thirteenth glumly told Acton at 12:05 P.M. "They are hot here."

The mob was equally hot on the West Side. At 10:50 A.M. the Sixteenth Precinct warned Acton that "all the stores are closing on Eighth Avenue, from fear of the mob in 17th Street." The troops under Sandford's control were advantageously placed to deal with this, and Acton immediately telegraphed the Twentieth Precinct, the nearest station to the Thirty-fifth Street Arsenal, to "tell General Sandford to send a force." But Sandford did nothing, and when news came that a mob was threatening Henry Jones's large soap and candle factory on Sixteenth Street, between Eighth and Ninth avenues, Acton decided he would have to rely on his own resources. Two hundred police, commanded by Captain Jeremiah Petty of the Fifth Precinct, were dispatched to sweep the area. The mob hastily decamped at the first glimpse of the advancing officers. Petty and his men rescued the four employees who had been defending the factory and probed as far as Nineteenth Street before returning to headquarters.[16]

The handful of police left in the Eighteenth Precinct were besieged in their station house on East Twenty-second Street. "The mob is very wild on the corner of 22nd Street and 2nd Avenue," the Eighteenth told Central at 11:20 A.M., and two minutes later: "I don't know but I will have to leave." At 11:40 A.M. the situation was desperate. "I must leave," telegraphed the Eighteenth. "The mob is here with guns." Acton urged them to hold on; relief was on the way. Just after noon, the reinforcements arrived, and the station was saved for the time being.

Late Tuesday morning, Governor Seymour arrived in the city, talked to Mayor Opdyke and General Wool at the Saint Nicholas Hotel, and went down to City Hall, where he made an impromptu speech which Republican propagandists rendered infamous. Led by Horace Greeley, they charged that Seymour had addressed the rioters as "my friends" and had weakly capitulated to mob violence by promising an end to the draft. Reports of what Seymour said vary enormously. The most complete of these was published in the *Herald*:

Hearing that there was difficulty in the city, I came down here, leaving the quiet of the country, to do what I can to preserve the public peace. . . . I come not only for the purpose of maintaining the laws, but also from a kind regard for the interests and the welfare of those who, under the influence of excitement and a feeling of supposed wrong, were in danger not only of inflicting serious blows to the good order of society, but to their own best interests. I beg you to listen to me as a friend; for I am your friend, and the friend of your families. I implore you to take care that no man's property or person is injured; for you owe it to yourselves and to the government under which you live to assist with your strong arms in preserving peace and order. I rely upon you to defend the peace and good order of the city; and if you do this, and refrain from further riotous acts, I will see to it that all your rights shall be protected. I will say a word about the draft. On Saturday last I sent the Adjutant-General of the State to Washington, urging its postponement. The question of the legality of the Conscription Act will go to the courts, and the decision of those courts, whatever it may be, must be obeyed by rulers and people alike. If the conscription shall be declared to be legal, then I pledge myself to use every influence with the State and city authorities to see that there shall be no inequality between the rich and the poor. I pledge myself that money shall be raised for the purpose of relieving those who are unable to protect their own interests. There is no occasion for resisting the draft, for it has not yet been enforced. And now, in conclusion, I beg you to disperse, leave your interests in my hands, and I will take care that justice is done to you, and that your families shall be fully protected.

All this was perfectly consistent with Seymour's attitude ever since Congress had authorized conscription. There was no capitulation to the mob here. It is not certain that Seymour ever used the words "my friends." One witness declared that Seymour began his speech: "Men of New York." Another recalled that someone in the audience shouted, "Governor, we are your friends," and Seymour replied, "If you are my friends, you will go to your homes like peaceable citizens." Talking about the speech with his family years later, Seymour said that he could not remember how he had begun, but the audience looked respectable enough, and he would have had no hesitation in calling them friends. In any case, such an opening to a speech was a mere formality. No one ever condemned the chief engineer, John Decker, for calling the mob at Third Avenue and Forty-sixth Street on Monday morning his "fellow citizens."

Defenders of Seymour have, of course, gone too far in arguing that the nearest riot at the time he spoke was more than a mile away uptown and that there were no rioters in his audience. Seymour himself thought the people who listened to him were law-abiding, and an eyewitness described the crowd as "an orderly respectable gathering, made up of old and young, merchants, clerks and others who were present in and about the Park—particularly about the bulletin boards of the several newspapers in Park Row, and hearing that the Governor was at the City Hall, had gone over to call him out."[17] But most rioters were respectable people with jobs and settled homes, who had never been arrested or involved in crime. Several times that morning, the police had broken up demonstrations outside the offices of the Republican newspapers. James H. Whitten, leader of the previous night's attack on the *Tribune*, had put in an appearance, trying to incite another attempt at storming and burning the paper's building.[18] Few other fighting men can have been on the ground, but it seems likely that many of Seymour's audience were supporters of the mob, the kind of people who would cheer on the hard-core of street fighters, shout a slogan, and perhaps even throw a few stones. In fact, while Seymour was speaking, they groaned and hooted a company of the Invalid Corps that formed on the steps of City Hall to keep the crowd back, and when the speeches were over, they gave groans for Nugent, Kennedy, and Lincoln. Any merchant, clerk, or member of the middle classes who had anything to lose would have been busy protecting his business premises or at home looking after his family on Tuesday morning, not hanging round City Hall Park.

While he was at City Hall, Seymour issued a proclamation declaring New York in a state of insurrection and ordering all those engaged in the "riotous proceedings" to return to their homes and work. He also wrote a letter to the Catholic Archbishop of New York: "Will you exert your powerful influence to stop the disorders now reigning in this city. I do not wish to ask anything inconsistent with your sacred duties but if you can with propriety aid the civil authorities at this crisis I hope you will do so."[19]

When Archbishop John Hughes received this, he was in the middle of composing a long diatribe complaining about Horace Greeley's misrepresentation of his views on conscription, and he added a postscript in response to the governor's request. He also paid off another old score against Greeley. An Irishman himself, Hughes was rabid at the *Tribune*'s aspersions on the loyalty of the New York Irish, and his letter, which was published in the *Herald* on Wednesday morning, both appealed for peace and dealt a blow at the editor of the offending paper:

In spite of Mr. Greeley's assault upon the Irish, in the present disturbed condition of the city, I will appeal not only to them, but to all persons who love God and revere the holy Catholic religion which they profess, to respect also the laws of man and the peace of society, to retire to their homes with as little delay as possible, and disconnect themselves from the seemingly deliberate intention to disturb the peace and social rights of the citizens of New York. If they are Catholics, or of such of them as are Catholics, I ask, for God's sake—for the sake of their holy religion—for my own sake, if they have any respect for the Episcopal authority—to dissolve their bad associations with reckless men, who have little regard either for Divine or human laws.

Early in the afternoon, Governor Seymour issued a list of places where men could report to join the volunteer companies that were aiding the police and troops. Many two-year men who had been discharged in May answered the call, and regiments like the Duryea Zouaves and the Ninth Regiment of the New York National Guard, which had entered federal service *en masse* in May 1861, as the Eighty-third New York Volunteers, were almost reconstituted. The Ninth New York Volunteers, Hawkins' Zouaves, was already in the process of reenlistment and reorganization, and the new recruits united with the veterans who had decided not to go back into the field, to serve against the mob. Men without military experience enrolled as special policemen, and by sunset Tuesday there were 1,200 of them on duty. On Tuesday afternoon, there were meetings at the Stock Exchange, Merchants' Exchange, and the Union League Club to organize groups of volunteers. One of President Lincoln's private secretaries, William O. Stoddard, who was on vacation in New York, joined a company he found being formed on the steps of the Sub-Treasury in Wall Street.[20]

Inside, there was a battery ready for action. The Assay Office, the Post Office, the Ordnance Office in Worth Street, and the Customs House were strongly garrisoned, and their clerks were armed and drilled. At the Customs House, Superintendent Hillyer had bombs with forty-second fuses placed in every window, set to be rolled out on attackers. The top of the building was occupied by the Bank Note Company, and the employees there prepared tanks of sulfuric acid for use if the place had to be defended. The gunboat *Tulip* anchored off the Battery, ready to open fire on Wall Street and Pine Street as soon as the assistant treasurer of the United States, John J. Cisco, gave the signal. The deposits in the Sub-Treasury and the money from the Clearing House were taken over to Governor's Island, and most of the banks sent their bullion and notes there, too.[21]

City Hall was protected by troops and artillery, and the *Tribune* building was turned into a fortress. The shattered doors and broken windows of the ground floor were blocked with huge bales of printing paper, thoroughly saturated with water to prevent their being set on fire. A hose was run up from the basement boiler so that the ground floor could be deluged with scalding steam in a minute. Howitzers and piles of hand grenades were placed in the upstairs windows. Gilmore went over to the Brooklyn Navy Yard and persuaded Admiral Paulding to let him have fifty forty-pound bombshells. A long wooden trough was knocked together, down which the bombshells could be rolled and launched into Printing House Square. Across the way, the *Times* had been reinforced by some sailors with a twenty-five-barrel rifle battery. One hundred employees of Lord and Taylor's marched to the arsenal to pick up arms and ammunition and then went back to fortify the store, using cases of goods to build makeshift ramparts.[22]

Groups of vigilantes were appearing in increasing numbers as neighbors banded together to protect their property. Such extra-legal organizations had been seen before in New York, at times when the city's northward movement had infected previously respectable neighborhoods with crime, and they had been particularly strong and numerous during the summer of 1857, when the new, undermanned Metropolitan Police could not provide security for life and property. The local home guards of 1863 were acting in a well-established tradition. Sometimes the volunteer fire companies turned out to patrol an area and drive off rioters. One such company was the Black Joke, whose members were probably thunderstruck at the Pandora's box of anarchy they had thrown open. Elbridge Gerry, nephew of the wealthy Peter Goelet, armed all the servants in his uncle's huge house at Broadway and Nineteenth Street, barricaded the windows, and even plucked the tail feathers from Goelet's pet peacocks, lest they attract the mob's attention. The owners of the Neptune Iron Works in the Eleventh Ward organized three hundred of their workmen, armed with muskets and sabers, to protect the district, and John Stephenson, who ran a carriage and railroad car factory on Twenty-eighth Street, handed out rifles to his workmen and fortified his premises with a couple of cannon.[23]

More and more information about the movements of the various bands of rioters was flowing into police headquarters from policemen who disguised themselves as ordinary laborers and went out to mingle with the crowds. Mrs. Martha Derby Perry saw the officer who usually patrolled her street sitting on a stoop "in his shirt sleeves without any sign of uniform, looking rough and disorderly, and talking to the strolling bands of rioters."[24] The members of the fledgling Detective Force were especially valuable in this role, since they were less likely to be recognized than a regular patrolman. Besides such intelligence work, the detectives raided six of the most notorious "lushing cribs" in the city and took thirty well-known burglars and thieves into custody for the duration of the riots. Although somewhat less than legal, their incarceration probably cut down the amount of crime in the city while the police were distracted from their regular duties.

Of all the two thousand men of the Metropolitan Police who battled the rioters, the members of the Telegraph Bureau were perhaps the most vital. The operators handled over 5,000 messages during the four days of disorder, and the superintendent of the Bureau, James Crowley, and his deputy, Eldred Polhamus, were constantly at work in the streets trying to mend broken wires and keep the lines open, all the while watching for the approach of rioters.[25] Without the telegraph, the police would have found it impossible to concentrate and move in strength against the various mobs.

Not the least of Commissioner Acton's problems was feeding and quartering his men and the hundreds of black refugees at the Central Office. During the riot week, the policemen, troops, and refugees at Central consumed 2,930 loaves of bread, 1,600 pounds of beef, 1,200 pounds of ham, 720 pounds of cheese, 600 pounds of butter, 1,200 pounds of crackers, and 5,000 gallons of coffee. Some merchants and householders generously supplied food and quarters on request, but when anyone objected, Acton simply seized what he needed and told the owner to send in an honest bill later.[26]

In Washington, the members of the federal government were awaking to the gravity of the situation in the nation's largest city. Secretary of War Stanton ordered the New York Seventh to return home and later decided to send four more New York militia regiments back.[27] Yet neither Stanton nor the chief of staff, General Halleck, realized quite how thin the forces in New York were stretched. "The Secretary of War requests that you will call out sufficient militia force to quell the riot," Halleck telegraphed Governor Seymour. "If absolutely necessary, troops will be sent from the field in Maryland, but this should be avoided as long as possible."[28] But, of course, every man of the New York militia who was fit to fight was in the field, under Stanton's control.

Tuesday was another searing hot day. A low haze hung over the city, and the fire bells rang incessantly. Hardly any cars or stages were running, and many of the downtown streets were ominously empty. The iron shutters of stores and hotels were securely fastened. Newsboys did a booming business, shouting strange and alarming phrases instead of their usual cries about carnage on the Potomac or at Vicksburg: "Horrible riot in the Second Avenue!" "Extra! Capture of Horace Greeley!" "Terrible battle in the Fourteenth Ward!"

As on the first day of the disorders, groups of toughs visited factories and stores, ironworks and shipyards, warning them to close up or be burned. The workmen took adzes, axes, saws, knives, and clubs, and fell in behind the leaders of the crowds. As they marched through the streets, they forced many passers-by and spectators to join them.[29] Mayor Opdyke's Proclamation was torn down and spat upon wherever it was seen, with curses for the "Black Republican thief that made it." One crowd in the Nineteenth Ward took a coffin from an undertaker's, chalked "Old Abe's Draft—Died Monday, July 13th, 1863" on the side, and carried it in triumph through the streets.

Rowdies from Brooklyn and New Jersey flocked to New York to join in the fun. Railroad tracks were torn up in both Third and Fourth avenues, and so were the Hudson River rails in Eleventh Avenue. A crowd collected a heap of paving stones at one end of the Fourth Avenue tunnel, ready to hurl down on the first train that emerged. Attacks continued on Republicans and everyone identified with the draft. A Ninth District enrolling officer named Charles H. Carpenter boarded at a house on Sixth Avenue. The mob paid him a visit and gutted the place. A grocery and feed store on Third Avenue was set ablaze because the owners were "damned Black Republicans." The home of a local Republican leader at Tenth Avenue and Forty-third Street was wrecked, and the banner of his club was burned in the street. Matthew Garragh, a storekeeper in Willett Street and a fervent Democrat, had put a sign reading "Republican Hall" over his establishment more than thirty years earlier. He had kept it up through all the political changes which had given the title "Republican" a very different meaning from what it had had in the 1820s, but now, fearing he might be burned out, he hastily took it down.[30]

More and more, as the riots went on, mere pillage and extortion became the overriding concern of the mobs. Liquor stores, saloons, tailors, pawnbrokers, and groceries were their favorite targets. Many businessmen had to pay for the privilege of not having their buildings burned. Several of the slaughterhouses and cattle dealers in the Twentieth and Twenty-second wards saved their premises in this way. The Eighth Avenue Railroad paid some rioters $1,200 to "guard" their stables.[31]

Adam Chairman, a tough who had served time in both German and American prisons, was in his element. On Tuesday morning, he went into John H. Soehnlin's liquor store at 84 Avenue B "and called for a glass of lager. . . . He drank the same and then refused to pay . . . saying at the time that he belonged to a gang that was going to burn the premises occupied by Aron Hexter as a hardware store No. 78 Avenue B."[32] Hexter's store was attacked and wrecked, but one of the people who lived above it gave Chairman twenty-five cents and "begged of him not to set the house on fire on account of the innocent women and children in said building . . . then gave him a glass of lager beer and said Chairman said well I will let it stand."

Michael Solinger, a partner in a clothing store at 17 Avenue B, gave Chairman some money to go away when he threatened to burn the place down, but a short time later he came back at the head of a mob. Some of Solinger's friends tried to defend the store. Jacob Sanders testified:

I saw the crowd and went into it. . . . I struck 2 or 3 of the boys and thought to drive them away home . . . [Chairman] was in the crowd he had a grey coat on. . . . Frederick Smith was also there he struck at me I then ran when Smith bellowed out at me to kill that son of a bitch there was also another man in the crowd whose name I don't know but whom I can point out to the officer [John Stepphan]—he said we must have clothes and we will go over to Solinger's and get them. After the crowd left the store I saw . . . [Chairman] go up 2nd Street he had two women's hooped skirts hung around his neck and over his clothes.

Daniel Schwartz, another spectator, later testified to a grand jury:

I know Chairman, would recognize him anywhere. . . . Chairman is from the same part of Germany with me and I remember when he was in States Prison but I did not see him whilst in prison. Remember all the neighbors talking out, how he escaped in a wagon full of hay . . . I saw him in the crowd at Sollinger's [*sic*] store he made a speech to them I heard the sound of his voice and saw him gesticulating I was not so near him as to know whether he spoke in German or English there was only a lot of boys there first when prisoner came up with about 60 or 70 loafers—full grown men, after making the speech the crowd say Hurrah he then said in English now is our time boys and then he threw a stone which knocked down three of the shutters the mob then rushed into the store and Chairman seemed to be boss of the crowd. He gave a parcel of clothing to one and another parcel to another.[33]

Lewis Chamberlain, a hay, grain, and coal dealer whose place of business was on the Hudson River waterfront at Thirtieth Street, fell foul of William Watson, a young man "of a wild and villainous aspect of countenance" who worked as a painter.[34] Chamberlain was going to his business when Watson came up to him on Eleventh Avenue, grabbed him by the collar with both hands, and demanded money. "He said he would kick my damned bowels out if I did not give it to him and burn the buildings. I thought it was the safest way to give him what money I had until I could put myself in shape . . . I discovered quite a number of his friends around him. I felt in my pockets to see what I had, I only found a small amount of postal currency[35] and in the course of five or ten minutes I made up my mind to give it to him he committing me on a half-promise that I should give him more the same day. I gave him the money and started to come downtown. He was as good as his word, he did not disappoint me and met me again in the afternoon nearly at the same place corner of Thirtieth Street and Eleventh Avenue and again demanded the money and he had all these men around him." Chamberlain, however, had provided himself with a pistol this time. "I told [him] . . . I should not give him any money; he said if I did not he would burn up my buildings; I said 'there they are, burn them'; he pressed me for money, I showed him what I had with me and he finally concluded that I would get the start of him a little and he would not attempt to take it."[36]

Some rioters seemed to be less concerned about money than with savoring their sudden authority and new-found power. A man called Isaac B. Hammond was followed down West Thirty-sixth Street by five or six rowdies who threw stones at him, knocked him down, and threatened him with a bayonet. They forced him to kneel down in the street, beg pardon, and humble himself before their leader, who proclaimed himself to be Patrick H. Byrnes of Forty-second Street and Second Avenue.[37]

*I have a rendezvous with death*
*At some disputed barricade.*

—ALAN SEEGER

# 6

# The Reign of King Mob

In the middle of the day, Ellen Leonard and his sister ventured out to buy food and milk. The ruins of the armory in East Twenty-first Street were still smoldering, but people were grubbing about in the wreckage and carrying off charred beams, baskets of coal, iron rails, and muskets misshapen and twisted by the heat of the blaze. After a long search, the two girls found a store that was open and bought groceries and a newspaper. They wanted percussion caps and ammunition, too, but these were even harder to get. No one would admit that they possessed such things. Finally a friendly bookseller shared his supply with the Leonards, and they hurried home. The crowds along Second Avenue were thicker than ever, filling the street, clustering in doorways, leaning out of windows, peering from rooftops. The saloons and groggeries were thronged, and everywhere people were repeating that it was better to die at home than on some Virginia battlefield. "Everything," the girl thought, "indicated that a collision was approaching."[1] The second battle of the Union Steam Works was beginning.

Inspector Dilks had left a few men behind to hold the works when he took his force back to headquarters, and Captain Helme was sent there, with six platoons, to get the carbines that Dilks had failed to bring away. At two o'clock, word reached the Central Office that the mob had gathered at the works in greater force than before. Dilks took two hundred men and marched for Twenty-second Street, together with a company of the Twelfth United

States Infantry under Captain Walter Franklin's command.

Helme and his men had found the situation at the works every bit as bad as in the morning. They clubbed their way into the building, relieved the hard-pressed garrison, and routed out the rioters who had forced their way in. They commandeered a wagon and piled it high with the carbines. The crowds around the works were so thick that it looked as if Helme and his men would have to fight a pitched battle to get away, but just then Dilks's force and the troops came in sight. Helme and his men gave a heartfelt cheer and charged. The relief force did the same, and the mob, caught between two fires, gave way.

The two commands joined in front of the works and prepared to return to headquarters. Some of the police were sent down Twenty-second Street to make sure that the Eighteenth Precinct station house, near First Avenue, was all right. They came under heavy attack, and the whole force had to rescue them. Dilks and Franklin decided to teach these rebellious inhabitants of the Gashouse and Mackerelville a lesson. They formed their men into a column, the troops in front, the police behind and on the flanks, ready to deal with any attacks from the houses along their line of march. They went down Twenty-second Street and into First Avenue, the mob hurling taunts and paving stones and growing thicker every moment.

As the column wheeled into First Avenue, Franklin ordered the troops to fire, and they continued to blaze away until they reached the corner of Twenty-first Street. The rioters disappeared like leaves in an autumn wind, taking cover behind stoops and in area ways, in doorways and in the houses. The soldiers had to fire again at the corner of Twenty-first Street and Second Avenue, but a couple of volleys cleared the street, and a deathly hush descended on the area. The police and troops met no more opposition as they returned to headquarters. That night, in a vain gesture of defiance, rioters set fire to the Union Steam Works, now empty of guns.[2]

Although they were denied the arms at the works, the mob found plenty available in the gun stores. The onset of troops, who did not hesitate to fire, made many eager to obtain deadlier weapons than clubs or slingshots. All over the city, beginning about noon, bands of men broke into gun dealers' stores and armed themselves. "The mob came in and filled the store entirely," said Charles Plath, who kept a gun store at 552 Grand Street.

One of the crowd told me that they did not want to rob me, but wanted arms, and would return them when they got through with them, but at the same time they were smashing and breaking everything around; they then carried off all the things or articles; they carried off a great deal;–whatever they could get hold of; they were in the store an hour . . . one of the mob called the largest portion out of the store; me and my clerks drove the balance of them out; I tried to shut the store up the best way I could; I nailed up the shutters, with the assistance of the clerks, neighbors, etc.; the guns were all taken then, and a great many of the goods on the shelves; they came back in about three-quarters of an hour, and commenced smashing away again, and got in; the store was full again, consisting of boys, large and small, and commenced taking out the goods again; I fired guns at them; I fired over their heads, and did not hurt them; they then ran out.[3]

During the war, the number of gun stores in New York had multiplied, and they kept larger stocks on hand than in peacetime. The only saving graces were that the largest stores were in the heavily guarded Wall Street area and that the dealers did not keep large amounts of ammunition or powder; the mob had to seek them elsewhere, frequently without success. R. H. Lievesley's hardware store at 287 First Avenue was one place that rioters raided in a search for supplies. "I was standing seeing what was going on," recalled Carl Warwood, a youth who lived around the corner. "I was with the crowd at the time, and went into Mr. Lievesley's store; they wanted powder, and broke into the store; they looked for the powder, but could not find it; I saw them take things out; I said to them 'Do not take so much out'; they replied, 'You shut up, or we will cool yourself off.' "[4]

By Tuesday afternoon, the riot had taken the shape of class war. It was not safe for any well-dressed man to walk the streets. Cries of "Down with the rich men" and "There goes a $300 man" would greet him, and an attack would follow. Joseph Annin, a well-known lawyer from Jersey City, who happened to be in New York on business that day, was walking down Second Avenue, curious to see what was happening. At Thirty-sixth Street, he was stopped by a gang of rowdies. Annin made a dash for it, but was halted by a pistol shot from one of the gang. They left him lying on the sidewalk; some people in the neighborhood carried him into a drugstore, and at 5:30 P.M. he was taken to Bellevue Hospital. Surgeons found it impossible to remove the bullet, and Annin died at his brother's house in Brooklyn on August 18.[5]

Only a couple of blocks away, one of the most lurid tragedies of the riot took place a little later. Colonel O'Brien, who commanded the state troops in the engagement at Second Avenue and Thirty-fifth Street in the morning, lived nearby, and some of the mob had looted his house.[6] About two o'clock, O'Brien came back alone, driving a wagon, to see what he could salvage from his property. This was brave to the point of foolhardiness, for the people of the locality were furious over the death and wounding of the children hit by the volley that O'Brien's men had fired. Possibly O'Brien did not know of this or thought that the district was thoroughly pacified. Perhaps he reasoned that the arsenal was only six blocks away and that he could find help and shelter there in case of any trouble. At all events, O'Brien was attacked by some men as soon as he got out of his wagon. He scuffled with his assailants and drove them away. He was slightly cut in the fight and walked down to Von Briesen's drugstore on the corner of Second Avenue and Thirty-fourth Street to get some medication. While he was inside, the attackers came back, tried the door of the drugstore, and found it locked. Two of them went round to the back of the building and after a few moments one of those left in front hurled a stone through the drugstore window. O'Brien came out to see what was happening, and while he stood on the sidewalk, one of the men who had gone around to the back came out of the store, crept up behind him, and struck him with a club. The surprised O'Brien wheeled around, reaching for his revolver, but another blow laid him unconscious on the sidewalk. People gathered around and amused themselves kicking and beating him. Small boys pushed wads of paper under his head and hands and set them alight. From time to time, men grabbed his legs and pulled his bleeding body from one side of the street to the other. O'Brien was a man of enormous physical strength, and this kept him alive long after most people would have succumbed under the terrible atrocities of the crowd. A girl screamed and tried to stop them from torturing the dying man; some of the mob beat her and chased her home. Later, they came to her boardinghouse and stripped it. What they did not steal they burned in the street. Von Briesen tried to give O'Brien a drink of water. The colonel's tormentors drove him away and wrecked his drugstore. At last a Catholic priest, Father Clowry of Saint Gabriel's in East Thirty-sixth Street, arrived, gave O'Brien extreme unction, and had him carried into a house. At dusk, the mob brought the almost dead man out again, tossed him into an alleyway, and set fire to the whole block. Later Father Clowry took O'Brien's body to Bellevue Hospital on a wheelbarrow.[7]

On the upper West Side, groups of rioters had spent the morning tearing up the tracks of the Hudson River Railroad in Eleventh Avenue. At 11:30 A.M. a gang of boys led by an eighteen-year-old blacksmith called Peter Dolan invaded Mayor Opdyke's house on Fifth Avenue. They were only in possession a few moments. The neighbors, headed by Captain Manierre, drove them out, and some police completed the rout. The military sent to the scene found nothing to do. Alfred Goldsborough Jones was still on guard at the Sixth Avenue Railroad stables on Forty-third Street, and at twelve noon he had a visit from a crowd of toughs with long clubs, who wanted to know if any of his drivers were working. The stables were deserted, but they dragged Jones outside and paraded him up and down the street arm-in-arm with a drunken Irishman. He made a speech denouncing the draft, and his captors assured him that he was all right, and with much shaking of hands they let him go.[8]

About 11:40 A.M. the Eleventh Avenue mob surged up to Forty-third Street, forced the Higgins carpet factory and the Metropolitan Gas Works to close and set fire to Allerton's West Side hotel.[9] General Sandford roused himself to send a company of troops there, with four thirty-two-pound howitzers, under the command of Major Fearing. Arriving on the scene, they fired four volleys, but they were not given time to use the howitzers. The crowd suddenly charged forward and nearly overpowered them. Some of the soldiers broke and ran, and a rout was narrowly averted when an officer shot down the man who was leading the flight, Private Joseph Ruttgers of the Seventeenth New York Volunteers, and forced the rest of the runaways back into line. Fearing was hurt, and a number of his command were wounded. Several of them hid in houses round about. The rest made for the safety of the arsenal as fast as they could go, with the rioters in hot pursuit.

Although he had plenty of men and artillery, Sandford panicked and began sending frenzied messages to police headquarters, asking for two hundred police or all the federal troops.[10] General Brown sent a battery of the Fifth United States Artillery and some infantry up to the arsenal, and the mob scattered as soon as they saw the guns. But for Sandford's chronic timidity, his forces could have handled the situation themselves just as easily.

Commissioner Acton and General Brown were concerned about a number of targets in the Twentieth and Twenty-second wards that the mob might find tempting, and as soon as they could, they sent Captain George W. Walling and sixty men of the Twentieth Precinct force uptown. A company of the Twelfth United States Infantry, under Captain Putnam, was ordered to follow and give Walling support. They found a crowd raging around Dr. Ward's and other mansions at Fifth Avenue and Forty-sixth Street and spoiling for a fight. "Kill every man who has a club!" Walling roared at the top of his voice, hoping the mob would hear. "Double quick! Charge!" The police and troops crashed into the rioters like a steamroller and sent them scrambling for safety, though watching women were screaming at them to "give the police hell!" Only one soldier was seriously hurt in this melee, Private Morris Kibbe, who fell behind and was surrounded by about twenty rioters. They beat him severely before he was rescued and taken off to Jews' Hospital.[11]

Saint Luke's Hospital was now safe, since Dr. Muhlenberg had agreed to admit a couple of injured rioters. He made a speech to some of the mob who had brought in a young man shot by the troops, telling them "that the doors of the Hospital were freely opened to every wounded man needing help, whoever or whatever he might be, but that in doing such charity it was not expected that the house should be threatened with fire and storm. . . . What they were doing was altogether wrong. There might be two opinions about the draft. They were not obliged to think it good, but it was their duty, if they disliked it, to use peaceful measures to get it changed." The rioters cheered, and since their comrades were being treated in the hospital, they formed themselves into a vigilante group to protect Saint Luke's. Another hospital, the United States General at Lexington Avenue and Fifty-first Street, where 247 wounded Union soldiers were convalescing, was menaced during the afternoon, but some armed citizens—a rather more respectable group than Saint Luke's guardians—held them off.[12]

Vigilantes also saved the Good Shepherd Home, an institution for aged and infirm Negroes at Second Avenue and Sixty-fifth Street. A gang of men and unruly boys set fire to the gatehouse and broke some windows about 5:30 P.M., but the members of the vigilance committee quickly chased the rowdies away and put out the flames.[13] Columbia College was threatened with destruction again, too, but Father James McMahon, of Saint John Evangelist Church on East Fiftieth Street, persuaded the rioters to spare it by telling them that there was a church attached to the college buildings.

The mob in Yorkville was just about to burn a house on Prospect Hill, at the corner of Fourth Avenue and Ninety-third Street, when Father Walter Quarters of Saint Lawrence's Church appealed to them not to commit such an act of vandalism. The priest was well liked by the people of Yorkville; they stopped their work of destruction, and Father Quarters asked them all to come to a meeting on the Eighty-fourth Street bridge over the Fourth Avenue railroad tracks that afternoon. The leading citizens of Yorkville were so concerned about the burnings on Monday night and the tearing up of the railroad tracks that they enthusiastically agreed to help Father Quarters. An attorney called John Keynton drafted some resolutions which were put to the meeting:

Whereas, The present distracted and excited state of our community demands action of the most decided character in order to quiet the minds and restore the feelings of the people in relation to the draft ordered by the executive authority; and

Whereas, A great portion of the poor working men of the community will necessarily be compelled, under the provisions of the draft, if enforced, to leave their families in abject poverty, in consequence of the odious provision exempting from military duty any citizen having three hundred dollars; therefore,

Resolved, That the Mayor and Commonalty of the city of New York shall address the civil authorities a respectful letter or address, demanding of them earnestly, that no draft shall take place within the city and county of New York.

Resolve further, That if such draft shall take place in order to remove the odious provisions thereof in its especial workings upon the poor laboring classes, that the said Common Council shall, by corporation ordinance, forthwith enact that any poor man, or any other person not able to pay three hundred dollars shall have the same paid by the corporation of the city of New York, in order to avoid the necessity of the poorer classes leaving their families in almost abject starvation and poverty.

Resolved, That until we see whether the authorities will take cognizance of these our demands that we forbear in any further destruction of property by fire, the results of which upon our friends we are unable to forsee.

Resolved further, That we are good citizens of the United States—that we desire to uphold the constitution and the Union—but we demand from those in power the recognition of our rights as freemen, and we hereby declare that we are not slaves.

Resolved, that a committee of twenty-five persons be appointed by this meeting to wait on the Mayor and Common Council, to demand and to enforce by all proper means the foregoing resolutions.

The committee was named, and there were several speeches. Father Quarters said that since he was as a father to them he desired that they be obedient as children and that he was always ready to stand by his flock in anything that would exhibit their willingness to obey the laws of their country. He also trusted that they, as law-abiding citizens, would refrain from destroying any more property and hoped they would await the decision of the corporative powers in relation to the draft.

Keynton said that he was anxious to see this matter settled to the entire satisfaction of the laboring classes and stated that the idea of the poor man being compelled to shoulder the musket, while the rich man could buy his freedom by paying $300, was wrong. He hoped all men would be placed on an equal footing. After some more speeches, including one from a Methodist minister, the Reverend Dr. Osborn, praising Irish-Americans, the crowd went quietly home.

After their victory over Fearing's militia, the Eleventh Avenue mob turned their attention to the refreshment saloon at the Wee-hawken ferry on the waterfront at Forty-second Street. The saloon was owned by James O'Bryon, a well-known Republican politi-cian, and knowledge of this, as well as the prospect of free liquor, may have impelled the mob to attack the place. A passer-by de-scribed the scene: "I saw the rioters in the street—100 or 150 of them; some three or four stout boys with clubs attacked the win-dows and broke them in; they then mashed in the doors; then the crowd rushed in; they pitched out boxes of cigars and bottles, and in about 10 minutes the house was on fire." Barrels of ale were rolled out into the street and their heads knocked in. While some of the plunderers regaled themselves with this, others concentrated on carrying away demijohns and bottles of spirits. Several of the more enterprising stole boats that were tied up along the water-front, loaded them with liquor, and rowed away. The flames spread from the saloon to the ferry-house and a boat-building shop, while the incendiaries drank deep and made merry.[14]

At two o'clock, seven men, including John Corrigan, an Irish peddler, Patrick Burke, and a man called Lewis, walked into the stables of Pickford and Jackson, proprietors of the Red Bird line of stages, on Thirty-fifth Street, between Tenth and Eleventh av-enues. They helped themselves to a horse apiece, saluted Burke as their "colonel," and rode off to join a crowd one block up the avenue. Blowing a brass horn, Corrigan rode his horse into a saloon on the corner of Thirty-fifth Street; some rioters followed him and drank up the stock in trade.[15] They wandered down Tenth Avenue, with Burke in the lead, looted a jeweler's store, and finally joined a crowd that had been pillaging a feed-store in Ninth Av-enue, near Twenty-ninth Street. All this time, Corrigan was dashing up and down the avenue on his horse, emitting blasts on his horn. At one time, he joined a gang that was tearing down telegraph poles and breaking into a liquor store on the corner of Forty-second Street and then galloped back to Twenty-ninth Street.

A servant girl pointed out the house of James S. Gibbons in Lamartine Place, off West Twenty-ninth Street, and told some of the mob that Horace Greeley lived there. The story spread among the crowd, becoming garbled (some heard that Greeley's cousin owned the house). Gibbons, in reality, was not related to the editor of the *Tribune*, but he was a strong Republican, and his wife and one of his daughters were away nursing wounded soldiers at Point Lookout, Maryland. Greeley was a friend of the family and had stayed with them for a while when he was ill in 1861. Gibbons himself was not at home that afternoon. Two of his daughters who were there saw the mob coming and fled to the house next door. Through doors and windows, the rioters poured into the Gibbons's home. Everything portable was carried off, even the grate pans and kitchen pots. Mirrors were shattered, and tables thrown from the windows. Pieces of furniture too heavy to be moved were chopped to bits. Books were used for kindling fires. Joseph H. Choate, then a young lawyer, who knew the Gibbons family well, witnessed the destruction. Seeing that there were too many rioters to resist single-handed, he decided to make sure the Gibbons girls were safe and guided them over the rooftops to the next street, where he found a carriage and took them to his house in West Twenty-first Street. A neighbor of the Gibbons, a man called John Wilson, who bore an unfortunate resemblance to Horace Greeley, was spotted by the crowd. "Here he is, here he is, the abolition liar, give it to him!" screamed the rioters, and Wilson was beaten to within an inch of his life before he was rescued by his wife and some friends.

When Captain Franklin's company of the Twelfth Infantry returned from the Union Steam Works, Brown and Acton decided to dispatch it, with some police, over to the West Side. Realizing that the men were tired out with marching, Acton had sent some officers over to Broadway to seize all the stages they could find. Fourteen of them were waiting outside the Central Office. The first driver in the line muttered that he did not want to carry police. "Take him down and lock him up in No. 4," ordered Acton, and with his example before them, the other drivers took up their reins.[16] The police and troops were crammed into the stages, and they lumbered off to Eighth Avenue and Twenty-first Street. Everything was quiet there, so they went on, up Eighth Avenue, and discovered the crowd pillaging Gibbons's house.

A charge sent the looters flying in all directions, and the force turned to the east, toward Fifth Avenue. Two policemen went ahead to reconnoiter and were greeted by stones and shrieks from the women, promising them they would be killed like rats before they left the ward. A man came rushing up to tell them that the mob had returned to the Gibbons house, and the two officers ran back to report to Captain James Z. Bogart, the police commander, and Captain Franklin. The force wheeled around, and double-timed it back to Twenty-ninth Street. The police went in first, and the military were held in reserve.

Once again, the street was cleared, and the officers began to hunt the rioters through the house, which was on fire in several places. One burly looter jumped through the parlor window, was tackled, and disappeared under a pile of policemen. A woman, clutching her booty, tried to strangle and bite the policeman who stopped her. Officer John R. Hill grabbed a man who was brandishing a pistol; he fired and wounded Hill in the thigh. The shot alarmed some of the troops, who were trigger-happy after their experience at the Steam Works, and, without orders, they opened fire. Several of the police who were struggling with looters in front of the house or in the doorway were hit. Officer Henry Dipple of the Broadway Squad was seriously wounded and died the following Sunday. Officer Joshua Hodgson took three slugs in his arm, and Officer Albert D. Robinson was hit in the thigh. Officer Peter Rice was hit in the groin and had two bullets through his thigh.[17] They were hurried off to hospital, and the rest of the force returned to headquarters. Some of the neighbors went into the Gibbons house with buckets of water and put out the fires. Later, some of the looters returned and went on ransacking the house far into the night, looking for something worth stealing. When Gibbons visited his home the next day, the only thing he was able to salvage was a toothbrush.[18]

During the sack of Gibbons's house, another group of rioters, led by two drunken Irishmen, Michael O'Brien and John Fitzherbert, was busy tearing an American flag to pieces in West Twenty-eighth Street. Fitzherbert's cries of "Damn the flag!" ceased as Andrew Houser, who lived at Number 336, came walking down the street. Houser was far from popular in the neighborhood, and the rioters knocked him down, beat him, and stole $70. Houser managed to get to his house and probably escaped through the backyards; the rioters turned the place upside down, but could not find him. Finally, Fitzherbert and O'Brien stole Houser's horse and wagon from his stable and drove off down the avenue, O'Brien brandishing an ax, and Fitzherbert shrieking "Three cheers for Jeff Davis!" "It serves you right, you long-necked Yankee bitch!" a woman called Flannigan, who lived on the opposite side of the street, shouted at the disconsolate Mrs. Houser, "I am glad of it." The career of Fitzherbert and O'Brien soon came to an inglorious end, however: they drove so wildly that they were stopped and arrested by a police patrol.[19]

On Sixth Avenue, a crowd rolled a barrel of beer out of a looted saloon, and "a seedy-looking character, evidently a retired knight of the buskin," ascended it. "Pelt the nigger!" shouted a boy. "Dislike me not for my complexion," declaimed the orator. "Fellow bummers! We live in a happy day. I am happy to be able to address so respectable and intelligent an audience as that now before me. We, fellow bummers, are the foundation of New York City, and if the foundation moves, you know, the structure falls." "It is falling," shouted his audience. "Bully for you!" "Go on!" "That's what's the matter!" Someone who liked beer better than speechmaking knocked the thespian off his perch, and the crowd fell to carousing.

Late in the afternoon, rioters on both the East and West sides began to build barricades. The area between Eleventh and Fourteenth streets, from First Avenue to the East River, was turned into a rioters' redoubt. Here, for the first time, the disturbances took a Luddite aspect. Two patent street-sweeping machines parked in the old cemetery of Saint Mark's Church at Eleventh Street were seized and burned.[20] Speakers, led by a man who announced that he was a returned soldier but that he sympathized with the South since the emancipation of the "niggers," denounced grain elevators as "labor-saving machines." They put poor men out of work, and they ought to be destroyed, like the street-sweeping machines.

On the West Side, a series of barricades was thrown up along Ninth Avenue, from Thirty-sixth Street up to Forty-second. Telegraph poles were cut down and laid across the avenue, and carts, wagons, lumber, boxes, bricks, rubbish heaped on top. The Mackerelville fortifications were not strategically important, and Commissioner Acton and General Brown contented themselves with sending some troops to protect the gasworks in Fourteenth Street. They were joined by a group of vigilantes, and though the gashouse had previously been threatened all was quiet while they were on guard. The Ninth Avenue barricades were a more serious matter. Rioters would be able to dominate most of the upper West Side from such a stronghold, and Captain Walling of the Twentieth Precinct police was ordered to clear the streets as soon as possible. A company of federal troops under Captain Wilkins was sent to help him. No aid was forthcoming from General Sandford, and Walling had to wait impatiently for Wilkins's arrival. At six o'clock, the federal troops appeared. They had stopped on their way uptown to chase some looters out of the Gibbons house, and from Twenty-ninth Street to Thirty-fifth they had repeatedly had to stop, turn about, and fire at crowds following them. Together, the police and troops marched on the Rue Saint Jacques of New York.

Crowds of people lined the sidewalks of the avenue and watched from the rooftops as the police deployed to left and right and the troops lined up across the road. A fusillade of pistol shots and an occasional bullet from a musket greeted them, but when the troops moved forward, firing volley after volley, the men at the barricade hastily retreated. The soldiers surged over the barricade, halted, and kept up a covering fire while the police tore it down. Four times the scene was repeated, until the avenue was clear. Beyond the last barricade, the troops and police suddenly found themselves under a hail of stones and bricks from the houses on either side of the avenue. The soldiers sent a volley of bullets into the houses, and all at once everything was calm. As dusk fell, the rioters slipped away and the crowds broke up.[21]

When Walling got back to his station house, he found that the night's work was not over. Several women had come there with news that they had wounded soldiers from the detachment that had been routed in Forty-second Street that afternoon concealed in their homes. Walling decided to try and rescue them without attracting attention. He commandeered a carriage from John Callahan's livery stable in West Thirty-third Street and sent it off to bring in the injured troops, with only a single policeman as escort. Two of the soldiers were picked up without trouble, but while a third was being helped into the carriage at Forty-second Street and Tenth Avenue, a group of desperadoes came in sight. Flourishing clubs and throwing stones, they made for the rescuers, and the policeman promptly took to his heels. Fortunately, Callahan was a popular and well-known figure in the area, and when the driver was able to make the attackers understand the coach belonged to him, they let the battered vehicle pass.[22]

Under cover of darkness, the Metropolitan Gas Works at the foot of Forty-second Street was set ablaze. This was a small concern which only supplied a very limited area of the city, but its destruction left part of the West Side in Stygian blackness. At 11:30 P.M. some Negroes who lived on West Thirty-sixth Street, near Seventh Avenue, were driven from their homes. They went to the Twentieth Precinct station house for shelter, but Walling's premises were already overflowing with refugees, and he sent them to the Sixteenth Precinct station on West Twentieth Street. Just before midnight, Walling heard that a crowd was threatening a Negro church on West Thirtieth Street. He called out his men, and using some fire engines as a cover, they were able to get within a block of the church before the rioters saw them. Shooting broke out, but the police replied with their revolvers and then charged with clubs flailing. After a sharp struggle, the neighborhood was cleared, and the upper West Side was quiet the rest of the night.[23]

At 7:40 P.M. General Brown resolved to pry the federal troops at the Thirty-fifth Street Arsenal out of Sandford's control and put them to work. Through the Twentieth Precinct, he sent a message to Colonel Nugent, ordering him to have the federal commanders at the arsenal report at police headquarters. At the same time, Brown made one last attempt to get Sandford and his men into action, "To Major-General Sandford, at Arsenal," he telegraphed. "I am in command of the U.S. troops in the city. Will you come to this office to consult with me?" But Sandford did not reply, and the militia continued to sit out the riots.

The bloody victory won by the police and the troops in the second battle of the Union Steam Works had left the population of the Twenty-first Ward in a white-hot fury. Speakers harangued the crowds. One man climbed to an awning and urged his audience to avenge the women and children who had been killed. They had not fought right, he said. They should go on the housetops and hurl bricks from the chimneys at the enemy. "All we want is a leader," he cried, "and then we will go to victory or the devil." He called on them all to follow him and punish the aristocrats of Fifth Avenue. On the corner of Twenty-first Street and Second Avenue, a middle-aged woman berated the men for their cowardice when attacked by the police. They ought to be ashamed to show their faces, she jeered. There were as many of them with carbines in their hands as there were of the police, but instead of bravely defending themselves, they had thrown down their weapons, and abjectly whined, and allowed themselves to be pummeled and struck to the ground.

At 10:30 P.M. the rioters of the Twenty-first Ward burned the home of Sinclair, the publisher of the *Tribune*, at 24 East Twenty-third Street, and half an hour later, they stormed the Eighteenth Precinct station house. The four policemen who had been left to guard the building pried the iron bars from a cell window and escaped through it into East Twenty-third Street. The attackers set the station on fire and soon a great column of flame and smoke shot up into the sky. George Templeton Strong went out to watch, and found himself "in a crowd of Keltic spectators disgorged by the circumjacent tenement houses . . . exulting over the damage done to 'them bloody police.' " Ellen Leonard peeped anxiously out of her window at the cheering mob holding back the firemen and the watching people on the rooftops, standing like burnished bronze statues in the glare of the fire.[24]

At eight o'clock, Inspector Leonard, Sergeant Polly of the Eleventh Precinct, and a patrolman had a narrow escape when they tried to make an arrest at Broadway and Chambers Street. A crowd was hooting and jeering Lieutenant Ryer's detachment of federal troops as they marched up Broadway, and it seems that Leonard lost his temper and grabbed one of the most prominent demonstrators. The police station at City Hall was only a short way off, but the crowds pressed so thick around the three policemen it seemed they would never reach it. "Kill them!" "Kill them!" "We'll give you what we gave Kennedy!" the furious crowd yelled. The three officers struggled into City Hall Park and were rescued by a charge of the police who were on duty at the hall. In the melee, the demonstrator whose arrest had caused all the trouble escaped.

Between half-past eight and nine o'clock, crowds gathered at the corner of Cherry and Catherine streets in the Seventh Ward. Three undercover policemen were recognized and badly beaten before they could escape. A plumber's shop was broken into, and the crowd mounted an attack on Brooks Brothers store. Brooks's management had the reputation of being hard employers (the previous March, four hundred of their tailors had gone on strike for higher wages), and the firm had been involved in a scandal over supplying shoddy uniforms to the army.[25] Such considerations may have turned some rioters' minds to thoughts of attacking Brooks's establishment, but as the largest clothing store in the area, it probably would have been sacked anyway. Police from the Fourth Precinct chased the crowd away once, but as soon as the officers marched off, the attackers returned and fell to work again.

Edwin Granville, a porter at the store, reported:

The attack was made at half-past nine o'clock in the evening, at that time a young man named Theo. Betts, salesman, was with me in the store; he slept in the store; the first signs of an attack were small stones thrown through the window, over the door; then commenced a great deal of banging and thumping against the doors and windows on Cherry Street side, then the panels of the doors were broken in, and they put their heads in and called me names, and said if I did not open they would hang or shoot me; it was a general cry; then when I saw them break the second panel, in order to raise the bar, I thought it was time for me to leave; there was one head at a time at each panel; there was great confusion in the street; I went to the custom-room, got a rope and let myself down into the back yard; I then went and changed my clothes to disguise myself, so they should not know me; then I went home; did not go near the mob for fear they would kill me.

While Granville was making his escape, the rioters were smashing glass cases and ransacking the store. Great heaps of garments were tossed into the air and piled on the floor. Bolts of cloth were thrown through the windows and the street outside was festooned with lengths of material. Cherry Street was covered with hats, suits, coats, pants, overalls, jackets, vests, clothes of all kinds and colors and sizes. Rioters laden with plunder were staggering away down the streets. In the middle of the carnival, 150 police, commanded by Inspector Carpenter, came up and charged into the crowd. Rioters opened fire, and Sergeant Finney of the Third Precinct was shot in the face. With club and revolver, the police cleared a path to the door of the store, re-formed, and charged again. The mob fell back, and Carpenter, dividing his force into four platoons, ordered an advance down each of the streets that met in front of Brooks Brothers store: Catherine, Hamilton, Cherry, and Oak. The crowds were pushed back and disappeared into the side streets and alleys of the waterfront. When Brooks Brothers took stock of their losses, they found that over $50,000 worth of clothing had been stolen or ruined.[26]

To the north, another mob was breaking into stores along Division and Grand streets. The barkeeper in the saloon at 474 Grand saved his employer's place by offering the rioters free drinks. Next door, at 476, Nathan Abrahams and his cap-maker, Harris Newfield, were frantically carrying everything they could upstairs, and this stratagem was successful. When the raiders broke into Abrahams's ready-made clothing store, they took everything there was in the store and the backroom and broke up the fixtures, but they did not look upstairs. Elias Silberstein, a partner in a clothing store at 456 Grand, was less resourceful. He was standing in the street when he saw the crowd come round the corner, armed with axes and shovels, and begin to attack his premises. He rushed up and asked them what they thought they were doing. The attackers told him it was none of his business, threatened to kill him, and chased him down to the corner of Clinton Street. Silberstein ran to the Thirteenth Precinct police station and begged for help, but nearly all the officers had been called away. When he got back to his store, he found the shelves bare. There was nothing left but one coat and some neckties the intruders had dropped on the floor. At one place, the looters met resistance. Bartholomew Ward, a clerk in the City Comptroller's office, was in a saloon opposite Bernhard Stern's clothing store at 446 Grand Street, having a drink with Oscar Bogart, who had formerly worked for the county clerk. Coming out of the saloon, Ward saw that Stern's place was being plundered. He had known Stern for five years and quickly resolved to stop the robbery. Drawing a revolver, he ran over to the store, followed by Bogart. They forced the looters outside, and Ward shouted that he would shoot the first man who stepped into the store. Some firemen from a nearby engine-house joined Ward and Bogart, and they guarded the store until the danger was past. At 1:30 P.M. a detachment of police arrived and swept the area.[27]

In the red-light district at the tip of Manhattan Island, the previous night's attacks on black prostitutes and the dance halls and stews they frequented had broadened into an attack on all brothels. Possibly this was because raiding such places could prove extremely lucrative. One householder in this locality lost $500 in gold, and $50 worth of furs belonging to his wife. On the other hand, personal enmity could sometimes be the motive. Maria Casey, who kept "one of the lowest of bawdy saloons," recognized three of the gang who attacked her place. "They had been at my house before; the door had been broken into before by the same party, about a month previous; one of them had a grudge against me, and he stole my watch; his name is John Carroll; he brought the men who broke in my door this time."[28]

Houses in James, Washington, and Rector streets were invaded and wrecked, and the mob began to work its way down Greenwich Street. Theodore Osterstock, a sometime circus rider turned saloon-keeper, temporarily diverted them into attacking a shoe-maker's at Number 161. The owner, Samuel Roesner, put up a fight, but he was shoved out of the way and his place thoroughly looted. Four hundred pairs of boots and five hundred pairs of shoes, worth $2,000 were stolen. Next, the crowd sent a salvo of bricks crashing through the window of Whitehead's drugstore opposite and plundered that too. Then they returned to their primary concern. Next door to Roesner's was a bordello kept by John Smith, and they broke in, drank up all the liquor in the bar, chased the girls away, and set fire to the place. A police patrol drove the rioters out of the district for the time being, but half an hour later they returned and attacked Smith in his private room. Smith shot one of the leading intruders, a longshoreman called Michael Haley, and escaped in the confusion. He went to the Twenty-seventh Precinct station house, but when the sergeant in charge there heard his story, he advised Smith to leave the city for a while. He did, staying away for a couple of weeks. Haley died a couple of minutes after he was shot, and Smith's act was later ruled justifiable homicide when the grand jury refused to indict him.[29]

Attacks on stores and the homes of Negroes went on during Tuesday night, as they had done all day. No part of the city was safe. The Seventh District draft office at 68 Third Avenue was ransacked. The Dry Dock Savings Bank on East Fourth Street, near Avenue C, was attacked; the watchman held the mob off until the police arrived. Police were sent to secure the Western Hotel at Liberty and Cortlandt streets against capture, and so many reports came in that rioters were planning to seize the North River ferries that the authorities in Jersey City were asked to stop the boats running. A huge iron-clad ram, the *Dunderberg*, was urder construction for the navy at Webb's shipyard on the East River waterfront at Seventh Street, and rumors spread that the mob meant to burn it. One hundred and sixteen men of the Twenty-second Regiment reserves joined the seventy men of the Seventh Regiment reserves, and together they set out for the yard. The people of the Eleventh Ward jeered and cursed them as they marched through the streets, but an order to fix bayonets was enough to deter a threatened attack. They reached the yard safely and stood guard there for the next couple of day.[30]

At ten o'clock, a threatening crowd gathered outside the Fifth Precinct police station on Leonard Street. Shots were fired and preparations made to set the station ablaze. There were four hundred black refugees there, but only two policemen: all the rest had been called away. Sergeant Higgins gave the Negroes guns and was anxiously calculating the chances of making a successful defense, when Inspector Carpenter arrived with one hundred and fifty men, and dispersed the mob. As soon as his force had left, the rioters gathered again, but Higgins was able to get help from the soldiers guarding the government stores in Worth Street, and this time the crowd was chased away for good. Armed Negroes guarded their homes in Minetta Lane, singing psalms and keeping watch from rooftops.[31]

Where Negroes had already fled, rioters made sure they would never return. Numbers 73 and 75 Roosevelt Street were burned down; three buildings on the corner of Roosevelt and Batavia streets were pulled down, the debris piled in the street and set on fire. Where the blacks still held on, attempts were made to rout them out. At the heart of the Negro district in Greenwich Village was "the Arch," a row of tenements that ran from Thompson to Sullivan Street, between Grand and Broome, and named for an open archway that ran under the buildings. Between one and two o'clock on Wednesday morning, a gang of rowdies led by William Rigby, a hack driver who lived a short distance away in Lispenard Street, came down Sullivan Street, breaking windows, destroying and stealing property in houses whose occupants had fled, and raiding a cigar store. When they reached the Arch, one of the crowd produced a large bag of straw and shavings. Camphene was poured over it, Rigby set it on fire, and the rioters threw it onto a barrel. Flames shot up, and the Arch might have burned down if a fire company on their way to a call further downtown had not seen the blaze and stopped to put it out.[32]

William James, a shipbroker, left his home on East Twenty-ninth Street at ten o'clock and walked across Fourth Avenue to get a pitcher of ale. Outside number 68, he was stopped by a youth waving a pistol, who told him, "There is a nigger living here with two white women, and we are going to bring him out and hang him on the lamp post, and you stop and see the fun." Jeremiah G. Hamilton, who lived there, was actually a white man, but he had spent nearly all his life in the West Indies, and his deeply tanned complexion made his neighbors believe he was black. Luckily for him, he had already made his escape, and the rioters contented themselves with pillaging his house.[33]

About eight o'clock that Tuesday night, a mob led by a small-time Democratic politician and grocer called William Cruise attacked 25 Thomas Street, in the Fifth Ward. This was the home of Mary Burke, a white prostitute who catered to Negroes. The rioters were "hallooing & screaming . . . running through the streets picking up stones and firing them at the houses." Cruise "ordered them to go in and burn the house down. . . . They stoned and broke the panels out of the door. He holloed for them to go and get some straw lying in the ash box. The boys got it and put it round the door. He holloed for them to go and get some matches." "Irish sons of bitches!" shrieked Mary Burke from the rooftop. She fired a shot at the crowd below, and Cruise drew a pistol and fired back. A lone policeman from the Fifth Precinct, Officer Richard Field, arrived and tried to persuade Cruise to go away. Cruise replied that the "nigger prostitute" ought to be burned out, and Field, seeing it was hopeless, gave up. He went into the house and guided the woman to safety across the roofs and through backyards. Meanwhile, Cruise had set fire to the straw and led the crowd round the corner into Worth Street. Among those who followed him was James Best, an Irish laborer who lived in Leonard Street; Michael Bannin, a sixteen-year-old schoolboy who lived in West Broadway; Charles Tooker, aged fifteen, a plumber who lived two doors down from Bannin; and a man called Moses Breen.

Cruise's objective was the rear house at 11 Worth Street, where a Negro named William Derrickson lived in the basement with his white wife and their two children. Derrickson, who worked as a loader in a packinghouse, had known Cruise for three or four years and sometimes supplied him with meat. They had quarreled before the riot. "All I know," Derrickson said later, "is one time I was standing just next to his door—I was talking with Mrs. ———'s girls.[34] He came out and wanted to know what in Hell I was doing there and if I didn't go about my business he would give me some ———." Possibly this is why Cruise led the mob to Derrickson's home; possibly he believed that Derrickson had immoral purposes in his employment of a white maid, Ellen Foos, a former prostitute who had served several terms in prison.

At any rate, Cruise led his followers straight to the Derricksons' home. "Here's where the niggers live, in the rear," he shouted. "Come down, we'll go after old Derrickson. He's the big nigger we want. We'll hang him to the lamp-post." Derrickson had put out the light when he heard the mob coming, and when they began to batter the door down, he dived out of the back window and escaped. Though the mobs had beaten and killed numbers of black men, they had not harmed women or children, and Derrickson believed that his family was not in danger. But Cruise and his gang were exceptionally vicious. "There's one of them!" shouted Best as they rushed in, pointing to the little boy Alfred. Cruise hit him over the head with an ax, and Best gave him another blow with a heavy iron-bound cart-rung. "For God's sake," screamed Mrs. Derrickson, "kill me and save my boy." She fell right over her son, trying to protect him with her body. Best, enraged, showered blows on her with the cart-rung, dragged the unconscious boy outside, and tore his clothes off. Mrs. Derrickson followed and again threw herself over him. Cruise beat her, pulled the boy out, and beat him, too. Moses Breen threw a rope over a lamppost to hang him, but Best had another idea. "Let's burn the nigger!" he yelled, waving the kerosene lamp from the house and kicking the child.

At that moment, Frederick Merrick, who kept the grocery next door, took a hand. Armed with a pistol, he went up to Cruise and Best. He recalled:

I said it was a shame for you to hit that boy, you great big men to come here and attack a boy, why don't you hit men, if you want to fight, so a man came and jumped up on the stoop and asked me what I had to do with it. I said I had as much to do with it as this–that if the[y] didn't desist I should try and make them–that there were enough to make them leave the street soon. He said if you don't look out we will hang you to the lamp-post–There is a rope. . . . I said, No you won't, you know better than that. Finally I said if you don't desist I will get help enough to me–we are all ready and will make you leave anyway. I saw they were earnest and I called all the Germans up there to help me in case they should attack me. I went amongst them–I was not afraid– but I said in case they should attack me to come and help me. This man said I am the man who hit him what do you want? . . . When I said that we would give them all hell if they didn't desist, So this Jim Best stood in the street and had this big stick of wood looked like a Cart rung I don't know what it was He said come on boys there is no use in standing here any longer–there is another nest of niggers round in Leonard Street–let's clear them out. So they gave three cheers for Leonard Street[35] and off they went.

The boy was left lying in the gutter, covered with blood. He recovered from his injuries, but his mother did not. On August 20, Mrs. Ann Derrickson died of peritonitis, brought on by the beating she had received. Early Wednesday morning, James Best came back to the house and asked Ellen Foos "if that nigger was dead yet, saying if he was not, he would come around that night and make sure of him, and that he had nine lives like a cat."[36]

*I have often heard the nature and condition of the colored people discussed by my shopmates in America. I have met with a few well-conditioned men who looked upon the blacks as rational beings; but the strongly expressed view of the majority was, that they are a soulless race, and I am satisfied that some of these people would shoot a black man with as little regard to moral consequences as they would a wild hog.*

—JAMES DAWSON BURN
*Three Years among the Working Classes in the United States during the War.*[1]

# 7

## City for Conquest

WEDNESDAY was the most critical day of the riot. The police and the federal troops were worn out with constant marching and fighting, and no help had arrived from the Army of the Potomac. The newspapers told of trouble over the draft in Boston and Hartford, Newark and Jersey City, Hastings, Tarrytown, and Rye. Things were most serious in the Massachusetts capital, where gun stores were ransacked, an armory attacked, and troops were called in. Reports said that at least three people had been killed and several wounded.

Elsewhere in the newspaper columns, there was more encouragement for the rioters. The city judge, John H. McCunn, whose name was a by-word for venality and the political perversion of justice, had declared the Draft Act unconstitutional. The case in question concerned an enrolling officer, William L. Stephens, who had arrested a man called Henry Biesel for refusing to give his name. McCunn declared that Stephens had no legal authority to make an arrest and pointed out that the Draft Act did not make refusal to give one's name to an enrolling officer an offense. But not content with this, McCunn went on to say that the whole Draft Act was *ultra vires*. It violated the rights of the people, made an illegal distinction among the citizenry, and directly contravened the Constitution.

In tangled reasoning, McCunn argued that the Constitution, authorizing Congress "to raise and support armies," provided only for the standing armies of the country. It did not provide for volunteer and temporary forces that any emergency might demand, for Article I of the Constitution authorized Congress to call out the militia when needed "to execute the laws of the Union, suppress insurrections and repel invasions." And the Second Amendment declared: "A well-regulated militia being necessary to the security of a free State, the right of the people to keep and bear arms shall not be infringed." The president was commander-in-chief of this militia when it was called into the service of the United States. But, said McCunn, the conscription law did not make the force it raised a militia force of the states, nor was it part of the standing army of the United States. Therefore, it was unauthorized by the Constitution. McCunn closed his opinion by saying that he deeply regretted that the people had not had patience and patriotism enough to wait until the courts had pronounced on the legality of the draft. The courts were able and equal to the duty of sustaining the rights of the citizens, and it was through the courts alone that their rights and safety were fully protected. There was, of course, no question that the government would appeal McCunn's decision to a higher court, but its appearance at the height of the disorders gave the mob's actions a partial color of legality.

From two o'clock until six, the city was quiet. A lumberyard on the corner of Avenue C and Fourteenth Street was set ablaze at 2:40 A.M., and houses belonging to two prominent Republicans were set on fire, one in Harlem and one in Yorkville. A Baptist church at Fifth Avenue and 125th Street was the target of three attempts at arson. Elsewhere, an uneasy calm prevailed, as another overcast and muggy day dawned. About eight o'clock, there was a heavy thundershower. Unfortunately for the authorities, the rain did not last long enough to clear the streets of rioters. Reports of trouble were coming in from all over the city by then, and detachments of police were sent to the most disturbed precincts. Commissioner Acton watched them from the front of the Central Office. "Go on, boys!" he shouted as the columns of weary officers marched off. "Go on! Give it to them, now! Quail on toast for every man of you, as soon as the mob is put down. Quail on toast, boys!"[2]

At half-past six that morning, James Costello, a Negro shoemaker who lived at 97 West Thirty-third Street, ventured out. In West Thirty-second Street, he was spotted by William Mealy, a volunteer fireman who belonged to Number 18 Engine Company.[3] Costello ran, and Mealy followed, close on his heels. Near Sixth Avenue, Costello turned, drew a revolver, and shot Mealy.[4] "Murder!" screamed his mother, who was watching the chase. Costello dived into the nearest house, and five or six whites, attracted by the shot, went in and pulled him out. "Kill the nigger!" they shouted, as they beat and kicked him, jumped up and down on his body and threw stones at him. Finally, he seemed to be dead, and they went to help Mealy, who was lying on the sidewalk. "He's moving!" called a boy who saw the Negro stir. A couple of the attackers came running back and started beating Costello again. They dragged him over to a large pothole full of water, put his face down into it, and emptied a barrel of ashes over his head. Someone got a rope and tied it around the Negro's neck. They hauled him over to a tree and hanged him from it.[5]

By this time, a crowd had gathered and they set on fire the house in which Costello had tried to hide, although the people who lived there had never seen him before. A woman told the mob that Negroes lived in some rear houses along Thirty-second Street, and they swarmed into them. They were looted and burned, and the rioters roamed up and down Sixth Avenue in search of Negroes and Negroes' homes.[6] "I was with my mother at No. 105 West 27th Street," Harriet L. Sandford recalled, "the mob came in the house and drove me out . . . they burst the door of my room open; I was on the walk two hours in 28th Street; I asked a head rioter if I could come back; he said I could, but must leave in fifteen minutes; I returned; my things were in a bundle; they were gone."[7] Mrs. Mary Alexander was driven out of her home at 94 West Twenty-eighth Street by a gang of rioters headed by James Cassidy, an Irish laborer, who lived nearby. "All you damned niggers get out of here in five minutes," bellowed Cassidy, "or we will burn down the house over your heads." Mrs. Alexander asked if she could get some clothes. "Yes, damn you," growled Cassidy, "go in and bring every thing you have got in there out, and don't never show your face in this street again." John Alexander had jumped from a third-story window when he heard the crowd's shouts,

"Turn out, you black sons of bitches! We're going to burn your house!" He hid in a neighbor's yard until nightfall. The white owner of a building occupied by Negroes at 273 West Twenty-eighth Street rushed over to the Twentieth Precinct station house to get help only to be told "We can't take care of ourselves" by the police.[8]

Many of the Negro homes were empty, and looters had a field day. A couple of plunderers with a hand cart carried away three trunks, two cases, a new cot bed, some bedding, and two tables. Others, after searching 270 Seventh Avenue for Negroes, broke into the butcher's shop on the ground floor and stole all the meat. When twenty or thirty rioters invaded the home of Mrs. Margaret Robinson, they stripped all the clothes off her young son and daughter.[9]

General Brown scraped together some troops to send to the area: some cavalry under Colonel Thaddeus P. Mott, one hundred artillerymen who had been armed with rifles, and a couple of guns, all commanded by Brigadier General Charles C. Dodge. They reached Thirty-second Street at eight o'clock and cut down Costello's body. The crowd scattered, and the troops marched on to the Thirty-fifth Street Arsenal without having to fire a shot. Almost as soon as they had reached the arsenal, though, word came that the mob had gathered again. Back most of the troops marched to Thirty-second Street (half the artillerymen stayed at the arsenal) and rescued fourteen Negroes, who were besieged in one of the houses. The rioters made a rush at the troops, but a couple of volleys sent them reeling back. Dodge decided to use the guns, but the rain had drenched the ammunition so that it was useless.

At that moment, Captain Shelley's company arrived, and General Dodge resolved to sweep the area. Shelley's men marched down Seventh Avenue, dispersing the mob as they went. Mott and his cavalry galloped up the avenue, and in West Thirty-third Street, they came across a Negro called Augustus Stuart being chased by a gang of toughs. Stuart, terrified and dazed from the blows he had received, thought the soldiers were going to attack him, too. He fired a wild shot at them, and a trooper cut him down with his saber. Stuart died in the hospital on Blackwell's Island on the twenty-third.

All the troops went back to police headquarters, except the artillerymen. They returned to the Thirty-fifth Street Arsenal to re-join the other half of the command. While they had been gone, the commander of the detachment at the arsenal, Lieutenant Joyce, had raided a house on Broadway where arms were said to be concealed and had discovered seventy-three Enfield rifles there.[10] As soon as the soldiers had left West Thirty-second Street, the crowds reappeared. They hung Costello's body from the tree again and resumed their search for Negroes and their sacking of Negroes' homes. Later in the morning, a detachment of police cut down Costello's body and took it away, but this, too, only caused temporary interruption of the pogrom.

In the middle of the afternoon, some rioters headed by George Glass, an Irish laborer who lived in West Twenty-seventh Street, broke into a house on the corner of Twenty-seventh and Seventh Avenue and discovered Abraham Franklin, a crippled black coachman, and his sister Henrietta there. Glass and his men dragged them out, roughed up the girl, and beat and kicked her brother for nearly a block, until they came to a lamppost on the corner of West Twenty-eighth Street. They shouted for a rope; Mark J. Silva, a Jewish tailor from England, hoisted the Negro up, and they hanged him from the lamppost. The approach of some troops from the Thirty-fifth Street Arsenal made the mob scatter and the soldiers cut Franklin down and rescued the girl. But as soon as the military marched on, Franklin's body was hung from the lamppost once more, with loud cheers for Jeff Davis. Later the body was taken down again, and Patrick Butler, an Irish butcher, sixteen years of age, grabbed it by the genitals and pulled it through the streets as the crowd cheered and yelled.[11]

At the same time that Franklin was murdered, a black waiter at the Howard House named Charles Jackson decided to try to escape from the city by the Newport boat. He testified:

I started from the Howard House 20 minutes of 4 to go to pier No. 3. I wanted to get to the boat before much of a crowd came. I met a man in Broadway and asked him how the crowd was; he said it was pretty bad and he said he would go down with me; we started and went down Second street below the Howard House; it was a white gentleman that went with me down to the wharf; we stepped into a hotel on the corner and got a glass of beer; we went down towards the wharf; before I got close to those fellows I heard one of them say, "Halloe John, here comes a nigger; we will hop on him." The first fellow I came across had a cap and side whiskers. [He was an Irish seaman who called himself Joseph Marshall, though his real name was Timothy Duggan, and he had been hanging around the waterfront ever since his arrival from New Orleans in the spring.] He came across and grabbed me by the coat and three or four others came across the street; in that instant I was knocked down with a brickbat or something. I thought Marshall said, "O you black son of a bitch I'll give you hell." I did not know anything until I was swimming up under the edge of the dock; they throwed me overboard; my clothes was all off me. I had a daguerrotype of my wife in my side coat pocket for which I paid 75 cents; a watch I paid $40 for in Washington, a coat that cost $28.00, a hat I paid $3.00 for, and a pair of pants worth $8.00. I had $36.00 in Treasury notes and $2.00 in postage currency in my pants pocket. I saw Marshall frequently for the last couple of months; I used to go down to the boat every day when I was at the Howard house.

Jackson hid under the wharf and stayed there all night.[12]

On Wednesday, as on the two days before, there was no safety for a Negro anywhere in New York. And as before, stores were robbed, factories forced to close, telegraph poles chopped down, and groups of rioters tried to extort money from people, though vigilantes provided a measure of protection in many areas.[13] On Wednesday morning, a gang led by John Halligan, a laborer; Adam Schlosshauer, a German gardener; and Martin Hart, who had arrived from Ireland only six weeks before, rambled through Harlem demanding money. Said Marcellus E. Randall, who had a business on 121st Street:

I first noticed them opposite my place of business on the other side of Avenue, one of them was playing a flute; they came across Third Avenue from opposite my place. They came from Mr. Lytle's place to our office. Hartt [*sic*] said "We want some money." I told him that I had none; said so for the purpose of getting rid of them. He said he knew a damn sight better and we had money. He then asked again if we were going to give him any money. I gave him the same answer as before. He then said, "We'll attend to you tonight." Halligan asked the same question of Mr. Porter who told him he had money but would not give him any and said he exercised the right to do with his money as he saw fit Halligan then made the same remark that he would fix us that night.

They then went out of our place and stopped at Sherwood & Conners about 25 feet from our office.—While they were standing there Halligan came back and took a good survey of the building from top to bottom from the outside. I saw Sherwood, of the firm of Sherwood & Conners pay them money—from there they went to Mrs. Brown's dry goods store & to a Lager Beer saloon I saw them go in Sheridan's tin smith shop and Mitchell's grocery store—then they crossed 125 Street and went in Hopes and then in Mrs. Coleman's dry goods store, and in Levi Adams factory and from there into Mr. Houston's. . . . As soon as they went out Mr. Porter and I went into Lytle's to get him to go with me to arrest them. He did not go with us. Porter said if he could get five men he would arrest them.

Some members of the local home guard overpowered Halligan and Hart on the corner of 122nd Street a few minutes later and gave them a good thrashing before turning them over to the police. Michael Mulray, who took Hart to the police station said that "several persons were beating and clubbing . . . Hart . . . he then got up and fled into the store on the . . . corner." Mulray "arrested him in order to rescue him from his assailants . . . he seemed to be badly injured and was crying for mercy." [14]

Some people exploited the riots to gain personal revenge. A man called Doherty, a laborer in Central Park, had asked Josiah Porter, who lived at Fifth Avenue and Sixty-first Street, if he could build a shanty on Porter's land. Porter refused, and during the riots Doherty convinced several men that Porter was an Orangeman and a Republican. They burned his house down and told his wife "if they found him in the house they would cut him in four quarters and throw him in the flames." [15]

Resentful Catholics took advantage of the riots to wreck a couple of Protestant missions in tenement districts: one maintained by Saint George's Episcopal Church, Stuyvesant Square, at 283 Avenue B, and another at the Five Points. Other rioters attacked anyone connected with the authorities. Seven men burst into the home of Joseph Hecht, an enrolling officer, at 229 Avenue A. "They took hold of me," testified Hecht, "and called me Mr. Lincoln; they swore at me." They beat him bloody and stole his watch, chain, and money. Down the avenue, at Number 173, some women leaned out of the window and waved their handkerchiefs when they saw some soldiers marching by. When the troops had gone, rioters attacked the house and sacked the store on the ground floor. Private Francis J. Menninger of the Twelfth Regiment was on guard outside the armory at Broadway and Fourth Street when a man called Patrick Carroll came up "and called him a damned son of a bitch said he would be killed if he went out and that he would mark [him]." Menninger called out the guard and Carroll was subdued after a struggle in which he tried to attack the regiment's commander with an iron ice pick.[16]

In the often surrealist fashion of riots, some people carried on their everyday life, though the city around them was in chaos. Michael Mayer was a policeman who was on duty battling rioters all through the disorders. Yet, on Wednesday morning, his wife decided to move their furniture from 212 East Twenty-third Street down to their new home at 297 Third Street, as they had planned days before. All went well until the removers' cart was loaded. "When I was about to leave," the cartman remembered, "three fellows pulled me off my cart and took hold of my horse; I begged them to stop; they threatened to kill me with a large knife which they put to my heart; they then took the horse and cart to the corner of First Avenue and 23rd Street; a great crowd threw all the things from the cart on to the street; there were men, women and children; the three fellows allowed me to go off, and gave me the bureau, and said I could have it myself." When the crowd had taken their pick of the Mayers' furniture, the rest was piled up and set on fire.[17]

At police headquarters, the telegraph brought news of trouble from precinct after precinct. A threatening crowd gathered at the Fourteenth Street gashouse and the garrison there drove them off at the point of the bayonet. Police had to be sent to hold the three United States government warehouses in the city. Rioters made a move on one of them, at the corner of Greenwich and Albany streets, where 20,000 muskets were stored, but they were driven back in time. Captain Franklin's company of troops and fifty police were sent up to Harlem by boat, and a force was dispatched to Yorkville.[18] At eleven o'clock, Captain John Jourdan and a detachment from the Sixth Precinct broke up a mob at Centre and Worth streets.

Early in the afternoon, Major Nevers, who was in command at the Seventh Regiment armory at Tompkins' Market, heard that a mob was attacking Negroes on East Thirty-fifth Street. He had about a hundred men of the regimental reserve on hand, and he turned them out and led them up to the Twenty-first Precinct police station. Sergeant Brackett and thirty-five policemen joined the troops there, and the united force marched over to Second Avenue, which was packed with people. Nevers wanted to open fire at once, but Brackett insisted on giving the crowd a warning. Stepping forward, he called on them to go home and avoid the fearful tragedy that would occur if the troops had to shoot into a throng containing many women and children. For the only time during the riots, the crowd obeyed such an admonition and even gave the sergeant a cheer as they straggled off.

Brackett, well satisfied, took his police back to the station, and the Seventh started down Third Avenue. After they had gone a couple of blocks, it became obvious that the real hard core of the East Side mob was here. By the time the troops reached Twenty-eighth Street, brickbats and flowerpots were falling on them like raindrops, and though the Seventh opened fire, the rioters rallied and returned to the attack. Nevers and his men pushed on to Twenty-sixth Street, where they met Captain Putnam's company of regulars, sent out on patrol by General Brown. Putnam marched his company to the front, and the rioters began to pepper them with musket and revolver shot. Putnam put riflemen on each flank, ordered them to fire at will, and advanced up the avenue, driving the crowd before him. They slipped away into the side streets, and Putnam and his men marched partway up Fourth Avenue and back. On the way back to headquarters, the mere sight of the soldiers was enough to scatter another mob in Third Avenue.[19]

That afternoon, after talking it over with Governor Seymour and General Wool, Mayor Opdyke issued a proclamation:

To the citizens of New York: I am happy to announce to you that the riot which for two days has disgraced our City, has been in good measure subjected to the control of the public authorities. It would not have interrupted your peace for a day but for the temporary absence of all our organized local militia. What now remains of the mob are fragments prowling about for plunder, and, for the purpose of meeting these, and saving the military and police from the exhaustion of continued movements, you are invited to form voluntary associations under competent leaders, to patrol and guard your various districts. With these exceptions you are again requested to resume your accustomed daily avocations. This is as necessary to your personal security as to the peace of the City.

The various lines of omnibuses, railways and telegraphs must be put in full operation immediately. Adequate military protection against their further interruption will be furnished on application to the military authorities of the State.

Fellow citizens, the laws must and shall be obeyed; public order shall not be broken with impunity. Our first duty now is to restore the public peace and preserve it unbroken, and to pursue and punish the offenders against the majesty of the laws.[20]

"Bosh," commented George Templeton Strong about Opdyke's assertion that the riot was practically over, and in fact there was some hard fighting still to be done before peace was restored.[21] There are some signs that Mayor Opdyke himself realized he would have to work hard to make his claims come true. When he sent the proclamation to the newspapers, he added a letter he had just received from Stanton:

Five regiments are under orders to return to New York. The retreat of Lee, now became a rout, with his army broken and much heavier loss of killed and wounded than was supposed, will relieve a large force for the restoration of order in New York.

Intelligence has just reached here of the auspicious commencement of General Gilmore's operations against Charleston.

All but one fort on Morris Island have been captured, and that will speedily be reduced, after which Sumter must follow.

If the news of federal victories and veteran regiments returning to New York did not end the riots, the suspension of the draft might. Colonel Fry, the provost marshal general, had telegraphed Colonel Nugent formal orders to stop the draft on Tuesday, although the mob had, of course, long since made drafting impossible. On Wednesday, Nugent was called to the Saint Nicholas Hotel, where Governor Seymour asked him if he had any orders from Washington about halting the draft. He said he had, but could not publish them without Fry's authorization. Seymour, Opdyke, and Collector Barney all tried to persuade Nugent to publish Fry's telegram, saying it would calm the public mind. Finally he agreed to make an unofficial announcement in next day's newspapers, over his own signature, that the draft was suspended in New York and Brooklyn.[22]

That morning the Common Council had taken some measures of its own to end the riots. It passed Alderman Hardy's ordinance appropriating $2.5 million to pay the fee of $300 for any poor New Yorker who was drafted and who could not find the money himself.[23] If a drafted man did agree to serve, then the $300 would be paid to him, as a bounty. There was little opposition. Alderman Mitchell said he was opposed to the draft, which was unequal; but he did not like to have the Common Council dictated to by a mob of infuriated thieves and plunderers. In his district the mobs were pillaging and burning the houses of respectable and civil men, merely for the sake of booty. But, since the members present all favored the passage of the ordinance right away and since his vote was needed for the passage, he would vote aye. Several members of the Board of Councilmen denounced the idea of any draft at all. One, Councilman Sandford, argued that neither men nor money should be given to the corrupt Lincoln administration. But in the end, they too voted for the ordinance, and it passed unanimously.

Lieutenant Ryer and his artillerymen-turned-infantry spent all afternoon at the Thirty-fifth Street Arsenal, until four o'clock, when news came that a mob was on the rampage at Forty-second Street and Tenth Avenue. This area had been a trouble spot all day. A detachment of Hawkins' Zouaves, sent to disperse a mob at the Hudson River Railroad depot in Forty-sixth Street at nine o'clock in the morning, had been forced to open fire in West Forty-fourth Street. Then, early in the afternoon, a detachment of police had gone there and cleared the locality. But, as so often happened, the mob gathered again as soon as the police left. Captain J. C. Slott, who was in command of the police on the upper West Side, sent to the arsenal for some troops, and General Sandford asked Ryer to go and help. Taking fifty men, Ryer joined the police, and they hurried off. Along West Forty-second Street, they were vehemently groaned at and hissed, and at Tenth Avenue, a hail of stones and bullets came down on them from the housetops and the windows, as well as from the crowds in the street.

Lieutenant Ryer wheeled his men left and right, half of them facing up the avenue, and the other half facing down, with the police in the middle. Both Ryer and the police commander, Sergeant Aldis, shouted at the mob that if they did not disperse, they would be shot. Obscenities and yells of defiance answered them, and Ryer gave the order to fire. Five volleys crashed out, and the crowd in the streets melted away like snow in a furnace, though snipers still kept up a desultory fire from roofs and windows. Ryer sent ten of his men into the houses on either side of the avenue; the gunfire died away, and after a few moments the soldiers reappeared, dragging a couple of prisoners with them. Ryer decided to return to the arsenal, but his force had not gone half a block before a gang of rioters made a sudden rush at them. He let them get close and then quickly faced the rear ranks about and let them have two volleys at point-blank range. The artillerymen left their prisoners at the Twentieth Precinct police station and went back on guard at the arsenal until General Brown recalled them to police headquarters next day.[24]

Late in the afternoon, Judge Connolly of the local police court turned up at the arsenal and demanded that General Sandford tell him the name of the officer who had commanded the troops in the Tenth Avenue fight. They had killed women and children, Connolly alleged, and if he could find out the lieutenant's name he would arrest him. Sandford diplomatically replied that he did not know it. Thereupon Connolly said that if troops were kept out of the Twenty-second Ward, he would disperse the rioters himself. Sandford had not done much about putting down the mob, but he did have enough good sense to decline this offer.

Brooklyn had remained quiet while anarchy reigned in New York. The city across the East River was so scandalously underpoliced that any mob outbreak would have met almost no opposition.[25] Fortunately, many of those most likely to riot went over to New York to fight and pillage there. Some small-scale disorders did occur. On Monday night, Brooklyn Negroes were attacked and beaten on their way home from work. Houses occupied by Negroes were stoned, and a few of them were looted. Large numbers of blacks fled to the rural districts of Queens County or took refuge in the police stations.

The sheriff of King's County appealed for volunteers, and a couple of hundred men responded. Reserve members of the National Guard were called out, and veterans were asked to return to the colors for temporary duty. As in New York, special policemen were sworn in and home guards were organized in many neighborhoods. At the Brooklyn Navy Yard, the walls were manned and mounted with guns. Two thirty-two-pounders commanded the main gate, and thirteen eighteen-pounders were trained on Flushing Avenue, the approach a mob would be most likely to use.[26]

Columns of smoke rising from burning buildings in New York could be clearly seen from the Brooklyn waterfront, and the city held its breath. But the uneasy calm was broken by only one major incident. Since 1861 several grain elevators had been built at the Atlantic Dock. With these machines, wheat could be quickly unloaded, weighed, and reloaded onto ships at the dock or out in the river, and they put hundreds of grain shovelers out of work. In July 1862 there was a bitter strike: grain shovelers and laborers came out, demanding that the use of elevators be abandoned. They were joined by longshoremen and stevedores, but the employers used sailors as strikebreakers, and the work stoppage collapsed. Use of the elevators continued until Wednesday night of the riot week, when a mob invaded the Atlantic Dock and burned two of the obnoxious machines, as well as a dredge tied up at the slip.[27]

In Manhattan a lull in the fighting in late afternoon was followed by an eventful evening. Colonel Wakeman took three companies of citizen volunteers and a couple of howitzers from Tompkins Market to patrol the length of the East Side. They went up Third Avenue to Thirty-fifth Street, then took Second Avenue as far as Sixtieth Street. It was here, on the fringe of the city, that they met opposition. A volley and a bayonet charge forced the rioters back, but the howitzers had to be brought into play before they ran for cover. The volunteers swung over to Avenue A (now York Avenue), chased another gang of rioters up to Seventieth Street, and then marched back downtown.

At 6:40 P.M. the First Precinct telegraphed Central: "Captain Wilson is here, and wishes you to inform Commissioner Acton that the residents are leaving Carmansville and Fort Washington. They think the mob will be there tonight, and he would like to take his force up." "Tell him he can go," replied Acton, and Wilson and his men from the Thirty-second Precinct took a steamboat and set off for the northern tip of Manhattan, where they dispersed a crowd in Carmansville.

Some of the police were unhappy about going out to meet rioters who were armed with rifles, while they had only clubs and revolvers. General Brown had suggested giving the police muskets on Tuesday, but Commissioner Acton would not hear of it. The police, he said, were "thoroughly drilled to the use of the club, but would be raw troops with rifles. It would only turn them from good police into poor militia. They can do their best work with the weapons they are trained to." He was much more blunt when, at 6:40 P.M., the Eighth Precinct inquired, "Will you allow us to have muskets if we find them ourselves?" "No. Acton." was the reply.

Early in the evening, George Templeton Strong went to the Union League Club, where he found "George Biggs, full of the loudest and most emphatic jawing. 'General Fremont's house and Craven's to be attacked tonight, Croton mains to be cut, and gas works destroyed,' and so on." Strong went home, and had all the bathtubs, pots, kettles, and pails in the house filled with water. "Here's an illustration of the vanity of human labors," he reflected in his diary, "a man writing diligently in his journal for the instruction of posterity, and quite uncertain whether his house will be burned over his head and journal and all with it by morning."[28]

A short distance from Strong's house in Gramercy Park, the mob was carrying all before it. Just before six o'clock, Major Nevers of the Seventh Regiment reserves heard that the rioters were gathering in strength on First Avenue, between Eighteenth and Nineteenth streets. As a militia officer, he automatically reported the news to General Sandford, instead of sending it to Commissioner Acton and General Brown. Sandford, showing more energy than on either of the previous days, ordered Colonel Cleveland Winslow and 150 of his citizen volunteers to the scene. Many of these men had served two years in the field under Winslow in the

Fifth New York Volunteers, the "Duryea Zouaves," and some of them had reenlisted in the veterans' regiment he was organizing.

With them went a couple of howitzers manned by Colonel Edward Jardine and some men of the Hawkins' Zouaves. On East Nineteenth Street, Ellen Leonard watched the mob. "Great excitement prevailed. There was loud talking with fierce gestures. Some ran thither with fire-arms, some with poles and boards. Then some one shouted 'They are coming!' and a small band of soldiers appeared marching up our street. The mob seemed to swell into vast dimensions, and densely filled the whole street before them. Hundreds hurried out on the rooftops, tore up brickbats, and hurled them with savage howls at the approaching soldiers. Shots were fired from secret ambushes, and soldiers fell before they had fired. Then they charged bravely into the mob, but their force was wholly inadequate." Winslow ordered the guns unlimbered and loaded, and ten rounds of grape and canister flushed the mob from the street. But the shooting from the rooftops and windows still went on, and numbers of the soldiers dropped to the ground. The wounded were carried into the houses up the street, in the middle class area near Second Avenue. Dr. Simon Hirsch, at 179 East Nineteenth Street, took in five; the Leonards gave refuge to several, including Colonel Jardine, dangerously wounded in the thigh.

Winslow might have sent some of his force to clear the houses, as Ryer had done that afternoon in Tenth Avenue. But he was unsure how long his men would stand fast under the heavy fire of the rioters, and he was worried about losing the two howitzers. The artillerymen had left their guns and taken cover once already, and though Winslow had been able to get them back to their pieces, he might not be so lucky a second time. He ordered a retreat, and the shattered and dispirited force withdrew, as the rioters cheered. As soon as he saw his men safe, Winslow rushed over to the Saint Nicholas Hotel to see Governor Seymour. He ordered Winslow to go to police headquarters and place himself under General Brown's orders. As soon as the latter heard that Winslow had left the wounded men behind, he resolved to try and rescue them. Captain Putnam was ordered out and led his company and Captain Shelley's, with some men from the Thirtieth Regiment and a gun, up to the scene of Winslow's defeat.

At the Leonards', the injured men had their wounds dressed by Jabez P. White, the former surgeon of the Hawkins' Zouaves, who had volunteered for service again with Jardine, his old commander. This time they were caught in a situation more dangerous than anything they had experienced in the Army of the Potomac. Any moment, the mob might come hunting for them. Jardine decided that resistance was out of the question. Their only chance of safety lay in disguising that they were soldiers. Guns and uniforms were hidden; the soldiers who could walk were ordered to escape over the rooftops. Surgeon White was ordered to go with them, but he insisted on staying. Jardine was concealed in the cellar, and another wounded man was put in a room at the top of the house. After what seemed an eternity of waiting, the bell rang, there was a loud pounding on the door, and a group of rioters demanded to search the house. Surgeon White was found and hauled out into the street, and a moment later they discovered Colonel Jardine's hiding place. He coolly assured them he was a civilian accidentally wounded during the fight. He played his part so convincingly that the intruders were thoroughly persuaded, and they left, even offering to station a guard at the door of the house to prevent his being annoyed by any more searches. Surgeon White's luck had been good, too. There were a couple of veterans of Hawkins' Zouaves in the mob, and when they recognized him, they got him away to safety.

Shortly, the crackle of musketry announced that Putnam's forces were fighting their way up First Avenue. While two companies held off the rioters, Captain Putnam began to search for Colonel Jardine. The Leonards had heard the troops approaching and welcomed them "with tears of joy and gratitude. . . . There was no time for inquiries or felicitations. The wounded men were our first care. Our young soldier in his delight had hobbled to the stairway, and was borne down in triumph by his sympathizing comrades, while a larger company brought the Colonel from the cellar. A pitiful sight he was all bleeding and ghastly, shivering with cold and suffering great pain. Both soldiers were placed carefully in the carriage brought for their conveyance, and then we ladies were requested to accompany them immediately. It was unsafe to remain in the house, soldiers could not be spared to protect

it, and it was best for us to go at once to the Central Police Station."
Sending a final volley down the street, the column moved off,
stopping from time to time to fire down the side streets or send out
skirmishers. The mob in the Eighteenth Precinct was far from subdued, and Captain Shelley's company was sent to Gramercy Park
after an hour's rest. Everything was quiet when the soldiers reached
the area, but at four o'clock there was an alarm: rioters were plundering a store in Fourth Avenue. Shelley immediately led his troops
there and attacked, and the mob disappeared like flies in winter.[29]

Despite Winslow's defeat, more attacks on Negro dwellings, including the Arch in Sullivan Street and more pillaging of stores in
Broad and Stone streets, a mood of optimism spread through police
headquarters on Wednesday night. Reinforcements were at last arriving. The Sixty-fifth Regiment of the New York National Guard
had reached the city at five o'clock, with four howitzers belonging
to the Eighth Regiment, and had run into trouble at once, when a
mob tried to seize two of the Eighth's Negro cooks. Brown put the
Sixty-fifth at Center Market and sent two of its companies to guard
the United States Sub-Treasury and two more to disperse rioters
in Union Square. The crack Seventh Regiment was expected during the night. There had been rumors that rioters might sabotage
the railroad tracks in northern New Jersey to stop troops reaching
New York, and so the Seventh had taken a ship from Amboy. At
4:40 A.M. the Twenty-eighth Precinct flashed the welcome news to
police headquarters: "The Seventh Regiment has arrived foot of
Canal Street. They are on their way to Broadway."[30]

No sleep. The sultriness pervades the air
And binds the brain—a dense oppression, such
As tawny tigers feel in matted shades,
Vexing their blood and making apt for ravage.
Beneath the stars the roofy desert spreads
Vacant as Libya. All is hushed near by.
Yet fitfully from far breaks a mixed surf
Of muffled sound, the Atheist roar of riot.
Yonder, where parching Sirius sets in drought,
Balefully glares red Arson—there—and there.
The town is taken by its rats—ship-rats
And rats of the wharves. All civil charms
And priestly spells which late held hearts in awe—
Fear-bound, subjected to a better sway
Than sway of self; these like a dream dissolve,
And man rebounds whole aeons back in nature.
Hail to the low dull rumble, dull and dead,
And ponderous drag that shakes the wall.
Wise Draco comes, deep in the midnight roll
Of black artillery; he comes, though late;
In code corroborating Calvin's creed
And cynic tyrannies of honest Kings;
He comes, nor parlies; and the Town, redeemed,
Gives thanks devout; nor, being thankful, heeds
The grimy slur on the Republic's faith implied,
Which holds that Man is naturally good,
And—more—is Nature's Roman, never to be scourged.

—HERMAN MELVILLE
*The House-top. A Night Piece. July, 1863*[1]

# 8

## Peace in Warsaw

THURSDAY brought respite to the battered city. More troops arrived—the Twenty-sixth Michigan Volunteers, the 152nd New
York Volunteers, and the Seventy-fourth Regiment of the New
York National Guard. By the end of the day, there were over 4,000
soldiers in New York. Under their protection, life began to return
to normal. Stores that had been closed and barred for forty-eight
hours reopened, and people hurried to buy fresh milk and ice.
Candles and turnips were much in demand, too, since the newspapers carried an appeal to New Yorkers to exercise care and economy in their use of gas. Their employees, the company explained,
had been driven away by the mob, and no gas was being made.[2]

The previous afternoon, Governor Seymour had asked the
streetcar and stage companies if they would resume service, and
they all agreed to try. Early Thursday morning, the cars began to
run, and there were only three interruptions. A gang of rowdies
halted one Fourth Avenue car and relieved the conductor and
passengers of their cash and jewelry. Another gang stopped a
First Avenue car at Seventeenth Street, until one of their number
shouted that if the Third Avenue Railroad, an abolition concern,
was allowed to run, it was only fair that the First and Second
Avenue cars, which were owned by a good Democratic company,
should be allowed to run, too. His fellows gave three cheers and let
the car go on. And at eight o'clock, a mob stopped the Second
Avenue cars at Twenty-third Street and ordered them back to the

depot. Sergeant Vaughan, who was in command of the Twenty-first Precinct, called for help, and a force of troops and police under Inspector Carpenter and Captain Putnam came. They cleared the area without any difficulty, and the cars resumed operations.[3]

In the upper West Side wards, things went on almost as usual. There was only one mob outbreak there all day.[4] The factories and workshops were open, and most of their operators reported for work. The Hudson River Railroad tracks were relaid, and trains reached the city on schedule.[5] The telegraph lines to Boston were repaired. Downtown, it was like a Sunday afternoon. Most places of business could not open for lack of staff, and the docks were almost deserted. Some Negro stevedores who had come to see if there was any chance of a job were chased and beaten in Broad Street, but policemen quickly rescued them and drove their attackers away. At half-past one, a longshoreman called Edward Downing mounted a barrel on the sidewalk in Rector Street and began to harangue the passers-by, calling on them to resist the authorities. Once again, the police were swiftly on the scene, arrested Downing, and moved his audience along. The least tranquil area of the city was the upper East Side, especially the district between Third Avenue and the river, from Twenty-first to Fortieth streets. None of the factories or shipyards were open here, and very few of the stores.[6] About seven o'clock in the morning, a Negro called Samuel Johnson was chased through the streets to the Thirty-fourth Street ferry, beaten senseless, and thrown into the river to drown.

Home guards and vigilance committees continued to patrol many neighborhoods throughout the day. Not all the rioters they had to deal with were as stupid as James Purdy, an English-born sailor who lived in Cedar Street. John W. Willson of 131 East Forty-fifth Street and a group of his neighbors "were engaged to protect their property and said Purdy came up and said let us burn a house evidently mistaking the parties who he was speaking to deponent and the others let him go on when he led the way to deponent's house and rang the bell deponent's wife came to the door and asked who was there when said Purdy replied damn you open the door or I will burst it in and proceeded to do so when deponent and his friends arrested him."[7]

Home guards took over many of the responsibilities of the police, freeing the officers for other duties or for some badly needed rest.[8] In one or two precincts, it was possible for officers to begin searching for stolen property. Negroes were still seeking refuge at station houses, and just before noon, Commissioner Acton sent out a general order to all precincts: "Receive colored people as long as you can. Refuse nobody." During the day, four hundred Negroes from the most crammed station houses were taken over to Blackwell's Island on the police steamboat.[9] Going to the boat along Thirty-fourth Street, they formed the center of a strange and melancholy procession. First came a strong force of police. Behind them trotted the children from the burned orphanage, boys in front and girls behind. Next came the refugees: old and young, men and women, a few carrying babies in their arms. Many of them were laden down with bundles of clothing and pieces of light furniture, all they had been able to save from the wreck of their homes. Hawkins' Zouaves marched alongside them, while a company of the Tenth New York Volunteers and another squad of police brought up the rear. The police also rescued Charles Jackson, the Negro who had been mobbed and thrown off Pier Four, North River, the previous day. Officers Hey, McClusker, and Darrow of the Twenty-seventh Precinct found Jackson hiding under the pier, clutching a huge rock, and ready to fight for his life. It took the police some time to convince him that they were friends and had come to rescue him.

Acting on a tip, five members of the Detective Squad raided a house in East Eleventh Street in the middle of the morning and captured John U. Andrews, the Virginian who had made a speech to the mob during the burning of the Ninth District draft office on Monday.[10]

During the day, Governor Seymour received startling news from Riker's Island. At the army camp there, 350 recruits had mutinied and locked up their officers. A day or two earlier, this might have been disastrous, and even now it was serious enough, for the governor did not want to send troops out of the city if he could possibly help it. Seymour appealed to Admiral Paulding, who sent the gunboat *Union* up to the island. Under the threat of bombardment, the mutineers gave in and returned to obedience.[11] Seymour took good care that no word of the mutiny reached the press, lest other troops became infected.

Like everyone else in the city, Governor Seymour had become convinced that General Sandford was not fit to command troops in combat, and as the New York regiments returned from Pennsylvania and Maryland, he put them under the orders of General Brown. Early in the morning Brown decided to use the three unassigned companies of the Sixty-fifth Regiment to garrison some of the most important munitions works on the East Side. Colonel Berens and his men reached East Twenty-fourth Street without any trouble, left one company and a howitzer at the Hotchkiss shell factory there, and headed for their next objective, Seward's shell factory on East Seventeenth Street. The nearer they got to the factory, the denser and uglier the crowds became. But no one made a move to attack the troops, and Berens left a company and a howitzer at Seward's, as he had been ordered. The other company and the last gun were meant to guard Jackson's foundry on East Twenty-eighth Street, and Berens led them up First Avenue. At Twenty-second Street, they came under fire from rioters. Berens wheeled his men into line and unlimbered the howitzer, and the rioters' fighting spirit oozed away. The shooting ceased, and the *franc-tireurs* retreated out of range. The troops pushed on, only to run into a heavy cross-fire at Twenty-third Street. Berens ordered them to return the fire as they marched, but he realized that his little force of twenty-eight men would not be able to hold the foundry without help, and he sent his quartermaster back to police headquarters to ask for reinforcements.

The crowds were thick at Twenty-eighth Street and Second Avenue, and the men of the Sixty-fifth had to make a charge to reach the foundry. Once they got there, they found the doors were locked. There was no time to be lost; they smashed them open and thankfully rushed inside. Constant fire and a surprise charge down East Twenty-eighth Street were needed to keep the mob at bay, but at two o'clock, the quartermaster arrived with two companies, and the worst was over.

The rioters were still circling around the foundry all the afternoon, and at five o'clock, a Catholic priest came to Berens as an emissary from the mob. He urged the colonel to evacuate the place, saying that the mob would not harm it if the troops left. But if they stayed, it would be burned to the ground. "He implored me to accept the proposal," recalled Berens, "saying that he feared for the worst consequences; that the mob was about 4,000 strong, altogether too large for my weak force to resist, and he could not control or restrain them."

Berens reported the mob's offer to General Brown. The owners of the foundry, who had been begging for troops to protect their property the day before, were now equally anxious to have them gone, but General Brown declared that he would not be dictated to by a mob and ordered Berens to hold the foundry at all costs. As it happened, the rioters failed to make good their threats. When an attack seemed imminent early in the evening, a couple of volleys from the soldiers sent them scrambling for cover, and the foundry was not threatened again that night.[12]

The company of the Sixty-fifth that was set to guard Seward's shell factory did not acquit itself nearly so well. The funerals of two people killed in the riots, Patrick Flannigan and Mrs. Julia Hennessey, were being held that day, and the corteges passed near Seward's. The company commander, Captain John Irlbacher, jumped to the conclusion that the crowds watching the funeral processions were going to attack his force, and he immediately discovered compelling reasons why he should take himself elsewhere, leaving his men to fend for themselves. His second-in-command, Lieutenant Caspar Meyer, decided that the best thing to do under the circumstances was to withdraw. He gave orders to abandon the factory and return to police headquarters. When General Brown discovered what had happened, he was furious and had both Irlbacher and Meyer arrested for cowardice.[13]

At noon, news came that there was trouble on the far West Side, at the very edge of the city. The mob was in force at Fifty-second Street and Eleventh Avenue with artillery. This sounded serious, and General Brown dispatched Captain Shelley's company uptown to check into the matter. Shelley found that a crowd of rioters, searching for ammunition, had broken into a bullet factory on Fifty-second Street and ransacked the place. As so often happened, though, a great deal of the ammunition was the wrong caliber for their guns. They had also taken a cannon they discovered in the factory and pulled it out into the street. Shelley's men made short work of the mob; a bayonet charge sent them flying and put the troops in possession of the gun. Shelley telegraphed General Brown asking what he should do with it. "Use it against the enemy" was the reply. As things turned out, Shelley never had the chance to follow this order. No rioters appeared, though he and his company stayed at the Twenty-second Precinct police station all night, ready to protect the Eighth and Ninth Avenue Railroad depot and stables, which the mob had threatened to burn.[14]

During the afternoon, Judge Connolly and State Senator Bradley called on Governor Seymour and asked him to keep the troops out of the Eighteenth Ward.[15] They argued that the peaceable middle-class population of the area would be able to calm and control the rioters if they were left alone.[16] The governor agreed to try their suggestion and gave them a letter to the Police Commissioners saying that he hoped their request would be granted. But when Bradley and Connolly went over to police headquarters and showed Commissioner Acton the letter, he was violently indignant. "It can't be done," he barked at them. "I would not do it to save your lives. The Eighteenth Ward is a plague spot, and it must be wiped out. We have been fighting a week, and are going to keep on until every man, white or black, can go anywhere on this island in perfect safety. You, John Bradley, dare not go East of Fourth Avenue today. Go back and tell the Governor I won't do it, and then go and tell your constituents who sent you to him that Tom Acton won't do it." General Brown gave the senator and the judge even shorter shrift, dismissing them with the remark, "There's been too much temporizing with rebels already, and I'll not move a man unless Mr. Acton tells me to."[17]

Irlbacher's desertion, Meyer's ignominious retreat, and Senator Bradley's proposal were not the only things that strained General Brown's temper that day. About four o'clock, Colonel Thaddeus Mott, whose cavalry force was stationed in Gramercy Park, led eighty of his men (on foot) in a probe down East Twenty-second Street. Between Second and Third avenues, they ran into intense fire from rioters blocking the way and barricaded in houses on either side of the street. Mott hastily ordered a retreat, which became a rout as the cavalrymen ran for dear life toward the safety of the park. One man, Sergeant Charles Davids, was killed and his body left lying in the street.

Mott sped down to police headquarters to announce his misfortune. With his gaunt features and bristling shock of white hair, General Brown bore a strong resemblance to Andrew Jackson, and when he heard what Mott had to say, he flew into a rage that would not have disgraced Old Hickory himself. "What are you doing here, sir?" bellowed the infuriated old soldier. "Go, sir. Your place is with your men." Commissioner Acton calmed Brown, and they put together a mixed force of police and 160 federal troops under Captain Putnam to go and recover the sergeant's body.

When they reached Gramercy Park, they found Mott's troops under fire from snipers.[18] Picking out the house from which the shooting was coming, Putnam sent Lieutenant Joyce and half a dozen men to clear it. But, as they broke in at the front, all the snipers but one, a man called Martin Moran, escaped over the back fence. He was taken into custody, and after warning the women left in the house that any more shots would be answered with artillery, Putnam ordered his command to march on.

They found the body of Sergeant Davids lying on the sidewalk in East Twenty-second Street. An uncanny stillness hung over the area as Putnam sent for a livery stable keeper and ordered him to supply a carriage. The man was understandably nervous about helping the authorities and said that the mob would kill him. Putnam replied that if he provided the carriage he would be protected; but if he refused, he would be shot on the spot. The horses were harnessed in double-quick time, and the body of Davids lifted into the carriage.

Just at that moment, rioters appeared at the windows and on the rooftops of the houses all around and opened a murderous fire. Ordering his skirmishers to cover them, Putnam sent the rest of his men charging into the houses. In hand-to-hand fighting, the rioters were driven from room to room, putting up a desperate resistance. Out in the street, more rioters appeared at the corner of Second Avenue. Once the houses were cleared, the troops advanced down the street and up the avenue, driving the mob before them. At Thirty-first Street, they came under heavy fire. Here, too, the houses were fortified and held by rioters, and the soldiers had to break down the doors and battle through darkened passages and rooms again before the shooting died away. Putnam formed up his men, with the prisoners captured in the houses in their midst, and marched off.

At police headquarters, there were cheers for the troops and the police who had gone with them, and jeers and threats for the prisoners. Commissioner Acton was delighted with Putnam's success and told him that he would promote him to brigadier general if it were in his power. Though no one knew it at the time, Putnam's forces had fought the last pitched battle of the riots.[19]

The Seventh Regiment was sent to patrol the East Side from Fourteenth Street to Thirty-fifth that night. At seven o'clock, Officer Hiram Chandler of the Twenty-first Precinct was beaten up by a gang of rioters at Second Avenue and Thirty-fourth Street, and a company of the Seventh took him to Bellevue Hospital. Private Charles Dalemetta of the Thirteenth New York Cavalry was not so lucky. He was caught and killed at Third Avenue and Forty-second Street. From ten o'clock until midnight, the Seventh's patrols were frequently harassed by shots winging at them from the side streets and rooftops, especially on Second Avenue. But the volleys which the troops poured into the snipers' nests quickly silenced opposition, and after twelve o'clock, all was quiet. At two o'clock on Friday morning, Commissioner Acton was able to lie down and get some sleep for the first time since the riots began.[20]

On Friday, Mayor Opdyke issued a proclamation which contained a great deal more truth, and far less wishful thinking, than his announcement on Wednesday:

To the citizens of New York: The riotous assemblages have been dispersed, Business is running in its usual channels. The various lines of omnibuses, railway and Telegraph have resumed their ordinary operations. Few symptoms of disorder remain, except in a small district in the Eastern part of the city, comprising a part of the Eighteenth and Twenty-first Wards. The Police is everywhere alert. A sufficient military force is now here to suppress any illegal movement, however formidable. Let me exhort you, therefore, to pursue your ordinary business. Avoid especially all crowds. Remain quietly at your homes, except when engaged in business or assisting the authorities in some organized force. When the Military appears in the streets, do not gather about it, being sure that it is doing its duty in obedience to orders from superior authority. Your homes and your places of business you have a right to defend, and it is your duty to defend them at all hazards. Yield to no intimidation and no demand for money as the price of your safety. If any person warns you to desist from your accustomed business give no heed to the warning, but arrest the person and bring him to the nearest station house for punishment as a conspirator. Be assured that the public authorities have the ability and the will to protect you from those who have conspired alike against your peace, against the Government of your choice, and against the laws which your Representatives have enacted.[21]

Bills posted in the lower part of the city on Thursday evening and announcements in Friday's morning newspapers carried a message from Archbishop Hughes "to the men of New York, who are now called in many of the papers Rioters." He was not able, he said, to visit them, due to rheumatism, but that was no reason why they should not visit him. He invited them to come and hear him speak from the balcony of his house at Madison Avenue and Thirty-sixth Street, at two o'clock on Friday afternoon. Since it was signed "+John Hughes" rather than simply "+John," some people assumed that the announcement was a hoax, but a crowd of several thousand turned out to hear the venerable prelate.[22] The archbishop was not strong enough to stand; he had to make his speech from a chair, but he was in fine voice. Unfortunately, he had little to say. He rambled on for nearly an hour, praising the Irish, pointing out that any property destroyed would have to be paid for by the taxpayers, and advising his audience to keep out of crowds. He asked them to preserve peace and order, saying that in the United States they could change the government by democratic means. He expressed his confidence that there were no rioters in his audience—"I cannot see a rioter's face among you"—and appealed to them to go quietly to their homes. The police and troops had been given strict orders not to interfere with people going to hear the archbishop, and there were no incidents.[23]

To no one's surprise, General Wool was relieved of his command and placed on the retired list by orders that arrived from Washington on Friday. But many people were shocked to find that

General Brown had suffered the same fate. It remains a mystery why the Lincoln administration inflicted such shabby and unceremonious treatment on the man who, with Commissioner Acton, saved New York.[24] Of the three commanding generals in the city during the riots, only the incompetent Sandford survived.

Wool was replaced as commander of the Department of the East by John A. Dix. A politician as well as a soldier, Dix had served in the army from 1812 to 1828, risen high in New York's Democratic politics, and served as senator and secretary of the treasury. He was well suited for the delicate task of trying to bring harmony between Lincoln and Seymour. As for the command of the federal troops in the city and harbor, Brown was superseded by Brigadier General E. R. S. Canby, a dour, colorless professional soldier who had served ably as commander of the Department of New Mexico, where he had defeated a Confederate attempt at invasion.

During the day, reinforcements continued to arrive, until there were about 6,000 troops in the city. Superficially, the life of the city was back to normal.[25] Only here and there were there reminders of the four days' struggle: the black ruins of burned buildings; the looted stores; the walls pockmarked where they had been struck by bullets; and howitzers standing incongruously among the green trees of Gramercy Park. But the authorities were nervous about new outbreaks. Acton did not think it safe for individual policemen to appear on the streets in uniform. When the Third Precinct telegraphed headquarters at 5:35 A.M. to ask "Do you think it safe for four colored women with children to go uptown to 61st Street to their homes?" the answer was a simple "No."

But for the most part, the day passed off quietly. The Seventh Regiment was billeted in a disused rubber factory on East Thirty-third Street. "The neighborhood is not a very select one," Private Henry Martyn Congdon told his father, "but it might be worse and our force is strong enough and determined enough to resist thousands." Like all the members of the Seventh, Congdon was longing for a wash and clean clothes. "I have not had my shoes off for nearly two weeks," he reflected. For the time being, however, he and the rest of the Seventh kept the watch on Third Avenue.[26]

The few incidents that did occur amounted to very little. Ten men who called at James Taylor's foundry on Goerck Street, and threatened to burn it down unless they were given $50, were quickly rounded up by the police. At nine o'clock, Captain John H. Howell was driving up Seventh Avenue, when somebody recognized him as the officer who had commanded the artillery in the fight in Thirty-second Street on Wednesday morning. "There's the man who fired on us!" came the cry. "Hang him!" Captain Howell ordered the driver to whip up his horses, and they escaped under a fusillade of stones, the captain emptying his revolver at the crowd.

Colonel Mott indulged in some blatant coat-trailing to see how well the East Side was pacified. "One of my officers, Lieutenant Robinson of [the] 1st N.Y. Mounted Rifles proceeded mounted and in uniform up the 1, 2, 3 and 5 Avenues & returned through Avenues B and C as far as 63rd Street," he reported. "He found everything quiet with the exception of a crowd of some 30 on the corner of 37th Street and Fourth Avenue, who undertook to take him from his horse, throwing stones, &c–He shot one of the mob & proceeded on his way unmolested." [27]

Early on Friday, Commissioner Acton received a "Black Hand" letter:

> Commissioner
> and Conspirator against
> Your State and the
> People,
> *Prepare to meet*
> *Your God!*
> By advice of
> THE COMMITTEE

The Commissioner, said the *Herald*, was "not known to have been particularly affected by the reading of his 'death warrant.' He anticipates the exercise of the pardoning power."

Next day, the city continued quiet, and the police were able to resume regular patrol. The "bloody week" was over.

# THE
# AFTERMATH

*The sea of a mighty population, held in galling fetters,*
*heaves uneasily in the tenements. Once already our city, to which*
*have come the duties and responsibilities of metropolitan*
*greatness before it was able to fairly measure its task, has felt*
*the swell of its resistless flood. If it rises once more, no*
*human power may avail to check it. The gap between the classes*
*in which it surges, unseen, unsuspected by the thoughtless, is*
*widening day by day.*

—JACOB RIIS
*How the Other Half Lives*[1]

# 9

# *The Harvest of Riot*

A WEEK AFTER he had been chased out of his office at Third Avenue and Forty-sixth Street, Captain Jenkins sent some men up to its ruins to see if they could salvage the safe, which contained all the draft lists, ballots, and papers. Due to a misunderstanding between Nugent and Canby, no soldiers were available to guard the expedition, but all went well. A crowd gathered and jeered as Jenkins's men lifted the safe out of the rubble and got it on to a cart, but no one made a move to attack them.[2] The city continued in this tense and sullen, but quiet, state for the next few weeks.

Requests for protection and reports of threatened violence flooded into the mayor's office. Dread of more violence was so great that not a single property owner in the Fifth District would rent Captain Duffy an office to replace his burned-out premises at 429 Grand Street. Mayor Opdyke was worried enough to write to a gun store owner who had been selling hand grenades to anyone who asked for them, requesting him to sell only to people who could produce a recommendation from the mayor's office.[3]

There were a few examples of unusual lawlessness in the days after the riot. Reports came in that attempts would be made to stop the street sweepers, and on the morning of Monday, the twentieth, extra police were stationed along Broadway to prevent any trouble. About midnight, a man named Gallagher was arrested after he drew a pistol on a sweeper who refused to listen to his counsel to stop work. Next day, James O'Neil, a heeler in the

Fourth Ward, stopped a Broadway sweeping machine at the point of a gun and ordered the driver off. He refused, and when O'Neil's pistol misfired, ran for the police, who took O'Neil into custody.[4] Some Negroes who worked for the Erie Railroad were attacked in the course of Tuesday, and at midnight that night a gang of thieves stopped a Second Avenue car at Nineteenth Street and robbed the passengers of their valuables, including the rings the ladies wore on their fingers.[5] But no serious disorders erupted. As the days went by, the militia regiments were mustered out, the federal troops withdrawn to the forts in the harbor or the fringe of the city, and New York lost the look of an occupied city.[6]

Demonstrations against the draft had taken place in many of the towns and villages around the metropolis during the riot week. Rioters broke into the provost marshal's office in Jamaica, Long Island, dragged thirty cases of uniforms which were stored there out into the street, and set fire to them. Later they attacked some stores in the village and looted them. On Tuesday morning, a band of about seventy or eighty toughs, some of them locals, some from New York, marched along the Harlem Railroad permanent way from Mott Haven to the junction with the New Haven line, a mile or so above Williamsbridge. They tore up the track in several places, and at the Williamsbridge depot, they wrecked the ticket office, smashed the telegraph apparatus, and cut down three or four telegraph poles. At Hastings a crowd of laborers forced the Hudson River Sugar Refinery to close. On Staten Island mobs burned Negroes' homes, invaded two militia drill rooms and stole rifles, and set fire to a car barn belonging to the Staten Island Railroad.[7]

General Canby feared that there might be further trouble unless something was done to demonstrate that the authorities were firmly in control of the situation,[8] and he asked the Police Commissioners to join him in sending a mixed force of troops and police up the Hudson as far as Peekskill. Two companies of the Seventy-fourth New York Volunteers and a force of police under Captain John F. Dickson of the Twenty-eighth Precinct set out on Sunday, the nineteenth, and spent three enjoyable days showing the flag in the river towns. Dickson's police later went to Staten Island and then to Flushing, Long Island, on the same errand.[9]

On Saturday, July 25, General Sandford issued an address to his men, a notable piece of historical fiction which lavished praise on himself and included the assertion that "the rioters were everywhere beaten and dispersed, on Monday afternoon, Monday night and Tuesday morning, and the peace of the city would have been entirely restored in a few hours, but for the interference of Brevet Brig.-Gen. Brown who, in disobedience of Gen. Wool, withdrew the detachments belonging to the General Government and thereby so materially diminished the force under the orders of the Major-General [Sandford], as to limit most seriously his operations against the rioters."[10]

General Brown was quick to respond and left little of Sandford's self-glorification standing. The Police Commissioners, who had already remarked in their address to the force that "in the judgement of this board the escape of the city from the power of an infuriated mob is due to the aid furnished the police by General Brown and the small military force under his command," backed him up, and so did the officers of his former command. Some of the most prominent Republicans in New York, including Mayor Opdyke, David Dudley Field, Horace Greeley, and Postmaster Wakeman, sent a letter to Stanton praising General Brown's "vigilance, fidelity and ability" and saying that he deserved special honor, not ignominious dismissal. But no word of thanks ever came from the War Department. All that Brown ever got for his services during the riots was a silver dinner service, presented to him by grateful citizens of New York.[11]

Others, besides Sandford, were busy rewriting history in the weeks after the riots. The *Commercial Advertiser*, which had noted the role played by John Masterson in starting the uprising, announced on July 31 that it was all a mistake and that Masterson had been out of the city at the time.[12] What pressures were brought to bear on the editor to falsify the record can only be conjectured.

Many people, scared out of their wits by the riots, called for President Lincoln to declare martial law in New York, and some of them urged that General Benjamin F. Butler ought to be put in command of the city.[13] Fortunately, Lincoln was too level-headed to inflict the explosive mixture of "the Beast" and unlimited personal authority on the nation's largest city. To such appeals, he sensibly replied that he thought the New York authorities were performing competently, and he would not intervene unless it became obvious that they could not keep order.[14]

When the draft was resumed on Wednesday, August 19, the government mobilized massive force and poured in men until on August 25 there were twelve regiments of regular infantry, twenty-three regiments of volunteer infantry, and eight regiments of volunteer artillery in the city, with five more volunteer infantry regiments on the way.[15] Great pains were taken to conciliate Governor Seymour; when he questioned the accuracy of the enrollment figures and claimed that New York and Brooklyn were being asked to provide more than their fair share of men, Lincoln substantially reduced their quota. Drafting was completed district by district, and everything went smoothly.[16]

Mayor Opdyke had vetoed the Common Council's proposal of Wednesday, July 15,[17] but a new ordinance was passed raising $2 million to procure substitutes or pay $300 to exempt any drafted firemen, policemen, member of the militia, or indigent New Yorker who could prove that his induction into the army would cause hardship to his family.[18] If such a law had been on the books in July, the men of the Black Joke would never have gone on the rampage, and the Draft Riots would never have occurred.

No such public aid was offered to the Negro refugees of the riot, many of whom had lost everything. A Merchants' Relief Committee was established to help them and raised $42,600 during the months after the riot. Vincent Coyler, who had been responsible for the welfare of the Negroes at New Bern, North Carolina, when General Burnside commanded there, was appointed secretary, and under his direction a depot was opened on East Fourth Street, where refugees could apply for money and clothing. "Ward missionaries" were employed to visit people at home, working closely with the visitors of the Association for Improving the Condition of the Poor. Altogether, 6,392 Negroes were helped by the Merchants' Relief Committee.[19]

The blacks who had lost their possessions during the riot could, of course, claim compensation from the county of New York. But the Riot Claims Committee would only pay people what their goods were worth in July, not what they would cost to replace, and since Negroes were likely to own well-worn furniture or second-hand clothes given them by white employers or friends, they fared badly. Some claims were dismissed because the Negroes had abandoned their homes without waiting to be attacked by rioters, leaving their goods to be stolen by their neighbors or by ordinary thieves. And some of the examiners employed by the committee were by no means unprejudiced themselves and were inclined to assume that Negro claimants were trying to cheat the county and pad their claims.[20]

Those Negroes who returned to New York found it hard to get work. For a short while after the riots, it was fashionable for well-to-do Republican families to fire their Irish servants and hire Negroes instead, but the fad died quickly. A number of firms refused to take their Negro employees back after the riots, fearing more trouble in the future. Streetcar conductors refused to carry blacks, which made it impossible for them to work far from their homes. When the Merchants' Relief Fund was exhausted, many Negro families faced a desperately hard winter. "Cases of extreme destitution are frequent" among Negroes, the Association for Improving the Condition of the Poor noted in its 1864 report. "Seventy families have been aided within the limits of a single block."[21]

Most white New Yorkers continued to nourish an intense hatred of Negroes. Samuel Gompers's father was nearly lynched on his arrival at Castle Garden emigrant depot on July 29 for shaking hands with a Negro who had helped him during the voyage. When the Union League Club decided to raise a black regiment, no one would rent the recruiting officers a building, no band in the city would parade with the troops, and even some members of the club balked at dining with the regiment's black chaplain.[22] When Lincoln's funeral procession passed through New York in 1865, the mayor at first refused to allow a black delegation to take part; and when he was overruled by the governor, the Negroes had to be accompanied by a strong force of police to protect them from harm.[23] Small wonder, then, that by 1865 New York City's Negro population was only 9,943, down 20 percent from the total of 12,581 blacks who lived there in 1860. A reporter for the *Evening Post*, visiting the refugees at police headquarters after the riots, remarked to the pastor of the African Methodist Bethel Church on Thirtieth Street that his race had a hopeful future. "Yes," said the clergyman, "in the next world." [24]

Under a state law of 1855, municipalities in New York were liable for property destroyed in a popular commotion, and a special committee of the New York County Board of Supervisors was set up to consider claims for damages due to the Draft Riots. Examiners appointed by the committee investigated each claim and made a recommendation. The committee then decided how much to award. The comptroller, who could reduce the amount set by the committee, had the final word. Unlike most of New York's public financial dealings, the riot claims seem to have been handled with reasonable honesty and efficiency. If anything, those in charge erred on the side of underpayment. Claims by corporations and individuals for loss of time or trade due to the riots were quickly squelched, as were businessmen's claims for not only the wholesale price of goods stolen but also for the estimated profit on their sale.[25] Some of the examiners went to considerable lengths to find reasons why claims should not be paid. Most claims were settled by the end of 1864, although a few people chose to go to court and sue for heavier sums than the committee was inclined to grant them. Altogether, the riots cost New York County $1,516,423.99, which was raised by the issue of bonds.[26]

Immediately after the riots, the authorities began to search for stolen property. On the morning of Friday, July 17, the entire Seventh Regiment surrounded the block between Thirty-seventh and Thirty-eighth streets, and Second and Third avenues, while police searched the houses. The process was repeated several times, and as the troops and police gradually worked their way down Second Avenue, 250 rifles and a large amount of stolen clothing were discovered. Unfortunately, the manpower was not available for such thorough measures to be taken all over the city. The police had to investigate on their own or with only a small detachment of troops to help them. During the first few days after the riots, many looters threw the goods they had stolen out of their windows into the street as soon as they saw a policeman in the offing, or went to the station houses with furniture and clothing they claimed to have found. But as time went on, the police had less and less success. For months after the riots, officers on duty in the tenement districts would find tapestry carpets, valuable rugs, and rich curtains decorating the most squalid and wretched rookeries in New York. Colonel Nugent's sword of honor, stolen from his apartments on Monday night, was found in the hands of a little boy on the East Side, the blade broken and the jewels pried from the hilt.[27]

Very few of the rioters were ever brought to justice. Witnesses were afraid to come forward, grand juries would not indict, the judicial authorities proved somewhat less than dedicated. Complainants suddenly found that they did not want to press charges, after all. On Friday, July 17, ten men were arrested for threatening to burn James Taylor's foundry unless he gave them money. The next day Taylor discovered that it was all "a harmless joke. Instead of burning my place they were men who would defend it."[28] Someone asking Mayor Opdyke for better police protection on upper First Avenue remarked that "several of the Inhabitants in this part of the city know some of the late rioters but from the unprotected state of their neighborhood they are afraid to give information against them."[29]

On the night of Wednesday, July 15, two Irish laborers called John Larkin and Thomas Lyons robbed Hermann Harjes, a grocer on Second Avenue, of $100. On July 30, they reappeared at Harjes's store and warned him he "would be sorry, and would get the worst of it, if he made a complaint against them." A leading rioter in the Gashouse district was a man called Michael Cronin. The week after the riots, Cronin heard that Michael and Mary Rafferty, a couple who lived in a tenement at 343 First Avenue, were thinking of denouncing him to the authorities. On Saturday night, July 25, Cronin burst into the Rafferty's apartment "armed with an axe and broke every article of furniture belonging to the comp[lainan]t viz. chairs, tables, bedstead, crockery, glass, pictures and small ornaments and after making an undescribable wreck of everything in the place he attacked and struck comp[lainan]t with the said axe over the left eye causing a very severe wound—the Complt being wounded fled and was pursued by the Deft. The Defendant subsequently returned to the premises armed with a knife, sword or bayonet and attempted to stab Mary Rafferty the wife of complt."[30]

If force did not work, perhaps money would. One of the people accused of murdering Abraham Franklin was an eighteen-year-old carman called Dennis Carey. Charles Swift, a prosecution witness, told the assistant district attorney Samuel Garvin:

Mrs. Carey the mother of the prisoner came around to my house in the evening about ½ past 6 or 7 o'clock about two weeks ago. She was under the influence of liquor at the time. She tried to induce me to accept of my wages for the week if I would leave the City thinking the trial would come on last Monday. I told her I would give her an answer next evening and in the mean time I promised to see James Fitzsimons the other witness in this case. I spoke to Fitzsimons and we came to this conclusion we would not accept of it. I done this merely to see what she was about as I was determined to follow this case up I went around as promised and told her we declined accepting it as if I went for a week on my return I would be locked up in the house of Detention the only way I could do would be to go to California for instance on afternoon of the 7th I again saw her by appointment her brother was present he brought in brandy wanted me to drink and commenced arranging with me to go to California. I declined to go that the expense would be $175.[31]

Under such circumstances as these, it was extremely difficult to get evidence that would stand up in court, even after Mayor Opdyke offered $500 reward for information leading to the arrest and conviction of anyone who committed murder or arson during the riots.[32] Out of the 443 people arrested as suspected rioters, 221 were released without any charges being brought against them. Ten more were discharged by the judge at their preliminary hearing, due to insufficient evidence. Another, John McDermott, escaped from the New York Hospital the day after he was arrested. Two more were found to be deserters. One, a man called Cole, was handed straight over to the military authorities. An indictment was sought against the other, Charles Dowd, but the grand jury refused to indict him and he was turned over to the navy. Thirteen men were allowed to enlist, and charges against them were dropped.[33] "Sir I have made up my mind to enlist," Matthew Powers, who was accused of taking a leading part in burning Josiah Porter's house, told Alderman Matthew T. Brennan, "if you will be so kind as to arrange it I am not under the impression I will be convicted but laying in here another month I do not like."

Powers subsequently wrote to Brennan, saying that he was enjoying life in garrison at Beaufort, South Carolina.[34] Two of the enlistees, John Larkin and Joseph Stehel, had partners in crime whose cases were interwoven with their own, and charges against them were dropped, too.[35]

Of the rest, three men, Wesley Adams, Caspar Henry, and Patrick Merry, jumped bail after they were indicted. Only Adams was recaptured, and he was not brought to trial on the charge of grand larceny during the riots. In thirty-six cases, the grand jury threw out the bill and refused to indict; seventy-four people were indicted, but never brought to trial.

Eighty-one alleged rioters enjoyed their day in court. Fourteen were acquitted, and sixty-seven convicted—an impressive figure, until it is subjected to analysis. Twenty-five of those found guilty were convicted in the Court of Special Session, where three of the city's police judges decided minor cases that did not require a jury trial. The stiffest sentence a convicted rioter received in this court was six months in the City Penitentiary.[36] Forty people were convicted in the Courts of General Sessions or Oyer and Terminer.[37] Then as now, plea bargaining was extensively practiced to keep the courts from becoming impossibly clogged. If everyone had insisted on their right to a trial on every indictment, the court system would have collapsed under the burden. So only thirteen of those convicted were actually tried;[38] the other twenty-seven agreed to plead guilty to a lesser charge or to only one of the several charges on which they were indicted.[39]

Adam Chairman was indicted for first-degree robbery, second-degree arson, and three counts of riot and assault and battery. He pleaded guilty to one charge of riot and assault and battery and was sentenced to six months in the City Penitentiary. James Best was indicted on three charges: riot and assault and battery on Alfred Derrickson, felonious assault and battery on Alfred Derrickson, and the first-degree murder of Ann Derrickson. He pleaded guilty to a charge of assault with intent to kill on Alfred Derrickson and received two years in the State Prison, Sing Sing. Michael McCabe, indicted on two counts of first-degree robbery, pleaded guilty to one charge of assault and battery, and the judge fined him six cents. Peter McGeough was even luckier. Indicted for riot and first-degree robbery, he agreed to plead guilty of petty larceny. Judgment was suspended, and he was discharged.[40]

The law enforcement of the 1860s was designed to protect property rather than life, and the sentences the rioters received reflected this. Mary Fox, who stole 120 pairs of gloves, agreed to plead guilty of an attempt to commit grand larceny and was sentenced to two years in the State Prison. James Best, who pleaded guilty to a charge of assault with intent to kill, received the same punishment.[41] The heaviest sentences meted out to convicted rioters were fifteen years' hard labor each in the State Prison for John Conway and Michael Doyle, who stole a hat worth three dollars.[42] John Hagan and Patrick Sherron, who stole a gold watch worth $50, were each sentenced to ten years in the State Prison. William Watson, who extorted thirty-five cents from Lewis Chamberlain, received the same sentence. Only one of those who attacked or murdered Negroes during the riots received a heavy sentence: Joseph Marshall, who was sent to the State Prison for ten years. This was because of two accidents. First, Marshall had not only beaten Charles Jackson and tried to drown him, he had also robbed him. Second, though District Attorney Hall only asked for a verdict of guilty of a felonious assault and battery with intent to rob in his summing up, the jury disregarded him and found Marshall guilty of first-degree robbery, as he had been charged in the indictment.[43]

Some of the fourteen acquittals were the result of sheer incompetence by the prosecution. John Everett, for example, was charged with stealing bedticks, a quilt, and other property from the Colored Orphan Asylum. At his trial in the Court of Special Session on July 22, no one from the orphanage was there to identify the stolen property, and so the judges had no choice but to acquit. When William Rigby, who had tried to set fire to the Arch, was tried for first-degree arson on October 22, the prosecution presented its case so badly that the jury, without leaving their seats, acquitted the defendants on technical grounds, a variance between the indictment and the proof.[44]

Most of the witnesses to the murder of William Williams in Leroy Street agreed that two of the three men who killed him were rather similar in appearance, stout and tall, with bushy black beards and dark complexions. The third man was about five feet, eight inches tall, clean-shaven, with sandy hair. The police arrested a man answering this description; but they also arrested *three* tall men with bushy black beards and dark complexions.[45]

One of these men, John McAllister, was brought to trial in the Court of Oyer and Terminer on Thursday, October 8. During the day, it emerged that only one of the prosecution witnesses, a man called Caleb Lawrence, identified McAllister as one of the killers; some of the other witnesses flatly denied it. McAllister admitted he had walked by the top of Leroy Street that morning and had seen the Negro's dead body, but insisted that he had no part in the murder. Lawrence did not stand up well under cross-examination:

Q. Do you recollect seeing a young miss by the name of Emma Flandreau at the Coroner's inquest?
A. Yes, sir.
Q. Did you ever have any conversation with her in regard to this matter?
A. I did.
Q. Did you ask her if she was a witness in this case?
A. Yes, sir.
Q. Did she say, Yes, to that?
A. Yes, sir.
Q. Did you ask her which one she thought it was that committed the murder?
A. No, sir, I don't think I did.
Q. You did not, I want you to be positive?
A. I don't think I did, I might.
Q. Will you swear positively you did not?
A. I will not.
Q. You might have said so?
A. I might.
Q. Did you ask her which she thought it was that threw the stones?
A. No, sir.
Q. Will you swear positively you did not?
A. I think I will—I could not say whether I did or not.
Q. Do you recollect saying you thought it was McAllister?
A. Yes, sir.
Q. Do you recollect of seeing Mrs. Taylor there?
A. No, sir.

Q. Mrs. Taylor, stand up. Did you see that woman there?
A. Yes, sir, I believe I did.
Q. Do you recollect having any conversation with her about the matter?
A. I spoke to Miss Flandreau right in her presence.
Q. Did you speak to Mrs. Taylor?
A. I don't think I did.
Q. Will you swear you did not?
A. I don't know I might.
Q. Is your memory good?
A. Well, pretty good.
Q. I want you to tell me whether you spoke to Mrs. Taylor or not.
A. I couldn't say.
Q. You might, or might not.
A. I might or might not, I speak to a good many.
Q. Do you recollect anything to this effect, or like this to Mrs. Taylor, "I am very glad to think that I have found out I am mistaken & that McAllister was not the man"?
A. No sir, no sir.
Q. Did you say anything like this; "I was not myself sure that Mc-Allister was the man."
A. No, sir.
Q. Did you furthermore state to Mrs. Taylor; "That you were glad you found out you were mistaken before you were sworn"?
A. No, sir.

Later, Lawrence admitted that he had mentioned to a friend of his called James Rider that he thought he could identify one of the killers. Rider told him to go to the police, and they would share the reward between them. When Lawrence balked, Rider contacted a policeman who was investigating the Williams case, Officer Timothy Golden, and arranged for him to interview Lawrence. A few days later, Lawrence was served with a subpoena to testify in the coroner's court.[46]

Before the end of the day, McAllister's counsel had William Butney and James Lamb, two of the other accused, brought into court, and he pointed out to the jury that it was practically impossible to tell them and McAllister apart. Next morning, Judge Barnard stopped the trial. He "addressed the jury, and said it was not his practice to take a case from the jury, and never without consultation with his brethren and the District Attorney . . . after a careful examination of this case, and a consultation with his brethren, and in accordance with their opinion, he could not charge the jury to find the prisoner guilty of a crime which might send him to the gallows or to a state prison for life. The Court would direct a verdict of not guilty."[47]

A case that set an important precedent came up in the Court of General Sessions on Saturday, August 8, when Dennis Welsh was tried for grand larceny. He was accused of stealing a mattress from the Gibbons house on Tuesday, July 14, and while he admitted the theft, he claimed he was forced into it by the mob.

The counsel for the prisoner begged the jury to throw aside any prejudice against the prisoner as having been engaged in the riot. The prisoner was compelled to take the mattress, but violence having been used to make him take the property, he was not therefore guilty. . . . While the mob was opposing the conscription, they were themselves conscripting men into their ranks, and the prisoner was one of them. The case was summed up for the people by the District Attorney. If the jury believed that the prisoner was a soldier in the rebel army, who had been conscripted and who deserts at the first opportunity, then there was no ground for a conviction, he not being morally guilty. . . . The Recorder charged the jury that there was a strong doubt in his mind in regard to the guilt of the prisoner, and while he did not know that he ought to express a doubt as to the prisoner's guilt, still in time of excitement like the present the jury should be careful and not act from prejudice, but if they had a doubt of the prisoner's guilt he should have the benefit of it. The jury retired for nearly an hour, when they returned a verdict of not guilty.[48]

Nearly every rioter could have plausibly made the same plea, and why they did not is a mystery explicable only by a lack of competent legal counsel.

Some of those indicted did make the mob's coercion their excuse for rioting,[49] and this is unquestionably why some of the riot indictments were never followed up by the district attorney's office.[50] But it is equally undeniable that after an example had been made of the first couple of dozen rioters unfortunate enough to have been selected for prosecution, the district attorney lost all interest in bringing the rest to justice.[51] No one was ever tried for

the murders of Colonel O'Brien, William Jones, or James Costello. Only Patrick Butler was punished for Abraham Franklin's
lynching.

William Cruise, who led the attack on the Derricksons, was tried
and convicted of assault with intent to kill on Alfred Derrickson
in the Court of Oyer and Terminer, December 21–23. The jury
added a recommendation to mercy, but the judge handed down the
heaviest sentence possible, two years and four months in the State
Prison.[52] William Williams's killers escaped scot-free.[53] Neither
Edward Canfield nor James Lamb was ever brought to trial. William Butney was tried at the December sitting of Oyer and Terminer, but the jury deadlocked; six for conviction, six for acquittal.[54]
He might have been retried, but for some reason District Attorney
Hall sent to New Orleans for an officer of the *Belvidere*, Butney's
ship, to come and identify him. The second mate came to New
York for this purpose and declared that he did not know Butney
and had never seen him on board the *Belvidere*. Perhaps he did
not want to get involved; perhaps he genuinely did not recognize
Butney.[55] Whether he did or did not was utterly irrelevant in deciding Butney's guilt, but Hall seized upon this fact to justify the
prisoner's discharge:

This being the last day of term & a motion having been made to discharge Butney I accede to it for the following reason. The evidence
against him is *pure* identity. He had a careful trial. 6 Jurors were for
acquitting him which raised a great doubt. One other was (of his co-
defts) acquitted. Two others discharged by court and self. But to make
the case more doubtful the party referred to in the within letter came
on and did *not* identify but denied Butney as being on board of the vessel in question to which the negro belonged and the killer went. Always
fearful of cases of mere identity the increasing doubt impels me to discharge him. A. Oakey Hall, D.A., April 28, 1864.[56]

One rioter was tried in federal court. This was John U. Andrews, the Virginian who had harangued the mob at the burning
of the Ninth District draft office. The Lincoln administration offered District Attorney Hall the chance to prosecute Andrews for
riot, before he was tried for treason against the United States. But
Hall curtly replied that "he declined being a party to the scheme

for putting a man twice in jeopardy for the same offence"; later he said that he did not want to take any responsibility for Andrews's months of imprisonment in Fort Lafayette. A recently converted Democrat, Hall was not about to endorse the administration's policy of arbitrary arrests without trial.[57]

Andrews was indicted on four charges: treason; conspiracy to levy war against the United States and resist the execution of United States laws; inciting, setting on foot and engaging in a rebellion and insurrection against the United States; and resisting and counseling and aiding resistance to a draft. He was brought to trial on the second charge in the United States Circuit Court, before Supreme Court Justice Samuel Nelson, on May 24, 1864.

The government alleged that a conspiracy had existed to stop the draft in the Eighth and Ninth New York districts; that Andrews had spoken to the mob, calling on them to arm themselves and follow him; and that he led them to the Eighth District draft office in Broadway and incited them to burn it down. The prosecution got off to a bad start when both Jenkins and Manierre, the Ninth and Eighth District provost marshals, admitted that they had never seen Andrews before. Three prosecution witnesses claimed to have heard Andrews's speech and gave their versions of it. One of them said that the Virginian had led the mob down to Broadway and Twenty-ninth Street to attack the Eighth District office, and a fourth witness said that he saw Andrews commanding the rioters in Lexington Avenue.[58]

Andrews was defended by a court-appointed attorney who seems to have been rather less than enthusiastic about his assignment.[59] He called no witnesses for the defense and failed to point out that the most damaging account of Andrews's speech given by a prosecution witness differed considerably from reports published in the newspapers on July 14.[60] Andrews himself was allowed to address the court and said:

On that day I heard that a riot was proceeding uptown, and came to the conclusion, as I never had seen a riot, I went there merely to look on, and without intending to take any side or part. I will proclaim the freedom of speech, the right to criticize any law, to form any judgment about it, and to express that judgment. When that right was taken away the avenue of freedom was barred to everyone. On that day I was recognized there by the crowd; they knew my principles, that I had always been a States Right Democrat. They insisted that I should make a speech and I was taken to the shed and there made a speech. If it be treason, if it be conspiracy to express my opinion, then I am guilty. The best legal authority upholds me in my position. Men charge me with treason. I am not a native of New-York. I was born in Virginia and have lost every cent I had in the world. I never corresponded with the South. I told those people that the draft was iniquitous, and they must proceed constitutionally against it and not by violence. And I told them to meet me at the Cooper Institute, where I would lead them legally and constitutionally in resistance to the law.

It took the jury only fifteen minutes to bring in a verdict of guilty. Andrews spoke to the court again before sentencing and said:

Without intent to combat the United States Government, I merely expressed my opinion. I did not use the language attributed to me. If I am to suffer for the expression of my opinion, I suffer willingly and freely. I stand here as a sovereign citizen, possessing a right to express my feelings. I did it on that day. I never lead a mob, and God is my witness that I begged the mob to resort to every legitimate means before resorting to violence. I stand here a victim to freedom of speech. If I am to spend the rest of my life in a prison I would still stand here and speak the truth. I now say that here, if I must be punished, let it be done quickly, for I would rather it were a dagger to my heart. I am a wreck, a broken man, ruined in health and strength. I have but a few days more to live.

Justice Nelson told Andrews that the time he had already spent in Fort Lafayette would be taken into consideration in sentencing him. It was obvious, he added, that Andrews must have been much excited when he allowed himself to be placed at the head of such a mob. Perhaps he was not aware of words he then uttered. The court, said Nelson, regretted much his allowing himself to become so excited as to forget himself in this manner, with this violent mob and unlawful assemblage. They [the court] would have been much gratified if the evidence could have allowed the court to have arrived at any other conclusion. He was a leader, was looked up to by the crowd. The court was therefore obliged to make an ex-

ample of him, to warn the community. Taking the previous imprisonment into consideration, Nelson sentenced Andrews to three
years' imprisonment at hard labor.[61]

So ended the court proceedings against the rioters of July 1863.
More might have been brought to trial if it had not been necessary
to keep their cases out of the September term of the Court of
General Sessions, when Judge McCunn was on the bench, but no
one showed any great zeal for prosecuting rioters after the first
fine careless rapture. The judges made no move to hold extra sessions of their courts; Governor Seymour did nothing about creating a special tribunal to try riot crimes; and even Republican
newspapers forgot all about the trials after writing editorials about
"the rapidity and certainty with which punishment has followed
upon the commission of the crimes" in August.[62]

The news of the riots encouraged the Confederacy and its foreign friends. Many Southerners were delighted. "We have awful
good news from New York," a clerk in the Confederate War
Department exulted, "an INSURRECTION, the loss of many lives,
extensive pillage and burning, with a suspension of the conscription!" The *Richmond Enquirer*, however, warned against thinking
that the riots would have much effect on the war, at least for some
time to come. Internal revolution, it pointed out, need not weaken
a nation's potential for foreign aggression. The example of Revolutionary France proved that. The New York riots certainly por-
tended the downfall of the whole rotten structure of Yankee
society. "Yet, the process may be long; and in the meantime, the
desperate energy of their war for conquest of the Confederacy
may grow more furious for a season." The South must redouble
its efforts and eventually it would see "the giant, but hollow bulk
of the Yankee nation bursting into fragments and rushing down
into perdition in flames and blood. Amen."[63]

The *Richmond Daily Dispatch* was much more euphoric. The
report of the riots, it declared, was far more welcome and much
more important than news of foreign intervention. There would
be more riots, and the draft would have to be abandoned. This
would mean no reinforcements for the federal army—and it had
already been shown that the present Union forces could not sub-
due the South. The *Montgomery Daily Advertiser*, too, gleefully

predicted more riots, and the *Mobile Daily Advertiser and Register* thought that the riots proved the Northerners now saw that they had been forced into an unholy war against the South.[64] There were no more uprisings in the North, and southern papers ceased to mention the riots. But the news of the four days' battle in New York did something to raise Confederate morale in the dark days after the fall of Vicksburg.

Abroad, reports of the riots dissipated much of the effect produced by the news of Gettysburg and Vicksburg. The Confederate cotton loan, which had been at 5 percent discount on the London Stock Exchange, rose 3 percent, and both the *Times* and the *Post* declared that the riots proved that the Northerners were against the war. The Liberal *Star* argued that "every negro murdered by the pro-slavery savages of . . . [New York] city will be worth a thousand soldiers to the cause of the Union and the proclamation of freedom. Henceforth it will be a point of honour with every decent citizen to stand by the government that is assailed by incendiaries and butchers." But every other paper, except for the *Daily News*, assumed that the draft would have to be abandoned and that the northern war effort would ultimately collapse for lack of troops.[65]

John Bigelow, the American consul general in Paris, was visiting Guizot, when he glanced at a newspaper and saw "to my mortification and grief that a fierce and bloody resistance to the conscription has been made in New York." The *Patrie* argued that the riots proved the Northerners were against the war and urged a speedy peace on the basis of a separation of North and South. The *France* carried two editorials on two successive days, headed "The Revolution in New York," which predicted that the North would soon dissolve into total anarchy and said Lincoln had the choice of either resigning or being driven from power. The *Constitutionnel* and *Pays* both predicted a second civil war, in the North this time.[66] Both in France and England, pro-Confederate opinion took new heart on hearing of the riots.

In their report for 1863, the Police Commissioners proposed that a riot squad should be organized, consisting of a quarter of the force, trained and organized like soldiers, and armed with rifles and light artillery. Nothing was ever done to put this idea into practice, but the Draft Riots left an enduring legacy in the New York Police Department. Even today, the training given to recruits emphasizes use of the nightstick and a high standard of drill. "During the Draft Riots of 1863," reads a departmental booklet describing the New York Police Academy, "the training of policemen paid off. Disciplined, well-drilled cops took rapid-fire military orders."[67]

According to the mythology that soon developed about the riots, the mob was all Irish and the disorders were the result of a Confederate conspiracy. Such accusations of disloyalty added fuel to the already ardent dislike of the native-born middle and upper classes for the Irish. "Sam, Organize!" read handbills posted all over the city in the days after the riot.[68] Nothing came of this appeal to revive the Know-Nothing crusade of the 1850s, but the doubts cast on the patriotism of Irish immigrants led Tammany Hall to put a heavy emphasis on red, white, and blue Americanism in the years of its greatest power,[69] played a part in making fervid patriotism a characteristic of Irish-Americans, and may have eased the passage of Negro suffrage. Recalling the riots, native-born whites may have been more inclined to agree with Frederick Douglass's remark that if a Negro knew as much when sober as an Irishman knew when drunk, he was fit to vote.

One immediate result of the riots was the demise of New York's volunteer fire department. Commissioner Acton and Superintendent Kennedy took the lead in the campaign for a paid department, and ten police captains produced well-publicized affidavits denouncing the volunteers' lawlessness, brawling, and thieving. An act to create a professional Metropolitan Fire Department was approved by the state legislature in January–March 1865, and the new organization went into operation on June 22. To everyone's surprise, the fire laddies accepted the change peacefully; there were no riots, no violent demonstrations, and no refusals to do duty. The commissioners of the new department announced that they would give preference to veteran volunteers in making appointments, and this was certainly a strong inducement to good behavior. But in the middle of the final legislative struggle over abolition of the volunteer system, Commissioner Acton told an investigating committee of the state senate that the Draft Riots had been started by volunteer firemen and that he knew who the guilty parties were. The fact that he gave no names makes it clear that this was a warning to Masterson and all the other volunteers who rioted in July 1863 not to resist the downfall of their power.[70]

The year after the Metropolitan Fire Department came into being, the Metropolitan Board of Health was born, when the state legislature finally yielded to years of lobbying by physicians like John H. Griscom and Stephen Smith, welfare organizations like the Association for Improving the Condition of the Poor, and reform groups. It is unlikely that the Draft Riots played a major role in the board's creation.[71] A few people, of course, may have seen the riots as a fearful warning of what would happen again and again if something was not done to clean up the slums, but the vast majority of New York's upper classes were out of town in July 1863, and the disorders do not seem to have had much impact on them. The cholera epidemic of 1865–1866 probably did much more than the riots to convince influential New Yorkers that better public health was a necessity.

The Draft Riots haunted Governor Seymour all the rest of his political life. In 1863, when seats in the state legislature and a secretary of state were to be elected; in 1864, when he ran for reelection as governor; and in 1868, when he was the Democratic candidate for president, Republican propagandists twisted Seymour's behavior during the riots, and especially his speech at City Hall, into damning evidence that he and his ticket should be rejected. In 1863 and 1864, Seymour and the Democrats would probably have lost anyway on the issues, but 1868 was a different matter. Seymour lost to Grant by very narrow margins in several northern states, and he may well have been the choice of a majority of the white voters. Without the Republican charges that he encouraged the mob, without Thomas Nast's devastating cartoons, he might well have done better.[72] If so, the Draft Riots may have cost Horatio Seymour the presidency of the United States.

*There are ten thousand stout fellows that would spend
the last drop of their blood against Popery that do not know
whether it be a man or a horse.*

—DANIEL DEFOE

# 10

## *The Reckoning*

ONE HOT August night in 1865, George Templeton Strong came home after chatting with Superintendent Kennedy at the Union League Club. "Mr. Superintendent Kennedy," he later recorded in his diary, "tells me that there were killed, during the riots of 1863, 1,155 persons, exclusive of those who were supposed to have been smuggled to their graves. He thinks there were many deaths besides from injuries received in the course of that performance, because the number of deaths by sunstroke reported during August and the latter half of July, 1863, was more than double the number of deaths from that cause during all the twenty-one summer months of the next preceding seven years. He supposes that many of our Keltic fellow citizens returned to their hod-carrying too soon after their heads had been broken by the locusts of his myrmidons."[1]

Tall tales about the numbers killed and wounded in the riots began to sprout almost as soon as the fighting ended. Judge Barnard, sentencing a rioter in Oyer and Terminer, referred to the "800 people killed." Governor Seymour, in his second annual message to the state legislature, passed on a police estimate that a thousand people had died. A detective working for the War Department gave the death toll as 1,462. Everyone had a motive for inflating the size of the count. The police wanted to demonstrate how brave and efficient they had been; Democrats wished to show how unpopular the draft and the rest of Lincoln's policies were;

and Republicans hoped to persuade the federal government to declare martial law in New York City.[2]

The true number of deaths was much smaller than any of these figures. Using the official records, it can be definitely proved that 105 people lost their lives in the Draft Riots. Three people were reported missing. Three more died in falls from a roof or windows, and it is possible that they may have been taking part in the rioting. Two deaths were attributed by the press to injuries sustained during the riots, but the New York County Coroners did not do so. And a number of deaths can be related to the riots. Peter Husten, Lydia Vanthorn, and Charles Watson were already ill, and the treatment they received during the riots accelerated their demise. It did not cause it. Other factors must have intervened to kill Terence Slavin, John Starkey, and John T. Van Buren. Perhaps they were victims of the primitive medical care of the period; perhaps the injuries they received during the riots left them so debilitated that they could not resist other diseases or the winter cold.

Probably few would argue that William W. Yates, a black who hanged himself out of fear of the mob, should be counted as a casualty of the riots. Nor would the two boys killed when the wall of the burned-out Eighteenth Precinct police station house fell on them, Terrence Boyle, sixteen years of age and John Kennedy, nine years of age, be listed as riot victims. Even including every doubtful case, the death toll for the riots only reaches 119. This still makes the Draft Riots the worst civil disorder the United States has ever known, but it is a far cry from some of the casualty figures bandied about.[3]

In the days after the riots, rumors were rife that many dead rioters were being concealed in the tenement districts until they could be smuggled out to the country and buried there or were being interred in yards and vacant lots. All such stories can be confidently dismissed.[4] Anyone burying a body in a garden or a lot uptown would have had to dig so deep and labor so long that they would have invited the very public attention they were seeking to avoid.[5] And anyone trying to smuggle a corpse out of Manhattan would have incurred considerable expense, much more than most tenement dwellers could afford. They would have been in constant danger of discovery while on the ferries or trains; in the hot summer of 1863, anyone with a nose would have been able to tell something was wrong. Finally, once they were in the country they would still have faced the problem of finding a concealed spot where they could bury the body. There was no reason on earth why any rioter's family or friends should have gone to such trouble and, for those who were Catholics, have incurred the penalties prescribed for burying a coreligionist in unconsecrated ground, when they could simply declare that the deceased was only a spectator of the riots who had been accidentally killed.[6] Similarly, there is no reason to look beyond the unusually high temperatures of late July and August 1863 to explain the many cases of sunstroke in New York during those months.

In the course of the riots, thirty-five soldiers and thirty-two policemen were seriously wounded, and thirty-eight soldiers and seventy-three policemen were lightly wounded. One hundred and twenty-eight civilians, both rioters and their victims, were hurt. One can be reasonably certain that the count of wounded for the troops and police is accurate. The civilian figure is a different matter. The total 128 probably includes all, or nearly all, of the people seriously wounded in the riot. Many of those lightly wounded had their injuries treated by general practitioners or by druggists who advertised themselves as physicians. And large numbers of Negroes who were beaten probably did not receive any medical attention at all.

Three hundred and fifty-two people can be identified as rioters. No information, except their names, is available on ninety-two of them. Of the remaining, 241 were male and nineteen female. Three of the latter were young girls: Mary Ann Carmody, 10; Honora Murphy, 11; and Catharine Waters, 12.[7] The age of 235 of the rioters can be ascertained: 66 were under 21; 87 were between 21 and 30 years of age; 40 were between 31 and 40; 27 were from 41 to 50 years of age; 13 were from 51 to 60; and two, Luke Featherston and Matthew Zweick, were over 60. The 63 males under 20 and the 29 over 45 years of age were not liable to the draft.

One hundred and sixty-six rioters can be traced to an exact address in New York City. Most came from the uptown wards, with the Eighteenth and the Twentieth in the lead. The Gashouse and Hell's Kitchen began in 1863 to earn the reputation that would make them infamous by the 1890s. A surprising number of rioters came from the rural Twelfth Ward, and especially from the village of Harlem. Three rioters, James Lee, Richard Balensburg, and Patrick Dougherty, lived in Brooklyn and came across the East River to take part in the New York troubles. Henry Fellbein lived in Hoboken, and Thomas Sutherland in Jersey City. Joseph Marshall and Jeremiah Tracy had no fixed address.[8]

The occupation of 168 rioters can be determined. Five, perhaps eight, of them could be described as middle-class or professionals of some kind. The most distinguished rioter was R. S. McCulloh, professor of mechanics and physics at Columbia College. He had strong southern sympathies, and a few months later he crossed the lines to throw in his lot with the Confederacy.[9] Nelson Edwards was a dentist. Two were somewhat tarnished characters: John U. Andrews, a shyster lawyer, and Thomas Fitzgerald, "a Physician, it is said, of some education and skill, but accustomed to drinking and bad company." James W. Collier was an actor, a calling still not regarded as quite respectable. William Spalding was a real estate agent; Thomas Kiernan a contractor, and Patrick Garvey a merchant. There is no way to determine if these descriptions accurately reflected the scope of their activities, or if "merchant," for example, was only a pompous way of saying "storekeeper." Forty-seven had occupations that required some skill or training: tailor, carpenter, plumber, blacksmith, boilermaker, stonemason, barber, cabinet maker, shoemaker, rope maker, brass-finisher, bricklayer, glass-cutter, gunsmith.[10] Fifty-seven rioters held jobs calling for no special skills: carman, peddler, barkeeper, cartman, housewife, washerwoman, domestic, street paver, gardener, hostler, milkman.[11] And fifty-six were laborers or factory workers.[12] Out of the eighty-three rioters questioned about their literacy, forty-three could not read or write. This was a mob of the industrial age, with the people at the bottom of the social pyramid predominating.[13]

An overwhelming percentage of the rioters were Irish. Out of 184 whose country of birth can be determined, 117 were born in Ireland, forty in the United States, sixteen in Germany, seven in England, and one each in France, Canada, Denmark, and Switzerland.[14] Most of the American-born were from New York.

Theodore Osterstock was from Pennsylvania, Charles Dowd from Massachusetts, and Francis X. Crawley and John U. Andrews from Virginia. John Conway and Michael Doyle were born in Philadelphia, James H. Whitten was from Frederick, Maryland, and Painter Springstein from New Jersey.

Until July 1863, most of the rioters had led quiet, respectable lives. Very few had any records of involvement with the law. Some, like John Hussey, "the Terror of the Hook," may have had a reputation as brawlers, but only a handful of the rioters can be called professional criminals: Wesley Allen, Charles Smith, Michael Doyle, John Conway, and possibly Adam Chairman. The manner in which Henry Fellbein and Mary Fox operated suggests that they were also experienced thieves. Two of the rioters, Dowd and Cole, were deserters; two more, Patrick Oatis and Francis Cusick, were ex-policemen. Only a few had served in the army: William Joyce, Maurice Fitzgerald, Daniel Donnelly, William Carson, Patrick Sweeney, William Stanton, John O'Hara, Matthew Powers, and John C. Henry, who was shot dead in West Thirty-sixth Street by members of his old regiment, the Hawkins' Zouaves.[15] John McDermott and James English were serving in the army in July 1863 and must have been on furlough when they were caught up in the rioting.

After the riots, Mayor Opdyke said that "while the riot was ostensibly a resistance to the draft, the rioters themselves were not, in general, persons liable to be drafted. A great proportion of them were persons under twenty years of age, and many were convicts, thieves and abandoned characters, the scum of this great city, and the hasty importations from other cities."[16] There was a certain measure of truth in the first part of his analysis, but hardly any at all in the second. The rioters were a fair cross-section of New York's younger male working class.

Most of the roaming bands of rioters who looted stores, wrecked Negroes' homes, invaded brothels, and beat up Republicans were quite small, numbering from twenty to fifty people. George Templeton Strong and Professor Wolcott Gibbs were dining at the Maison Dorée on the evening of Monday, July 13, when "there was an alarm of a coming mob, and we went to the window to see. The 'mob' was moving down Fourteenth Street and consisted of just thirty-four lousy, blackguardly Irishmen with a tail of small boys." "I kept a restaurant and boarding house," testified Lewis Ward, ". . . I was inside, alone, when the riot commenced; the first I knew of the riot was a stone flying through the window; two gangs of rioters, one consisting of nine and the other of seventeen men, rushed in." Some gangs of rioters were even smaller than this: "ten or twelve" attacked Michael Newman's cigar store at 217 Division Street on Wednesday, the fifteenth, and Joseph Hecht, an enrolling officer, was thrashed by seven of them. Typically, numbers of "half-grown boys" would tag along with the adult rowdies. The longer police or troops took to arrive at a place offering rich pickings, like Brooks Brothers' store or the Gibbons house, naturally the more people would join the looters, but the attacks were always initiated by small groups.[17]

The mobs who met the police and troops in pitched battle were larger, but it does not seem that there were more than three hundred hard-core street fighters gathered in one place at any time during the riots. The *New York Times* estimated that the whole number of real rioters was only from two to three thousand.[18] The crowds who filled the streets were mostly spectators,[19] though numbers of them might take a marginal part in the rioting: adolescent boys by throwing stones, women by shrieking obscenities and threats at the police and soldiers or, more rarely, by putting stones in their stockings to make slingshots.[20]

"At the burning of the Orphan Asylum," wrote an eyewitness, "at the destruction of the fine block corner of Broadway and 29th Street; and at the attack upon the *Tribune* office, there were not more than a hundred actual rioters at work—not so many at the last two places. . . . Following and abetting the hundred or so of active rioters, there was, at either place, a crowd of boys and women, numbering perhaps five hundred, and of spectators, of various sympathies, several thousand." Reporters watching the battles on Third Avenue at Monday noon thought there was a nucleus of about three hundred desperadoes who did nearly all the fighting. One man watching the mob go down Broadway late Monday afternoon thought it consisted of "about 150 ragamuffins"; James Parton thought they numbered about two hundred.[21]

The Draft Riots were fundamentally an insurrection of anarchy, an outburst against any kind of governmental control by the people near the bottom of society. The temporary powerlessness of the authorities released a flood of violence and resentment that was usually kept repressed. As the hours went by, the riot itself created a devil-may-care mood of euphoria that led to more rioting. A wild melange of motives drove the mob on. Obviously, there was strong opposition to the draft and to the war. Rioters cheered for Jefferson Davis and planned to hang Horace Greeley if they could catch him. Enrolling officers and reporters for Republican newspapers were beaten. Revenge for the deaths caused by his troops was the motive for the murder of Colonel O'Brien, and after being roughly handled by the police, or fired upon by the troops, other rioters may well have felt the same way. Something for nothing is always an attractive proposition, especially if other people seem to be getting away with it. "I took said property because every one else took it," said Theodore Arnold when he was arrested for looting.[22]

Some took advantage of the breakdown in law and order to settle old grudges, like Peter Doherty, or to extort money. William Watson tried to get money from Lewis Chamberlain at the urging of his companions, who told him that "the old fellow wouldn't say nothing." "[He] kept, and keeps now, a grocery-store on the Northeast corner of Division and Essex streets," reported an examiner on John Weschusen's claim for damages. "It appears that he had made himself obnoxious to that class of men and boys who usually congregate about corner groceries; as a consequence, his store was sacked." Weschusen was known as a miser in his neighborhood, and the rioters tore his place apart until they found $500 in gold.[23]

One extremely strong and persistent motive was deep-rooted hatred of Negroes. Many of those arrested for attacks on Negroes or their houses knew their victims before the riots or lived close to them. The implication is clear that they had long been envious of some Negroes' relative prosperity or resented having to dwell in the same neighborhood.[24] Mrs. Mary Alexander lived at 94 West Twenty-eighth Street until July 15. She related:

A large crowd of men and boys came there and ordered deponent to leave said house together with other persons in said house. That deponent with others were obliged to leave said place, not being able to take any of their house-hold effects whatever, through fear of personal violence from said mob. That on the seventeenth day of July 1863 she went to the house and then saw that it had been sacked & robbed of all its contents the deponent then went to the house or appartments [*sic*] of Frank A. Shandley whose family lived in the lower part of said 94, West 28th Street, and then and there met James Shandley the son of said Frank who said to her as soon as he saw deponent, "Oh, Mrs. Alexander, we have got most all of your things in our house." That deponent then asked him if his mother was home to which he replied in the affirmative, that he then went up stairs to the rooms of his said mother Anne Shandley and that his mother opened the door and let him in but immediately closed and fastened it & refused to let deponent in although requested to do so several times, that she denied having anything belonging to deponent except her husband's likeness and told deponent that what things she had she would not give up until she saw what other people done with the things they had. That deponent has since identified a large number of articles consisting of household furniture and clothing at the 29th Precinct Station House as her property which deponent is informed by officer Clark of the 29th Precinct were found in the house of said Frank A. Shandley and Anne Shandley.[25]

At times, with the destruction of the street-sweeping machines and the grain elevators at the Atlantic Docks, the riots took on a Luddite aspect; at times, with the attacks on well-dressed "$300 men," they became class war.

Some people simply drifted into rioting, aided by liberal quantities of drink. On Monday, the thirteenth, William Stanton was hired by the keeper of the local prison attached to the Fourth District Police Court to guard the drugstore in the building from rioters. The next day, he was arrested himself for tearing up the track of the Fourth Avenue Railroad. Martin Hart, who had arrived in New York from Ireland on June 1, went to live in Harlem and took a job laying gas pipes at Kingsbridge. On the morning of July 15, he went to the dock at 130th Street and Third Avenue, as usual, to take the riverboat to work. Because of the riots, the boat was not running, and after waiting several hours, Hart gave up and started for home. On the way, he fell in with a crowd of rowdies, had several drinks with them, "from the effect of which he became intoxicated and then danced several times for the amusement of the crowd." Eventually, they straggled into Harlem and began demanding money from storekeepers. A few moments later, Hart was in jail.[26]

One or two members of the mob seem to have gone along with their friends to try and restrain them from serious rioting. Mrs. Ann Martin, a white woman married to a Negro, describing what happened on the night of Wednesday, July 15, said:

The first [thing] that attracted my attention was four men hallooing in 121st Street opposite Mr. Woods house they came down the street, and when they got to the second lamp West of my house, they stooped down and pointed to my house, and said that is the house Thomas Kumiski[27] now here was one of the four men, Patrick Henrady now here was one of the four men, and Daniel McGovern now here was one of the four also. Patrick Henrady had a club in his hand. The four men went first to the house next door to me, towards. Av. A, and caught hold of the old woman by the handkerchief on the shoulders and said they wanted either meat or bread, they also said they either wanted liquor or money, she said a devil of a cent would she give them if she had her pocket full of money. They caught hold of her by the handkerchief again, when Kuminski said come away come away respect old age don't do that. They called for Laine two or three times she said Laine was out. They called for liquor then, and she said she would give them none and then they came up to my place. They came up to my place and they asked me for money and liquor and I told them I had none. They said, By God, if they do not get some, they would set fire to the House and they would kill all the damned negroes in the house. They asked if there were any Negroes upstairs. I told them they were none. They said By God they would set fire to the shanty. They asked me for a match. Patrick Henarady put his hand to his pocket and took out a match and scratched it twice and it did not take fire. There are three scratches on the jam where he scratched the matches. The match did not light he scraped it so hard Kumiski stood by me, apart from them and said to them to come away that he did not like to see a poor man's house injured that he was a working man himself and he knew how hard it was to get it. He said he belonged to the Fire Company but then he did not go in for destroying any man's property. McGovern took hold of the door, and said he would pull it of the hinges if I did not give them money or liquor and when I told them I had none to give, he said to Henarady, God Damn it Put it through set fire to it, and with that Henarady took another Match out of his pockets and scraped it again on the door and the match would not light. He asked for matches again, and cursed the Matches they would not light and asked me for more matches. I told him I had none to give, he was inside the house, and dragged down the window curtain and said come boys we will put the shanty through tonight I asked Kumiski if he would take them away, and he said I can't do anything with them Mrs. Martin. Henarady broke and smashing the window from the outside said come Boys what are you about, set the House afire. McGovern took hold of me, and asked me to come into the entry that he wanted to speak to me, I told him that I would not go into a dark entry with any man, That if he had anything to say to me to say it there Then, when I would not go in, these two went into the house together, and turned out again, and went next door to ask Mary for matches and liquor, she said she had none. Then the Gentlemen from down the street came and took them. When Kumiski heard the men coming up from Mr. Ebling's he ran over into the lot opposite my house. The other man ran away I do not know where. There are vacant lots behind my house, that man that ran away talked as bad as the rest of them. Five or ten minutes after the difficulty was over Kumiski came over to my house from the lot into which he had run, and said to me, he said to me, Well I did all I could to protect poor People's Property. When the boys would not be said by me, to go Home. I said I was very thankful to him. He said "I done all I could to them," he bid me good-night. Kumiski took hold of no one and the others took hold of each other and dragged each other threatening to put the shanty through at once and kill the God Dam Negroes all except Kumiski threatened the Negroes and McGovern kicked my dog, saying it was a Nigger's dog and to kill it. Kumiski said nothing and did nothing that I have not stated it was one of them that stooped down and pointed out my house, as I have before stated. Hanaday was there between 4 and 5 o'clock the day before, with two other men, he had a stick in his hand and slapped it on the table, and said do you know what we want, we want you to clear out of this house do you know the constitution I said no, I did not know the constitution he says Well will I tell you what the constitution is To rip and tear everything in the house, and tear the Shantys down upon the Negroes, give me some money says he, and he said money and drink. I told him I had none yes said he you have, and we won't go without it, so I took out my pocket book and showed it to him, and said see Boys I have none and if I had I would give it to you he swore then the shanty would be set fire to that night, and that only it had rained the night before it would be afloat now, and he gave me notice to be out of it by twelve o'clock that night.

Then one of the men who was with him said that Martin was a good man, that he was a hard-working man, and that he had never done any injury to any man in Harlem, and giving me his hand, said that he would go bail, that the shanty should not go down, while he was on the route that night, I thanked him, and he coaxed Hanaday not to burn it, and Hanaday said he wouldn't and the other man aforesaid said I had worked hard for the House as well as my husband. He said I was a good woman, and was a pity to burn it, and he would not burn it that night, that he would go bail. Then Hanaday said rapping the table What is the Constitution to me – I did not say anything and one of the others said rip and tare so then they went away.[28]

There was also a certain element of what can only be called sexual vigilantism present in the riots. Several of the Negroes who fell foul of the mobs were married to white women. "What made you marry a nigger?" Daniel McGovern asked Mrs. Martin. "I told him I could marry who I liked – That he could marry who he liked," Mrs. Martin recalled. "The first thing he said when he came to my place was that if he did not get liquor he would drag the hinges off the door that I was married to a god damned nigger & he meant to smash him."[29] Bordellos and prostitutes catering to Negroes were attacked, and eventually this broadened into an attack on all brothels.[30]

Unlike most American outbreaks of mass violence, the Draft Riots were directed initially against the state. Occurring in the summer, in the middle of a heat wave, they followed a familiar pattern, but there were one or two unusual features about the Draft Riots. First, rioting tended to diminish as darkness fell, instead of becoming more intense. Second, during most disturbances, fighting rises to a crescendo during the early morning hours, when people are going to work, and in the late afternoon, when they are going home. Except on the afternoon of the first day, Monday, July 13, this was not true of the Draft Riots. The paralysis of economic activity was complete, and few Negroes were foolhardy enough to risk going to their jobs.

Thoughts of conspiracy and subversion seem reasonable in times of great internal conflict and uncertainty, and just as the Gordon Riots were attributed to the machinations of French and American agents, and as the Jacobites were blamed for stirring up the London riots of 1736 over cheap Irish labor and the Gin Act, so many Republicans assumed that the Draft Riots were the result of a Confederate plot.[31] "It is evident," Secretary of the Navy Gideon Welles told Senator Charles Sumner, "that this demonstration into Pennsylvania, Morgan's into Indiana, the coming out of the *Atlanta*, the mission of Stevens [*sic*], etc., are all part of a great scheme that was to take effect in the first half of July when our draft was to be made, and a concerted movement to resist it in all the larger cities was to have taken place had the other party been successful. They failing the mobs here failed."[32] Some argued that Governor Seymour was implicated in the plot.[33] Needless to say, there is not the slightest evidence to support any of these paranoid fantasies.

Several months after the riots, that perpetual odd-man-out Orestes A. Brownson published an article in his *Quarterly Review* which charged that the Catholic priesthood and press had upheld slavery and offered only lukewarm support at best to the Union's struggle for survival. The rioters of July, concluded Brownson, had "only acted out the opinions they had received from men of higher religious and social position than themselves." There was a severely limited amount of truth in this accusation. The church had held rigidly aloof from the abolitionist movement, influenced by its doctrine that slavery was an evil to be borne, by its opposition to violent, revolutionary cures for social ills, and by the strong ties between abolitionism and militant Protestantism and rationalism. Some Catholic newspapers bitterly opposed the draft. But their circulation and influence was small. And the church's emphasis on loyalty to a country's legitimate government made the clergy support the Union when war came. Archbishop Hughes went to Europe at the request of President Lincoln to work for the Union cause at the Vatican and in Paris. In 1862 he urged the federal government to adopt conscription. During the riots, many of New York's Catholic priests went out into the streets and used all their influence to abate the fury of the mob. Once the fighting was over, they went from house to house in the tenement districts, trying to persuade people to give up stolen property.[34]

The argument, sometimes heard, that the riots were sparked and fueled by white workers' (especially longshoremen's) fears of competition from cheap black labor will not stand up to examination. Only three longshoremen can be identified as rioters, and none of them was involved in attacking Negroes. John Hussey was wounded while leading the mob against the troops in Pitt Street; Michael Haley was shot dead when he broke into a German brothel in Greenwich Street; and Edward Downing was arrested for trying to make an incendiary speech in Rector Street. Only one Negro longshoreman, William Johnson, is known to have been beaten during the riots.[35] Three Negro longshoremen had their homes wrecked and looted, but there is no sign that their occupation was the cause of the attack. Two of them were not at home when the mob made its assault.[36] Nor is there any sign that any other type of worker was worried about the threat of former slaves flooding into the North. Logically, if the mobs had been fearful on this score, they would have sought out and attacked establishments that employed Negroes. But there were no such onslaughts.[37]

In fact, it was the Negroes of New York City who were being undercut by competition from cheap labor. Employers preferred to hire immigrants, especially Germans, who would work long hours for low pay. In the 1850s and 1860s, Negroes were even being forced out of menial positions traditionally assigned to them, such as waiters' and barbers' jobs. "Every hour," wrote Frederick Douglass, "sees the black man elbowed out of employment by some newly arrived immigrant whose hunger and whose color are thought to give him a better title to the place." "The only chance for the colored man North nowadays," said Henry Ward Beecher in 1862, "is to wait and shave, and they are being driven from that as fast as possible."[38]

The bogey of cheap black labor competition was not new in 1863. The prediction had long been used by the Democrats as ammunition against the Republicans. In 1861 Fernando Wood had campaigned for reelection as mayor by arguing that "this war . . . is a war of the abolitionists against Southern men and their rights. They are very willing to spend Irish and German blood to secure a victory, and when they have secured it, they will bring the black laborer up into the North to steal the work and the bread of the honest Irish and Germans."[39] Significantly, such appeals did not work: Wood lost the election. And anyone willing to believe such threadbare, shopworn rhetoric in 1863, when everything showed that precisely the opposite was happening, must have been credulous and gullible indeed. There is no evidence for thinking that fear of black labor competition played any significant part in causing the Draft Riots.[40] The intense racial prejudice of white New Yorkers in the 1860s is enough to explain all.

The authorities did not show up well during the riots. Even allowing for the disruption of communications by bad weather, the federal government was lamentably slow in getting reinforcements to New York. General Sandford was utterly unfit to command, and the fact that he could reach and keep high rank demonstrated the workings of the militia system at their very worst. The police were brave enough, but the riots showed clearly that their training was grievously inadequate. Well-disciplined police officers should be able to control crowds much larger than their own numbers; but the police never won a battle during the Draft Riots unless they were numerically equal or superior to the mob.

To the surprise of some and the relief of many, all but a very few of the large number of Irish Catholics on the Metropolitan force remained faithful and did their duty. After the riots, eleven officers were charged with dereliction. Officer Herring, accused of being absent from the ranks during the fight on Third Avenue on Monday July 13 was able to show that he had fought well until he was knocked down and carried into a house on East Fortieth Street to recover and that he had reported for duty as soon as he was able to walk. Officer Ware was charged with being absent without leave from the sixteenth to the eighteenth. He, too, had fought hard until he heard that the house where he lived was going to be attacked because some Negroes lived there. His sergeant had refused him permission to go home, but he went anyway.

Several of his fellow patrolmen testified that Officer Kelly had said that he was in favor of the riots and that his heart was with the mob. At the Union Steam Works, Kelly had stood with his club by his side and refused to use it, saying that it was a shame to beat men so. Officer Murdock was charged, and substantially admitted, that he had said after the mob's attack on the *Tribune*, "that it was a shame to beat innocent men, and that the *Tribune* office ought to be burnt down, as it had helped to bring on the present troubles." And Officer O'Rourke was charged with saying that the police attack on the Union Steam Works "was a cowardly and murderous assault upon innocent citizens, and he was glad he had nothing to charge himself with, as he did not use his club on them."

Officer Westervelt, who was absent without leave during the riots, produced a weak defense: he was hurt during the first day of the disorders, and besides, he lived at Harlem, and since the cars were not running, he would have been compelled to walk all the way downtown to report. Officer Egan faced a charge of allowing a prisoner to escape.[41] Ordered to take some captured rioters to the Tombs, he let a man called Riley remain unshackled, saying that he was "too good-looking" to be chained with the others. On the way, they passed some men skylarking in John Street, and Riley took advantage of the distraction to escape.

Three senior officers were charged. Sergeant Jones refused to take in black refugees when he was left in command at the Twenty-ninth Precinct station house. Sergeant Fulmer stayed at the Nineteenth Precinct station house on Monday, instead of reporting at headquarters as ordered. On Tuesday he reported there, went out with the force for two hours, and then went back to the station house, where he stayed for the rest of the riots. He offered no explanation of his odd behavior, although witnesses testified that he did his best to protect life and property while he was at the station house. Captain A. S. Relay, commander of the Twelfth Precinct, sent all his men downtown on receiving the order to concentrate at headquarters, but refused to go himself. He stayed and organized a home guard in Harlem.[42]

Some of the high-ranking officers made serious tactical blunders during the riots: Captain Palmer, in not holding the Ninth District draft office against the rowdies of the Black Joke; Captain Cameron, in ordering the Broadway Squad to evacuate the armory; Inspector Dilks, in failing to haul all the guns away immediately after the first battle of the Union Steam Works. Commissioner Acton seems to have been badly rattled on the first day of the disorders. He sent the reinforcements up to Third Avenue and Forty-sixth Street in penny packets, and as a result, the mob chewed them up piecemeal. He ordered the whole Brooklyn force over to Manhattan on Monday evening and then decided to send them back as soon as they reached headquarters.[43] But after this, he settled down and performed well, and so did General Brown. It is hard to fault their handling of the disturbances after Monday evening. Unquestionably it would have been better if many of the troops tied down on garrison duty at important buildings could have been sent against the mobs, but the inadequacy and uncertainty of the communications available to Acton and Brown, and the extent of the disorders, meant that they could not take the risk of leaving these buildings unprotected. The only objection that could be made is that the police from the Thirty-second Precinct, who usually patrolled on horseback, should have been mounted when they were called down to the city to fight rioters. After noon on Monday, the situation had deteriorated so badly that only saturation of the city with massive force could have ended the riots. With the relatively small number of men at their command, Acton and Brown had no choice but to adopt the fire-brigade strategy of rushing detachments from place to place to break up mobs as they formed. If Sandford had cooperated with Acton and Brown, his militia could have been backed up with regulars and police, and setbacks like Fearing's rout in West Forty-second Street or Winslow's defeat in East Nineteenth Street might have been avoided, but it is not likely that the riots would have been put down any sooner.

In the early 1870s, riots ceased in New York City. Though immigrants flooded in and poverty, misery, and overcrowding were worse than ever, there were no outbreaks of mass violence. Many reasons can be adduced to explain why this new state of peace came about. A professional fire department replaced the roistering volunteer fire laddies; compulsory education and child labor kept many potential adolescent rioters busy. Industrial expansion and long spells of prosperity meant that, until the 1890s, there were usually few unemployed in New York. The new immigrants of 1870–1914 came from countries where political police were powerful and political activity was repressed. The rise of professional baseball and football provided an alternative to rioting as a form of communal weekend entertainment, and the establishment of working-class amusement centers like Coney Island supplied another safety valve. "We have to have it," an English visitor was told, "yes, sir, without it New York itself would burn, the people would go mad, there would be nothing to work off the general cussedness; New York without an outlet like Coney Island would soon be an inferno."[44] Cheap transportation—the bicycle and rapid-transit lines—made it possible for tenement dwellers to escape from the city now and again. There are indications that the police adopted a policy of aggressive patrol in the late 1880s.[45]

All these developments helped in greater or lesser degree to keep the peace in New York City. But the main reason why New York was free of major civil disturbances in the last quarter of the nineteenth century and the first years of the twentieth is that in the mid-1870s Honest John Kelly put together on a permanent basis the machine that Fernando Wood had tried to create and that Boss Tweed had temporarily succeeded in building. Kelly and Croker broke up the ward gangs, which only strengthened the district leaders and made it possible for them to rebel against the Tammany leadership.[46] Under that leadership, the interests of the city's multifarious ethnic groups, the police, and the politicians were harmonized. The result was a corrupt, but peaceful, city, free of the violent conflicts of the mid-nineteenth century. Riots did not resume until the machine faltered and failed to adapt to the needs of a new wave of immigrants, a group harder to assimilate than the Irish and Germans, Italians and Jews who had gone before, and whose demands may yet prove American democracy to be a rope of sand.

# APPENDIXES

# I

## *The Dead*

HENRY ALBOHM, shot by John Piper on Tuesday, July 14, and died August 15.

MATTHIAS ANGEHOVEN, shot at the armory, Second Avenue and 21st Street, on Monday, July 13, and died the same day.

JOSEPH ANNIN, shot by a rioter in Second Avenue on Tuesday, July 14, and died August 18.

THOMAS BAKER, shot at Seventh Avenue and 31st Street on Wednesday, July 15, and died July 17.

GARRETT BARRY, shot by John Lamb in a quarrel over loot in East 32nd Street on Wednesday, July 15, and died the same day.

JANE BARRY, struck by a bureau thrown from a window of the Colored Orphan Asylum and fatally injured, Monday, July 13.

MARCUS BOCHMAN, died July 14 of burns received the day before at the armory, Second Avenue and 21st Street.

PATRICK BOYLAN, shot in Pitt Street on the morning of Tuesday, July 14, and died August 2.

WILLIAM BOYLE, shot by troops at Third Avenue and 22nd Street on the night of Thursday, July 16, and died the next day.

THOMAS BRANNIGAN, died July 14 of burns and other injuries received at the armory, Second Avenue and 21st Street, on Monday, July 13.

JAMES BRODERICK, shot by troops in Ninth Avenue and died July 16.

BROWN, Lieutenant, killed in East 19th Street, Wednesday, July 15.

PIERCE CAHILL, shot by troops in Third Avenue, between 20th and 21st streets, on Wednesday, July 15, and died on July 18.

MARY ANN CARMODY, shot and killed in West 41st Street on Wednesday, July 15.

WILLIAM WALLACE CARPENTER, a soldier, died July 17. No details available.

WILLIAM CARSON, fatally injured jumping from a window of the burning armory, Second Avenue and 21st Street, on Monday, July 13.

PATRICK CASEY, shot and killed in West 42nd Street on Wednesday, July 15.

HUGH CLENK, died on Monday, July 13.

WILLIAM CONWAY, died July 14 of gunshot wounds.

MARY CORCORAN, shot and killed by troops on Thursday, July 16. "She was standing on the sidewalk, when one of the mob fired a pistol at the military, and they instantly fired a volley at the rioters, killing her among others."

JOHN COSTELLO, died July 14 of burns and other injuries received at the armory, Second Avenue and 21st Street, on Monday, July 13.

LAWRENCE CUNNINGHAM, died July 14, of "injuries received while at the riot in 2nd Avenue and 21st Street."

PATRICK CURLEY, shot at Second Avenue and 21st Street on Tuesday, July 14, and died the next day.

CHARLES DALEMETTA, Private, Co. G, 13th New York Cavalry, captured and killed by rioters at the corner of Third Avenue and 42nd Street on the night of Thursday, July 16.

BERNARD DALEY, shot by troops on Wednesday, July 15, and died July 17.

CHARLES DAVIDS, Sergeant, Co. G, 13th New York Cavalry, shot and killed by rioters in East 22nd Street, between First and Second avenues, on Thursday, July 16.

ANN DERRICKSON, died August 20 of peritonitis "caused by blows from James Best, William Cruise and other persons unknown on the night of July 14th."

HENRY DIPPLE, patrolman, Broadway Squad, Metropolitan Police, accidentally shot by troops while he was clearing rioters from the Gibbons house in West 29th Street on the afternoon of Tuesday, July 14, and died July 19.

PATRICK DOUGHERTY, shot and killed by troops on Tuesday, July 14.

LOUIS EBERSPACHER, died of gunshot wounds on July 14.

PETER FARRELL, shot in Tenth Avenue, probably on July 14.

LUKE FEATHERSTON, died of gunshot wounds on July 14.

CHARLES FISBECK, JR., shot and killed at Second Avenue and 21st Street on Tuesday, July 14.

PATRICK FLANNIGAN, died of gunshot wounds on July 14.

JOHN GAFFNEY, shot in Pitt Street on the morning of Tuesday, July 14, and died July 19.

PATRICK GAHERTY, shot in Tenth Avenue, between 41st and 42nd streets, on Wednesday, July 15, and died the following day.

PATRICK GARVEY, shot and killed by troops in Pitt Street on the morning of Tuesday, July 14.

PATRICK GARVEY, shot and killed at the corner of Tenth Avenue and 41st Street on Wednesday, July 15.

THOMAS GIBSON, shot and killed by troops at Second Avenue and 21st Street on Tuesday, July 14.

JOHN GOTZ, died July 17 of "a gunshot wound in the abdomen while standing in his yard door in 3rd Avenue near 32nd Street, July 15th, 1863."

JOHN GRAY, shot at Tenth Avenue and 42nd Street on Wednesday, July 15, and died July 20.

MICHAEL HALEY, shot and killed by John Smith while attacking his premises at 157–159 Greenwich Street on the night of July 14–15.

JAMES HAND, died July 14 of a fractured skull received at Second Avenue and 21st Street.

JULIA HENNESSEY, died of gunshot wounds on July 14.

JOHN C. HENRY, shot and killed by troops in Seventh Avenue on Wednesday, July 15, 1863.

VALENTINE HETTLIN, died of gunshot wounds on July 15.

JAMES HUGHES, shot at Second Avenue and 21st Street on Tuesday, July 14, and died the following day.

JEREMIAH HURLEY, died on July 15.

WILLIAM JOYCE, shot at the corner of First Avenue and 15th Street on Thursday, July 16, and died early the next day.

HENRY KACHELL, shot and killed by troops at the corner of Ninth Avenue and 39th Street on Tuesday, July 14.

BERNARD KANE, shot and killed at the armory, Second Avenue and 21st Street, on Monday, July 13.

PHILIP KEARNEY, soldier, died August 8.

MICHAEL KEEGAN, shot by troops at the corner of Seventh Avenue and 37th Street and died August 20.

ELLEN KIRKE, shot and killed on Tuesday, July 14.

DELIA LAWRENCE, shot in West 41st Street, near Tenth Avenue, and died July 16.

JAMES LEE, clubbed at Second Avenue and 23rd Street on Tuesday, July 14, and died July 25 of "compression of the brain from blows received during the riot."

FREDERICK LEIDER, of Avenue A, between 11th and 12th streets, fatally injured on Monday, July 13, when jumping from a third-story window at the armory, Second Avenue and 21st Street, and died the following day.

RICHARD LYMAN, died July 14 of a "pistol shot wound at the hands of John Leary." No further details available.

FRANCIS MCCABE, shot by troops at the corner of Ninth Avenue and 36th Street on the night of Tuesday, July 14, and died July 27.

EDWARD MCDEVITT, of 32 Lewis Street, shot and killed by troops on Tuesday, July 14.

PETER MCINTYRE, patrolman, 29th Precinct, Metropolitan Police, died August 9 of injuries received during the riots.

JOHN MCKINNA, Private, 15th Co., 1st Battalion, U.S. Invalid Corps, died July 14 of a fractured skull received at the corner of Sixth Avenue and 51st Street on Monday, July 13.

JAMES MCLAUGHLIN, shot on Thursday, July 16, and died the following day.

HUGH MCMAHON, shot on Tuesday, July 14, and died the following day.

PATRICK SHEEDY MCNAMARA, clubbed at the door of his home in 47th Street, between Fifth and Sixth avenues, on Tuesday, July 14, and died of the resulting head injuries the following day.

ELIZABETH MARSHALL, shot and killed on Wednesday, July 15.

JOHN MATSON, beaten on Tuesday, July 14, and died of his injuries the same day.

WILLIAM MEALY, of West 32nd Street, near Seventh Avenue, shot near his home by James Costello on the morning of Wednesday, July 15, and died July 25.

GEORGE MILLER, shot and killed by troops on Tuesday, July 14.

PETER MILLER, shot and killed by troops on Tuesday, July 14.

EDWARD MURPHY, died of gunshot wounds, July 14.

HONORA MURPHY, died of gunshot wounds, July 14.

WILLIAM MURRAY, shot Tuesday, July 14, and died the following day.

HENRY F. O'BRIEN, Colonel, 11th New York Volunteers, beaten to death Tuesday, July 14, in East 34th Street.

PATRICK O'DONNELL, shot and killed by troops, Tuesday, July 14.

PHILIP O'REILLY, of 51 Willet Street, shot and killed by troops in Pitt Street on the morning of Tuesday, July 14.

ELLEN PERKINSON, died July 16.

PETER QUINN, of 264 West 37th Street, shot at the corner of Ninth Avenue and 44th Street, and died July 14.

JOHN REILLY, received head injuries on Tuesday, July 14, and died the same day.

MICHAEL H. RYAN, of 180 West 25th Street, shot in Ninth Avenue, near 29th Street, on Tuesday, July 14, and died the following day.

ANTON SCHMIDT, died of gunshot wounds on Tuesday, July 14.

WILLIAM STEVENS, of 225 Water Street, shot by troops in Pitt Street on the morning of Tuesday, July 14.

ALEXANDER STEWART, received a serious saber cut from a soldier in West 33rd Street on Wednesday, July 15, and died on July 23.

MICHAEL SULLIVAN, of 326 First Avenue, shot by troops in First Avenue on Wednesday, July 15, and died July 18.

WILLIAM HENRY THOMPSON, of 38 Sheriff Street, shot and killed by troops in Pitt Street on the morning of Tuesday, July 14.

JEREMIAH TRACY, shot at Second Avenue and 21st Street on Tuesday, July 14, and died later the same day.

UKELL, Captain, killed in East 19th Street, Wednesday, July 15.

RICHARD WELCH, shot at Seventh Avenue and 32nd Street on Thursday, July 16, and died later the same day.

CATHARINE WATERS, of 252 East 18th Street, shot by troops in First Avenue on Tuesday, July 14, and died August 8.

William Cooper Williams, of 25 Clinton Avenue, Brooklyn, an on-looker, shot in First Avenue on Tuesday, July 14, and died the same day.

Edward Zugenbuhler, shot at the corner of First Avenue and 24th Street, July 15, and died the same day.

Together with the fourteen unidentified bodies whose deaths can be attributed to the riots, this gives a definite death toll of 105. Five of these fourteen bodies whose names could not be discovered at the time can be identified as:

James Costello, of 97 West 33rd Street, beaten and hanged by the mob in West 32nd Street on Wednesday, July 15.

Abraham Franklin, of Seventh Avenue and 27th Street, beaten and hanged by the mob at Seventh Avenue and 28th Street on Wednesday, July 15.

Samuel Johnson, beaten and thrown into the East River to drown, Thursday evening, July 16.

William Jones, beaten and hanged by the mob in Clarkson Street on Monday evening, July 13.

William Williams, beaten to death by rioters in Leroy Street on Tuesday morning, July 14.

A sixth body can be tentatively identified as Fireman McGonigal of No. 17 Engine Company, killed at the burning of the armory at Second Avenue and 21st Street. Four more of the unidentified lost their lives in the fire there, too. Of the others, one died of head injuries after being clubbed; one was shot in the head at the corner of Second Avenue and 24th Street; one was a young boy about 13 years of age who died of injuries received at Second Avenue and 21st Street on Tuesday, July 14; and one was found shot dead on the corner of Second Avenue and 22nd Street on the night of Thursday, July 16.

None of these bodies fitted the descriptions of three men reported missing:

Robert Proctor, Private, 19th Co., 1st Battalion, U.S. Invalid Corps, who was never seen again after the battle in Third Avenue on Monday, July 13.

Jeremiah Robinson, beaten to death by the mob in Madison Street. His body was thrown into the river.

Joseph Thompson, of 105 West 27th Street, vanished during the riots and was never seen again.

Three people died in circumstances which suggest that they may have been taking part in the rioting:

Catherine Carbery, died July 22 of "injuries accidentally received by falling out of a window."

Lawrence Culboy, died by "falling from the window of House No. 355

West 29th Street July 13th, 1863 accidental or intentional the jury are unable to determine."

MARY DONAHUE, died July 15 at 123 First Avenue of "injuries accidentally received from falling off the roof of the above premises."

Two men were described as victims of the riot in the newspapers:

CHARLES E. DAVIS, died August 7 of a gunshot wound received in 21st Street, near Sixth Avenue.

WILLIAM JOHNSON, died July 22 of a beating received on Tuesday, July 14, near Burling Slip.

But the coroners did not describe these deaths as caused by the riots. Then there are six deaths related to the riot:

PETER HUSTEN, died July 27. "The jury found that his death was the result of congestion of the liver, accelerated by blows received at the hands of the mob."

TERENCE SLAVIN, of 296 West 45th Street, shot by troops in Tenth Avenue, between 41st and 42nd streets, on Tuesday, July 14, and died October 29.

JOHN STARKEY, a volunteer special policeman, clubbed in Second Avenue on Thursday, July 16, and died January 20, 1864.

JOHN T. VAN BUREN, patrolman, 8th Precinct, Metropolitan Police, received a broken leg on Monday, July 13, and died November 7. The coroner's jury brought in a verdict of "exhaustion from injuries received while engaged in suppressing a riot July 13th, 1863."

LYDIA VANTHORN, "residing at No. 121, Broome Street, was driven from her house by the rioters while suffering under illness, and took refuge in a police stationhouse. That place, however, was already overcrowded, and she was compelled to seek protection elsewhere, but fell in the street in consequence of weakness. She failed rapidly after this, and died" in early August.

CHARLES WATSON, of 94 Attorney Street, died August 21. "Deceased was consumptive, and the beating he received at the hands of the rioters accelerated his death."

It is possible that out of the ten men, one woman, two female children, and one male child whose unidentified bodies were washed up around the shores of New York City and Brooklyn from July 15 to July 31, some may have been victims of the riots. Vincent Colyer, in his report on the relief operations among Negro refugees sponsored by the Merchants' Committee, mentions four more victims of the mob: Joseph Jackson, Joseph Reed (aged 7), William Henry Nichols, and a three-day-old baby. None of these deaths can be documented from any other source. It is possible that some refugees thought they would receive more aid if they could boast a death in their family.

# II

## *The Wounded*

*A.   Soldiers*

H. AHRENS, 3rd Hussars, shoulder dislocated.

JOHN ALCOCK, Private, 15th Co., 1st Battalion, U.S. Invalid Corps, left arm broken and beaten by the mob in East 40th Street on Monday, July 13. Brought to Bellevue Hospital at 3:30 P.M. that day by Officer Frost of the 21st Precinct from 133 East 40th Street, where he was hidden in a basement. Transferred from Bellevue to the General Hospital Ladies' Home, July 31, 1863, for convalescence, and returned to duty October 20, 1863.

JAMES F. ARLIS, 5th U.S. Artillery, admitted to the New York Hospital with a gunshot wound in the hand July 17 and discharged July 20.

FREDERICK ASMUS, Private, 19th Co., 1st Battalion, U.S. Invalid Corps, beaten Monday, July 13, in the fight at Third Avenue and 43rd Street.

ATCHISON, seriously injured. No further details available.

MYRON AUSTIN, a volunteer with the Hawkins' Zouaves, a veteran of the Eighth Regiment, New York National Guard, shot in the knee Wednesday night in the fight at First Avenue and East 19th Street.

JOSEPH BARBER, Co. A, 9th New York Volunteers, gunshot wound in the head and facial contusions.

THORNTON BIRDSALL, volunteer member of Colonel Winslow's command, seriously injured at the battle in East 19th Street on the evening of Wednesday, July 15.

LUDWIG BORCHESS, Private, 19th Co., 1st Battalion, U.S. Invalid Corps, beaten Monday, July 13, in the fight at Third Avenue and 43rd Street.

GODFREY BROWENSTEIN, Co. C, 12th New York Artillery, broken leg.

JAMES BRUNTON, Private, 19th Co., 1st Battalion, U.S. Invalid Corps, beaten Monday, July 13, in the fight at Third Avenue and 43rd Street.

ROBERT CALLAGHAN, Co. C, 37th Regiment, gunshot wound in the leg.

CARDOE, Sergeant, Co. F, 12th U.S. Infantry, minor flesh wound in the hand received at Second Avenue and 31st Street on the evening of Thursday, July 16.

HENRY CLAY, Co. A, 12th New York Artillery, lacerated head wound and gunshot wound in the arm.

NICHOLAS DIRARD, 31st New York Volunteers, ribs fractured.

TIMOTHY DUNN, Private, 19th Co., 1st Battalion, U.S. Invalid Corps, beaten Monday, July 13, in the fight at Third Avenue and 43rd Street.

FEARING, Major, received lacerated wounds on the head and a fractured skull in a fight at 42nd Street and Tenth Avenue on Tuesday, July 14.

PATRICK FITZPATRICK, Co. B, 12th New York Artillery, contused wounds on the head.

DANIEL GALVIN, Co. A, 12th New York Volunteers, concussion of the brain from blows on the head.

NICHOLAS GERARD, Co. B, 31st New York Volunteers, bruises.

JOHN E. HARRINGTON, 8th New York Artillery, gunshot wound in the arm.

JAMES A. D. HOPPS, Private, 19th Co., 1st Battalion, U.S. Invalid Corps, contusion of knees from beating received in the fight at Third Avenue and 43rd Street on Monday, July 13. Taken to the New York Hospital; transferred to the General Hospital Ladies' Home July 19 for convalescence and returned to duty September 1.

JACOB HORLACHER, Corporal, 19th Co., 1st Battalion, U.S. Invalid Corps, beaten in the fight at Third Avenue and 43rd Street on Monday, July 13.

JARDINE, Lieutenant Colonel, 9th New York Volunteers, Hawkins' Zouaves, shot in the thigh on Wednesday evening, July 15, in East 19th Street, near First Avenue.

EMILE JERRASSE, 5th New York Volunteers, fractured skull and gunshot wound in the arm.

MICHAEL JOYCE, 31st New York Volunteers, contused wounds.

JAMES KANE, 4th Sergeant, 19th Co., 1st Battalion, U.S. Invalid Corps, lacerated face wound received in the fight at Third Avenue and 43rd Street on Monday, July 13. Taken to Bellevue Hospital, transferred to the General Hospital Ladies' Home July 19 and returned to duty July 23.

WILLIAM KAVANAGH, Private, 19th Co., 1st Battalion, U.S. Invalid Corps, beaten in the fight at Third Avenue and 43rd Street on Monday, July 13.

MORRIS KIBBE, 12th U.S. Infantry, received a scalp wound in the fight at Fifth Avenue and 46th Street on the afternoon of Tuesday, July 14. Taken to Jews' Hospital by Officer Demarest of the 20th Precinct; discharged July 23; returned to duty September 23.

ERNEST KOBER, Private, 19th Co., 1st Battalion, U.S. Invalid Corps, beaten in the fight at Third Avenue and 43rd Street on Monday, July 13.

CHARLES KOLB, 8th New York Artillery, scalp wound, admitted to Jews' Hospital July 14, discharged July 29.

KROUSE, Private, 12th U.S. Infantry, slightly wounded in East 22nd Street, Thursday night, July 16.

JOHN LUCAS, Co. C, 12th New York Artillery, contused wounds on the head.

JAMES MCLANE, 17th New York Volunteers, contused wound on the head.

HENRY MCMAHON, Private, 17th New York Veteran Volunteers, received head injuries at Second Avenue and 22nd Street on Tuesday, July 14. Went to Bellevue Hospital by himself at 4:15 P.M.; transferred to the General Hospital Ladies' Home on July 20; transferred to the Convalescent Hospital at Fort Wood, Bedloe's Island, where he deserted, August 13. (The *New York Tribune* reported that McMahon was attacked by some rioters because he was wearing the U.S. Army uniform, but there is a certain possibility that he was a rioter. Why was he not with his regiment? And why was he on the spot at the time of the Union Steam Works battle? On the other hand, he may have been on his way to report for duty and simply blundered into the mob by chance.)

HENRY MALTSEY, Co. G, 1st New York Volunteers, contused wounds on the head.

JAMES MANNELLY, Corning Cavalry, admitted to the New York Hospital with debility July 16 and discharged August 4.

THOMAS MARSDEN, 2nd Co., Light Cavalry, admitted to the New York Hospital with a bayonet wound in the thigh July 14. Discharged July 25.

DENNIS MULLIN, gunshot wound in the head.

THOMAS NEILL, Private, Co. A, 11th New York Volunteers, badly bruised about the face.

WILLIAM NEILL, Private, 19th Co., 1st Battalion, U.S. Invalid Corps, beaten in the fight at Third Avenue and 43rd Street on Monday, July 13. Admitted to the New York Hospital with fractured ribs and contusion of the back, transferred to the General Hospital Ladies' Home July 19 and returned to duty September 7.

CORNELIUS O'KEEFE, Private, 19th Co., 1st Battalion, U.S. Invalid Corps, beaten in the fight at Third Avenue and 43rd Street on Monday, July 13.

ORLANDO PATRICK, a citizen volunteer, formerly a lieutenant in the Army of the Potomac, invalided out after being wounded at Fredericksburg. Seriously wounded at 34th Street on Wednesday, July 15.

AUGUST RENNAN, 31st New York Volunteers, admitted to Jews' Hospital with a scalp wound July 14 and discharged July 31.

CHRISTOPHER ROBERTS, 31st New York Volunteers, admitted to the New York Hospital with a gunshot wound of the arm.

CHARLES ROEDEL, Private, 19th Co., 1st Battalion, U.S. Invalid Corps, beaten in the fight at Third Avenue and 43rd Street on Monday, July 13.

DANIEL RUBSAMEN, Private, 19th Co., 1st Battalion, U.S. Invalid Corps, scalp wound received in the fight at Third Avenue and 43rd Street on Monday, July 13. Taken to Bellevue Hospital at 10:10 P.M. by Officer Smith of the 21st Precinct from the precinct station house. Transferred to the General Hospital Ladies' Home July 19 and returned to duty July 23. (In April 1864 Rubsamen was again in the General Hospital Ladies' Home and was discharged from the service due to disability on May 12, 1864. Possibly his riot wound caused or contributed to the disability.)

RUNK, 17th New York Volunteers, shot in the leg and severely wounded in First Avenue on the night of Wednesday, July 15.

JOSEPH RUTGER, Co. A, 17th New York Volunteers, shot in the face and hand. (This was the soldier who was running away in 42nd Street on Tuesday, July 14.)

DANIEL SALVIS, Co. A, 12th New York Artillery, bruises.

ADAM SCHWEND, Co. C, 65th New York State National Guard, slightly injured in the knee.

JOHN SELLEGER, 178th New York Volunteers, scalp wound, admitted to Jews' Hospital July 14 and discharged July 29.

ALFRED SKINNER, 178th New York Volunteers, contused wounds.

JOHN SMITH, Co. A, 9th New York Volunteers, contused wounds.

CORNELIUS SNEDECKER, Co. A, 9th New York Volunteers, contusion.

AUGUST SOLGERT, Co. H, 7th New York Volunteers, lacerated wounds on the head.

SAMUEL STERN, a citizen volunteer, contused wound on the head.

CHARLES STOLTZ, 17th New York Volunteers, contused wounds on the head. Treated at the 35th Street Arsenal, then sent to the General Hospital Ladies' Home on July 17. Returned to duty July 29.

ALEX. TATE, Co. G, 13th New York Cavalry, contused nose wound.

WILLIAM TAYLOR, Co. G, 9th New York Volunteers, contused wounds of the head.

JOHN THOBY, Private, 19th Co., 1st Battalion, U.S. Invalid Corps, received a scalp wound in the fight at Third Avenue and 43rd Street on Monday, July 13. Taken to the New York Hospital July 14, transferred to the General Hospital Ladies' Home July 19, returned to duty August 18.

UPTON, Lieutenant, wounded in East 19th Street, July 15.

FERDINAND WESTERMON, Private, U.S. Invalid Corps, accidentally wounded by gunshot in the knee, Monday, July 13.

JABEZ P. WHITE, Assistant Surgeon, 9th New York Volunteers, received a head wound when captured by the mob, First Avenue and 19th Street, on the evening of Wednesday, July 15.

MARTIN WOODS, Co. A, 31st New York Volunteers, contused wounds on the head.

In addition, the surgeons at the 35th Street Arsenal failed to obtain the names of five militiamen whom they treated for head wounds, one they treated for fractured ribs, one man of the 11th New York Volunteers who had been shot in the foot, and one citizen volunteer who had been shot in the arm.

This gives a total of 35 soldiers seriously wounded and 38 slightly wounded.

## B. *Police*

Except where noted, the wounded officers were patrolmen:

JAMES ADAMS, 7th Precinct, accidentally shot in the thigh, Monday, July 13.

JOSEPH ADAMS, 8th Precinct, slightly hurt.

JOHN C. ANDRE, 8th Precinct, head cut, Third Avenue, 12:30 P.M., Monday, July 13.

ARNOUX, 18th Precinct, beaten on the morning of Monday, July 13.

HUGH BARKLEY, 8th Precinct, head cut.

H. BASSFORD, 28th Precinct, scalp wounds, received in Third Avenue, 11:30 A.M., Monday, July 13.

JOHN M. BENNETT, 15th Precinct, beaten, Third Avenue, 11:30 A.M., Monday, July 13, and taken to St. Luke's Hospital.

BERTHOLF, 12th Precinct, badly beaten while reconnoitering in Harlem early on the morning of Tuesday, July 14.

EDWIN BODINE, 15th Precinct, beaten, Third Avenue, 11:30 A.M., Monday, July 13.

RICHARD BOLEMAN, 28th Precinct, injured by the mob, Lexington Avenue and 43rd Street.

BLACKWOOD, 9th Precinct, three ribs broken.

EDWARD T. BROUGHTON, 15th Precinct, cuts and an eye injury, Third Avenue, 11:30 A.M., Monday, July 13.

JOHN H. BRYAN, 28th Precinct, scalp wounds received in Third Avenue, 11:30 A.M., Monday, July 13.

SIMON BURNS, 8th Precinct, head wound received in Third Avenue, 12:30 P.M., Monday, July 13.

HIRAM CHANDLER, 25th Precinct, head injury received on the corner of First Avenue and 34th Street, Thursday, July 16. Taken to Bellevue Hospital. "He was escorted to the Hospital by a large detachment of police and a force of the 7th Regiment, to protect him from the mob."

CHERRY, Sergeant, 1st Precinct, beaten, New Street, Monday, July 13.

CHOLWELL, 9th Precinct, back injury.

WILLIAM J. COLE, 18th Precinct, slightly wounded on Monday, July 13.

JOHN COOK, 19th Precinct, seriously injured at the Ninth District draft office, Monday, July 13, trying to protect Chief Clerk Vanderpoel.

GEORGE CROLINS, Roundsman, 8th Precinct, dangerously stabbed in two places, Third Avenue, 12:30 P.M., Monday, July 13.

CROCKER, 9th Precinct, head injury.

FREDERICK DAPKE, 28th Precinct, beaten, Third Avenue, 11:30 A.M., Monday, July 13.

DAVIS, 4th Precinct, beaten by the mob, July 14.

T. A. DELANEY, 15th Precinct.

DEMAREST, 15th Precinct.

D. DIDWAY, 15th Precinct, beaten and eye injured, Third Avenue, 11:30 A.M., Monday, July 13.

FREDERICK ELLISON, Sergeant, 8th Precinct, badly cut and beaten, Third Avenue, 12:30 P.M., Monday, July 13.

DANIEL FIELD, 3rd Precinct, wounded in the right arm at Brooks Brothers.

ALANSON FINCH, Sergeant, 17th Precinct, severe gash on the forehead, Third Avenue, noon, Monday, July 13.

FINNEY, Sergeant, 3rd Precinct, shot in the face at Brooks Brothers, Cherry and Catharine streets, on the night of Tuesday, July 14.

L. A. FLEMING, 29th Precinct, head injury received on Third Avenue, Monday, July 13. Taken to Bellevue Hospital by Officer Gunner of the same precinct, 3:05 P.M.

FOLLIS, 27th Precinct, arm injury received at the Union Steam Works on the afternoon of Tuesday, July 14.

CHARLES FOLSOM, a volunteer special, wrist broken.

FORTIER, 15th Precinct.

EDWARD FOSTER, 15th Precinct, cut and beaten, Third Avenue, 11:30 A.M., Monday, July 13.

GABRIEL, 15th Precinct, beaten, Third Avenue, 11:30 A.M., Monday, July 13.

GARDINER, 26th Precinct, leg injury received in the fight at the *Tribune* office, Monday, July 13.

GASS, 11th Precinct, struck on the head by stones.

JOHN GIBBS, 15th Precinct, beaten and seriously injured in Third Avenue, 11:30 A.M., Monday, July 13. Taken to St. Luke's Hospital.

GRUBELSTEIN, 18th Precinct, beaten by the mob and sprained his ankle escaping from them in East 24th Street, Monday, July 13.

JOHN HART, 8th Precinct, head cut.

THOMAS HENDERSON, 29th Precinct, head injury received at the armory, Second Avenue and 21st Street, on Monday, July 13. Taken to Bellevue Hospital at 5:45 P.M.

HERRING, knocked unconscious by a stone, Third Avenue, Monday, July 13.

HILL, 17th Precinct, hurt at Third Avenue and 46th Street, Monday, July 13.

JOHN R. HILL, 26th Precinct, accidentally shot by troops while clearing rioters from the Gibbons house in West 29th Street on Tuesday, July 14. Taken to the New York Hospital.

JOSHUA HODGSON, Broadway Squad, accidentally shot by troops while clearing rioters from the Gibbons house in West 29th Street on Tuesday, July 14. Taken to the New York Hospital.

JOHN HOLLEY, 28th Precinct, beaten and received a broken finger, Third Avenue, 11:30 A.M., Monday, July 13.

W. J. HOLMES, 29th Precinct.

HOPKINS, Roundsman, 6th Precinct, struck on the head by a stone, Broome and Mott streets, Monday, July 13.

THOMAS JARVIS, injured.

KENNEDY, 4th Precinct, beaten by the mob on the night of Tuesday, July 14.

JOHN A. KENNEDY, Superintendent, severely beaten, Third Avenue, Monday, July 13.

TERENCE KIERNAN, 15th Precinct, beaten on Third Avenue, 11:30 A.M., Monday, July 13.

JAMES KNIGHT, 28th Precinct, chest injury received on Third Avenue, 11:30 A.M., Monday, July 13.

LARKIN, 9th Precinct, head cut.

LARUE, 18th Precinct, beaten on Third Avenue, noon, Monday, July 13.

CHARLES R. LAW, 8th Precinct, head injury received in Third Avenue, Monday, July 13. Taken to Bellevue Hospital at 1:50 P.M.

CHARLES C. LEAYCROFT, 29th Precinct.

DAVID MCCALL, 8th Precinct, beaten and foot injured in Third Avenue, 12:30 P.M., Monday, July 13.

JOHN MCCARTY, 29th Precinct, badly injured on Monday, July 13.

MCCORD, 26th Precinct, clubbed by mistake when on plainclothes duty at the *Tribune* office, Monday, July 13.

MCCLEARY, Sergeant, 1st Precinct, badly beaten while trying to rescue a Negro from the mob in New Street, Monday night, July 13.

ROBERT A. MCCREDIE, Sergeant, 15th Precinct, struck on the wrist by an iron bar in the fight on Third Avenue, 11:30 A.M., Monday, July 13.

MCDONALD, 9th Precinct, three teeth knocked out.

CHARLES MCDONNELL, 6th Precinct, beaten and his face badly cut, Mott and Centre streets, Wednesday, July 15.

MCMAHON, 11th Precinct, badly injured, Roosevelt and Batacia streets, night of Monday, July 13.

GEORGE MAGGASUPPI, 8th Precinct, head wound received on Third Avenue, 12:30 P.M., Monday, July 13.

MANGIN, Sergeant, 9th Precinct, abdominal injuries.

EDWARD MASON, 3rd Precinct, thrown from a housetop by rioters.

C. W. MEHRER, 8th Precinct, beaten on Third Avenue, 12:30 P.M., Monday, July 13.

W. H. MINGAY, 15th Precinct, beaten on Third Avenue, 11:30 A.M., Monday, July 13.

PATRICK MORRISON, 29th Precinct.

CORNELIUS MURRAY, a volunteer special, shot in the groin during the battle in East 22nd Street on Thursday, July 16.

NILDEBERGER, 8th Precinct.

O'BRIEN, 15th Precinct.

MICHAEL C. O'BYRNE, 29th Precinct, clubbed by John McDermott while trying to arrest him, Tuesday, July 14.

FRANCIS PALMER, 8th Precinct, struck by a stone in the fight on Third Avenue, 12:30 P.M., Monday, July 13.

J. PHILLIPS, 15th Precinct.

N. G. PHILLIPS, 15th Precinct, beaten, gashed on the ear, and stabbed in the arm, Third Avenue, 11:30 A.M., Monday, July 13.

FRANCIS PLATT, 4th Precinct, knocked unconscious while clearing the mob from Brooks Brothers' store, Tuesday evening, July 14.

DANIEL POLHAMUS, 28th Precinct, scalp wounds received on Third Avenue, 11:30 A.M., Monday, July 13.

REGAN, 14th Precinct, injured escaping from the mob in Oak Street, night of Tuesday, July 14.

RHODES, 27th Precinct, head injury, Broadway and Amity Street, Monday, July 13.

ALBERT D. ROBINSON, Broadway Squad, accidentally shot in the thigh by troops while clearing rioters from the Gibbons house in West 29th Street on Tuesday, July 14.

ROE, Sergeant, 15th Precinct, tip of a finger shot off, Leonard Street and West Broadway.

RODE, Sergeant, 4th Precinct.

PETER RICE, 26th Precinct, accidentally shot by troops while clearing rioters from the Gibbons house in West 29th Street on Tuesday, July 14.

ROTHSCHILD, 17th Precinct, struck on the head by stones.

JOHN RUSSELL, 9th Precinct, ankle injury.

SANDERSON, 18th Precinct, beaten on Third Avenue, noon, Monday, July 13.

SANDFORD, 10th Precinct, injured in Second Avenue, Tuesday morning, July 14.

JOHN W. SIEBERT, 28th Precinct, received a broken arm in the fight on Third Avenue, 11:30 A.M., Monday, July 13.

S. B. SMITH, Sergeant, 9th Precinct, severely injured in the fight on Third Avenue, 12:30 P.M., Monday, July 13.

JOHN B. SUTHERLAND, 15th Precinct, seriously injured in the fight on Third Avenue, 11:30 A.M., Monday, July 13, and taken to St. Luke's Hospital.

SWAINSON, 29th Precinct.

TRAIN, 29th Precinct.

WILLIAM H. TRAVIS, 15th Precinct, injured, Third Avenue, 11:30 A.M., Monday, July 13, and taken to St. Luke's Hospital.

JOHN WALSH, 9th Precinct, head injuries; taken to the New York Hospital.

JACOB B. WARLOW, Captain, 1st Precinct, foot injured, Second Avenue, Tuesday morning, July 14.

H. N. WARREN, 11th Precinct, struck on the head by stones at the battle in East 34th Street, Tuesday, July 14.

WARTTEMIRE, 9th Precinct, left arm dislocated.

WILLIAM H. WELLING, Sergeant, 1st Precinct, shot in the back by rioters at the *Tribune* office on the night of Monday, July 13.

WEIL, 17th Precinct, hurt at Third Avenue and 46th Street, morning of Monday, July 13.

WOLFE, Sergeant, 28th Precinct, head injury received in Third Avenue, 11:30 A.M., Monday, July 13.

THOMAS WYNNE, 18th Precinct, head injury and stab wound in the right arm received in Third Avenue, noon, Monday, July 13. Taken to Bellevue Hospital at 2:20 P.M. by Officer Duryea of the same precinct.

This gives a total of 32 policemen seriously hurt and 73 slightly wounded.

## C.   Rioters and Victims

JEREMIAH ALLEN, clubbed at Second Avenue and 22nd Street on Tuesday, July 14, and taken to Bellevue Hospital at 5 P.M. with head injuries.

ELIZABETH ANDERSON, an "aged" Negro, "badly beaten about the head by Irishwomen, who attacked her in her own yard." Taken to New York Hospital.

JAMES HENRY ARMSTRONG, Negro, beaten by rioters in their attack on 72 Roosevelt Street on Monday, July 13.

WILLIAM ARMSTRONG, Negro, badly beaten by rioters in their attack on 74–76 Roosevelt Street on Monday, July 13, and taken to the New York Hospital.

GEORGE BARKER, beaten by the mob for harboring injured police in his house, corner of Lexington Avenue and 41st Street, Monday, July 13.

CORNELIUS BARRETT, 11, shot in the leg during the First Avenue riot, Thursday, July 16.

STEPHEN BENSON, Negro, beaten by the mob and had his thumb broken at 74 Roosevelt Street, Monday, July 13.

BERRY, Negro, daughter of Mrs. Sarah Berry of 223 West 26th Street, broke her arm when jumping out of a back window to escape the rioters at 11 P.M., Monday, July 13.

PATRICK BOYLE, shot and taken to the New York Hospital.

FRANCIS BRADY, 15, shot in the right arm by troops on the corner of Ninth Avenue and 41st Street, Tuesday, July 14. Taken to Bellevue Hospital by his father, 9:30 P.M.

JOHN BROWN, Negro, beaten by the mob at 84 Roosevelt Street, Monday, July 13.

BUHRER, Ex-Lieutenant in the 7th New York Volunteers, beaten at East 45th Street and Lexington Avenue on the afternoon of Monday, July 13.

AUSTIN BULGER, shot in the left arm by troops in East 24th Street on Thursday, July 16.

CHARLES BURKE, taken to the New York Hospital with a gunshot wound in the neck.

HENRY CANON, taken to the New York Hospital with gunshot wounds.

ELLEN CLYNE, taken to Bellevue Hospital with a head wound received on the corner of Avenue A and Eleventh Street on Thursday, July 16.

JOHN CONROY, badly beaten about the head and taken to the New York Hospital.

MARY CRAWFORD, injuries received when struck by a brick while the mob was battling police on Third Avenue at noon, Monday, July 13.

CULLEN, wounded in the shin while watching the mob in Pitt Street, Tuesday, July 14.

MARIA DE LAMASTANY, shot in the hip in Second Avenue on the evening of Thursday, July 16, and taken to Bellevue Hospital.

C. L. DE RENDANNI, a merchant from Bassa County, Liberia, beaten by rioters on Tuesday, July 14.

WILLIAM DEVINE, shot and taken to the New York Hospital.

DANIEL DONNELLY, a discharged soldier, admitted to Bellevue Hospital with an arm injury July 13 and left hospital on July 23.

FREDERICK DUGGANS, a small boy, shot in the leg in First Avenue.

ELIZA ELLIOTT, 9, taken from her home at 110 East 27th Street to Bellevue Hospital with a gunshot wound of the face on Thursday, July 16.

JAMES ENGLISH, a serving soldier, brought to Bellevue Hospital by his wife at 6:15 P.M., Tuesday, July 14, with injuries received when he was clubbed at First Avenue and 22nd Street. Left hospital July 27.

JOHN ENNIS, 16, came to Bellevue Hospital by himself at 12:30 P.M., Tuesday, July 14, with head injuries caused by clubbing.

BRIDGET FARLEY, received a head wound in Washington Street, July 15.

MARY FEEKS, Negro, beaten severely by the mob.

LEWIS FREEMAN, 11, taken to Bellevue Hospital at 2:40 P.M., Tuesday, July 14, after being shot in the right hip at Second Avenue and 22nd Street.

GIBSON, shot in the hand in Grant Street, Tuesday, July 14.

ADDISON GRANT, beaten by the mob at Third Avenue and 45th Street.

JOHN GETTY, shot and taken to the New York Hospital.

JAMES HAGGERTY, shot through the lung in First Avenue.

CHARLES HAVERING, shot in 42nd Street between Ninth and Tenth avenues and taken to Bellevue Hospital.

WILLIAM HENRY HEATH, Negro, badly beaten at 63 Roosevelt Street on Monday, July 13, and taken to the New York Hospital.

JOSEPH HECHT, beaten by rioters who invaded his home at 229 Avenue A because he had been an enrolling officer.

MICHAEL HEWITT, shot in the neck by troops in Pitt Street, Tuesday, July 14, and taken to Bellevue Hospital.

HEWITT, priest, severely injured by a slingshot while attempting to calm a mob.

WILLIAM W. HILL, Negro, hurt jumping out of a third-story window in a burning house, 62 Roosevelt Street, Monday, July 13.

MICHAEL HUGHES, shot in the neck in Pitt Street, Tuesday, July 14, and taken to Bellevue Hospital.

JOHN HUSSEY, shot in the leg by troops in Pitt Street, Tuesday, July 14.

CHARLES JACKSON, Negro, beaten and thrown in the river at the foot of Morris Street.

HENRY JOHNSON, Negro, beaten and part of his left ear bitten off, Monday, July 13.

THOMAS JOHNSON, Negro, broke his arm jumping from an upper window in a burning building, 62 Roosevelt Street.

L. L. JONES, shot; apparently a bystander.

MICHAEL KAGAN, admitted to the New York Hospital with a gunshot wound in his thigh.

VALENTINE KASE, badly beaten by rioters at Second Avenue and 36th Street, Monday, July 13.

JAMES KEEGAN, a fireman, injured.

WILLIAM KELLY, 14, shot in the left thigh in Pitt Street, Tuesday, July 14. Taken to Bellevue Hospital at 12:45 P.M. by Officer Nixon of the 7th Precinct.

PATRICK KINLON, a fireman, injured.

JOHN LAMB, clubbed in a looters' quarrel, Thursday, July 16, and taken to Bellevue Hospital.

JOHN LANE, Negro, beaten outside his home, 273 West 28th Street.

LAWRENCE, infant son of Mrs. Delia Lawrence, shot when his mother was killed.

J. LEONARD, beaten by rioters, Wednesday, July 15.

THOMAS LEWIS, Negro, beaten in Monroe Street, near Market, and taken to Bellevue Hospital with head injuries by Officer Wilkinson of the 7th Precinct, noon, Tuesday, July 14.

WILLIAM LIPMAN, beaten by rioters while defending his clothing store at 424 Third Avenue.

MARGARET LIVINGSTON, wounded in the thigh by a shot, reportedly from the 35th Street Arsenal, between 7 and 8 A.M., Wednesday, July 15, when she was coming out of a grocery store at Seventh Avenue and 26th Street.

DANIEL McAULIFFE, shot in the groin at the corner of Third Avenue and 35th Street, Thursday, July 16, and taken to Bellevue Hospital.

MICHAEL McCANN, attacked on Thursday, July 16, by Patrick Oatis, who bit off his left ear and part of his right.

MICHAEL McCARTY, clubbed at Second Avenue and 22nd Street and taken to Bellevue Hospital at 12:30 P.M., Tuesday, July 14.

BARNEY MacKAY, shot in both legs by troops, Ninth Avenue, between 39th and 40th streets, Thursday, July 16.

EMANUEL McCONKEY, Negro, beaten by the mob at 76 Roosevelt Street, Monday, July 13.

JOHN McDERMOTT, a serving soldier, clubbed and had his arm broken while resisting arrest, Tuesday, July 14, near City Hall. Escaped from the New York Hospital the following day.

ANGUS McDONALD, bruised head and broken rib received in Franklin Street, taken to the New York Hospital.

JOHN McDONALD, shot by troops, Thursday, July 16.

FRANCIS McLASKEY, shot in the head in West 41st Street and taken to Bellevue Hospital.

THOMAS MACKIN, taken to New York Hospital with a bayonet wound inflicted by the sentinel at Lafayette Hall.

JOSEPH MCMULLEN, wounded in Pitt Street, Tuesday, July 14, and taken to the New York Hospital.

PATRICK MCSWEENEY, shot in both legs by troops in East 19th Street and taken to Bellevue Hospital at 3:30 P.M., Tuesday, July 14.

MICHAEL MAHAN, shot in the left shoulder at the corner of First Avenue and 17th Street, Thursday, July 16, and taken to Bellevue Hospital.

MARCELLA MAHONEY, shot in the left breast at Second Avenue and 22nd Street and taken to Bellevue Hospital by her sister at 7:15 P.M., Tuesday, July 14.

WILLIAM MALCOLMSON, badly beaten and shot in the forehead in East 34th Street; taken to Bellevue Hospital.

JOHN MILLER, shot in the left leg in First Avenue, Thursday, July 16, and taken to Bellevue Hospital.

PATRICK MORGAN, shot in the left arm in East 18th Street.

JOHN MORTON, taken to the New York Hospital, suffering from "over excitement" while engaged in a fight in 22nd Street, near Second Avenue.

JOHN MULHARE, 8, shot in the right eye while standing at a window looking at the rioters and military in East 35th Street. Taken to Bellevue Hospital by his brother, 12:30 P.M., Tuesday, July 14.

DENNIS MURPHY, a fireman, injured.

HOWARD MURPHY, shot in the right arm at Second Avenue and 22nd Street and taken to Bellevue Hospital by Officer Schofield of the 18th Precinct at 3:55 P.M., Monday, July 13.

JOHN MURRAY, taken to Bellevue Hospital suffering from burns received at the armory, Second Avenue and 21st Street, Monday, July 13.

JOHN NICHOLSON, shot in Clarkson Street, Monday, July 13, by a Negro whom he was chasing. Taken to the New York Hospital and discharged in mid-August.

JOHN O'CONNOR, shot in the right thigh at Second Avenue and 22nd Street and taken to Bellevue Hospital.

MICHAEL O'CONNOR, beaten in Oliver Street. Taken to the New York Hospital.

Mrs. MARY OLWELL, wounded in the right arm while watching the mob in Pitt Street, Tuesday, July 14.

R. PETTIGREW, head cut when attacked by rioters at Third Avenue and 46th Street, July 13.

EDWARD PLUMMER, beaten about the head in Second Avenue. Taken to Bellevue Hospital, treated, and discharged.

JACOB PRICE, a discharged soldier, formerly a member of Co. C, 4th Delaware Volunteers, beaten and taken to Bellevue Hospital, Thursday, July 16. Left hospital on July 24.

CORNELIUS REGAN, 11, shot in the left breast in East 19th Street, between First and Second avenues, and taken to Bellevue Hospital at 3 P.M., Tuesday, July 14.

HARMON RENNER, stabbed in the thigh by a Negro and taken to the New York Hospital.

JOHN ROGON, shot in the head at the *Tribune* office and taken to the New York Hospital.

JAMES SCANFIELD, 13, shot in the left arm and left foot at the corner of First Avenue and 22nd Street on Thursday, July 16, and taken to Bellevue Hospital.

JAMES SCOTT, Negro, badly beaten about the head in Roosevelt Street on Monday, July 13, and taken to the New York Hospital.

ERASMUS SCRENDSON, shot in the left foot at the corner of Third Avenue and 21st Street on Thursday, July 16, and taken to Bellevue Hospital.

HENRY E. SEARLES, attacked and robbed by Patrick Sheron and John Hagan at 1 A.M., Tuesday, July 14.

JOHN SHEEHY, shot in the right side in West 74th Street, near Ninth Avenue, Thursday, July 16, and taken to Bellevue Hospital.

TIMOTHY SMITH, beaten by the mob at the corner of Prince and Elizabeth streets, Monday, July 13.

STADIGER, beaten at East 45th Street and Lexington Avenue on the afternoon of Monday, July 13, when he went to the aid of ex-Lieutenant Buhrer.

RICHARD STAFFORD, shot in the right arm at the corner of Eleventh Avenue and 42nd Street and taken to Bellevue Hospital.

BURRIS STEDWELL, Negro, beaten at 99 West 33rd Street, Tuesday, July 14.

CORNELIUS SULLIVAN, shot in the right leg at 46th Street and First Avenue and taken to Bellevue Hospital.

JEREMIAH SULLIVAN, taken to Bellevue Hospital with gunshot wounds of the back and arm received on Thursday, July 16, at First Avenue and 19th Street.

LOUIS TREMAIN, 11, shot in the thigh by troops in East 22nd Street.

JOHN TURNER, Negro, badly beaten about the head at 74 Roosevelt Street, 8 P.M., Monday July 13, and taken to the New York Hospital.

EDWARD S. VANDERPOEL, Chief Clerk, Ninth District Provost-Marshal's Office, beaten by the rioters at Third Avenue and 46th Street, Monday, July 13.

R. VAN FITCH, beaten in Warren Street.

DR. VAN KLEECK, attacked while attending to an injured policeman on July 13.

WILLIAM WATSON, Negro, taken to the New York Hospital with head injuries.

ANDREW WELLEY, shot in the right thigh at First Avenue and 23rd Street and taken to Bellevue Hospital at 3 P.M., Tuesday, July 14.

GEORGE WASHINGTON WILLIAMS, a Negro living in Brooklyn. Beaten by rioters near Fulton Ferry on Tuesday, July 14.

MARY WILLIAMS, Negro, hurt jumping from an upper window of a burning building, 74 Roosevelt Street, and taken to Bellevue Hospital.

JOHN WILSON, Negro, badly beaten at Fulton Ferry, Tuesday, July 14.

In addition, eleven civilians were treated by the surgeons at the 35th Street Arsenal, but did not give their names. Seven had suffered minor injuries; one had an injury of the hips; one had a fractured skull; one had been shot in the groin, and one in the arm. Four unidentified patients were treated at Bellevue. One was a boy who had been clubbed. He stayed the night, ate breakfast, and then jumped over the wall and escaped. The other three were men: one with a fractured skull received in a fight on the corner of First Avenue and 23rd Street; one shot in the forehead at the same place and brought to the hospital at 4 P.M., Tuesday, July 14; and the third was brought in at 1:15 P.M., Monday, July 13, by Officer Kealy, suffering from burns and injuries received at Second Avenue and 40th Street.

Why their names were not recorded is not clear. They may, of course, have died and been listed by the coroners under their names. Alternatively, they may have been unconscious when they were brought in and only gave their names later, when public interest in the riots had flagged. Since the Bellevue records of this period have been destroyed, this possibility cannot be investigated. The New York Hospital records exist, but the authorities there will not allow them to be examined, which makes it impossible to find out more about a nameless man admitted there who had been clubbed by a policeman. A fifteen-year-old boy was admitted to St. Luke's Hospital with concussion on July 13 and discharged the following day. (Because of restrictions imposed by the authorities of St. Luke's, his name cannot be published.)

This gives a total of 128 people injured in some way during the riots.

# III

## The Arrested

WESLEY ADAMS, alias Charles Williams, alias Charles Allen, indicted for grand larceny (stealing a gold watch in a Second Avenue car), August 5. Jumped bail August 7 and was not recaptured until February 1865. Never tried on this charge. Habitual criminal.

GEORGE AMMERMAN, no charges preferred, released.

JOHN H. ANDERSON, no charges preferred, released.

JOHN U. ANDREWS, indicted by a federal grand jury, February 27, 1864, on four charges: treason; conspiracy to levy war against the United States; inciting, setting on foot, and engaging in a rebellion and insurrection against the United States; resisting and counseling and aiding resistance to a draft. Tried in U.S. Circuit Court on the second charge, May 24, 1864, found guilty and sentenced to three years' imprisonment at hard labor.

THOMAS ARMSTRONG, no charges preferred, released.

THEODORE ARNOLD, an illiterate German peddler, 18 years of age. When examined, said "I took said property because everyone else took it." Indicted for grand larceny, pleaded guilty, and was sentenced to five years' hard labor in the State Prison.

ROBERT BAKER, a juvenile, tried and found guilty of petty larceny in the Court of Special Session, July 31. Sent to the House of Refuge.

RICHARD BALENSBURG, arrested at the Catherine Ferry in Brooklyn, with three others, and accused of stealing goods from Brooks Brothers. No charges preferred, released.

MICHAEL BANNIN, a 16-year-old schoolboy, suspected of complicity in the attack on the Derrickson family at 11 Worth Street on Tuesday, July 14. The grand jury did not indict him.

BRIDGET BARRETT, accused of stealing a couple of bars of soap from Henry H. Jones's factory in West 16th Street. The grand jury laid her case over and never took it up again.

MICHAEL BARRY, no charges preferred, released.

FRIEDRICH BASS, no charges preferred, released.

GEORGE BAUER, indicted for first-degree robbery, October 22, 1863, although he claimed to have been forced into it: "A big man caught hold of me by the left hand and coat and compelled me to go with him, and he had a cartrung in his other hand: he said 'If you don't go, I'll strike you.' I went with him because I was afraid of my life." Never brought to trial.

JOSEPH BAVOKE, no charges preferred, released.

MARTIN BEACH, accused of being a leader in the attack on the Union Steam Works and the theft of the guns stored there. When examined, said "I have nothing to say. If a man swears false against me I can't help it." Indicted for riot and assault and battery, October 22, but never brought to trial.

JOHN BECKERLY, no charges preferred, released.

FREDERICK BEILSTEIN, accused of stealing furniture and other articles. No charges preferred, released.

JAMES BEST, indicted October 17 on three charges: riot and assault and battery on Alfred Derrickson; felonious assault and battery on Alfred Derrickson; first-degree murder of Ann Derrickson. Agreed to plead guilty to a charge of assault with intent to kill Alfred Derrickson on January 6, 1864, and was sentenced to two years in the State Prison on January 8, 1864.

JOHN BOYLE, arrested for threatening the destruction of Taylor's foundry in Goerck Street on Friday, July 16. No charges preferred, released.

MICHAEL BOYLE, arrested as a sniper in the West Side riots. No charges preferred, released.

ROSE BOWMAN, indicted for grand larceny, but never brought to trial.

JOHN BRADY, arrested in East 22nd Street as a rioter, Thursday, July 16. No charges preferred, released.

PATRICK BRADY, no charges preferred, released.

MICHAEL BRAY, no charges preferred, released.

THOMAS BRENAN, alleged to have fired repeatedly on the police and troops during the riots on the East Side. No charges preferred, released.

FERGUS BRENNAN, alleged to have been a leader in the West Side mobs. Indicted for riot, August 5, but never brought to trial.

DANIEL BROWN, 15, charged with stealing from a store in Third Avenue which had been broken open by the mob. Said he was innocent. Indicted for burglary, August 11; found guilty and sent to the Juvenile Asylum, August 15.

HUGH BRYAN, accused of taking a leading part in the attack on the Ninth District draft office at 46th Street and Third Avenue. The grand jury refused to indict him.

JOHN BUCKLEY, arrested for possession of property stolen from 1190, 1192, 1194, and 1198 Broadway on Monday, July 13. Tried and found guilty in the Court of Special Session on July 17 and sent to the House of Refuge. A juvenile.

WILLIAM BURNEY, indicted for the first-degree murder of William Williams, a Negro seaman, in Leroy Street on Tuesday, July 14. Tried in Oyer and Terminer, December 9–11, and the jury deadlocked, six for acquittal, six for conviction. Never retried and finally discharged on April 28, 1864.

ALEXANDER BURNS, arrested for possession of property stolen from 1190, 1192, 1194, and 1198 Broadway on Monday, July 13. Tried and found guilty in the Court of Special Session on July 17 and sent to the House of Refuge. A juvenile.

JOHN BURNS, arrested by a patrol of the 16th New York Cavalry for illegally entering a store in Third Avenue. No charges preferred, released.

GEORGE W. BURROWS, indicted for riot and assault and battery on October 28, but never brought to trial.

PATRICK BUTLER, 16, accused of complicity in the murder of Abraham Franklin at Seventh Avenue and 28th Street on Wednesday, July 15. When examined, said "I am not guilty, all I done was to take hold of his private parts." The authorities originally contemplated charging Butler with murder, but as a notation on the indictment papers observed, "Want a name for the crime, August 5, 1863." On August 11 Butler was indicted for an offense against public decency. Next day, he pleaded guilty and was sent to the House of Refuge.

PATRICK BYRNES, accused of attacking Isaac B. Hammond on Tuesday, July 14. Grand jury refused to indict him.

CORNELIUS CALLAGHAN, accused of looting and burning the house of Hiram B. Gray at Third Avenue and 88th Street. Grand jury refused to indict him.

MARY CALLAHAN, no charges preferred, released.

WILLIAM CALLAHAN, no charges preferred, released.

EDWARD CANFIELD, indicted October 17 for the first-degree murder of William Williams, a Negro seaman, in Leroy Street on Tuesday, July 14. Never brought to trial.

DENNIS CAREY, indicted August 4 for the first-degree murder of Abraham Franklin at Seventh Avenue and 28th Street on Wednesday, July 15. Never brought to trial.

PATRICK CARLE, arrested for riotous behavior, Tuesday, July 14. No charges preferred, released.

PATRICK CARNEY, accused of organizing the tearing up of the railroad tracks at Third Avenue and 83rd Street. Grand jury refused to indict him.

JOHN CARR, accused of being one of a mob in Thomas Street. Tried in the Court of Special Session on July 31, found guilty, and sentenced to five days in the City Prison.

JOHN CARRIGAN, no charges preferred, released.

MARIA CARROLL, accused of stealing from a house in West 32nd Street which was attacked and set on fire by the mob on Wednesday, July 15. Grand jury refused to indict her.

MICHAEL CARROLL, no charges preferred, released.

PATRICK CARROLL, indicted for riot and assault and battery, November 17. Never brought to trial.

WILLIAM CARROLL, indicted on two charges on August 11: riot and assault and battery; and third-degree burglary. Never brought to trial.

JAMES CASEY, no charges preferred, released.

MARY CASEY, no charges preferred, released.

JAMES CASSIDY, indicted on two charges on October 22: riot and assault and battery; and second-degree robbery. Never brought to trial.

MICHAEL CAVANAUGH, a juvenile, arrested for participation in the riot—throwing stones, using threatening language, breaking windows and furniture. Tried in the Court of Special Session, July 31, found guilty, and sent to the House of Refuge.

ADAM CHAIRMAN, a habitual criminal, indicted for first-degree robbery, second-degree arson, and three counts of riot and assault and battery. He was charged with, but not indicted for, extortion and looting a store. He pleaded guilty to one count of riot and assault and battery in Oyer and Terminer on October 12 and was sentenced to six months in the City Penitentiary.

MICHAEL CHRYSTIE, no charges preferred, released.

JOHN CLAFF, no charges preferred, released.

BERNARD CLARK, charged with complicity in the burning of Josiah Porter's house in 53rd Street, near Lexington Avenue, on Wednesday, July 15. August 5, indicted for first-degree arson; August 7, indicted for riot and assault and battery. Never brought to trial.

EDWARD CLARY, accused of trying to shoot a policeman. Grand jury refused to indict him.

PATRICK CLOONEY, accused of stealing clothes from Brooks Brothers' store. No charges preferred, released.

PATRICK COADY, a juvenile, accused of possession of stolen goods. No charges preferred, released.

JOHN COBRICK, accused of receiving stolen goods. No charges preferred, released.

LAWRENCE CODY, no charges preferred, released.

PATRICK COFFEE, accused of complicity in the murder of William Jones in Clarkson Street on Monday, July 13. No charges preferred, released.

COLE, a deserter from the 79th New York Volunteers, accused of participation in the riots. No charges were preferred against him by the civil authorities, so presumably he was handed over to the army.

PATRICK COLEMAN, accused of stealing clothes from Brooks Brothers' store. August 4, indicted for grand larceny. Discharged September 18 to enlist.

OLIVER COLINBUSH, no charges preferred, released.

JAMES W. COLLIER, charged with attacking Dr. Oliver A. Jarvis on Monday, July 13. Collier claimed he did not assault Jarvis, though the mob had forced him to join them. Indicted for felonious assault and battery, October 22, but the district attorney entered a nolle prosequi on this case on February 16, 1864: "Satisfied after a full examination that Mr. Collier was not a rioter and that the motives of complainant were mercenary in preferring the charge . . . A. Oakey Hall."

THOMAS CONNERS, accused of stealing from the Gibbons house in Lamartine Place, off West 29th Street. Indicted for grand larceny, August 5; agreed to plead guilty to petit larceny, August 11, and in consideration of his previous good character received a sentence of three months in the City Penitentiary.

DANIEL CONROY, accused of being one of the mob that beat Private John Alcock of the Invalid Corps at Third Avenue and 43rd Street on Monday, July 13. The grand jury refused to indict him.

JOHN CONWAY, of Philadelphia, indicted for first-degree robbery on August 4. Tried, found guilty, and sentenced to fifteen years imprisonment at hard labor in the State Prison.

THOMAS COONEY, accused of throwing stones and brickbats at the police and troops in Ninth Avenue and of possessing carpet taken from Allerton's Hotel on the West Side. Indicted for grand larceny and for riot and assault and battery. Pleaded guilty to the second charge and was sentenced to one year in the City Penitentiary and a fine of $250.

ROBERT CORDACK, no charges preferred, released.

SIMON CORNER, no charges preferred, released.

JOHN CORRIGAN, accused of taking a leading part in the West Side riots on Tuesday, July 14. The grand jury refused to indict him.

JOHN COSTELLO, no charges preferred, released.

EGBERT COX, 19, accused with others of storming a Negro tenement at 28 Cornelia Street on Monday, July 13. Tried in the Court of Special Session, found guilty, and sentenced to sixty days in the City Prison.

FRANCIS X. CRAWLEY, accused of cheering on the rioters at the attack on the Eighth District draft office on Monday, July 13. Indicted for riot and assault and battery, August 4, but never brought to trial.

PATRICK CRONAN, no charges preferred, released.

DAVID CRONIN, no charges preferred, released.

WILLIAM CRUISE, accused of leading the attack on the Derricksons. October 17, indicted for riot and assault and battery on Alfred Derrickson and for the first-degree murder of Ann Derrickson. Tried in Oyer and Terminer, December 21–23, and found guilty of assault with intent to kill Alfred Derrickson. The jury added a recommendation to mercy, but the judge handed down the heaviest sentence possible, two years and four months' imprisonment at hard labor in the State Prison.

THOMAS CUMISKIE, indicted for first-degree robbery on August 5 and for second-degree arson and two counts of riot and assault and battery on August 7. Pleaded guilty to riot and assault and battery in Oyer and Terminer on October 13 and was sentenced to two months in the City Penitentiary.

ROBERT CUNNINGHAM, accused of robbery. The grand jury refused to indict him.

PATRICK CURLY, no charges preferred, released.

PATRICK CURRAN, a juvenile, arrested on suspicion of looting. No charges preferred, released.

FRANCIS CUSICK, accused of rioting, highway robbery, grand larceny, felonious assault and battery, and attempted murder of Superintendent John A. Kennedy. The grand jury refused to indict him.

JOHN L. CYPHERD, no charges preferred, released.

FREDERICK DEDRICK, no charges preferred, released.

ROBERT DE FORREST, arrested for possession of a loaded rifle. No charges preferred, released.

CATHERINE DELANEY, accused of stealing a few bars of soap from Henry H. Jones's factory on Tuesday, July 14. The grand jury refused to indict her.

CHARLES DENNIN, accused of taking a leading part in the rioting on Third Avenue on Monday, July 13. Indicted for riot and assault and battery, October 14, but never brought to trial.

THOMAS DEVINE, no charges preferred, released.

PETER DOLAN, accused of leading the attack on Mayor Opdyke's house, 79 Fifth Avenue, on Tuesday, July 14. Tried in the Court of Special Session, July 24; pleaded guilty and was sentenced to four months in the City Penitentiary.

THOMAS DONAHUE, no charges preferred, released.

CHARLES DONALDSON, accused of being a leader in the attacks on Negroes and their homes on the West Side on Tuesday, July 14, and Wednesday, July 15. The grand jury refused to indict him.

JOHN DONNELLY, accused of threatening Taylor's foundry in Georck Street on Friday, July 17. No charges preferred, released.

MICHAEL DONNELLY, arrested in Greenpoint on July 17 for possession of stolen guns and clothing. Discharged on grounds of insufficient evidence.

MICHAEL DONOHUE, no charges preferred, released.

CHARLES DOWD, 18, accused of robbing Mrs. Magdalena K. Brown. The grand jury refused to indict him, but he was "delivered to Officer Jacob Depuy as a deserter."

GEORGE DOWLING, no charges preferred, released.

EDWARD DOWNING, a longshoreman, accused of making "an incendiary address." No charges preferred, released.

DENNIS DOYLE, no charges preferred, released.

ELLEN DOYLE, accused of robbing Mrs. Magdalena K. Brown. The grand jury refused to indict her.

MICHAEL DOYLE, of Philadelphia, indicted for first-degree robbery, August 4. Found guilty and sentenced to fifteen years at hard labor in the State Prison.

MARY ANN DRISCOLL, of 274 Water Street, accused of stealing furniture and bedding from Dr. William Powell's Globe Hotel at 2 Dover Street. No charges preferred, released.

FRANCIS DUFFY, charged with felonious possession of clothing and books taken from the 18th Precinct station house. No charges preferred, released.

NICHOLAS DUFFY, charged with breaking into the Magdalen Asylum on East 88th Street and stealing money and jewelry, Monday, July 13. Indicted for first-degree burglary, August 5. Jumped bail, but was brought in and committed to the City Jail, August 10. Never brought to trial.

EUGENE DUGAN, no charges preferred, released.

WILLIAM DUGAN, charged with stealing two coats; found guilty in the Court of Special Sessions, July 24, and sent to the House of Refuge.

MICHAEL DUNN, indicted for riot and assault and battery on Josiah T. Porter, October 17. Never brought to trial.

NELSON EDWARDS, born in England, a dentist at 720 Broadway, "charged with making inflammatory speeches to several of the mobs, telling them to give the d—— abolitionists the silent knife, and offering to lead them down town and show them what places to burn." No charges preferred, released.

JAMES ELLIOTT, a notorious thief, pulled in during the Detective Squad's sweep of the lushing cribs. No charges preferred, released.

ULYSSES ELY, indicted for grand larceny, but never brought to trial.

LEONARD ENGLE, no charges preferred, released.

JAMES EVANS, charged with possession of stolen property—the books of Henry H. Jones & Co., 429 West 16th Street, and a few boxes of their soap. No charges preferred, released.

JOHN EVERETT, charged with stealing twelve bedticks, a quilt, and other property from the Colored Orphan Asylum on Monday, July 13. Tried in the Court of Special Session on July 22. No one appeared to identify the property found in Everett's possession, so the judges were obliged to acquit him.

MICHAEL EYERS, 11, accused of taking some liquor from the store of Barney Murtha, 259 Tenth Avenue, after the mob had broken it open. No charges preferred, released.

BERNARD FAGAN, charged with complicity in the burning of Josiah T. Porter's house, indicted for first-degree arson on August 5 and for riot and assault and battery on August 7. Never brought to trial.

CHARLES FARLEY, indicted for robbery, but never brought to trial.

JOHN FARLEY, a juvenile, arrested for possession of stolen goods. No charges preferred, released.

ANN FARRELL, 60, Irish, arrested for stealing from a store in 18th Street. No charges preferred, released.

GEORGE FARRELL, a juvenile, indicted for theft, but never brought to trial.

JAMES FARRELL, a juvenile, arrested for possession of stolen goods. No charges preferred, released.

JOHN FAY, a notorious Philadelphia thief, charged with beating and robbing a soldier in City Hall Park. Discharged on grounds of insufficient evidence.

THOMAS FAY, no charges preferred, released.

MOSES FEENEY, no charges preferred, released.

HENRY FELLBEIN, charged with stealing 120 pairs of gloves, etc., from the store of Lucas Thompson, July 13, with Mary Fox. Indicted for grand larceny, August 12. With the complainant's agreement, he was released October 10 to enlist in the army.

JAMES FINGLETON, 18, accused of stealing clothes from the store of Morris Levy, 377 Third Avenue. The grand jury refused to indict him.

EDWARD FISHER, a juvenile, charged with possession of property stolen from 1190, 1192, 1194, and 1198 Broadway. Tried in the Court of Special Session on July 17, found guilty, and sent to the House of Refuge.

MARTIN FITZGERALD, accused of stealing clothes from the store of Morris Levy, 377 Third Avenue. No charges preferred, released.

MORRIS FITZGERALD, accused of tearing up the track of the Third Avenue Railroad at East 83rd Street on Tuesday, July 14. Tried in the Court of Special Session on July 31, found guilty, and sentenced to the Penitentiary for two months. Fitzgerald had served in the 88th Regiment of Meagher's Irish Brigade, had been wounded, and honorably discharged.

THOMAS FITZGERALD, "a physician, it is said, of some education and skill, but accustomed to drinking and to bad company." Accused of setting fire to Edgar Ketchum's house at Harlem. Indicted for second-degree arson, but never brought to trial.

JAMES FITZGERRON, arrested for suspicious behavior near the *Tribune* building, 3 A.M., July 14. No charges preferred, released.

JOHN FITZHART, no charges preferred, released.

JOHN FITZHERBERT, accused of being a leader in a mob that beat Andrew Houser in West 28th Street and robbed him of a horse and wagon worth $100 and Treasury notes to the value of $70. October 12, indicted for riot, first-degree robbery, and third-degree burglary, but was never brought to trial.

FRANK FITZPATRICK, indicted for murder, never brought to trial.

HUGH FITZPATRICK, no charges preferred, released.

JOHN FITZPATRICK, indicted on August 11 for riot and assault and battery. Released to enlist, October 9.

THOMAS FITZPATRICK, no charges preferred, released.

JOHN FITZSIMMONS, no charges preferred, released.

THOMAS FITZSIMMONS, accused of being in the mob that attacked Jackson's foundry at Second Avenue and 28th Street on Thursday, July 16. The grand jury refused to indict him.

PHIL FITZSIMONS, arrested as a rioter in East 22nd Street on Thursday, July 16.

MICHAEL FLANAGAN, indicted for assault and battery, never brought to trial.

PATRICK FLANAGAN, charged with rioting at Broadway and 4th Street on Monday, July 13. Tried in the Court of Special Session, July 22, found guilty and sentenced to six months in the City Penitentiary.

BENJAMIN FLANIGAN, no charges preferred, released.

JAMES FLANIGAN, indicted for riot on December 18, but never brought to trial.

TIMOTHY FLYNN, no charges preferred, released.

WILLIAM FOSTER, no charges preferred, released.

MARY FOX, also known as Mary Fuchs, accused with Henry Fellbein for stealing from the store of Lucas Thompson and indicted for grand larceny, August 12. Tried in General Sessions, August 13, and pleaded guilty to a charge of attempting to commit grand larceny. Sentenced to two years' imprisonment at hard labor in the State Prison.

BURT FRANCIS, no charges preferred, released.

FRANCIS FRASER, no charges preferred, released.

BRYAN FRIEL, a juvenile, accused of being one of the mob and of striking Charles A. Scher on the head with a stone, Wednesday, July 15. Tried in the Court of Special Session, July 28, found guilty, and sent to the House of Refuge.

RICHARD FRISCOE, charged with stealing goods from Brooks Brothers. Tried in the Court of Special Session on July 31, found guilty, and sent to the City Penitentiary for two months.

STEPHEN GANNON, accused of being one of the mob that attacked the Union Steam Works, Second Avenue and 22nd Street, on Tuesday, July 14. No charges preferred, released.

MILES GARRITY, accused of being one of the mob and of attempted extortion. The grand jury refused to indict him.

OWEN GIBNEY, no charges preferred, released.

GEORGE GLASS, charged with complicity in the murder of Abraham Franklin. The grand jury refused to indict him.

JOHN GLEASON, sentenced to two years in the penitentiary on pleading guilty to a charge of grand larceny.

PATRICK GOLDING, charged with being in the mob that burned the Colored Orphan Asylum and with threatening to kill Alderman Terence Farley and burn his house. Indicted for riot and assault and battery, but never brought to trial.

THOMAS GRACE, indicted for manslaughter, never brought to trial.

BERNARD GRAHAM, no charges preferred, released.

GEORGE GRAY, no charges preferred, released.

JAMES GREEN, accused of having been one of a mob in Thomas Street. Tried in the Court of Special Session, July 31; found guilty and sentenced to five days in the City Prison.

JOHN HAGAN, charged, together with Patrick Sheron, with highway robbery. Indicted for first-degree robbery, August 4. Tried in General Sessions, August 11. The jury found him guilty without leaving their seats, and he was sentenced to ten years' imprisonment at hard labor in the State Prison.

MICHAEL HAGERTY, charged with Martin Luhs with possession of a number of Enfield rifles. No charges preferred, released.

PATRICK HAGGERTY, no charges preferred, released.

MARY HALL, accused of stealing from Henry H. Jones's soap and candle factory in West 16th Street, Tuesday, July 14. The grand jury refused to indict her.

JOHN HALLIGAN, one of the Harlem extortion gang, indicted on August 5 for first-degree robbery and attempted robbery and on August 7 for riot and assault and battery. He pleaded guilty to the last charge and was sentenced to thirty days in the City Prison.

FREDERICK HAMMERS, accused of complicity in the burning of Josiah Porter's house, August 5, indicted for first-degree arson; August 7, indicted for riot and assault and battery. Never brought to trial.

PATRICK HARMON, no charges preferred, released.

HUGH HARRIS, no charges preferred, released.

JAMES HART, no charges preferred, released.

JOHN HART, sentenced to two years in the City Penitentiary for robbing a man of a gold chronometer worth $650 near the Colored Orphan Asylum on Monday, July 13.

MARTIN HART, one of the Harlem extortion gang, indicted for first-degree robbery and attempted robbery on August 5, and for riot and assault and battery on David Houston, August 7. Pleaded guilty to the riot charge in General Sessions on August 13 and was sentenced to ten days in the City Prison.

WILLIAM HARTLEY, charged with extortion from storekeepers in Brooklyn. No charges preferred, released.

JOHN HARTIGAN, no charges preferred, released.

EDWARD HASE, no charges preferred, released.

GEORGE W. HAYWECK, no charges preferred, released.

JAMES HEFFMAN, accused of being one of the mob that attacked the house of Josiah Porter. No charges preferred, released.

DAVID HENNESSEY, a juvenile, indicted for theft. Never brought to trial.

PATRICK HENRADY, a leader of the rioters in Harlem, indicted for first-degree robbery on August 5 and for attempted arson and riot and assault and battery on August 7. Pleaded guilty to the riot charge on August 13 in General Sessions and was sentenced to two months in the City Penitentiary.

CASPAR HENRY, indicted for petty larceny, August 11. Jumped bail and was never recaptured.

CHRISTOPHER HIGGINS, no charges preferred, released.

GARRETT HILL, 12, charged with attacking a Negro tenement at 28 Cornelia Street on Monday, July 13. No charges preferred, released.

PATRICK HIRSCHOTT, no charges preferred, released.

SAMUEL HOGAN, indicted for assault and battery. Never brought to trial.

JOHN HOLLAND, no charges preferred, released.

MICHAEL HOLLAND, no charges preferred, released.

JAMES HOWARD, no charges preferred, released.

WILLIAM J. HURLEY, no charges preferred, released.

JOHN HUSSEY, "whom the 13th Ward police characterize as a desperate and notorious bully, and who called himself the 'Terror of the Hook,' " charged with leading the mob in Pitt and Delancey streets on Tuesday, July 14. The grand jury refused to indict him.

CATHARINE JACOBS, no charges preferred, released.

NATHAN JACOBS, accused of stealing a sewing machine on Wednesday, July 15. Tried and convicted in the Court of Special Session and sentenced to twenty days in the City Prison.

WILLIAM JOHNSON, no charges preferred, released.

JOHN WILLIAM JOYCE, charged with being one of the mob and stealing about $1,300 worth of firearms, clothing, and jewelry from Jonathan Green's pawnbroker's shop, 405 West 42nd Street, on Tuesday, July 14. Released to join the navy, October 7, and all charges dropped.

THOMAS KANE, convicted of grand larceny and sentenced to one year's imprisonment in the City Penitentiary.

WILLIAM KEAGAN, no charges preferred, released.

MICHAEL KEBRICK, charged with stealing from the Gibbons house. The grand jury refused to indict him.

PATRICK KEEGAN, charged with the murder of Colonel O'Brien. Indicted for first-degree murder on November 24, but never brought to trial.

SARAH KEEGAN, arrested for looting. No charges preferred, released.

EDWARD KEHOE, arrested in Brooklyn for trying to incite a mob on Tuesday night. No charges preferred, released.

HERMAN KELLER, charged with stealing two revolvers. Tried and convicted in the Court of Special Session.

BRIDGET KELLEY, no charges preferred, released.

JOHN KELLOMAN, no charges preferred, released.

ANDREW KELLY, accused of being one of the mob that sacked John Greene's house in Tenth Avenue, near 35th Street, on Tuesday, July 14. No charges preferred, released.

JAMES KELLY, indicted for riot, but never brought to trial.

JOHN KELLY, arrested as a rioter in East 22nd Street on Thursday, July 16. No charges preferred, released.

MICHAEL KELLY, no charges preferred, released.

MARY KENNEDY, accused of stealing from the Gibbons house. Indicted for grand larceny on August 4, but never brought to trial.

JOHN KERRIGAN, no charges preferred, released.

JACOB KESNER, accused of stealing on Tuesday, July 14. Tried and convicted in the Court of Special Session on July 31 and sentenced to six months in the City Penitentiary.

PATRICK KIERNAN, charged with complicity in the burning of Josiah Porter's house. August 5, indicted for first-degree arson; August 7, indicted for riot and assault and battery. Never brought to trial.

THOMAS KIERNAN, charged with being one of the mob that beat Private Alcock of the Invalid Corps at Third Avenue and 43rd Street on Monday, July 13. The grand jury refused to indict him.

JACOB KRESLING, accused, with John Weidel, of extorting money from a baker, Frederick R. Schneider of 311 West 44th Street, by threatening to burn his premises. No charges preferred, released.

FRANCIS LAMB, accused of throwing a paving stone at a policeman on Wednesday, July 15. Tried in the Court of Special Session on August 4 and acquitted by a vote of two to one. The dissenter, Judge Quackenbush, would have sent Lamb to the City Penitentiary for four months.

JAMES LAMB, accused of taking part in the murder of William Williams in Leroy Street on Tuesday, July 14. October 19, indicted for first-degree murder, but never brought to trial.

JOHN LARKIN, accused, with Thomas Lyons, of extorting $100 from Herman Harjes, a grocer of 499 Second Avenue, by threatening to burn his place down. Larkin enlisted October 12, and the charges were dropped.

JOHN LEARY, SR., accused of looting the house of Jeremiah Hamilton. October 28, indicted for riot and assault and battery, first-degree burglary, and grand larceny. Never brought to trial.

JOHN LEARY, JR., 13, accused of looting the house of Jeremiah Hamilton October 28, indicted for riot and assault and battery, first-degree burglary, and grand larceny. Never brought to trial.

MICHAEL LEARY, accused of possession of property stolen from the Gibbons house. August 4, indicted for grand larceny. Never brought to trial.

JAMES LEE, accused of stealing from William Lipman's clothing store on Third Avenue. August 5, indicted for grand larceny. Tried in General Sessions on August 7, but the jury failed to agree on a verdict. Enlisted, September 18 and charge dropped.

MARTIN LEEKE, no charges preferred, released.

PETER LEONHARD, no charges preferred, released.

JAMES LEVERISH, arrested as a rioter in East 22nd Street on Thursday, July 16. No charges preferred, released.

JOHN LING, no charges preferred, released.

JACOB LONG, 14, accused of taking part in the murder of John Costello by throwing stones at him as he lay in the street. August 11, indicted for murder, but never brought to trial.

THEODORE LUBEE, no charges preferred, released.

MARTIN LUHS, arrested with Michael Haggerty for possession of a number of Enfield rifles. No charges preferred, released.

RICHARD LYNCH, accused of highway robbery and invading the Magdalen Asylum. Pleaded guilty in the Court of Special Session to a charge of assault with intent to commit robbery and was sentenced to ten months' imprisonment in the City Penitentiary. August 5, indicted on three counts of first-degree robbery and also indicted for first-degree burglary and grand larceny. Lynch pleaded guilty in General Sessions to one of the robbery charges and was sentenced to five years' imprisonment at hard labor in the State Prison.

THOMAS LYNCH, no charges preferred, released.

MATTHEW LYONS, accused of trying to incite a gang of bakers to leave their work. No charges preferred, released.

THOMAS LYONS, accused with John Larkin of extortion. Charges against Larkin were dropped when he enlisted, and no further action was taken afterwards against Lyons.

JOHN MCALLISTER, accused of taking part in the murder of William Williams in Leroy Street on Tuesday, July 14. Tried in Oyer and Terminer, October 8–9. When court opened on the ninth, the judge stopped the trial and directed the jury to bring in a verdict of not guilty.

JAMES MCBRIDE, no charges preferred, released.

MICHAEL MCCABE, indicted on two counts of highway robbery on August 7. On one indictment, alleging that he assaulted William Mitchell and stole $2.00 from him on Wednesday, July 15, McCabe agreed to plead guilty to a charge of assault and battery. Thursday, August 13, 1863, "ordered that judgment be suspended. Sept[ember], 25, 1863, the like judgment to pay a fine of six cents."

OWEN MCCAFFREY, no charges preferred, released.

FLORENCE MCCARTHY, no charges preferred, released.

WILLIAM MCCARTHY, accused of stealing from Brooks Brothers. August 7, indicted for grand larceny. Pleaded guilty to a charge of attempting to commit grand larceny and was sentenced to two years and two months imprisonment at hard labor in the State Prison.

ANN MCCARTY, accused of stealing furniture and other property from the house of W. N. Dickenson, 9 York Street. Tried and found guilty in the Court of Special Session, July 24. Sentenced to three months in the City Penitentiary.

JOHANNA MCCARTY, no charges preferred, released.

JOHN MCCARTY, no charges preferred, released.

BARNARD MCCONNELL, no charges preferred, released.

PATRICK MCCORMACK, no charges preferred, released.

KATE MCCORMICK, no charges preferred, released.

HUGH MCCLUSKEY, a juvenile, accused of possessing property stolen from 1190, 1192, 1194, and 1198 Broadway. Tried and convicted in the Court of Special Session on July 17 and sent to the House of Refuge.

P. MCCULLOUGH, no charges preferred, released.

JAMES MCDADE, indicted for riot and assault and battery, August 11. Never brought to trial.

JOHN MCDERMOTT, accused of attacking Officer Michael C. O'Byrne of the 29th Precinct near City Hall. Escaped from the New York Hospital, Wednesday, July 15, and never recaptured.

HUGH MCDONALD, alias Jack Curry, charged with petty larceny and riot. Tried in the Court of Special Session on July 28 and acquitted.

JAMES MCDONALD, indicted for riot and assault and battery, October 22. Never brought to trial.

DAVID MCGARVAN, no charges preferred, released.

PETER MCGEOUGH, accused of robbing Catherine M. Sternward of forty cents. August 11, indicted for first-degree robbery; October 8, pleaded guilty to petty larceny; October 12, "judgment suspended, prisoner discharged."

NEIL MCGORHEN, no charges preferred, released.

DANIEL MCGOVERN, accused of rioting in Harlem. Indicted for first-degree robbery on August 5 and for riot and assault and battery on August 7. Pleaded guilty to the second charge in General Sessions, August 11 and sentenced to two months in the City Penitentiary.

MARY MCGOVERN, accused of rioting and possession of stolen property— a carpet belonging to Officer Lawrence of the 20th Precinct. The grand jury refused to indict her.

JAMES MCGOWAN, no charges preferred, released.

LOUIS MCGRATH, no charges preferred, released.

WILLIAM MCGREGOR, no charges preferred, released.

JAMES MCGUIRE, indicted for grand larceny and petty larceny, August 13. Pleaded guilty to attempted grand larceny in General Sessions, September 9, and sentenced to two years' imprisonment at hard labor in State Prison.

THOMAS MCGUIRE, no charges preferred, released.

THOMAS MCKAY, alias Thomas Turner, 12, accused of taking liquor from the store of Barney Murtha, 259 Tenth Avenue, after the mob had broken the place open. No charges preferred, released.

PATRICK MCKENNA, indicted, with Thomas Mollet, for larceny from the person. Never brought to trial.

OWEN MCKINNEY, charged with complicity in the murder of Abraham Franklin. No charges preferred, released.

PHILIP MCLAUGHLIN, no charges preferred, released.

MICHAEL MCLOUGHLIN, accused of threatening Taylor's foundry in Georck Street on Friday, July 17. No charges preferred, released.

JAMES MCMAHEN, accused of rioting on Tuesday, July 14. No charges preferred, released.

JOHN MCMANUS, no charges preferred, released.

MARY MCNAMARA, no charges preferred, released.

WILLIAM MCNALLY, a juvenile, arrested in Brooklyn and accused of destroying Negroes' furniture. Discharged on grounds of insufficient evidence.

ROSS MCPOOL, no charges preferred, released.

EDWARD MCSWEGAN, no charges preferred, released.

JOHN MCWELLMAN, no charges preferred, released.

BARNEY MACKAY, accused of being a leader of the West Side rioters. No charges preferred, released.

JAMES MADONER, no charges preferred, released.

JOHN MAHER, accused of attempting to rescue a prisoner from an officer on July 15. Tried in the Court of Special Session on August 4 and acquitted by a vote of two to one. The dissenter was Judge Quackenbush, "being of opinion that the evidence was sufficiently conclusive to warrant some correction for the prisoner."

P. MAHERT, no charges preferred, released.

OWEN MALLEY, no charges preferred, released.

PATRICK MALONEY, charged with rioting on Tuesday, July 14. No charges preferred, released.

JOHN MARTIN, accused of robbery, Tuesday, July 14. The grand jury refused to indict him.

MARSH, a notorious Philadelphia thief, accused of beating and robbing a soldier in City Hall Park. Discharged on grounds of insufficient evidence.

JOSEPH MARSHALL, alias Timothy Duggan, charged with attacking Charles Jackson and throwing him off Pier 4, North River, on Wednesday, July 15. August 4, indicted for first-degree robbery. Tried, convicted, and sentenced to ten years' imprisonment at hard labor in the State Prison.

W. MAXWELL, no charges preferred, released.

JOHN MEEHAN, no charges preferred, released.

MICHAEL MENAHEN, accused as a rioter. No charges preferred, released.

PATRICK MERRY, accused of leading the attack on the Eighth District draft office in Broadway on Monday, July 13. Indicted for third-degree burglary and two counts of second-degree arson. Jumped bail and was never recaptured.

HUGH MINNICK, accused with rioting in Second Avenue. No charges preferred, released.

GEORGE MILLER, no charges preferred, released.

HENRIETTA MILLER, no charges preferred, released.

JAMES MINOR, a juvenile, arrested in Brooklyn and accused of destroying Negroes' furniture. Discharged on grounds of insufficient evidence.

ROBERT MITCHELL, indicted for riot and assault and battery and for third-degree burglary, August 11. Never brought to trial.

THOMAS MOLLET, indicted with Patrick McKenna for larceny from the person. Never brought to trial.

BRIDGET MONAHAN, accused of possessing stolen goods. No charges preferred, released.

PATRICK MONAHAN, accused of assaulting a man with a bayonet to force him to join the mob, Tuesday, July 14. Indicted, August 7, for assault and battery with intent to kill. Pleaded guilty in General Sessions, August 11, and in consideration of his previous good character he was sentenced to three months in the City Penitentiary.

MONTGOMERY, a notorious Philadelphia thief, arrested for beating and robbing a soldier in City Hall Park. Discharged on grounds of insufficient evidence.

ANN MOORE, arrested at Catherine Ferry, Brooklyn, and accused of stealing from Brooks Brothers' store. No charges preferred, released.

JOHN MOORE, accused of rioting on Tuesday, July 14. No charges preferred, released.

MARTIN MORAN, arrested as a sniper, Third Avenue and 20th Street. No charges preferred, released.

THOMAS MULCHAY, indicted as a juvenile thief, never brought to trial.

MULLAN, accused of beating and extorting money from a publican named Purdy who lived on the Bloomingdale Road, near 81st Street. Tried and convicted in the Court of Special Session and sentenced to one month in the City Prison.

EDWARD MURPHY, accused of leading a mob that invaded a hardware store at 668 Third Avenue to steal axes with which to cut down telegraph poles. Murphy was discharged to enlist, October 6.

JOHN MURPHY, charged with riotous conduct on the complaint of William B. Astor and Hugh Stinson. The charges were not pressed.

JOHN MURPHY, accused of tearing down 107 Rivington Street on Tuesday, July 14. Tried in the Court of Special Session, July 31. Witnesses testified to seeing Murphy with boards in his hands, but other witnesses failed to appear, and so he was acquitted.

JOHN MURPHY, a juvenile, indicted as a thief, never brought to trial.

PATRICK MURPHY, pleaded guilty to a charge of riot and sentenced to two years in the City Penitentiary.

WILLIAM MURPHY, no charges preferred, released.

MYERS, a notorious Philadelphia thief, arrested for beating and robbing a soldier in City Hall Park. Discharged on grounds of insufficient evidence.

JOHN NICHOLSON, accused of murdering William Jones in Clarkson Street on Monday, July 13. Indicted for murder, October 17, but never brought to trial.

JOHN NUGENT, accused (with Thomas Nugent) of stealing from Brooks Brothers. Tried in the Court of Special Session on July 24 and acquitted.

THOMAS NUGENT, accused (with John Nugent) of stealing from Brooks Brothers. Tried in the Court of Special Session on July 24, convicted, and sentenced to two months in the City Penitentiary.

PATRICK OATIS, accused of attacking and gravely disfiguring two people during the riots. Discharged to enlist, October 5.

ELLEN O'BEIRNE, pleaded guilty to attempted grand larceny, sentenced to two years in the City Penitentiary.

MICHAEL O'BRIEN, accused of taking a leading part in beating Andrew Houser in West 28th Street on Tuesday, July 14, robbing of Treasury notes worth $70, and stealing his horse and wagon. October 12, indicted for riot, first-degree robbery, and third-degree burglary. Never brought to trial.

PATRICK O'BRIEN, accused of the murder of Colonel O'Brien. Indicted for first-degree murder, November 24, but never brought to trial.

SAMUEL O'CONNOR, no charges preferred, released.

TERENCE O'CONNOR, no charges preferred, released.

SAMUEL O'DONNELL, arrested for threatening Taylor's foundry in Goerck Street on Friday, July 17. No charges preferred, released.

JOHN O'HARA, charged with stealing a watch during the riots. August 5, indicted for petty larceny. Tried in General Sessions and pleaded guilty. O'Hara claimed to be a discharged soldier, and though the judge said he had some doubts about the genuineness of this claim, he would give O'Hara the benefit of the doubt and sentence him to three years' imprisonment at hard labor in the State Prison.

JOHN O'KEEFE, accused of taking a leading part in firing the premises of Severn and Moulton in East 49th Street. Indicted October 28 for attempted arson and third-degree burglary, but never brought to trial.

OWEN O'MEARA, no charges preferred, released.

KATE O'NAGAN, no charges preferred, released.

PATRICK O'NEILL, accused of taking part in the burning of Josiah Porter's house; indicted, October 17, for riot and assault and battery. Never brought to trial.

CONRAD OLLWEIDER, no charges preferred, released.

THEODORE OSTERSTOCK, charged with taking a leading part in the sacking of Samuel Roesner's shoe store in Greenwich Street on Tuesday, July 14. Indicted, August 5, for grand larceny and for riot and assault and battery. Tried and convicted on the latter charge in General Sessions on August 7; the judge said he thought there was still some doubt, and so he would sentence Osterstock to three months in the City Penitentiary.

SAMUEL OTTENBURG, no charges preferred, released.

JOHN PARKER, a juvenile, arrested for possession of stolen goods. No charges preferred, released.

WILLIAM PATTEN, accused of being the leader of a gang of rioters who robbed stores and forced factories to close on the Upper West Side. August 5, indicted for riot and assault and battery. At first, he pleaded guilty; then, changed his plea to not guilty. Never brought to trial.

WILLIAM PERRY, no charges preferred, released.

MARIA PILKIN, 272 Water Street, accused of stealing furniture and bedding from Dr. William Powell's hotel at 2 Dover Street on Tuesday, July 14. No charges preferred, released.

PETER PINE, accused of looting, indicted for larceny and receiving stolen property on August 11. Never brought to trial.

SARAH PINE, accused of looting, indicted for larceny and receiving stolen property on August 11. Never brought to trial.

JOHN PIPER, accused of extortion, indicted for riot and assault and battery on Thomas White. Never brought to trial.

MARY POLLOCK, no charges preferred, released.

MARGARET POTTER, accused of stealing furniture, etc., from the house of W. N. Dickenson at 9 York Street. Tried and convicted in the Court of Special Session, July 24, and sentenced to three months in the City Penitentiary.

MATTHEW POWERS, accused of complicity in the burning of Josiah Porter's house. A discharged soldier. August 5, indicted for first-degree arson. Released to enlist.

GEORGE H. PULLEN, arrested on Thursday, July 16, in a house on East 22nd Street where arms were discovered. Having proved a good character, he was released.

JAMES PURDY, accused of trying to raise a mob to burn houses on Thursday, July 16. The grand jury refused to indict him.

ELIZABETH QUINN, accused of stealing furniture from the house of W. N. Dickenson at 9 York Street. Tried in the Court of Special Session July 24 and acquitted when it was shown that she was only a boarder in the house of the guilty party.

THOMAS QUINN, accused of taking part in the hanging of William Jones. No charges preferred, released.

JOHN REGNAR, no charges preferred, released.

PATRICK REILLY, no charges preferred, released.

OWEN REYNOLDS, accused of threatening Taylor's foundry in Goerck Street on Friday, July 17. No charges preferred, released.

TERENCE REYNOLDS, accused of complicity in the burning of Josiah Porter's house. The grand jury refused to indict him.

JAMES H. RIDER, accused of threatening Taylor's foundry in Goerck Street on Friday, July 17. No charges preferred, released.

WILLIAM RIGBY, accused of trying to set fire to the Arch. August 11, indicted for first-degree arson. Tried in General Sessions, October 22, and the jury acquitted him without leaving their seats on technical grounds—a variance between the indictment and the proof. Re-indicted for first-degree arson on October 28, but never retried, probably because of doubts about double jeopardy.

JAMES RILEY, arrested as a rioter on East 22nd Street on Thursday, July 16. No charges preferred, released.

JOHN RILEY, accused of breaking into Parr's hardware store on Eighth Avenue. Indicted for third-degree burglary, August 4. Never brought to trial.

LAWRENCE RILEY, no charges preferred, released.

THOMAS RILEY, accused of rioting in Harlem. No charges preferred, released.

ROGERS, accused of trying to incite a riot in Williamsburgh. Convicted and sentenced to six months in the Penitentiary.

PATRICK ROONEY, accused of leading the mob in an attack on 175 West 27th Street. Indicted for riot and assault and battery, but never brought to trial.

PATRICK RUSH, no charges preferred, released.

DAVID RYAN, accused of helping to set fire to the store of Pinckney and Moulton in East 49th Street on Tuesday, July 14. The grand jury refused to indict him.

JOHN RYDER, accused of taking part in the looting of a store in Grand Street, July 14. Indicted for riot and assault and battery and for third-degree burglary, August 11. Never brought to trial.

ROBERT SADLER, arrested in Greenpoint on July 17 for possession of stolen guns and clothing. Discharged on grounds of insufficient evidence.

FRANCES SCHENCK, accused of stealing furniture from the house of W. N. Dickenson at 9 York Street. Tried in the Court of Special Session on July 24 and acquitted.

OSWALD SCHENCK, accused of stealing four coats and a vest. Tried in the Court of Special Session, July 26, found guilty and sentenced to four months in the City Penitentiary.

ADAM SCHLOSSHAUER, accused of extortion in Harlem on Wednesday, July 15. August 5, indicted for attempted robbery and first-degree robbery. August 7, indicted for riot and assault and battery. Pleaded guilty to this charge and to a charge of petty larceny, October 8, in General Session. "Judgment suspended, prisoner discharged" by Recorder Hoffman, October 13.

JOHN SCHRECK, no charges preferred, released.

LEWIS SCHROEDER, no charges preferred, released.

JAMES SEDGWICK, no charges preferred, released.

JOHN SEIBACK, accused of rioting on Tuesday, July 14. No charges preferred, released.

MATTHEW P. SENNOTT, indicted for grand and petty larceny on October 12. Never brought to trial on these charges, but tried and convicted on another indictment for petty larceny, January 15, 1864.

EDWARD SHAREN, accused of riotous conduct. Discharged on grounds of insufficient evidence.

ANN SHANDLEY, accused of storming and looting a house at 94 West 28th Street. October 22, indicted for riot and assault and battery and for second-degree robbery. Never brought to trial.

FRANK A. SHANDLEY, accused of storming and looting a house at 94 West 28th Street. October 22, indicted for riot and assault and battery and for second-degree robbery. Never brought to trial.

JAMES SHANDLEY, 13, accused of storming and looting a house at 94 West 28th Street. Complaint dismissed, possibly because his parents, Frank and Ann Shandley, were held responsible.

ADAM SHAW, accused of rioting. The grand jury refused to indict him.

MARY SHAW, no charges preferred, released.

PATRICK SHERRON, accused of stealing a gold watch, 12:30 A.M., Tuesday, July 14. Indicted for first-degree robbery, August 4. Tried in General Sessions, August 10; the jury found him guilty without leaving their seats, and he was sentenced to ten years' imprisonment at hard labor in the State Prison.

PATRICK SHIELDS, no charges preferred, released.

CHRISTOPHER SIDNEY, a juvenile, accused of petty larceny. Tried and convicted in the Court of Special Session on July 26 and sent to the House of Refuge.

MARK J. SILVA, accused of taking a leading part in the murder of Abraham Franklin. Indicted for first-degree murder, August 4, but never brought to trial.

ANDREW SIMMONS, alleged to be the leader of the gang that threatened Taylor's foundry in Goerck Street, Friday, July 17. No charges preferred, released.

MARTIN SINK, accused of petty larceny. Tried in the Court of Special Session, July 26, and acquitted for want of direct testimony against him.

ANDREW SMITH, also known as Andray Schmidt, accused of extortion, Tuesday, July 14. The grand jury refused to indict him.

ANTHONY SMITH, arrested at Catherine Ferry, Brooklyn, and accused of stealing from Brooks Brothers. No charges preferred, released.

CHARLES SMITH, accused of highway robbery. Indicted for robbery and grand larceny, August 11. Allowed to enlist and charges dropped.

EDWARD SMITH, accused of leading a mob attack on a factory in West 25th Street on Wednesday, July 15. The grand jury refused to indict him.

FREDERICK SMITH, accused of taking part in the attack on the store of Goldschmidt and Solinger, 17 Avenue B, on Tuesday, July 14. The grand jury refused to indict him.

GEORGE SMITH, a juvenile, accused of stealing shoes and other property from the U.S. government stores on Broadway, between 28th and 29th streets. Indicted for first-degree burglary. Sent to the House of Refuge.

JACK SMITH, accused of threatening Taylor's foundry in Goerck Street on Friday, July 17. No charges preferred, released.

JAMES SMITH, no charges preferred, released.

JOHN SMITH, accused of rioting on Tuesday, July 14. No charges preferred, released.

JOHN SMITH, arrested for the fatal shooting of Michael Haley, a rioter who was attacking Smith's premises at 157–159 Greenwich Street. The grand jury refused to indict him.

THOMAS SMITH, arrested at Catherine Ferry, Brooklyn, for stealing from Brooks Brothers. No charges preferred, released.

WILLIAM SMITH, arrested for possession of a loaded rifle. No charges preferred, released.

WILLIAM T. SMITH, indicted for grand larceny, never brought to trial.

WILLIAM SPALDING, accused of stealing from Lucien Ayer. Indicted for grand larceny, October 27, but never brought to trial.

CHARLES SPENCER, accused of breaking into Parr's hardware store on Eighth Avenue. Indicted for third-degree burglary, August 4. Never brought to trial.

PAINTER SPRINGSTEIN, accused of looting Negroes' home in West 28th Street. Indicted for larceny and receiving stolen property, August 11. Never brought to trial.

RICHARD STAGE, a juvenile, accused of attacking Negro homes on Monday, July 13. Tried in the Court of Special Session and acquitted.

PATRICK STANTON, arrested in Greenpoint on July 17 for possession of stolen guns and clothing. Discharged on grounds of insufficient evidence.

WILLIAM STANTON, accused of tearing up the tracks of the Fourth Avenue Railroad. Indicted for riot and assault and battery. Tried in Oyer and Terminer, October 6; pleaded guilty and was sentenced to six months in the City Penitentiary. Had served two years in the 38th New York Volunteers and received an honorable discharge.

CATHARINE STAPLETON, indicted for grand larceny, August 12. September 9, pleaded guilty to a charge of attempted grand larceny and sentenced to six months in the City Penitentiary.

DANIEL STAPLETON, accused of rioting on Tuesday, July 14. No charges preferred, released.

JOHN STAPLETON, accused of rioting on Tuesday, July 14. No charges preferred, released.

PATRICK STAPLETON, SR., accused of rioting on Tuesday, July 14. No charges preferred, released.

PATRICK STAPLETON, JR., accused of rioting on Tuesday, July 14. No charges preferred, released.

JOSEPH STEHEL, accused of robbing and burning the house of John J. Dow in Lexington Avenue, between 44th and 45th streets, on Monday, July 13. Allowed to enlist in the army, September 21, and charges dropped.

SEBASTIAN STEHEL, charged with receiving stolen goods from Joseph Stehel, his son. The latter was allowed to enlist, and on September 22 charges against the father were dropped, too.

JOHN STEPPHAN, accused of taking part in the attack on the store of Goldschmidt and Solinger, 17 Avenue B, on Tuesday, July 14. The grand jury refused to indict him.

HENRY STEVENS, no charges preferred, released.

ISAAC STEVENS, no charges preferred, released.

CHARLES STUART, accused of possessing property stolen from the 28th Precinct police station. No charges preferred, released.

DANIEL SULLIVAN, accused of the murder of Joseph Annin in Second Avenue on Tuesday, July 14. He produced an alibi and was released.

MARY SULLIVAN, no charges preferred, released.

PATRICK SULLIVAN, accused of threatening Taylor's foundry in Goerck Street on Friday, July 17. No charges preferred, released.

THOMAS S. SUTHERLAND, accused of leading the mob in the attack on Allerton's Hotel, in 43rd Street, on Monday, July 13. Indicted for second-degree arson, August 11. Never brought to trial.

PATRICK SWEENEY, accused of trying to start a fire at the Arch on the night of Tuesday, July 14. A discharged soldier. Indicted for riot, August 5. Tried and convicted in General Sessions and sentenced to three months in the City Penitentiary.

ARCHIBALD TAYLOR, indicted for murder and arson and first-degree robbery, never brought to trial.

WILLIAM TENANT, no charges preferred, released.

DAVID TENELL, indicted for robbery and riot, never brought to trial.

GEORGE THOMPSON, tried and convicted in the Court of Special Session of attacking a Negro woman called Mary Johnson. Sentenced to four months in the City Penitentiary.

HENRY TILTON, accused of being one of the mob that plundered Colonel O'Brien's house and murdered the colonel himself. The grand jury refused to indict him.

CHARLES TOOKER, 15, accused of taking part in the attack on the Derricksons at 9 Worth Street. The grand jury refused to indict him.

PATRICK TOONEY, no charges preferred, released.

JOHN TRACEY, a sailor, accused of attacking Negroes in Brooklyn. Convicted, fined $20, and sent to jail because he could not pay.

JAMES TUITE, no charges preferred, released.

JAMES TULLY, no charges preferred, released.

CHRIS. VAGE, no charges preferred, released.

JOHN VAN HOUTEN, no charges preferred, released.

DANIEL VAUGHAN, accused of leading the mob that burned down a building at 49th Street and Third Avenue. October 12, indicted for riot and assault and battery and for third-degree burglary. October 17, indicted for third-degree arson. Never brought to trial.

HENRY WADE, accused of being a leader in the rioting. Enlisted September 21, and charges dropped.

JOHN WAGNER, no charges preferred, released.

JOHN WALKER, no charges preferred, released.

MICHAEL WALLACE, no charges preferred, released.

WILLIAM WALLACE, no charges preferred, released.

JOHN WARD, pleaded guilty to a charge of robbery and sentenced to one year in the City Penitentiary.

WILLIAM WATSON, accused of extorting money from Lewis Chamberlain. Indicted for first-degree robbery. Tried in General Sessions; the jury found him guilty without leaving their seats, and he was sentenced to ten years' imprisonment at hard labor in the State Prison.

BENJAMIN WEBB, no charges preferred, released.

JOHN WEIS, no charges preferred, released.

JOHN F. WELLS, accused of cutting down telegraph poles on First Avenue on Wednesday, July 15. August 11, indicted for riot and assault and battery. October 5, allowed to enlist and charges dropped.

DENNIS WELSH, accused of looting from the Gibbons house. August 4, indicted for grand larceny. Tried, August 8; he claimed he was forced to take the stolen items and he was acquitted.

JOHN WELSH, no charges preferred, released.

NANCY WESTBROOK, indicted for burglary and grand larceny, never brought to trial.

GEORGE WETHERAL, arrested for threatening Taylor's foundry in Goerck Street on Friday, July 17. No charges preferred, released.

JAMES H. WHITTEN, accused of leading the attack on the *Tribune* office. August 7, indicted for riot, second-degree arson, and third-degree burglary. Tried and convicted in General Sessions; sentenced to one year's imprisonment in the City Penitentiary and a fine of $250.

JOHN WIEDEL, accused of extorting money from Frederick Schneider of 311 West 44th Street by threatening to burn his bakery. No charges preferred, released.

MARY WILKINS, indicted for grand larceny, never brought to trial.

DOMINICK WILLIAMS, accused of rioting on Tuesday, July 14. No charges preferred, released.

MAGGIE WILLIAMS, indicted for grand larceny, never brought to trial.

PATRICK WOLFE, no charges preferred, released.

WILLIAM WOOD, charged with extortion from storekeeper in Brooklyn. No charges preferred, released.

JOHN WRIGHT, no charges preferred, released.

DANIEL WRITNER, no charges preferred, released.

MATTHEW ZWEICK, accused of complicity in the murder of John Costello. August 11, indicted for riot and an offense against public decency. October 17, indicted for first-degree murder. The district attorney refused to prosecute: "Not evidence enough—reward case!"

This gives a total of 443.

# IV

## *The Rioters*

WESLEY ADAMS, habitual criminal (arrested).

JEREMIAH ALLEN, 38, of 265 East 21st Street in the Eighteenth Ward; a laborer (wounded).

JOHN U. ANDREWS, 39, of 10 East 11th Street in the Seventeenth Ward; a lawyer; from Virginia (arrested).

MATTHIAS ANGEHOVEN, 41, born in Germany (dead).

THEODORE ARNOLD, 18, lived in 39th Street; a peddler; born in Germany; illiterate (arrested).

THOMAS BAKER, 45, of 310 West 26th Street in the Sixteenth Ward; born in England (dead).

ROBERT BAKER, a juvenile (arrested).

RICHARD BALENSBURG, of Brooklyn (arrested).

BRIDGET BARRETT, of 286 West 13th Street in the Ninth Ward (arrested).

CORNELIUS BARRETT, 11, of 189 First Avenue in the Seventeenth Ward (wounded).

GARRETT BARRY, 20, of 110 East 29th Street in the Twenty-first Ward; a carman; born in Ireland (dead).

GEORGE BAUER, 39, of 411 First Avenue in the Eighteenth Ward; a shoemaker; born in Germany; literate (arrested).

MARTIN BEACH, 37, of 141 East 24th Street in the Eighteenth Ward; a hostler; born in Ireland; illiterate (arrested).

FREDERICK BEILSTEIN, a German (arrested).

JAMES BEST, 21, of 19 Leonard Street in the Fifth Ward; a peddler; born in Ireland; illiterate (arrested).

MARCUS BOCHMAN, 29, of 306 Delancey Street in the Thirteenth Ward; a laborer; born in France (dead).

PATRICK BOYLAN, 33, of 34 Jackson Street (rear) in the Seventh Ward; a carman; born in Ireland (dead).

WILLIAM BOYLE, 23, of 106 East 22nd Street in the Eighteenth Ward; a laborer; born in Ireland (dead).

FRANCIS BRADY, 15, of 145 West 41st Street in the Twenty-second Ward (wounded).

THOMAS BRANNIGAN, 27, of 208 East 18th Street in the Eighteenth Ward; a laborer; born in Ireland (dead).

THOMAS BRENAN, a grocer; born in Ireland (arrested).

FERGUS BRENNAN, a laborer; born in Ireland (arrested).

JAMES BRODERICK, 44, of 76 East 31st Street in the Twenty-first Ward; a blacksmith; born in Ireland (dead).

DANIEL BROWN, 15, lived in Third Avenue; a harness maker; born in Ireland; illiterate (arrested).

HUGH BRYAN, 30, of 605 Third Avenue in the Nineteenth Ward; a plumber; born in Ireland (arrested).

JOHN BUCKLEY, a juvenile (arrested).

AUSTIN BULGER, 36, of 309 East 34th Street in the Twenty-first Ward; a machinist (wounded).

ALEXANDER BURNS, a juvenile (arrested).

PATRICK BUTLER, 16, lived in 28th Street; a butcher; born in Ireland (arrested).

WILLIAM BUTNEY, 25, lived in New York; a steamship fireman; born in Ireland; illiterate (arrested).

PATRICK H. BYRNES, 28, of 1390 Third Avenue in the Twelfth Ward; a painter; born in Canada; literate (arrested).

PIERCE CAHILL, 54, of 108 East 22nd Street in the Eighteenth Ward; a laborer; born in Ireland (dead).

CORNELIUS CALLAGHAN, "about 28," of Third Avenue, between 113th and 114th streets in the Twelfth Ward; born in New York City; occupation: "out of business at present"; literate (arrested).

EDWARD CANFIELD, "about 28," of Leroy Street in the Ninth Ward; a laborer; born in Ireland; illiterate (arrested).

DENNIS CAREY, 18, lived in 30th Street; a carman; born in New York; literate (arrested).

MARY ANN CARMODY, 10, lived in 42nd Street, between Eleventh and Twelfth avenues, in the Twenty-second Ward (dead).

PATRICK CARNEY, "over 50," of Yorkville; a stonemason; born in Ireland (arrested).

MARIA CARROLL, 37, lived in 33rd Street; occupation—"washing and ironing"; born in Ireland; illiterate (arrested).

WILLIAM CARSON, 34, of 217 East 23rd Street in the Eighteenth Ward; a laborer; born in Ireland (dead).

PATRICK CASEY, 10, of 331 West 43rd Street in the Twenty-second Ward; born in the United States of Irish parents (dead).

JAMES CASSIDY, 40, lived in 28th Street; a laborer; born in Ireland; illiterate (arrested).

ADAM CHAIRMAN, born in Germany; habitual criminal (arrested).

BERNARD CLARK, 37, lived at 64th Street and Fifth Avenue in the Nineteenth Ward; a laborer; born in Ireland; literate (arrested).

EDWARD CLARY, 18, lived in Thirteenth Street; a boilermaker; born in Ireland; illiterate (arrested).

HUGH CLENK, 35, born in Ireland (dead).

ELLEN CLYNE, 23, of 496 First Avenue in the Twenty-first Ward; a domestic (wounded).

PATRICK COADY, a juvenile (arrested).

PATRICK COLEMAN, 29, of 30 Oak Street in the Fourth Ward; a laborer; born in Ireland (arrested).

JAMES COLLIER, 28, of 101 Charles Street in the Ninth Ward; an actor; born in New York (arrested).

THOMAS CONNERS, 19, of 30 Little 12th Street in the Ninth Ward; a mattress maker; born in Ireland; literate (arrested).

DANIEL CONROY, 46, of East 38th Street in the Twenty-first Ward; a laborer; born in Ireland; illiterate (arrested).

JOHN CONWAY, 21, of 187 Avenue C in the Eleventh Ward; a cabinetmaker; born in Philadelphia; literate (arrested).

WILLIAM CONWAY, 14, of 598 West 48th Street in the Twenty-second Ward; born in New York (dead).

THOMAS COONEY, 50, lived in 33rd Street; a butcher; born in Ireland; literate (arrested).

MARY CORCORAN, 24, of 163 East 26th Street in the Twenty-first Ward; born in Ireland (dead).

JOHN CORRIGAN, 35, of 302 West 31st Street in the Twentieth Ward; a peddler; born in Ireland; illiterate (arrested).

JOHN COSTELLO, 12, of 266 First Avenue in the Eighteenth Ward; born in the United States (dead).

EGBERT COX, 19 (arrested).

FRANCIS X. CRAWLEY, 29, a clerk in a drugstore; born in Virginia (arrested).

WILLIAM CRUISE, 47, of 28 Thomas Street in the Fifth Ward; a storekeeper; born in Ireland; literate (arrested).

THOMAS CUMISKIE, 34, lived in 120th Street in the Twelfth Ward; a cartman; born in Ireland; literate (arrested).

LAWRENCE CUNNINGHAM, 25, born in Ireland (dead).

ROBERT CUNNINGHAM, 23, of 60 West Broadway in the Third Ward; a cartman; born in New York; illiterate (arrested).

PATRICK CURLEY, 25, of 128 East 25th Street in the Eighteenth Ward; a laborer; born in Ireland (dead).

PATRICK CURRAN, a juvenile (arrested).

FRANCIS CUSICK, 35, of 268 Avenue B in the Eleventh Ward; a stage driver; born in Ireland (arrested).

BERNARD DALEY, 50, of 197 East 28th Street in the Twenty-first Ward; a laborer; born in Ireland (dead).

MARIA DE LAMASTANY, 29, of 192 East 23rd Street in the Eighteenth Ward; a domestic (wounded).

PETER DOLAN, 18, a blacksmith (arrested).

DANIEL DONNELLY, 60, born in Ireland (wounded).

PATRICK DOUGHERTY, 35, of Conklin Alley, Brooklyn; born in Ireland (dead).

CHARLES DOWD, 18, lived in Washington Street; a seaman (and deserter from the U.S. Navy); born in Massachusetts; illiterate (arrested).

EDWARD DOWNING, a longshoreman (arrested).

ELLEN DOYLE, 45, of Washington Street; a housekeeper; born in Ireland; illiterate (arrested).

MICHAEL DOYLE, 22, of Mulberry Street in the Sixth Ward; a bricklayer; born in Philadelphia; literate (arrested).

MARY ANN DRISCOLL, of 274 Water Street in the Fourth Ward (arrested).

NICHOLAS DUFFY, 21, lived in 89th Street in the Twelfth Ward; a teamster on the Reservoir; born in New York; illiterate (arrested).

WILLIAM DUGAN, 20, of 21 Pitt Street in the Thirteenth Ward (arrested).

FREDERICK DUGGANS, a juvenile, of 285 First Avenue in the Eighteenth Ward (wounded).

LOUIS EBERSPACHER, 23, of 111 St. Mark's Place in the Seventeenth Ward; born in Germany (dead).

NELSON EDWARDS, of 720 Broadway in the Fifteenth Ward; a dentist; born in England (arrested).

JAMES ENGLISH, a serving soldier (wounded).

JOHN ENNIS, 16, of 139 East 29th Street in the Twenty-first Ward; a plumber (wounded).

MICHAEL EYERS, 11 (arrested).

BERNARD FAGAN, 20, lived in 57th Street, near Fifth Avenue, in the Nineteenth Ward; a laborer; born in Ireland; illiterate (arrested).

JOHN FARLEY, a juvenile (arrested).

ANN FARRELL, 60, born in Ireland (arrested).

GEORGE FARRELL, a juvenile (arrested).

JAMES FARRELL, a juvenile (arrested).

PETER FARRELL, 13, of 361 West 45th Street in the Twenty-second Ward; born in New York (dead).

LUKE FEATHERSTON, 65, of 254 First Avenue in the Eighteenth Ward; born in Ireland (dead).

MOSES FEENEY, of East 16th Street in the Eighteenth Ward (arrested).

HENRY FELLBEIN, 29, lived in Hoboken; a tobacconist; born in Germany; literate (arrested).

JAMES FINGLETON, 18, of 132 East 38th Street in the Twenty-first Ward; a baker; born in Ireland; illiterate (arrested).

CHARLES FISBECK, JR., 10, of 170 East 26th Street in the Eighteenth Ward; born in New York (dead).

EDWARD FISHER, a juvenile (arrested).

MARTIN FITZGERALD, 28, a carman; born in Ireland (arrested).

MAURICE FITZGERALD, lived in 81st Street, near Third Avenue, in the Nineteenth Ward (arrested).

THOMAS FITZGERALD, a physician (arrested).

JOHN FITZHERBERT, 28, of 408 Seventh Avenue, in the Twentieth Ward; a gunsmith; born in Ireland; literate (arrested).

THOMAS FITZSIMMONS, of 120 East 28th Street in the Twenty-first Ward; a carman; married (arrested).

PATRICK FLANNIGAN, 45, of 339 First Avenue in the Eighteenth Ward; born in Ireland (dead).

MARY FOX, 26, lived in Seventh Avenue; a housekeeper; born in Germany; literate (arrested).

LEWIS FREEMAN, 11, of 422 Ninth Avenue in the Twentieth Ward (wounded).

BRYAN FRIEL, a juvenile (arrested).

JOHN GAFFNEY, 25, of 252 Division Street in the Thirteenth Ward; a laborer; unmarried (dead).

PATRICK GAHERTY, 45, of 458 West 42nd Street in the Twenty-second Ward; a painter; born in Ireland (dead).

MILES GARRITY, 35, of 369 Eighth Avenue in the Twentieth Ward; a tinsmith; born in Ireland (arrested).

PATRICK GARVEY, 14, of 404 8th Street; born in England (dead).

PATRICK GARVEY, 40, of 488 Tenth Avenue in the Twenty-second Ward; a merchant; born in Ireland (dead).

THOMAS GIBSON, 21, of 14 Jackson Street in the Seventh Ward; a boiler-maker; born in Ireland (dead).

GEORGE GLASS, 53, of West 27th Street in the Twentieth Ward; laborer; born in Ireland; literate (arrested).

JOHN GLEASON, 22 (arrested).

JOHN GRAY, 58, of 449 West 42nd Street in the Twenty-second Ward; laborer; born in Ireland (dead).

JOHN HAGAN, 26, of 146 Essex Street in the Seventeenth Ward; a glass-cutter (arrested).

MICHAEL HALEY, 20, a longshoreman; born in Ireland (dead).

JOHN HALLIGAN, 27, lived in 110th Street in the Twelfth Ward; born in Ireland; a laborer; literate (arrested).

FREDERICK HAMMERS, 23, lived at 107th Street and Sixth Avenue in the Twelfth Ward; a laborer; born in New York; illiterate (arrested).

JAMES HAND, 25, born in Ireland (dead).

MARTIN HART, 30, lived in 112th Street in the Twelfth Ward; a laborer; born in Ireland; illiterate (arrested).

CHARLES HAVERING, 36, lived on the corner of 64th Street and Eleventh Avenue in the Twenty-second Ward; a rope maker (wounded).

DAVID HENNESSEY, a juvenile (arrested).

JULIA HENNESSEY, 35, of 209 East 20th Street in the Eighteenth Ward; born in Ireland (dead).

PATRICK HENRADY, 22, lived in 111th Street in the Twelfth Ward; a junk dealer; born in Ireland; illiterate (arrested).

JOHN C. HENRY, of 130 Seventh Avenue in the Sixteenth Ward (dead).

VALENTINE HETTLIN, 39, of 121 Third Street; born in Germany (dead).

GARRETT HILL, 12 (arrested).

JAMES HUGHES, 20, of 110 East 11th Street in the Seventeenth Ward; boilermaker; born in Ireland (dead).

MICHAEL HUGHES, 49, of 178 Monroe Street in the Seventh Ward; a laborer (wounded).

JEREMIAH HURLEY, 20, a baker (dead).

JOHN HUSSEY, a longshoreman; born in Ireland (arrested).

JOHN W. JOYCE, 17, of 263 West 42nd Street in the Twenty-second Ward; occupation–"drive peddler's wagon"; born in New York (arrested).

WILLIAM JOYCE, 19, of 141 East 11th Street in the Seventeenth Ward; a laborer; born in New York (dead).

HENRY KACHELL, 21, of 130 West 41st Street in the Twenty-second Ward; a German (dead).

BERNARD KANE, 30, born in Ireland (dead).

MICHAEL KEEGAN, 48, of 505 Seventh Avenue in the Twentieth Ward; a hostler; born in Ireland (dead).

WILLIAM KELLY, 14, of 616 Water Street in the Seventh Ward (wounded).

MARY KENNEDY, 44, lived in 36th Street; born in Ireland; illiterate; occupation–"I do nothing except wash, got 4 children" (arrested).

PATRICK KIERNAN, 18, lived in 57th Street, near Fifth Avenue, in the Nineteenth Ward; a laborer; born in Ireland; illiterate (arrested).

THOMAS KIERNAN, 40, of East 44th Street in the Nineteenth Ward; a contractor; born in Ireland; literate (arrested).

JAMES LAMB, 33, of 135 Leroy Street in the Ninth Ward; born in Ireland; a laborer; literate (arrested).

JOHN LAMB, 35, of Second Avenue, between 31st and 32nd streets, in the Twenty-first Ward; a carpenter (wounded).

JOHN LARKIN, 22, lived at Second Avenue and 32nd Street in the Twenty-first Ward; born in Ireland; illiterate; occupation: "I work in a car spring factory" (arrested).

JOHN LEARY, SR., 52, of 83 East 29th Street in the Twenty-first Ward; born in Ireland; a wheelwright and blacksmith; literate (arrested).

JOHN LEARY, JR., 13 of 83 East 29th Street in the Twenty-first Ward; born in New York; literate; occupation: "work with my father" (arrested).

MICHAEL LEARY, 23, of 330 Eighth Avenue in the Twentieth Ward; a shoemaker; born in Ireland; literate (arrested).

JAMES LEE, 19, of West 23rd Street in the Sixteenth Ward; born in Ireland (dead).

JAMES LEE, "about 24," lived in Brooklyn; kept a liquor and grocery store; born in Ireland (arrested).

FREDERICK LEIDER, 31, lived in Avenue A, between 11th and 12th streets, in the Seventeenth Ward; a basket maker; born in Ireland (dead).

JACOB LONG, 14, lived in 28th Street; born in New York; literate; occupation: "I work in a butcher's shop" (arrested).

RICHARD LYMAN, 23, born in Ireland (dead).

RICHARD LYNCH, 21, lived in 83rd Street; born in New York; a laborer; literate (arrested).

THOMAS LYONS, 30, lived in 33rd Street; a laborer; born in Ireland; illiterate (arrested).

DANIEL MCAULIFFE, 36, of 109 East 41st Street in the Nineteenth Ward; a laborer (wounded).

FRANCIS MCCABE, 18, lived in 40th Street, near Tenth Avenue; worked in a hoop-skirt manufactory; born in Ireland (dead).

MICHAEL MCCABE, "about 26," lived in Fifth Street; a workman; born in Ireland; illiterate (arrested).

WILLIAM MCCARTHY, 25, of 113 Cherry Street in the Fourth Ward; born in Belfast; illiterate; occupation: "sea-faring man" (arrested).

MICHAEL MCCARTY, 27, of 312 Avenue A in the Eighteenth Ward (wounded).

HUGH MCCLUSKEY, a juvenile (arrested).

R. S. MCCULLOH, Professor of Mechanics and Physics, Columbia College.

JOHN MCDERMOTT, a serving soldier (wounded).

EDWARD MCDEVITT, 27, of 32 Lewis Street in the Thirteenth Ward; a factory worker; born in Ireland (dead).

JAMES MCDONALD, 48, of East 25th Street in the Eighteenth Ward; a milkman; born in Ireland; barely literate (arrested).

PETER MCGEOUGH, 22, lived on 39th Street; born in Ireland; a peddler; illiterate (arrested).

DANIEL MCGOVERN, 19, lived at 127th Street and Eighth Avenue in the Twelfth Ward; born in Ireland; worked in the Harlem Candle Factory; literate (arrested).

MARY MCGOVERN, of 272 Tenth Avenue in the Twentieth Ward. "How old are you?–don't know . . . occupation: I keep house." Born in Ireland; illiterate (arrested).

JAMES MCGUIRE, 40, of Laurens Street in the Eighth Ward; a tailor; born in Ireland; illiterate (arrested).

JAMES MCLAUGHLIN, 58, of 243 East 30th Street in the Twenty-first Ward; born in Ireland (dead).

BARNEY MACKAY, born in Ireland (arrested).

THOMAS MCKAY, 12 (arrested).

HUGH MCMAHON, 33, of 277 First Avenue in the Eighteenth Ward; born in Ireland; a shoemaker (dead).

WILLIAM MCNALLY, a juvenile (arrested).

PATRICK S. MCNAMARA, 30, of 89 West 46th Street in the Twenty-second Ward; a laborer; born in Ireland (dead).

PATRICK MCSWEENEY, 24, of East 21st Street, near Avenue A, in the Eighteenth Ward; a barkeeper (wounded).

MICHAEL MAHAN, 39, of East 17th Street and Avenue A in the Eighteenth Ward; a laborer (wounded).

WILLIAM MALCOLMSON, 42, of 343 East 34th Street in the Twenty-first Ward; a hostler (wounded).

JOSEPH MARSHALL, 23, no fixed address; a seaman; born in Ireland (arrested).

JOHN MARTIN, 22, of 30 West Broadway in the Third Ward; a plumber; born in New York; literate (arrested).

JOHN MATSON, 49, of 30 Hamilton Street in the Seventh Ward; born in Denmark (dead).

WILLIAM MEALY, 19, of 32nd Street and Seventh Avenue in the Sixteenth Ward; a shoemaker; born in Ireland (dead).

MICHAEL MENAHEN, 20 (arrested).

PATRICK MERRY, 35, of 100 West 28th Street in the Twentieth Ward; a cellar-digger; born in Ireland (arrested).

GEORGE MILLER, 46, of 265 West 36th Street in the Twentieth Ward; a laborer; born in Germany (dead).

JOHN MILLER, 22, of 294 East 14th Street in the Eleventh Ward; a driver (wounded).

PETER MILLER, 30, of 190 East 38th Street in the Twenty-first Ward; born in Germany (dead).

JAMES MINOR, a juvenile (arrested).

PATRICK MONAHAN, 45, of 36th Street; a laborer; born in Ireland; illiterate (arrested).

THOMAS MULCHAY, a juvenile (arrested).

EDWARD MURPHY, 44, a laborer; born in Ireland (dead).

HONORA MURPHY, 11, of 229 East 20th Street in the Eighteenth Ward; born in Ireland (dead).

HOWARD MURPHY, 44, of 304 Monroe Street in the Seventh Ward; a laborer (wounded).

JOHN MURPHY, a juvenile (arrested).

JOHN MURRAY, 22, of 122 East 26th Street in the Eighteenth Ward (wounded).

WILLIAM MURRAY, 40, born in Ireland (dead).

JOHN NICHOLSON, 25, lived in Charlton Street in the Eighth Ward; a bricklayer; born in Ireland; illiterate (arrested).

PATRICK OATIS, 23, of 25th Street and Second Avenue in the Eighteenth Ward; a bricklayer; born in Ireland (arrested).

MICHAEL O'BRIEN, 38, lived in 30th Street; a cabinetmaker; born in Ireland; literate (arrested).

JOHN O'CONNOR, 22, of 251 East 21st Street in the Eighteenth Ward; a laborer (wounded).

PATRICK O'DONNELL, 24, born in Ireland (dead).

JOHN O'HARA, 21, of 93 Park Street in the Sixth Ward; a carpenter; born in Ireland; illiterate (arrested).

JOHN O'KEEFE, 21, of 42nd Street and Fourth Avenue in the Nineteenth Ward; born in the United States; literate (arrested).

PATRICK O'NEILL, 28, of Fifth Avenue between 56th and 57th streets in the Nineteenth Ward; a laborer; born in Ireland; literate (arrested).

PHILIP O'REILLY, 35, of 51 Willet Street in the Thirteenth Ward; born in Ireland; a carpenter (dead).

THEODORE OSTERSTOCK, 27, of 57 Greenwich Street in the First Ward; born in Pennsylvania; a circus rider, though he also kept a lager beer saloon (arrested).

JOHN PARKER, a juvenile (arrested).

WILLIAM PATTEN, a laborer; born in Ireland (arrested).

ELLEN PERKINSON, 53, born in Ireland (dead).

MARIA PILKIN, of 272 Water Street in the Fourth Ward (arrested).

PETER PINE, 58, of 50 West 30th Street in the Twentieth Ward; a store-keeper; born in the United States; illiterate (arrested).

SARAH PINE, 54, of 50 West 30th Street in the Twentieth Ward; occupation: "work at day work"; born in the United States; illiterate (arrested).

JOHN PIPER, 36, lived at 44th Street and Eleventh Avenue in the Twenty-second Ward; a teamster; born in New York (arrested).

MATTHEW POWERS, 24, lived in 67th Street, between Fourth and Fifth avenues, in the Nineteenth Ward; born in Ireland; a brass finisher; literate (arrested).

JAMES PURDY, 27, of Cedar Street in the First Ward; a sailor; born in England; literate (arrested).

PETER QUINN, 55, of 264 West 37th Street in the Twentieth Ward; born in Ireland (dead).

CORNELIUS REGAN, 11, of 215 East 13th Street in the Seventeenth Ward (wounded).

JOHN REILLY, 41, of 253 East 21st Street in the Eighteenth Ward; born in Ireland (dead).

WILLIAM RIGBY, 23, of Lispenard Street in the Fifth Ward; a hack driver; born in New York; illiterate (arrested).

MICHAEL H. RYAN, 27, of 180 West 25th Street in the Sixteenth Ward; born in Ireland (dead).

JAMES SCANFIELD, 13, of 170 West 34th Street in the Twentieth Ward (wounded).

OSWALD SCHENCK, "about 20" (arrested).

ADAM SCHLOSSHAUER, 48, lived in 115th Street in the Twelfth Ward; a gardener; born in Germany; illiterate (arrested).

ANTON SCHMIDT, 23, of 195 3rd Street in the Eleventh Ward; born in Germany (dead).

ERASMUS SCRENDSON, 25, of 144 East 21st Street in the Eighteenth Ward; a pianoforte maker (wounded).

ANN SHANDLEY, 45, of 94 West 28th Street in the Twentieth Ward; born in Ireland; housewife; illiterate (arrested).

FRANK A. SHANDLEY, 47, of 94 West 28th Street in the Twentieth Ward; a street paver; born in Ireland; illiterate (arrested).

JAMES SHANDLEY, 13, of 94 West 28th Street in the Twentieth Ward; born in Brooklyn; occupation: "work in fish market"; literate (arrested).

JOHN SHEEHY, 35, of 65th Street and Tenth Avenue in the Twenty-second Ward; a laborer (wounded).

PATRICK SHERRON, 25, of 11th Street; a blacksmith; born in Ireland; illiterate (arrested).

CHRISTOPHER SIDNEY, a juvenile (arrested).

MARK J. SILVA, 30, of 166 West 27th Street in the Twentieth Ward; born in England; Jewish; kept a tailor store; illiterate (arrested).

TERENCE SLAVIN, 25, of 296 West 45th Street in the Twenty-second Ward; born in Ireland (dead).

ANDREW SMITH, 29, of 75 Avenue B in the Eleventh Ward; a tailor; born in Germany; literate (arrested).

CHARLES SMITH, 18, of 143 East 40th Street in the Nineteenth Ward; a coach maker; born in New York; illiterate (arrested).

GEORGE SMITH, a juvenile (arrested).

WILLIAM SPALDING, 26, a real estate agent; born in New York; literate (arrested).

PAINTER SPRINGSTEIN, 35, of 50 West 30th Street in the Twentieth Ward; occupation: "anything I can get to do"; born in New Jersey; illiterate (arrested).

RICHARD STAFFORD, 17, of Eleventh Avenue, between 44th and 45th streets, in the Twenty-second Ward; a laborer (wounded).

WILLIAM STANTON, 28, of 87th Street and Fourth Avenue in the Twelfth Ward; born in New York; occupation: "laboring work in Central Park"; illiterate (arrested).

WILLIAM STEVENS, 13, of 225 Water Street in the Seventh Ward; born in New York (dead).

CORNELIUS SULLIVAN, 25, of 236 First Avenue in the Eighteenth Ward; laborer (wounded).

JEREMIAH SULLIVAN, 33, of 251 East 21st Street in the Eighteenth Ward; a laborer (wounded).

MICHAEL SULLIVAN, 25, of 326 First Avenue in the Eighteenth Ward; a laborer; born in Ireland (dead).

THOMAS S. SUTHERLAND, 27, of 250 South 4th Street, Jersey City; a boilermaker; born in England; literate (arrested).

PATRICK SWEENEY, 47, a laborer; born in Ireland (arrested).

WILLIAM HENRY THOMPSON, 10, of 38 Sheriff Street in the Thirteenth Ward (dead).

HENRY TILTON, 40, of 152 East 32nd Street in the Twenty-first Ward; a gardener who also kept a small grocery store; born in England; barely literate (arrested).

JOHN TRACEY, a sailor (arrested).

JEREMIAH TRACY, 41, of no fixed address; a laborer; born in Ireland (dead).

JOHN TRACEY, a sailor (arrested).

DANIEL VAUGHAN, 30, of 50th Street and Third Avenue in the Nineteenth Ward; a mason's laborer; born in Ireland; barely literate (arrested).

HENRY WADE, 32, lived in 25th Street; a boilermaker; born in Ireland; literate (arrested).

JOHN WARD, a barkeeper (arrested).

CATHARINE WATERS, 12, of 252 East 18th Street in the Eighteenth Ward (dead).

WILLIAM WATSON, 21, of 293 West 31st Street in the Twentieth Ward; a painter; born in New York (arrested).

RICHARD WELCH, 50, of 95 West 3rd Street in the Fifteenth Ward; a carpenter; born in Ireland (dead).

ANDREW WELLEY, 20, of 413 East 5th Street in the Eleventh Ward; a cartman (wounded).

DENNIS WELSH, 31, of 129 West 29th Street in the Twentieth Ward; a shoemaker; born in Ireland; literate (arrested).

JAMES H. WHITTEN, 52, of 150½ West 28th Street in the Twentieth Ward; a barber; born in Frederick, Maryland (arrested).

EDWARD ZUGENBUHLER, 30, of 340 West 39th Street in the Twentieth Ward; born in Switzerland (dead).

MATTHEW ZWEICK, 63, of 115 West 32nd Street in the Twentieth Ward; a laborer; born in Germany; literate (arrested).

There is also the 15-year-old rioter who, under the rules of St. Luke's Hospital, must remain anonymous.

No information is available on the following rioters:

Rose Bowman
Charles H. Burke
Peter Burke
George W. Burrows
Henry Canon
John Carr
Patrick Carroll
William Carroll
Michael Cavanaugh
John Conroy
Catherine Delaney
Charles Dennin
Charles Donaldson
Michael Donnelly
Francis Duffy
Michael Dunn
Charles Earley

Ulysses Ely
James Evans
John Everett
John Fay
Frank Fitzpatrick
John Fitzpatrick
Michael Flanagan
Patrick Flanagan
James Flanigan
Richard Friscoe
Stephen Gannon
Patrick Golding
Thomas Grace
James Green
James Haggerty
John Hart
William Hartley

Caspar Henry
Michael Hewitt
Samuel Hogan
Nathan Jacobs
Michael Kagan
Thomas Kane
Patrick Keegan
Herman Keller
James Kelly
Jacob Kesner
Jacob Kresling
Ann McCarty
James McDade
Thomas Mackin
Patrick McKenna
Francis McLaskey
Joseph McMullen
William McNally
[?] Marsh
James Minor
Robert Mitchell
Thomas Mollet
[?] Montgomery
John Morton
[?] Mullan
Edward Murphy
John Murphy
Patrick Murphy
[?] Myers

Thomas Nugent
Ellen O'Beirne
Patrick O'Brien
Margaret Potter
John Riley
[?] Rogers
John Rogon
Patrick Rooney
David Ryan
John Ryder
Robert Sadler
Matthew P. Sennott
Edward Smith
William T. Smith
Charles Spencer
Patrick Stanton
Catharine Stapleton
Joseph Stehel
John Stepphan
Charles Stuart
Archibald Taylor
David Tenell
George Thompson
John F. Wells
Nancy Westbrook
John Wiedel
Mary Wilkins
Maggie Williams
William Wood

I have used my own judgment in drawing up this list of rioters and have not necessarily been bound by what the grand jury or the courts decided. In view of the courage it took to make a complaint in the New York City of the 1860s, I have given complainants' evidence great weight. I have, however, excluded John McAllister, who was clearly a victim of mistaken identification. Among the wounded, I have given Henry McMahon the benefit of the doubt, and it is clear that John Mulhare, 8, and Eliza Elliott, 9, were too young to be rioters. L. L. Jones was a spectator, and Marcella Mahoney a passer-by. Among the dead, I have excluded Ellen Kirke, 2, and Elizabeth Marshall, 6, as too young. I have included Mary Carmody, 10, and Honora Murphy, 11, since the evidence seems to show that they were in the streets, some way from their homes. Delia Lawrence was carrying her baby when she was shot, and it does not seem probable that she would have the child with her if she were rioting. Everyone agreed that William Cooper Williams was a spectator. So, almost certainly, was John

Gotz, who was shot while standing in his own yard door. Patrick Sheedy McNamara was clubbed at his own door, but the coroner and the jury in that case were obviously convinced that the police and troops were justified in beating him. It is not easy to decide about John Gaffney, but since he did not move away when Lieutenant Wood ordered the crowd to disperse, he must be counted as a rioter. On the other hand, Jane Barry, the little girl who was crushed to death by a bureau thrown from the Colored Orphan Asylum, was clearly a spectator.

Catherine Carbery, Lawrence Culboy, Mary Donahue, and Charles E. Davis might have been included, but since it was not certain that they were rioters, it seemed better to leave them out.

# Notes

*Abbreviations*

Columbia – Special Collections, Butler Library, Columbia University.
Comptroller's Records – Office of the Comptroller of the City of New York, Municipal Building, Chambers and Centre Streets, New York, N.Y.
CCB – Records Room, Supreme Court, County of New York, State of New York, Criminal Courts Building, 100 Centre Street, New York, N.Y.
H.R. – Hall of Records, Chambers Street, New York, N.Y.
L.C. – Manuscripts Division, Library of Congress.
MARC – Municipal Archives and Records Centre, 23 Park Row, New York, N.Y.
N.A. – National Archives, Washington, D.C.
N.Y.H.S. – New York Historical Society.
N.Y.H.S.Q. – *New York Historical Society Quarterly*.
N.Y.P.L. – New York Public Library.
N.Y.S.L. – New York State Library, Albany.
St. Joseph's – Cardinal James Francis McIntyre Reading Room, Archbishop Corrigan Memorial Library, St. Joseph's Seminary, Yonkers, N.Y.

*Chapter 1*

1. Camille Ferri Pisani, *Prince Napoleon in America, 1861: Letters from His Aide-de-Camp*, trans. Georges J. Joyaux (Bloomington: Indiana University Press, 1959), pp. 37–38; W. E. Baxter, *American and the Americans* (London: G. Routledge, 1855), p. 16; "Lord Acton's American Diaries," *Fortnightly Review* 110 (1921): 727–28; Junius Henri Browne, *The Great Metropolis: A Mirror of New York. A Complete History of Metropolitan Life and Society, with Sketches of Prominent Places, Persons and Things in the City as They Actually Exist* (Hartford, Conn.: American Publishing, 1869), p. 60.

2. *Statistics of Population of the City and County of New York as shown by the State Census of 1865, with the comparative results of this and previous enumerations and other Statistics given by the State and Federal Census, from*

*the earliest period, prepared at the request of the Committee on Annual Taxes of the Board of Supervisors by Franklin B. Hough. Document No. 13, Board of Supervisors, August 15, 1866* (New York, [n.p.], 1866), pp. 30, 50 (hereafter cited as Hough); Robert G. Albion, with the collaboration of Jennie Barnes Pope, *The Rise of New York Port [1815–1860]* (New York: Charles Scribner's Sons, 1939), passim; *Harper's Weekly*, April 11, 1857; Edward Ewing Pratt, *Industrial Causes of Congestion of Population in New York City*, Columbia University Studies in History, Economics and Public Law, vol. 43, no. 1 (New York: Columbia University Press, 1911), p. 38; Hough, pp. 53, 54.

3. Joel H. Ross, *What I Saw in New York; Or, A Bird's Eye View of City Life* (Auburn, N.Y.: Derby & Miller, 1852), pp. 19–20; Thomas Adams et al., *Population, Land Values and Government: Studies of the Growth and Distribution of Population and Land Values, and of Problems of Government*, Regional Survey, vol. 2 (New York: Regional Plan of New York and Its Environs, 1929), p. 53; Charles Astor Bristed, *The Upper Ten Thousand* (New York: Stinger & Townsend, 1852), p. 37; *Harper's Weekly*, November 13, 1858; Ruffin, *Anticipations of the Future*, p. 142; Browne, *The Great Metropolis*, p. 25; Pisani, *Prince Napoleon in America*, pp. 53–54; *New York Leader*, June 16, 1860; *New York Herald*, September 6, 1857, and August 10, 1855; U.S. Works Progress Administration, Federal Writers Project, *New York City Guide* (New York: Random House, 1939), p. 60; [Henry Sedley], *Dangerfield's Rest; or, Before the Storm. A Novel of American Life and Manners* (New York: Sheldon, 1864), p. 195.

4. *New York Herald*, August 10, 1855, May 12, 1856, May 4, 1859, and March 25, 1863; *New York Journal of Commerce*, August 29, 1859; John J. Sturtevant, "Recollections," p. 27, N.Y.P.L. Reminiscences of William A. Prendergast, 1:6, Oral History Project, Columbia University; Diary of Philip Hone, May 31, 1850, N.Y.H.S.; Edward P. Mitchell, *Memoirs of an Editor: Fifty Years of Journalism* (New York: Charles Scribner's Sons, 1941), pp. 18–19; Bayrd Still, ed., *Mirror for Gotham: New York as Seen by Contemporaries from Dutch Days to the Present* (New York: New York University Press, 1956), pp. 176–77; Pisani, *Prince Napoleon in America*, p. 53; Browne, *The Great Metropolis*, p. 291.

5. WPA, *New York City Guide*, p. 146; Otho G. Cartwright, *The Middle West Side. A Historical Sketch*, Russell Sage Foundation West Side Studies (New York: Survey Associates, Inc., 1914), pp. 34–35, 37–39.

6. Quoted in Jane Jacobs, *The Death and Life of Great American Cities* (New York: Random House, 1961), p. 247.

7. *New York Herald*, May 12, 1856, and April 5, 1860; Edward W. Watkin, *A Trip to the United States and Canada: In a series of letters* (London: W. H. Smith and Son, 1852), p. 11; Albert Ulman, *Maiden Lane–The Story of a Single Street* (New York: Maiden Lane Historical Society, 1931), pp. 72–84; Robert A. Ernst, *Immigrant Life in New York City, 1825–1863* (New York: King's Crown Press, 1949), p. 82; Albion, *Rise of New York Port*, pp. 292–93; Lawrence Costello, "The New York City Labor Movement during the Civil War" (Ph.D. diss., Columbia University, 1967), pp. 38–39.

8. Pratt, *Industrial Causes of Congestion*, p. 15; J. D. B. De Bow, *The Seventh Census of the United States: 1850* (Washington: Robert Armstrong, Public Printer, 1853), p. 102; J. C. G. Kennedy, *Population of the United States in 1860: Compiled from the Original Returns of the Eighth Census* (Washington: Government Printing Office, 1864), p. 337; Francis A. Walker, *The Statistics of*

*the Population of the United States, Embracing the Tables of Race, Nationality, Sex, Selected Ages, and Occupations, To Which are Added the Statistics of School Attendance and Illiteracy, of Schools, Libraries, Newspapers and Periodicals, Churches, Pauperism and Crime, and of Areas, Families and Dwellings. Compiled from the Original Returns of the Ninth Census (June 1, 1870), under the direction of the Secretary of the Interior* (Washington: Government Printing Office, 1872), 1:212–13.

9. Fort Tryon Park and the west side of Morningside Park give an idea of the natural terrain of the area. Comptroller Andrew H. Green to Mayor William H. Wickham, November 15, 1875, Box 6051, Mayors' Papers, MARC; John J. Sturtevant, "Recollections," pp. 26–27; WPA, *New York City Guide*, p. 186; Theodore Lothrop Stoddard, *Master of Manhattan: The Life of Richard Croker* (New York: Longmans, Green, 1931), pp. 17–18; Croswell Bowen, *The Elegant Oakey* (New York: Oxford University Press, 1956), p. 270.

10. Charles Townsend Harris, *Memories of Manhattan in the Sixties and Seventies* (New York: Derrydale Press, 1928), p. 61; Diary of George Templeton Strong, February 13, 1865, Columbia; *Harper's Weekly*, December 12, 1863; *New York Leader*, March 31, 1860; I. N. Phelps Stokes, "New York City Slums," pp. 2121–22, N.Y.P.L., quoting *Letter of John I. Davenport, Esq., on the subject of the population of the City of New York, Its Density and the Evils resulting therefrom* (New York: Arcade Railway, 1884), pp. 16–17; *New York Journal of Commerce*, February 20, 1857, and January 14, 1860; *New York Evening Post*, March 28, 1863; Sedley, *Dangerfield's Rest*, p. 79.

11. Horace Greeley, quoted in Wheaton J. Lane, *Commodore Vanderbilt: An Epic of the Steam Age* (New York: Alfred A. Knopf, 1942), p. 205.

12. *New York Journal of Commerce*, April 5, 1864; *New York Daily Transcript*, March 3, 1863; Lane, *Vanderbilt*, pp. 204–5; Leonard Jerome to Mayor Edward Cooper, August 3, 1879, November [no day], 1879, Box 435, Rapid Transit, 1875–1886, Mayor's Papers, MARC.

13. *New York Journal of Commerce*, April 1, 1857, and July 16, 1858; *New York Times*, August 20, 1858; Diary of George Templeton Strong, September 11, 1858, Columbia.

14. Some 25,000 people commuted daily from Brooklyn to New York in the early 1860s. The *New York Herald*, September 10, 1855, put the figure at 20,000. Harold C. Syrett, *The City of Brooklyn, 1865–1898*, Columbia University Studies in History, Economics and Public Law, no. 512 (New York: Columbia University Press, 1944), pp. 11, 13, estimated that 10 percent of Brooklyn's populace worked in New York in 1865. That year Brooklyn had 295,440 people.

15. *New York Herald*, January 11, 1856, and November 20, 1858; *New York Journal of Commerce*, February 9, 19, 1856, and January 19, 1857; D. B. Steinman, *The Builders of the Bridge: The Story of John Roebling and His Son* (New York: Harcourt, Brace, 1945), pp. 292–98; *New York Herald*, February 28, 1863.

16. Mayor Opdyke to the Board of Aldermen, May 15, 1863, Mayor's Letterbooks, Box 5335, MARC.

17. *New York Journal of Commerce*, February 5, April 13, 1853, March 14, April 12, 1856, and August 17, 1858.

18. This figure includes equipment; James B. Walker, *Fifty Years of Rapid Transit, 1864–1917* (New York: Law Printing, 1918), pp. 10–11, 28.

19. *New York Journal of Commerce*, December 8, 13, 1864; *New York Mail and Express*, May 1, 3, 1895, enclosed in Charles T. Harvey to Mayor Strong,

May 3, 1895, Rapid Transit, 1890–1897, Box 437, Mayor's Papers, MARC; Cyrus Clark to Mayor William Wickham, May 10, 1875, Box 227, Letters to Mayor Wickham, May–July, 1875, Mayor's Papers, MARC; William Fullerton Reeves, "Rapid Transit Elevated Lines in New York City," N.Y.H.S.Q., 18, pt. 4 (January 1935):59–82; Robert Daley, "Alfred Ely Beach and His Wonderful Pneumatic Underground Railway," *American Heritage* 12 (June 1961):57.

20. Ross, *What I Saw in New York*, pp. 82–87; Stoddard, *Master of Manhattan*, p. 21; Oscar Handlin, *The Newcomers: Negroes and Puerto Ricans in a Changing Metropolis* (Cambridge, Mass.: Harvard University Press, 1959), pp. 11–16; Samuel B. Halliday, *The Lost and Found; Or, Life Amongst the Poor* (New York: Blakeman & Mason, 1859), pp. 56–58.

21. I. N. Phelps Stokes, "New York City Slums," pp. 1151–58, N.Y.P.L., quoting S. A. Raborg, "The Sanitary and Moral Condition of New York City," *Catholic World* 7 (1868):553–54; *New York Herald*, August 12, 1855; Halliday, *The Lost and Found*, pp. 90–91, 190–205.

22. *New York in Slices, by an Experienced Carver. Being the Original Slices Published in the N.Y. Tribune* (New York: W. F. Burgess, 1849), p. 22; Halliday, *The Lost and Found*, pp. 207–15. The city missionaries had done a little to improve the area by the mid-1850s; *Harper's Weekly*, February 21, 1857; [Solon Robinson], *Hot Corn: Life Scenes in New York Illustrated* (New York: De Witt and Davenport, 1854), pp. 208–9; Ladies of the Mission, *The Old Brewery and the New Mission at the Five Points* (New York: Stringer & Townsend, 1854), passim.

23. From 12½ to 25 cents. A New York pound was worth $2.50. See James F. Richardson, *The New York Police: Colonial Times to 1901* (New York: Oxford University Press, 1970), p. 17.

24. State of New York, *Report of the Select Committee appointed to examine into the condition of Tenant Houses in New-York and Brooklyn*, Assembly Doc. No. 205, March 9, 1857, p. 13–29; *New York Herald*, March 28, July 6, 1856; *Hot Corn*, pp. 70, 209–16, 311, 313, 314.

25. Samuel Gompers, *Seventy Years of Life and Labor*, rev. and ed. Philip Taft and John A. Sessions (New York: E. P. Dutton, 1957), p. 54.

26. *Report of the Select Committee*, pp. 20–22. State of New York, *Annual Reports of the Board of Commissioners of Metropolitan Police*, Assembly Document No. 226, January 27, 1863, pp. 19–20; Assembly Document No. 28, January 22, 1864, p. 78; Assembly Document No. 36, January 9, 1865, pp. 48–49, 53–54; Assembly Document No. 12, January 9, 1866, pp. 63–66; hereafter cited as *Report of the Police Commissioners; New York Journal of Commerce*, January 25, May 31, 1853, and August 7, 1856; Cartwright, *Middle West Side*, pp. 34–35; *New York Leader*, September 24, 1864; WPA, *New York City Guide*, p. 187.

27. *Report of the Select Committee*, p. 19; the Working Men's Home, running through the block from Elizabeth to Mott streets, charged $5.50 to $8.50 a month. Rooms at 98 Christopher Street cost from $5.00 to $7.00 a month. *New York Journal of Commerce*, September 16, 1856.

28. *New York Herald*, February 2, July 6, 1856.

29. *Report of the Select Committee*, pp. 19–20.

30. Ernst, *Immigrant Life*, p. 50.

31. *Report of the Police Commissioners*, January 9, 1866, pp. 17–19.

32. *New York Journal of Commerce*, November 26, 1864; the building of St.

Patrick's stopped in 1860, when Archbishop John Hughes ran out of money; see Katherine Burton, *The Dream Lives Forever: The Story of St. Patrick's Cathedral* (New York: Longmans, Green, 1960), pp. xi, 41–42.

33. Diary of George Templeton Strong, July 16, 1857, April 3, 1859, February 27, 1864, and October 22, 1867, Columbia; *New York Herald*, July 11, 13, 1857, and December 29, 1869; *New York Journal of Commerce*, April 28, 1853, March 27, 1855, July 22, 1858, June 25, August 8, and September 20, 1859; John J. Sturtevant, "Recollections," pp. 26–27, N.Y.P.L; "Squatter Life in New York," *Harper's New Monthly Magazine* 90 (September 1880): 563–69; Halliday, *The Lost and Found*, p. 150.

34. Charles Loring Brace, *The Dangerous Classes of New York, and Twenty Years' Work among Them* (New York: Wynkoop & Hallumbeck, 1872), pp. 151–53.

35. *Report of the Council of Hygiene and Public Health of the Citizens' Association of New York upon the Sanitary Condition of the City* (New York: D. Appleton, 1865), pp. x, xxxix–xl, lxx–lxxii; Report of the Board of Surgeons for the Year Ending November 1st, 1864, in *Report of the Police Commissioners*, January 9, 1865, pp. 48–51; Stephen Smith, *The City That Was* (New York: Frank Allaben, 1911), pp. 59, 123–24.

On March 13, 1861, the *New York Herald* carried a story about tenement conditions which included the following table:

| Wards | Number of houses containing 10 or more families each | Number of families | Number of people |
|:---:|:---:|:---:|:---:|
| 1 | 48 | 709 | 2,752 |
| 2 | 3 | 34 | 107 |
| 3 | 2 | 21 | 88 |
| 4 | 60 | 1,135 | 4,870 |
| 5 | 54 | 813 | 3,330 |
| 6 | 87 | 1,239 | 5,143 |
| 7 | 81 | 1,263 | 5,383 |
| 8 | 52 | 685 | 2,695 |
| 9 | 41 | 560 | 2,173 |
| 10 | 80 | 1,224 | 4,897 |
| 11 | 171 | 2,340 | 9,419 |
| 12 | 1 | 10 | 38 |
| 13 | 104 | 1,165 | 5,251 |
| 14 | 98 | 1,397 | 5,348 |
| 15 | 33 | 397 | 1,724 |
| 16 | 36 | 453 | 1,678 |
| 17 | 387 | 5,602 | 20,825 |
| 18 | 186 | 2,678 | 10,741 |
| 19 | 22 | 258 | 1,042 |
| 20 | 147 | 1,936 | 7,814 |
| 21 | 84 | 1,092 | 4,193 |
| 22 | 45 | 566 | 2,579 |
| TOTAL | 1,822 | 25,677 | 102,090 |

Of these 1,822 tenements housing ten families or more, 108 contained over twenty families, distributed by ward as follows: First, 6; Fourth, 15; Fifth, 7; Sixth, 5; Seventh, 15; Eighth, 2; Ninth, 1; Tenth, 11; Eleventh, 5; Thirteenth, 1; Fourteenth, 7; Seventeenth, 19; Eighteenth, 8; Twentieth, 3; Twenty-first, 3.

36. *New York Leader*, May 24, 1863; *New York in Slices*, pp. 82–83; *Report of the Council on Hygiene*, pp. 60–61; *New York Journal of Commerce*, January 9, 1860; *Report of the Select Committee*, pp. 25–26; Roy Lubove, "The New York Association for Improving the Condition of the Poor: The Formative Years," N.Y.H.S.Q. 43 (July 1959):312; John Duffy, *A History of Public Health in New York City, 1625–1866* (New York: Russell Sage Foundation, 1968), pp. 427–37.

37. *Report of the Council of Hygiene*, p. 101.

38. *Reports of the Police Commissioners*, January 9, 1865, pp. 48–51, January 9, 1866, pp. 68–69; *New York Evening Post*, April 3, July 1, 1863; *Report of the Council of Hygiene*, pp. xcix–ci, cviii–cx, 5–348 passim; Ernst, *Immigrant Life*, p. 22; Handlin, *The Newcomers*, p. 16; *New York Journal of Commerce*, March 12, 1856.

39. *New York Commercial Advertiser*, June 8, 1863; *Report of the Police Commissioners*, January 9, 1865, pp. 49–50; *Report of the Council of Hygiene*, p. cxxvii; *New York Journal of Commerce*, June 11, 23, 1863; *New York Herald*, July 24, 29, August 2, 5, 1856, and March 7, 1861; Duffy, *Public Health in New York City*, pp. 363–74; Edward Dicey, *Six Months in the Federal States* (London: Macmillan, 1863), 1:20; *New York Evening Post*, January 6, 1863; *New York Sunday Dispatch*, December 14, 1862; *New York Sunday Mercury*, April 12, 1863; *New York Journal of Commerce*, March 26, 1855; *New York Herald*, January 28, June 5, 1857, and February 23, 1860; *New York Commercial Advertiser*, May 27, 1863; *New York Journal of Commerce*, April 6, 1857.

40. *Report of the Police Commissioners*, January 9, 1866, pp. 9–10.

41. *Report of the Council of Hygiene*, pp. 147–48; *Report of the Police Commissioners*, January 9, 1865, pp. 48–49; *New York Journal of Commerce*, January 4, 1855, and January 6, 1857; Diary of George Templeton Strong, March 18, 1865, Columbia; "Squatter Life in New York," p. 562; *New York Herald*, August 24, 1855.

## Chapter 2

1. These were Election Riot, 1834; anti-abolitionist riots, 1834 and 1835; Stevedores' Riot, 1836; Flour Riots, 1837; Election Riot, 1842; Astor Place Riots, 1849; Labor Riots, 1850; Kaine Riots, 1852; Fourth of July Riots, 1853; Police Riots, 1857; Dead Rabbits-Bowery Boys Riots, 1857; Draft Riots, 1863; Orangeman's Day Riots, 1870 and 1871; and the Tompkins Square Riots of 1874.

2. Mayor Aaron Clark to the Board of Aldermen, January 28, 1839, City Clerk, Filed Papers, Box 3008, MARC; *New York Herald*, May 6, 24, June 15, July 8, 1836.

3. *New York Times*, August 2, 1864, and July 12, 1870.

4. *New York Journal of Commerce*, November 3, 1858.

5. Diary of Philip Hone, February 24, 25, March 21, 1836, and April 7, 1840, N.Y.H.S.; *New York Herald*, March 17, May 26, June 7, 15, 1836; Carl N.

Degler, *Labor in the Economy and Politics of New York City, 1850–1860: A Study of the Impact of Early Industrialism* (Ph.D. diss., Columbia University, 1952), pp. 80–82.

6. Diary of Philip Hone, July 10, 12, 14, 22, 1834, N.Y.H.S.; 1834 Riot Papers, N.Y.H.S.; Mayor Aaron Clark to the Board of Aldermen, January 28, 1839, Box 3008, City Clerk, Filed Papers, MARC; *New York Evening Post,* July 10, 11, 12, 1834. There were other anti-abolitionist outbreaks in New York in October 1833, May 1834, and June 1835. For a very inadequate attempt at analysis of these riots, see Leonard L. Richards, *"Gentlemen of Property and Standing": Anti-Abolition Riots in America in the 1830s* (New York: Oxford University Press, 1969).

7. Cases of Keziah Manning, Jesse Harrod and Henry Pier, Indictments, April 1837, CCB; *New York Evening Star,* April 13, 1837, quoted in *Baltimore Republican,* April 17, 1837; *New York Colored American,* April 15, 22, 1837; *New York Evening Post for the Country,* April 17, 1837; *New York Herald,* April 12, 13, 14, 19, 21, 25, 1837.

8. Ray A. Billington, *The Protestant Crusade, 1800–1860: A Study of the Origins of American Nativism* (New York: Macmillan, 1938), pp. 60, 303, 319; Edward Van Every, *Sins of New York: As Exposed by the Police Gazette* (New York: Frederick A. Stokes, 1930), pp. 83–85; *New York Herald,* November 28, 29, December 1, 2, 4–9, 11, 13, 1855.

9. *New York Herald,* May 23, 1836; Diary of Philip Hone, April 13, 1842, N.Y.H.S.; Diary of George Templeton Strong, April 13, 1842, Columbia.

10. *New York Times,* July 13, 1870; Diary of George Templeton Strong, July 13, 1870, Columbia. Two of the injured died from their wounds. *New York Times,* July 12, 1871.

11. *New York Times,* July 9–11, 1871; Diary of George Templeton Strong, July 10, 11, 1871, Columbia; *New York Herald,* July 11, 1871; *New York Tribune,* July 11, 1871; *New York Sun,* July 11, 1871; *New York Standard,* July 11, 1871; *New York Evening Post,* July 11, 1871; *New York Commercial Advertiser,* July 11, 1871.

12. *New York Times,* July 12–18, 1871; Diary of George Templeton Strong, July 12, 13, 15, 1871, Columbia; George William Wright to Neely Wright, July 10, 1871, Wright Papers, N.Y.H.S.; Diary of Edward N. Tailer, Jr., July 12, 1871, N.Y.H.S.; Diary of Andrew Lester, July 12, 1871, N.Y.H.S.

13. Diary of Philip Hone, October 13, 15, 17, 18, 1831, and June 19, 1832, N.Y.H.S.; *New York Evening Post,* October 14, 1831.

14. Diary of Philip Hone, July 10, 1834, N.Y.H.S.; Milo Osborne to Mayor Cornelius W. Lawrence, n.d., 1834 Riot Papers, N.Y.H.S.; *New York Evening Post,* July 10, 1834; Richards, *Gentlemen of Property and Standing,* p. 116. The mob looked upon abolitionism as a British plot to divide and disrupt the United States.

15. Diary of Philip Hone, October 14, 27, 1834, N.Y.H.S.; Anne Mathews to Charles J. Mathews, September 30, October 14, 30, 1834, printed in Anne Mathews, *Memoirs of Charles Mathews, Comedian* (London: Richard Bentley, 1839), 4:292–305.

16. Diary of Philip Hone, May 28, June 10, 1836, N.Y.H.S.; *New York Herald,* May 30, 1836; *New York Evening Post,* May 27, 28, 1836; *New York Leader,* April 11, 1863.

17. Richard Moody, *The Astor Place Riot* (Bloomington: Indiana University Press, 1958), passim; I. Prescott Hall et al. to William C. Macready, May 8, 1849, New York City Miscellany, N.Y.H.S.; Diary of Philip Hone, May 8, 10–12, 14, 1849, N.Y.H.S.; Diary of Edward N. Tailer, Jr., May 10, 11, 14, 1849, N.Y.H.S.; Diary of George Templeton Strong, May 11, 12, 14, 1849, Columbia; Petitions, Amount of Expenses and Minutes of the Meetings of Mayor and Aldermen regarding petitions, City Clerk's Papers, Box 2988, MARC; *The Diaries of William Charles Macready, 1833–1851*, ed. William Toynbee (New York: G.P. Putnam's Sons, 1912), 2:404–29.

18. Diary of Philip Hone, February 13, 14, 1837, N.Y.H.S.; Diary of Henry A. Patterson, February 13, 1837, N.Y.H.S.; Cases of John Windt, Ezra Porter, Edward Smith, Edmund S. Weeks, William S. Arents, John Gaw, Edward Eager, George Grant, William Louge, James Kelly, Elijah Olmstead, Francis Rosier, Henry E. Harrison, William Liner, Nick Billot, James Dandridge, John McLaughlin, James Chapman, Eugene Argon, William Wood, Sandford Thorn, Michael Kaser, Francis Barton, James Roach, Daniel Marshall, and Matthias Pearcher, Indictments, March 1837, CCB; see R.B. Rose, "Eighteenth Century Price Riots: The French Revolution and the Jacobin Maximum," *International Review of Social History* 4, pt. 3 (1959):432–45; "Eighteenth Century Price Riots and Public Policy in England," *I.R.S.H.* 6, pt. 2 (1961):277–92, and E.J. Hobsbawm, *Primitive Rebels: Studies in Archaic Forms of Social Movement in the 19th and 20th Centuries* (Manchester: Manchester University Press, 1959), pp. 108–25.

19. Diary of Philip Hone, May 15, 1843, N.Y.H.S.; Duffy, *Public Health in New York City*, p. 469; Billington, *Protestant Crusade*, p. 196.

20. Diary of Philip Hone, April 8, 1834, and November 3, 1840, N.Y.H.S.

21. Carleton J. Beals, *Brass Knuckle Crusade* (New York: Hastings House, 1960), p. 12; James L. Crouthamel, *James Watson Webb: A Biography* (Middletown, Conn.: Wesleyan University Press, 1969), p. 75; *New York Herald*, February 7, March 25, 1856; Diary of Philip Hone, December 2, 1839, January 21, 1843, and May 5, 1847, N.Y.H.S.; Diary of George Templeton Strong, February 1, 1857, Columbia.

22. *Report of the Select Committee*, pp. 13–14; see also Halliday, *The Lost and Found*, passim.

23. Diary of George Templeton Strong, July 7, 1851, Columbia; *New York Journal of Commerce*, March 15, 1853, and February 20, 1857; *Report of the Police Commissioners*, January 22, 1864, p. 9; Brace, *The Dangerous Classes of New York*, p. 194; Diary of Edward N. Tailer, Jr., January 25, 1864, N.Y.H.S.; Elizabeth Oakes Smith, *The Newsboy* (New York: J.C. Derby, 1854), pp. 11–71; *The Old Brewery*, pp. 155, 162, 167–69, 177–81; Halliday, *The Lost and Found*, pp. 138–39, 142; *New York Tribune*, July 13, 1857.

24. Costello, "The New York City Labor Movement," pp. 66–67; George G. Foster, *New York Naked* [New York: De Witt & Davenport, 185?], pp. 137–38, 152–53; Foster, *New York in Slices*, pp. 50–51; Philip S. Foner, *History of the Labor Movement in the United States: From Colonial Times to the Founding of the American Federation of Labor* (New York: International Publishers, 1947), p. 341.

25. Stoddard, *Master of Manhattan*, pp. 26–27; Alvin F. Harlow, *Old Bowery Days: The Chronicles of a Famous Street* (New York: Appleton, 1931), pp. 194–95, 306; *New York Tribune*, July 6, 1857.

26. Browne, *The Great Metropolis*, p. 564; John E. Hilary Skinner, *After the Storm; or, Jonathan and his Neighbors in 1865–66* (London: Richard Bentley, 1866), 1:15–16; Minute Book, 1863, Board of Fire Commissioners, N.Y.H.S.; *New York Leader*, July 16, 1859, November 19, 1864, and January 21, 28, 1865; *New York Journal of Commerce*, December 14, 15, 1864, February 9, 1865; Herbert Asbury, *Ye Olde Fire Laddies* (New York: Alfred A. Knopf, 1930), pp. 154–56, 166–68; *New York Herald*, September 28, 1857; *New York World*, July 26, 1860; Memorial of Henry B. Hinsdale and members of the New York Fire Department to the Common Council, January 27, 1840, City Clerk, Filed Papers, Box 3008, MARC; *Report of the Committee on the Fire Department*; adopted, Aldermen, September 13, 1852; Assistants, September 17, 1852; approved by Mayor Kingsland, September 18, 1852, City Clerk Documents—Approved, Box 2814, MARC; Augustine E. Costello, *Our Firemen: A History of the New York Fire Departments* (New York: privately published, 1887), pp. 97–100, 115–19, 161–62, 173–81, 183–86.

27. Billington, *Protestant Crusade*, pp. 231–32; John Francis Maguire, *The Irish in America* (London: Longmans, Green, 1868), pp. 440–42; Mayor Robert H. Morris to James Harper, May 9, 1844, Harper Papers, N.Y.H.S.

28. As Charles Tilly's *The Vendee* (Cambridge, Mass.: Harvard University Press, 1964) shows, marginal groups such as the Irish immigrants, cut off from the rural community and not integrated with the urban community, are especially prone to violence.

29. In theory, the groggeries were supposed to be closed, too, but the police rarely enforced this law; *New York Herald*, April 13, 1856, February 13, June 4, October 16, 1859, and September 28, 1860; *New York Journal of Commerce*, November 12, 1859, and March 31, June 6, 1863; *New York Leader*, April 21, 1860; John J. Sturtevant, "Recollections," p. 47, N.Y.P.L.; Alexander J. Wall, "The Sylvan Steamboats on the East River, New York to Harlem," N.Y.H.S.Q. 8 (October 1924):59–72; Vincent F. Seyfried, *The Long Island Rail Road: A Comprehensive History*, part 2, *The Flushing, North Shore & Central Railroad* (Garden City, N.Y.: privately published, 1963), p. 23.

30. *New York Journal of Commerce*, April 13, 1857, November 17, 1864, and February 22, 1865; *New York Herald*, January 3, 1855, January 28, 1857, October 28, 1858, November 20, 1859, January 4, 1860, and December 7, 1861; *New York Commercial Advertiser*, December 4, 5, 1863; *New York Evening Post*, January 5, October 26, 1863; *Harper's Weekly*, March 28, 1857; Mayor A. Oakey Hall to the Common Council, January 3, 1870, Mayor's Letterbooks, Box 5335, MARC; Diary of Philip Hone, April 12, 1848, N.Y.H.S.

31. *New York Herald*, November 11, December 1, 1858; *Harper's Weekly*, October 6, 1860; *New York Commercial Advertiser*, December 30, 1863; Diary of George Templeton Strong, June 10, 1859, and November 23, 1857; Theodore Roosevelt, *Autobiography* (New York: Macmillan, 1913), p. 63; Stoddard, *Master of Manhattan*, p. 13; James D. McCabe, *Lights and Shadows of New York Life; or, The sights and sensations of the great city. A work descriptive of the city of New York in all its various phases. . .* (Philadelphia: National Publishing Co., 1872), pp. 64–65.

32. *New York Herald*, March 10, 1855, November 17, 1856, November 9, 10, 11, 1858, October 1, 15, 1859, and January 24, 1860; *Plunkitt of Tammany Hall. A Series of Very Plain Talks on Very Practical Politics, Delivered by Ex-Senator George Washington Plunkitt, the Tammany Philosopher from His Rostrum—*

*the New York County Court House Bootblack Stand—and Recorded by William
L. Riordan* (New York: Alfred A. Knopf, 1948), p. 111; Alfred Connable and
Edward Silberfarb, *Tigers of Tammany: Nine Men Who Ran New York* (New
York: Holt, Rinehart & Winston, 1967), pp. 115–16; *New York Herald*, No-
vember 1, 1858, quoted in William M. Ivins, *Machine Politics and Money in
Elections in New York City* (New York: Harper, 1887), pp. 130–31; *New York
Journal of Commerce*, March 4, February 16, 1853.

33. *New York Herald*, February 2, November 17, 1856; *New York Journal
of Commerce*, November 26, 1855, and December 8, 1859; Diary of Philip Hone,
April 15, 1840, and April 12, 1843, N.Y.H.S.; *New York Tribune*, November 4,
1850, quoted in Seth Low, *New York in 1850 and 1890. A Political Study. An
Address Delivered Before the New York Historical Society on its Eighty-seventh
Anniversary, Tuesday, November 17, 1891* (New York: Printed for the Society,
1892), p. 19; Duffy, *Public Health in New York City*, p. 324; Case of Thomas
Reeves, Indictments, November 1856, CCB; Lyman Abbott, *Reminiscences*
(Boston: Houghton Mifflin, 1915), pp. 111–12; John I. Davenport, *The Election
and the Naturalization Frauds in New York City, 1860–1870* (New York: [n.p.],
1894), pp. 29–48.

34. James Parton, "The Government of the City of New York," *North American Review* 213 (October 1866):437, 451–52; Duffy, *Public Health in New York
City*, pp. 320–21, 324, 325, 368; *New York Herald*, September 25, October 9,
1855, June 6, November 14, 1856, October 26, May 7, October 27, 1858, October 4, 1859, and January 13, 1860; Connable and Silberfarb, *Tigers of Tammany*, pp. 118–19, 121, 122, 129.

35. Charles R. Miller to Salmon P. Chase, July 28, 1863, Chase Papers, L.C.;
Diary of George Templeton Strong, April 9, 1855, April 10, 1857, Columbia;
*New York Courier and Enquirer*, March 16, 1860, quoted in the *New York
Herald*, March 19, 1860; *New York Journal of Commerce*, March 30, 1860, and
November 26, 1864.

36. *New York Herald*, March 26, April 7, 1862; Diary of George Templeton
Strong, April 23, 24, 1863, Columbia; *New York Freeman's Journal*, May 2,
1863; *New York Daily Transcript*, May 9, 1863; Horatio Seymour to Samuel J.
Tilden, May 9, 1863, Samuel J. Tilden Papers, N.Y.P.L.; Diary of Edward N.
Tailer, Jr., Monday, April 16, 1860, N.Y.H.S.; *New York Journal of Commerce,*
March 12, April 17, 1860; *New York Herald*, March 15, 1860; Mountaineer
[Charles Wright], *The Prospect: A View of Politics* (Buffalo: privately pub-
lished, 1862), pp. 17–19.

37. *Harper's Weekly*, June 19, September 18, November 27, 1858; *New York
Journal of Commerce*, February 16, 1853, and January 14, 1856; Diary of
George Templeton Strong, July 2, 1852, Columbia; Diary of Philip Hone, May
17, 18, 1841; *New York Evening Post*, August 7, 1863; *New York Herald*,
January 6, 1837, December 6, 1855, April 13, December 8, 1856, February 2,
May 8, 11, October 2, 1857, and January 3, 1858.

38. The trial of Mrs. Burdell for the murder of Dr. Cunningham.

39. Nelson J. Waterbury to Horatio Seymour, December 26, 1864, Seymour
Papers, N.Y.H.S.; ironically, Reynolds was one of the few criminals to be
hanged in New York at this time, since he had no political connections, Harris,
*Memories*, p. 39.

40. *New York Herald*, April 11, 1856; Nelson J. Waterbury to Horatio Sey-

mour, December 26, 1864, Seymour Papers, N.Y.H.S.; *Buffalo Democracy*, May 18, 1855, quoted in the *New York Journal of Commerce*, May 21, 1855; *New York Journal of Commerce*, January 8, 1857; *Harper's Weekly*, May 15, December 4, 1858; *New York Herald*, January 20, 1860. The *Herald* gave the number of pardons granted as follows:

| YEAR | GOVERNOR | NUMBER PARDONED |
|------|----------|------------------|
| 1847 | Young | 129 |
| 1848 | Young | 139 |
| 1849 | Fish | 35 |
| 1850 | Fish | 62 |
| 1851 | Hunt | 160 |
| 1852 | Hunt | 186 |
| 1853 | Seymour | 207 |
| 1854 | Seymour | 249 |
| 1855 | Clark | 253 |
| 1856 | Clark | 277 |
| 1857 | King | 193 |
| 1858 | King | 233 |
| 1859 | Morgan | 84 |

41. *New York Herald*, October 9, 1859; State of New York, *Annual Report of Commissioners of the Metropolitan Police*, Assembly Document, No. 20, January 16, 1868, pp. 8–9; State of New York, *Report of Joint Committee on Police Matters in the City and County of New-York, and County of Kings*, Senate Document No. 97, March 4, 1856, pp. 137–38, 167–68.

42. Christopher Hibbert, *King Mob: The Story of Lord George Gordon and the London Riots of 1780* (New York: World Publishing Company, 1958), pp. 123–24; Patrick Pringle, *Hue and Cry: The Birth of the British Police* (London: Museum Press, 1955), pp. 12–13, 15; T. A. Critchley, *A History of Police in England and Wales* (London: Constable, 1967), pp. 36–38, 47–56; George Dilnot, *Scotland Yard: Its History and Organization, 1829–1929* (London: Geoffrey Bles, 1929), pp. 30–50.

43. Nor, of course, did a number of British forces, especially in towns with municipal problems similar to those of New York, such as Liverpool and Glasgow.

44. Richardson, *New York Police*, pp. 22, 37, 42, 48, and 65.

45. Ibid., pp. 45–46, 49–51, 53–55, 57, 60; Howard B. Furer, *William Frederick Havemeyer: A Political Biography* (New York: American Press, 1965), pp. 28–33; Nominations and Appointments of Policemen, City Clerk, Filed Papers, Boxes 3204 and 3205, MARC; John C. Covel to James W. Beekman, July 22, 1850; James G. Graham to Beekman, February 20, 1850; J. M. Miller to Beekman, February 17, 1851; James W. Gerard to Beekman, April 16, 1853 [?]—all in Beekman Papers, N.Y.H.S.; Foster, *New York in Slices*, pp. 29–30; Policemen of the City of New York Dismissed and Suspended from January 1, 1847, to January 1, 1848, City Clerk, Filed Papers, Box 3020, MARC; Charges against James Nesbit, November 13, 1845; charges against George W. Hunt, November 14, 1845—both in City Clerk, Filed Papers, Box 3198, MARC; *New York Herald*, January 1, March 21, December 8, 16, 1855; *New York Journal of Commerce*, March 17, 1855; *Report of Joint Committee on Police Matters*, March 4, 1856,

pp. 6–7, 31, 33, 35–38, 54–56, 65–66, 104–6; *Baltimore Patriot,* quoted in *New York Journal of Commerce,* December 17, 1855.

46. From September to May they wore a blue frock coat, striped blue trousers, leather body belt, stock, and trimmings. In the summer, the captain of each ward was allowed to prescribe the uniform for his men. Some chose white duck suits, others colors; some captains preferred straw hats, and others felt.

47. *New York Journal of Commerce,* February 15, 17, 28, April 15, 23, 1853; Circular, Commissioners of Police [1854], James W. Beekman Papers, N.Y.H.S.; *New York Herald,* January 1, 1855; Richardson, *New York Police,* pp. 64–65; Raymond B. Fosdick, *American Police Systems* (New York: Century, 1920), p. 71.

48. State of New York, *Report of Majority of Committee on Cities and Villages on bills relative to Police Departments of New York and Brooklyn,* Assembly Document No. 127, March 2, 1857, pp. 2–3; Fosdick, *American Police Systems,* pp. 80–81; *New York Herald,* December 29, 1855; David W. Mitchell, *Ten Years in the United States, Being an Englishman's View of Men and Things in the North and South* (London: Smith, Elder, 1862), p. 168; Charges against Chauncey Edwards and William Palmer, Complaints against Policemen, City Clerk, Filed Papers, Box 3212, MARC; Cases of William Foster, Joseph Petty, William Wilson, John E. Enright, Patrick Currie, Francis Bradley, Miles Sullivan, and Philip O'Brien, Indictments, November 1856, CCB; Richardson, *New York Police,* pp. 93–95.

49. General James W. Nye, speaking at the Republican State Convention, *New York Journal of Commerce,* October 1, 1857.

50. *New York Herald,* June 15, 1857; Diary of George Templeton Strong, June 17, 1857, Columbia; George Washington Walling, *Recollections of a New York Chief of Police* (Denver: Denver Police Mutual Aid Fund, 1890), pp. 54–60; Richardson, *New York Police,* pp. 96–108; *New York Herald,* June 16–20, 1857.

51. *New York Journal of Commerce,* July 7–11, 13, 1857; *New York Herald,* July 6–8, 10–12, 1857; *New York Times,* July 6–8, 11, 13, 1857; *New York Tribune,* July 6–8, 1857; *New York Evening Post,* July 6–8, 1857; Lyman Abbott to Cousin Abby, July 10, 1857, printed in *Reminiscences,* pp. 33–36; Diary of George Templeton Strong, July 5, 1857, Columbia; Diary of Edward N. Tailer, Jr., July 4, 1857, N.Y.H.S.

52. The chairman of the committee was State Senator Francis B. Spinola of Brooklyn, later described by the *New York Leader* as "quick in speech and in thought; quick to perceive acutely which side his bread is buttered on; . . . whenever any peculiarly quick party-work has to be done in short order by a steady and merciless hand, we know no political surgeon who can wield a knife with more prompt or unerring advantage" (September 3, 1859).

53. Frederick A. Tallmadge (May 1857–April 1859) and Amos Pilsbury (May 1859–February 1860).

54. As mayor of New York, Wood could claim a seat on the board ex-officio; *New York Herald,* August 7, October 20, November 23, 1857, May 11, August 14, 1858, and January 11, February 20, 1859; *New York Journal of Commerce,* July 15, October 26, 1857, October 29, 1858, January 17, 1859, and January 18, February 4, March 3, 6, April 14, 1860; *Harper's Weekly,* March 27, November 27, 1858; State of New York, *Report of the Select Committee appointed to investigate the affairs of the New York Metropolitan Police,* Senate Document No. 113,

April 2, 1859, pp. 3–5, 6–7, 13–15, 18–19; Fosdick, *American Police Systems*, pp. 81–87; Richardson, *New York Police*, pp. 109–18.

55. Fosdick, *American Police Systems*, pp. 87–89; Richardson, *New York Police*, pp. 119–22; *New York Leader*, August 18, September 15, 1860.

56. Brooklyn, with only 168 patrolmen for its population of 266,674, was notably under-policed, and Staten Island and Westchester County were hardly policed at all; *New York Daily News*, July 11, 1863.

57. *New York Herald*, December 13, 15, 19, 1860; *Report of the Police Commissioners*, January 22, 1864, p. 5.

58. *New York World*, January 3, 1863.

59. *New York Leader*, July 30, 1859; *New York Journal of Commerce*, January 14, 1859. Forty-three of the police came from England, seventeen from Scotland, three from Wales, eight from France, four from the British North American Provinces, and one each from Norway, Sweden, Denmark, the Netherlands, Poland, and Switzerland; Manuscript Census Returns, 1860, N.A.

60. As black policemen discover today, other blacks take more notice of the uniform than of identity of color; Nicholas Alex, *Black in Blue: A Study of the Negro Policeman* (New York: Appleton-Century-Crofts, 1969), pp. 144–46, 151–53.

61. See Philip Mason, *Call the Next Witness* (New York: Harcourt, Brace, 1945).

62. The city penitentiary on Blackwell's (now Welfare) Island.

63. *New York Herald*, May 25, 1858, and September 8, 14, 1860; *New York Journal of Commerce*, April 29, October 6, 1858, March 9, 16, and May 17, 1860, and May 20, 1863; *New York Sunday Dispatch*, December 14, 1862; *New York Leader*, September 8, 1860.

64. Some New York policemen on patrol in the unsettled parts of Manhattan were mounted; *New York Herald*, January 13, 1858; *Reports of the Police Commissioners*, January 22, 1864, pp. 44–45; January 9, 1865, p. 6.

65. Frederick C. Mather, *Public Order in the Age of Chartrists* (Manchester: Manchester University Press, 1959), pp. 102–4.

66. *New York Journal of Commerce*, July 14–17, 20, 23, 1857; Diary of George Templeton Strong, July 14, 16, 1857, Columbia; *New York Tribune*, July 13–15, 1857; *New York Times*, July 13–15, 1857; *New York Evening Post*, July 13–15, 1857; *New York Herald*, July 13–17, 1857.

67. Diary of Philip Hone, November 14, 25, 1831, October 17, 1839, June 23, 1846, N.Y.H.S.; *New York Herald*, October 14, 1837; W. P. Wainwright to James W. Beekman, January 17, 24, 1851, James W. Beekman Papers, N.Y.H.S.; W. P. Wainwright, Colonel, 22nd Regiment, N.Y.S.M., Orders No. 1, July 1851, Wainwright Family Papers, N.Y.P.L.; Augustus P. Green Autobiography, pp. 16–20, N.Y.H.S.; *New York Daily News*, June 5, 1855; Joseph H. Choate to his mother, September 7, 1856, printed in Edward Sanford Martin, *The Life of Joseph Hodges Choate: As Gathered Chiefly from His Letters* (New York: Scribner's, 1921), 1:193; *New York Journal of Commerce*, March 26, 1859.

68. *New York Journal of Commerce*, November 8, 1857.

## Chapter 3

1. "The luxury and comfort of New York and Philadelphia strike one as extraordinary after having lately come from Charleston and Richmond. . . . The streets

are as full as possible of well-dressed people. . . . They apparently don't feel the war at all here"; *New York Weekly Day Book and Caucasian*, October 17, 1863 – By a British Officer [Lieutenant-Colonel Arthur Fremantle], reprinted from *Blackwood's*. Fremantle's diary was published as *Three Months in the Southern States: April–June, 1863* (New York: John Bradburn, 1864). Other editions were published in London and Mobile. It was republished in 1954 as *The Fremantle Diary* (Boston: Little, Brown), edited by Walter Lord; Mitchell, *Memoirs*, p. 42; Browne, *The Great Metropolis*, p. 135; *New York in Slices*, pp. 13–15; Matthew Hale Smith, *Sunshine and Shadow in New York* (Hartford, Conn.: J. B. Burr, 1869), pp. 214–16.

2. Diary of George Templeton Strong, January 13, 24, 1863, Columbia.

3. *The Old Guard, A Monthly Journal Devoted to the Principles of 1776 and 1787* (January 1863) 1, no. 1, pp. 15–19; February 1863, 1, no. 2, pp. 29–35, 40–43; June 1863, 1, no. 6, pp. 128–32; Samuel J. Tilden to J. J. Taylor, February 23, 1863; Tilden to Martin Kalbfleisch (draft), June 11, 1863, Tilden Papers, N.Y.P.L.; *New York World*, March 3, 1863; *New York Daily News*, June 17, 19, July 7, 1863; General John Wool to Edwin M. Stanton, May 19, 1863, Letters Received by the Adjutant-General's Office (Main Series), 1861–1870, Records of the Adjutant-General's Office, R.G. 94, N.A.; *New York Leader*, March 7, 1863; James G. Randall, *Lincoln the President: Midstream* (New York: Dodd, Mead, 1952), pp. 224–28.

4. *New York Times*, January 8, 1863.

5. *New York Herald*, January 1, 3, 19, 1863; *Brooklyn Daily Eagle*, January 2, 1863; James G. Randall, *Lincoln the President: Springfield to Gettysburg* (New York: Dodd, Mead, 1945), 2:169–76.

6. John R. Commons, ed., *History of Labor in the United States* (New York: Macmillan, 1918), 2:15; U.S. Bureau of Labor Statistics, Wholesale Prices, 1913, no. 114, Appendix, quoted in Foner, *Labor Movement*, pp. 325–26; *New York Daily News*, June 15, 1863; *New York Leader*, February 13, 1864; *New York Times*, November 21, 1863; *New York Journal of Commerce*, July 18, 1864; *New York Weekly Express*, January 16, 1863; *New York Journal of Commerce*, March 25, April 2, 14, 15, 17, June 2, 9, 16, and 20, 1863; *New York Commercial Advertiser*, April 13, 1863; *New York Herald*, April 14, 15, 1863; *New York Evening Post*, June 9, 15, 1863. Costello, "The New York City Labor Movement," pp. 277–79.

7. Eugene Converse Murdock, *Patriotism Limited, 1862–1865: The Civil War Draft and the Bounty System* ([Kent, Ohio]: Kent State University Press, 1967), pp. 5–10; Randall, *Lincoln the President: Springfield to Gettysburg*, 2:289–93; Fred A. Shannon, *The Organization and Administration of the Union Army, 1861–1865* (Cleveland: Arthur H. Clark, 1928), 1:295–311; Marcus Cunliffe, *Soldiers & Civilians: The Martial Spirit in America, 1775–1865* (Boston: Little, Brown, 1968), pp. 31–62, 101–11.

8. U.S., *Congressional Globe*, 37th Cong., 3d sess., p. 1225. Similar attacks were made by Daniel W. Voorhees of Indiana, Robert Mallory of Kentucky, George Pendleton of Ohio, Samuel S. Cox of Ohio, and Elijah H. Norton of Missouri, ibid., pp. 1230–34, 1249–52, 1255–58, 1267–70, and 1273–75. In the Senate, James A. Bayard of Delaware, David Turpie of Indiana, Garret Davis of Kentucky, William A. Richardson of Illinois, and Willard Saulsbury of Delaware raised the same objections, ibid., pp. 1363–71, 1377–91.

9. *Frank Leslie's Illustrated Newspaper*, March 14, 1863; *Freeman's Journal*,

March 16, 1863; *Old Guard*, March 1863, 1, issue 3, p. 67; *New York World*, March 23, 1863; *Sunday Mercury*, February 22, 1863.

10. U.S., *Congressional Globe*, 37th Cong., 3d sess., p. 1292. Senator Powell of Kentucky tried to have the fee reduced to $150, ibid., p. 1390.

11. Ibid., p. 981.

12. Provost Marshal General to Senator Henry Wilson, July 25, 1863, Letter Book, Volume 1, Provost Marshal General's Office, R.G. 110, N.A. In the same letter, however, Fry remarked that the object of the Conscription Act was to raise men, not money. A draftee would be well aware that furnishing a substitute would exempt him from service for the next three years, while paying $300 would only exempt him from that particular draft. Therefore, those who could afford it would always provide a substitute, "and thus the object of the law is attained and the wants of the Government are provided for."

13. July 18, 1863, quoted in Foner, *Labor Movement*, p. 322; *New York Leader*, March 7, 1863; *New York Daily News*, July 11, 13, 1863.

14. E. A. Parrott, Colonel and Acting Assistant P.M.G. for Ohio to P.M.G., June 29, 1863, enclosing a report by Colonel Parrott, June 28, 1863; James L. Drake, Captain and P.M. 14th District, to Parrott, June 13, 26, 1863; Col. William Wallace, 15th Ohio Infantry, to Capt. John Green, Assistant Adjutant General, June 20, 1863; telegrams from John A. Sinnett, Captain and P.M., 13th District, to Parrott, June 19, 1863 (two); June 24, 1863, Records of the P.M.G.'s Bureau, Letters Received, Box 39, R.G. 110, N.A.

15. Colonel Conrad Baker, A.A.P.M.G. for Indiana, to P.M.G., June 11, 12, 1863; Baker to P.M.G., June 20, 1863, enclosing R. M. Thompson, P.M. 7th District, to Baker, June 18, 1863; Baker to P.M.G., June 16, 1863, enclosing Captain John N. Scott, Inspecting Officer, 9th District, to Baker, June 12, 1863; Baker to P.M.G., June 17, 1863; Baker to P.M.G., July 13, 1863, enclosing Captain Orris Blake to Baker, July 10, 1863; Baker to P.M.G., June 22, 1863, July 2, 1863, Records of the P.M.G.'s Bureau, Letters Received, Box 3, R.G. 110, N.A.

16. James Diefendorf, Surgeon, 1st District, Wisconsin, to P.M.G., June 1, 1863; Colonel Charles D. Lovell, A.A.P.M.G. for Wisconsin, to P.M.G., July 8, 1863; enclosing W. F. Drum, Inspector, 3rd District, report of July 8, 1863, Letters Received, Box 12; Lovell to P.M.G., May 28, June 2, 30, 1863, Letters Received, Box 29; J. M. Tillapaugh, P.M., 1st District, Wisconsin, June 2, 1863, Letters Received, Box 55, Records of the P.M.G.'s Bureau, R.G. 110, N.A.

17. Colonel J. Oakes, A.A.P.M.G. for Illinois, to P.M.G., July 1, 1863, enclosing Captain William James, P.M., 1st District, and J.L. Milliken, Commissioner, to Oakes, July 30, 1863, Letters Received, Box 26; Oakes to P.M.G., June 8, 1863, Letters Received, Box 36; Captain Edwin Wilmer to P.M.G., June 17, 1863, Letters Received, Box 59, Records of the P.M.G.'s Bureau, R.G. 110, N.A.; Randall, *Lincoln the President: Springfield to Gettysburg*, 2:294.

18. *New York Times*, June 4, 1863; *New York Herald*, June 4, 1863.

19. *New York Times*, July 6, 1863.

20. Captain Joel B. Erhardt, P.M. 4th District, to P.M.G., May 30, 1863, Letters Received, Box 15, Records of the P.M.G.'s Bureau, R.G. 110, N.A.; Augustine E. Costello, *Our Police Protectors: History of the New York Police from the Earliest Period to the Present Times* (New York: By the Author, 1885), p. 162.

21. *New York Times*, quoted in Murdock, *Patriotism Limited*, p. 69; *New*

*York Herald,* July 11, 13, 1863. Many people assumed that the real danger of resistance would come when conscripts who refused to report for duty were hunted down and arrested as deserters. Diary of George Templeton Strong, July 12, 1863, Columbia; *New York Times,* July 14, 1863; *Daily News,* July 11, 1863.

22. *New York Commercial Advertiser,* January 2, 5, June 16, 1863; *New York Journal of Commerce,* June 5, 1863; *New York Evening Express,* January 6, 1863; S. L. M. Barlow to Horatio Seymour, December 2, 1862; W. C. Prime to Seymour, December 3, 1862; James Gordon Bennett to Seymour, January 2, 1863; Smith Weed to Seymour, January 4, 1863; John A. Stewart to William McMurray, December 30, 1862, all in Fairchild Collection, Seymour Papers, N.Y.H.S.

23. Nugent to P.M.G., July 9, 1863, Letters Received, Box 35, Records of the P.M.G.'s Bureau, R.G. 110, N.A.

24. *New York Herald,* July 12, 1863; Lt. Frederick Barger to Nugent, July 11, 1863, Letters Received, Box 3, Records of the P.M.G.'s Bureau, R.G. 110, N.A.; Costello, *Our Police Protectors,* p. 162; *New York Journal of Commerce,* July 7, 1863.

25. *New York Herald,* July 13, 1863.

26. *Annual Cyclopaedia,* 1863, p. 811.

27. *New York Sunday Mercury,* July 12, 1863; *New York Evening Post,* July 11, 1863; *New York Commercial Advertiser,* July 31, 1863.

28. Except where noted, the following account is based on A Volunteer Special [William O. Stoddard], *The Volcano under the City* (New York: Fords, Howard & Hulbert, 1887), pp. 19, 21, 25–26, 30, 33–47; *New York Times,* July 14, 1863; *New York World,* July 14, 1863; *New York Daily News,* July 14, 1863; *New York Herald,* July 14, 1863; *New York Evening Post,* July 13, 1863; David M. Barnes, *The Draft Riots in New York. July, 1863. The Metropolitan Police: Their Services During Riot Week. Their Honorable Record* (New York: Baker & Godwin, 1863), passim; *New York Journal of Commerce,* July 14, 1863; *New York Commercial Advertiser,* July 13, 1863; *New York Caucasian,* July 18, 1863; *New York Irish-American,* July 18, 1863; *New York Tribune,* July 14, 1863.

29. Speech by Thomas C. Acton, printed in *Banquet given by the members of Union League Club of 1863 and 1864, to commemorate the departure for the seat of war of the 20th regiment of United States Colored Troops Raised by the Club* (New York: Union League Club, 1886), p. 41.

30. Claim of Cornelia Bucknor, *Communication of the Comptroller. . . On Account of the Damage Done by Riots of 1863, Documents of the New York County Board of Supervisors, 1868, Document No. 13* [hereafter cited as RC], 2: 625–27.

31. Claim of Emily A. Bucknor, RC, 2:607–9; Journal of Alfred Goldsborough Jones, Monday, July 13, 1863, N.Y.P.L.; Costello, *Our Police Protectors,* p. 205.

32. Case of Thomas Fitzsimmons, Grand Jury Dismissals, August 1863, CCB.

33. *New York Leader,* March 18, 1865; Provost Marshal Charles E. Jenkins to P.M.G., July 13, 1863, *War of the Rebellion,* Records, Series 1, vol. 27, part 2, Reports, pp. 905–6 [hereafter cited at O.R.].

34. Case of Hugh Bryan, Grand Jury Dismissals, August 1863, CCB.

35. Claim of Mary E. Edwards, RC, 1:80–81; Claim of Garrett S. Schanck,

RC, 1:97–99; Claim of Moritz Arnstein, RC, 1:614–17; Claim of Francis F. Rohlfs, RC, 1:694–96; Claim of Jeremiah Duane, RC, 1:1031–41; Claim of George E. Borst, RC, 1:1065–66; Claim of Jenny Jones, R.C., 2:512–13; Claim of Erastus Smith, RC, 2:528–29; Claim of Ellen Downey, RC, 2:687–89; Claim of Filippo Donnarumma, RC, 2:700–711; Claim of Joseph Warren, RC, 2:726–27; Claim of John B. Martel, RC, 2:738–41; Claim of Robert McQuhal, RC, 2:833–35; Charles E. Jenkins, Captain & P.M., 9th District, N.Y., to P.M.G., July 14, 1863, Letters Received, Box 26, Records of the P.M.G.'s Bureau, R.G. 110, N.A.

36. *Our Police Protectors*, p. 166.

37. Case of Francis Cusick, Grand Jury Dismissals, August 1863, CCB.

38. *New York Herald*, November 9, 1859.

39. The Sanitary Squad was charged with the enforcement of the laws regulating tenement houses, public nuisances, unsafe buildings, and care of the public schools. They examined steam boilers to make sure they were safe and issued licences to run steam engines.

40. Nugent to P.M.G., August 1, 1863, enclosing Nugent to P.M.G., July 19, 1863, and Lieutenant M. S. Reed to Nugent, July 18, 1863; Nugent to P.M.G., July 15, 1863, Letters Received, Box 35, Records of the P.M.G.'s Bureau, R.G. 110, N.A.; Assistant Adjutant General Henry Stone to Nugent, July 16, 1863, Letter Book, vol. 1, P.M.G.'s Office, R.G. 110, N.A.; Claim of Henry Holman and Wife, RC, 1:1064–65.

41. Fifteen of the Invalids were hurt badly enough to stop them doing duty for a time. They were Privates John Allcock, Frederick Asmus, Ludwig Borchess, James Brunton, Timothy Dunn, James Hopps, William Kavanagh, Ernest Kober, Cornelius O'Keefe, William Neill, Charles Roedel, Daniel Rubsamen, and John Thoby; Corporal Jacob Horlacher; and Sergeant James Kane.

Muster Rolls, 15th and 19th Cos., 1st Battalion, U.S. Invalid Corps; Veteran Reserve Corps, 10th, Field and Staff, Box 5066, Office of the Adjutant General, Volunteer Organizations, Civil War, R.G. 94, N.A.; N.Y. Register 407, New York Hospital, Civil, N.Y. City, April 23, 1861–January 15, 1870, R.G. 94, N.A.; N.Y. Registers 306 and 308, G.H. Ladies' Home, N.Y. City, in H., May 1863–May 1865; Apart from Procter, McKinna, and Allcock, William Neill, who had some ribs broken, came off worst.

42. Case of Thomas Kiernan and Daniel Conroy, Grand Jury Dismissals, August 1863, CCB; Bellevue Hospital, N.Y.C., Records, Class: Reg.; No. 403, Sick and Wounded, R.G. 94, N.A.; N.Y. Register 308, G.H. Ladies Home, N.Y. City, in H., May 1863–May 1865, R.G. 94, N.A.; Muster Rolls, August 31, October 31, 1863, Monthly Return, October 1, 1863, 15th Company, 1st Battalion, U.S. Invalid Corps, Veteran Reserve Corps, 10th, Field and Staff, Boxes 5065, 5066, Office of the Adjutant General, Volunteer Organizations, Civil War, R.G. 94, N.A.; Records of the Adjutant-General's Office, Compiled Records showing service of Military Units in Volunteer Union Organizations, 19th Co., 1st Battalion, U.S. Invalid Corps, R.G. 94 (Microcopy 594, reel 220), N.A.

43. A letter to the State Department, written in 1862 and signed "Notary Public," shows that Andrews was also acting as an agent for people applying for passports, especially those going to Cuba; John U. Andrews to William H. Seward, September 21, 1862, File 210, Turner-Baker Papers, M797, roll 8, R.G. 94, N.A.

44. This is the version of Andrews's speech printed in the *New York Daily News*, July 14, 1863, which seems to be the fullest report available. A rather different version was published in the *New York Caucasian*, July 18, 1863: "He told them that they were fighting for their rights, and he hoped to see them wipe out this Abolition Black Republican party. They should not touch the persons or property of private individuals, but all connected with this infernal draft should swing as high as Haman. He had always opposed this party, and he wished to see it crushed now. He finally offered himself as the leader of the multitude, advising them to form into files of twenty front, and march en masse down to the Eighth District, and wherever this accursed draft was being enforced to wreak their vengeance. He would lead them to death if necessary."

45. Chief engineer was the highest office in the department.

46. *New York Times*, July 15, 17, 1863; *New York Daily News*, July 14, quoted in the *New York Tribune*, July 17, 1863.

47. *New York Commercial Advertiser*, August 14, 1863.

48. Claim of Christian Kochne, RC, 1:192–93; Claim of Patrick Kearney, RC, 1:206–7; Claim of Frederick Schlafer, RC, 2:634–36.

49. Foster, *Fifteen Minutes around New York* (New York: De Witt and Davenport, 1854), p. 52; Diary of Edward N. Tailer, Jr., August 27, 1863, N.Y.H.S.; Ellen Leonard, "Three Days of Terror, or the July Riots in 1863," pamphlet reprint from *Harper's Magazine*, January 1867, p. 3.

50. Diary of George Templeton Strong, July 13, 1863, Columbia; *The Reminiscences of Augustus Saint-Gaudens*, ed. Homer Saint-Gaudens (New York: Century, 1913), 1:50–51.

51. Walling, *Recollections*, p. 78.

52. Claim of Mary Crawford, RC, 1:1142–43; Claim of Sergeant Frederick Ellison, RC, 2:141–42; Case of Charles Dennin, Indictments, October 1863, CCB.

53. Coroner's Journal, November 9, 1863, H.R.; *New York Tribune*, July 22, November 9, 1863; *New York Tribune*, July 14, 1863; *New York Evening Post*, August 10, 1863; Claim of George Barker, RC, 2:847–49; *New York Evening Post*, November 10, 1863; *New York Sunday Mercury*, August 2, 1863.

54. A policeman, Officer Terence Kiernan of the 15th Precinct, had sheltered in the Croton Cottage for a while an hour before, but the mob does not seem to have known this, and it was probably not the cause of the attack. Claim of John H. Starin, RC, 2:65–66; Claim of Jeremiah Walsh, RC, 2:686–87; Claim of Jacob Weeks, RC, 2:347–48; Claim of Lewis Jordan, RC, 2:697–701.

55. He was caught by the mob, beaten, and thrown over a stoop into an area where he broke the lock on the basement door, went inside, and escaped out of the back of the house. The mob stoned the house and broke all the windows, but did no further damage; Claim of Henry W. Larkin, RC, 2:71–72.

56. Diary of George Templeton Strong, Monday, July 13, 1863, Columbia; Claim of Wallace L. Turner, RC, 2:575–90; Claim of Ann Haskins, RC, 1:751–55; Claim of Joseph and Sebastian Stehel, Grand Jury Dismissals, July 1863, CCB; Martha Derby Perry, ed., *Letters from a Surgeon of the Civil War* (Boston: Little, Brown, 1906), pp. 58–60.

57. According to letters written by Seymour's nephew in 1888 and 1920, the governor received a telegram from Wool and Inspector General Miller at noon while on the road to Long Branch, and he immediately left for New York City. But if this were true, Seymour would have reached New York by the middle of

Monday afternoon. In fact, he did not arrive until late Tuesday morning. Two explanations of Seymour's actions can be offered. First, the governor did receive a telegram on the road to Long Branch and dismissed it as unimportant. Since it was sent quite early on Monday morning, it did not indicate how serious the disorders really were. Second, Seymour heard nothing about the riots until Monday night, when he returned to New Brunswick. New York City was regularly in turmoil, and no one expected the governor to come rushing down from Albany on hearing of the Astor Place Riot, or the Police Riot, or the 1857 Fourth of July troubles. So Seymour went to bed, deciding to return to Albany by way of New York the next day to see what was going on. When he reached the city the next morning, of course, he found that things were infinitely worse than he had expected. Alexander J. Wall, "The Administration of Governor Horatio Seymour during the War of the Rebellion and the Draft Riots in New York City, July 13–17, 1863, with the events leading up to them," N.Y.H.S.Q. 12 (October 1928): 97; Stewart Mitchell, *Horatio Seymour of New York* (Cambridge, Mass.: Harvard University Press, 1938), pp. 321–22; Horatio Seymour to Benson J. Lossing, N.D. [February 1888], Seymour Papers, N.Y.S.L.

58. Records, First Division, New York Militia, July 13, 1863, N.Y.P.L.; Opdyke to Seymour, June 29, 1863, Mayor's Letterbooks, Box 5335, MARC; Wool to Seymour, June 14, July 6, 1863, Fairchild Collection, Seymour Papers, N.Y.H.S.; Opdyke to Acton, July 13, 1863; Opdyke to Seymour, July 1863; Opdyke to General Wool, July 13, 1863 (two); Opdyke to General Sandford, July 13, 1863; two telegrams from Opdyke to Seymour, 1 P.M., 3:40 P.M., July 13, 1863; Mayor's Proclamation, 2:35 P.M., July 13, 1863; telegram from Opdyke to Stanton, July 13, 1863; Opdyke to Rear Admiral Hiram Paulding, July 13, 1863, Mayor's Letterbooks, Box 5335, MARC; Wool to Seymour, July 20, 1863, Fairchild Collection, Seymour Papers, N.Y.H.S.; Nugent to P.M.G., July 15, 1863, Records of the P.M.G.'s Bureau, Letters Received, Box 35, R.G. 110, N.A.

59. Claim of C. J. and E. De Witt, Agents, RC, 1:1155–58.

60. Leonard, *Three Days*, p. 3.

61. Captain N. R. Mills, the regular commander, was on vacation.

62. Claim of George W. Farlee, RC, 1:332–57; Claim of Alexander Foster, RC, 1:75–76; Claim of Emory S. Parsons, RC, 1:106–7; Claim of George F. Ingalls, RC, 2:777–78.

63. Claim of Mrs. Jane Boyd, RC, 1:119–22; Claim of Henrietta Strauss, RC, 1:234–36; Claim of S. W. Hoag, RC, 1:271–73; Claim of John Lawrence, RC, 1:609–12; Claim of Eliza Bell, RC, 1:839–40; Claim of S. S. Brintnall, RC, 2:490–91; Claim of Theophilus Taylor, Comptroller's Records. The dead were Matthias Angehoven, Thomas Brannigan, Marcus Bochman, John Costello, William Carson, Bernard Kane, Frederick Leider, Edward Murphy, and five unknown men. One of the unknowns can be identified as a fireman called McGonigal, a member of No. 17 Engine Company. Another was found to be a soldier, though his identity was never established. Coroner's Journal, July 14, 15, 1863, H.R.; *New York Tribune*, July 17, 20, 24, 1863; *New York Evening Post*, August 31, 1863; *New York Sunday Dispatch*, July 19, 1863; Bellevue Hospital, N.Y.C. Records. Class.: Reg.: No. 403, Sick & Wounded; N.Y. Register 411 (Civil) Hospitals in New York, 1861 to 1865, R.G. 94, N.A. The injured were Howard Murphy, John O'Connor, John Murray, and Officer Thomas Henderson of the

29th Precinct; *New York Tribune,* July 17, 20, 1863; *New York Commercial Advertiser,* July 20, 1863.

64. B. F. Manierre to P.M.G., July 14, 1863, Letters Received, Box 31, Records of the P.M.G.'s Bureau, R.G. 110, N.A. Nugent to P.M.G., July 15, 1863, Letters Received, Box 35, Records of the P.M.G.'s Bureau, R.G. 110, N.A.

65. Claim of Richard Murphy, RC, 1:876–78; Claim of Thomas Thornton, RC, 2:358–61.

66. Claim of Sarah B. Safford, RC, 1:428–32; Claim of Mrs. Frances A. Brennan, RC, 1:701–5; Claim of James Stephens, RC, 1:601–3; Claim of Julius Taylor, RC, 1:357–66.

67. Cases of Patrick Merry and Francis X. Crawley, Indictments, August 1863, CCB; Case of Adam Shaw, Grand Jury Dismissals, July 1863, CCB; Case of Edward Shaaren, Grand Jury Dismissals, August 1863, CCB; Claim of A. G. Newman, RC, 2:730–32; Claim of Newman, Onderdonk and Capron, RC, 2:812–15; Claim of William Hartley, RC, 1:479–85; Claim of C. Y. Bradley, RC, 1:224–26; Claim of Sarah H. Trotter, RC, 1:718–20; Claim of George E. Underhill, RC, 1:939–40; Claim of Zebedee M. Quimby, RC, 1:985–1000; Claim of E. P. Chargoies, RC, 1:1012–13; Claim of Brown & Harper, RC, 2:268–69; Claim of Marie Dietlin, RC, 2:934–46; Claims of Victor Magne and William Bierman, Comptroller's Records.

68. Claim of Hervey Sparks, RC, 2:896–904.

69. Cases of Thomas Sutherland and Theodore Arnold, Indictments, August 1863, CCB; Claim of George Fair and others, RC, 2:905–24.

70. Anne Ayres, *The Life and Work of William Augustus Muhlenberg, Doctor in Divinity* (New York: Thomas Whitaker, 1889), p. 348.

71. Torrey to Asa Gray, July 13, 1863, Historic Letter File, Torrey, J., 1851–1873, Gray Herbarium Library, Harvard University.

72. Ayres, *Muhlenberg,* pp. 346–51.

73. Chief Clerk Seth C. Hawley, quoted in *Our Police Protectors,* p. 208.

74. James R. Gilmore, *Personal Recollections of Abraham Lincoln and the Civil War* (Boston: L. C. Page, 1898), p. 171.

75. Claim of Chester Driggs, RC, 2:866–67; *New York Sun,* July 29, 1863.

*Chapter 4*

1. Brace, *The Dangerous Classes of New York,* p. 29. Except where noted, the following account is based on *Volcano under the City,* pp. 117–86; Barnes, *Draft Riots,* passim; *New York Times,* July 14, 15, 1863; *New York World,* July 14, 1863; *New York Daily News,* July 14, 1863; *New York Evening Post,* July 13, 14, 1863; *New York Journal of Commerce,* July 14, 1863; *New York Commercial Advertiser,* July 13, 14, 1863; *New York Caucasian,* July 18, 1863; *New York Irish-American,* July 18, 1863; *New York Tribune,* July 14, 1863; *New York Herald,* July 14, 1863.

2. *New York Weekly Day Book and Caucasian,* October 17, 1863.

3. John Torrey to Asa Gray, July 13, 1863, Historic Letter File–Torrey, J., 1851–1873, Gray Herbarium Library, Harvard University; *New York Evangelist,* July 23, 1863; Claim of William C. Payne, RC, 1:571–73; Claim of Lewis Ward, RC, 1:618–21; Claim of Patrick Martin, RC, 2:497–98; Claim of Jane Maria Herrick, RC, 2:568–70.

4. Unknown correspondent [probably Caleb Lyon of Lyonsdale] to Charles Sumner, August 1, 1863, Sumner Papers, Houghton Library, Harvard University; Walling, *Recollections*, p. 79; Claim of Lucy M. Clarke, RC, 1:941–43; Claim of Sarah K. Hare, RC, 1:1143–46; Coroner's Journal, July 14, 1863, HR; *New York Tribune*, July 20, 24, 1863.

5. *New York Commercial Advertiser*, October 17, 1863.

6. Mitchell, *Memoirs*, p. 61; Claim of Joseph Lynch, RC, 2:668–70.

7. *New York Herald*, January 25, 1861. In such major race riots as East St. Louis (1917), Chicago, and Washington, D.C. (1919), and Detroit (1943), the white mobs did not dare attack the heart of the black ghetto. They confined themselves to attacks on the fringes of the ghetto and assaults on Negroes found downtown or in white areas. Similarly, during the Gordon riots the London mob did not attack the most densely populated Catholic districts. The only exception to this ecological rule of riot is the Tulsa Riot of 1921, where whites stormed and completely destroyed the Negro quarter; Allen D. Grimshaw, "A Study in Social Violence: Urban Race Riots in the United States (Ph. D. diss., University of Pennsylvania, 1959), passim; George F. E. Rude, *The Crowd in History: A Study of Popular Disturbances in France and England, 1730–1848* (New York: Wiley, 1964), p. 62.

8. Claim of Emanuel McConkey, RC, 1:377–80.

9. Claim of Henry Beverly, RC, 2:792–804; Claim of Stephen Benson, RC, 1:735–37; Claim of William Green, RC, 1:576–77; Claim of Executors of Estate of Mahlon Day, RC, 2:145–47; Claim of James H. Armstrong, RC, 2:80–82; Claim of William Henry Heath, RC, 2:278–79; Claim of Margaret Dowling, RC, 2:306–7; Claim of Hester Scott, RC, 2:393–95; Claim of Ann Tice, RC, 2:728–30; Claim of Thomas M. McLean, RC, 2:790–92; Claim of Anthony Zabriskie, RC, 1:135–37; Claim of Sarah Halstead, RC, 1:151–52; Claim of Albert Luhrs, Comptroller's Records.

10. *New York National Anti-Slavery Standard*, July 25, 1863; Claim of William L. Chambers, RC, 1:299–301; Claim of Robert Spriggs, RC, 1:100–101.

11. Claim of Maria Prince, RC, 2:148–50; Claim of Anna C. Kane, RC, 2:142–43; Claim of John Ceasar, RC, 2:331–32; Claim of Josephine Ludlow, RC, 2:423–24; Claim of Mary Feeks, RC, 2:810–11; Claim of Catherine Tingle, RC, 1:161–62; Claim of Catherine Johnston, RC, 1:134–35; Claim of Theodore Kruse, RC, 1:169–71; Claim of Mary Smith Lowell, RC, 1:242–43; Claim of Peter Hollis, RC, 1:579–80; Claim of Hamlet Moore, RC, 1:603–6; Claim of Sarah A. Foreman, RC, 1:642–43; Claim of Sarah Berry, RC, 1:679–80; Claim of Anna Jasper, RC, 1:1067–69; Claim of Martha Verry and William Clark, Comptroller's Records.

12. Claim of Timothy Smith, RC, 1:1092–93; Claim of William Pasel, Comptroller's Records.

13. Claim of Mary Johnston, RC, 2:154–66; Claim of William Briggs, RC, 2:590–92; Claim of Joseph McKean, Comptroller's Records.

14. Case of John Nicholson, Indictments, October 1863, CCB.

15. Case of Patrick Oatis, Grand Jury Dismissals, October 1863, CCB.

16. *Report of the Committee of Merchants for the Relief of Colored People Suffering from the Late Riots in the City of New York* (New York: n.p., 1863), p. 15; *New York Commercial Advertiser*, July 16, 1863.

17. Coroner's Journal, July 27, 1863, H.R.; *New York Tribune*, July 17, 27, October 10, 1863; *New York Commercial Advertiser*, July 16, 1863.

18. Claim of John Ceasar, RC, 2:331–32.

19. Weeksville was centered on the block bounded by Pacific and Dean streets, Troy and Schnectady avenues in present-day Brooklyn; *New York Times*, July 2, 1969.

20. *Report of the Merchants' Committee*, p. 30; *Albany Evening Journal*, July 16, 1863; *New York Journal of Commerce*, July 20, 21, 1863; *Banquet. . . of the Union League Club*, p. 42; *New York Sunday Mercury*, August 9, 1863.

21. Walling, *Recollections*, p. 79.

22. Regimental Returns, July, August 1863, 5th U.S. Cavalry, R.G. 94, N.A.; Wool to Paulding, July 13, 1863 (two), enclosed in Wool to Stanton, July 20, 1863, OR, Series 1, vol. 27, pt. 2, pp. 882–83; Paulding to Commander R. W. Meade, July 13, 1863, Comdt., New York Yard to Officers, March 7, 1863, to November 13, 1863, Navy Department Records, R.G. 45, N.A.

23. *New York Leader*, July 23, 1859, August 18, 1860, and February 28, 1863; *New York Sunday Mercury*, November 29, 1863.

24. Sandford was encouraged in this by the state adjutant-general, who telegraphed: "Look out for the arsenal" and "I am anxious about the arsenal"; Telegrams from Sprague to Sandford, July 13, 14, 1863, OR, Series 1, vol. 27, pt. 2, p. 913.

25. First Division Records, July 13, 1863, N.Y. Militia, N.Y.P.L.

26. Captain Franklin to Brown, July 20, 1863, printed in Joel Tyler Headley, *Pen and Pencil Sketches of the Great Riots. An Illustrated History of the Railroad and other Great American Riots Including all the Riots in the Early History of the Country* (New York: E. B. Treat, 1882), p. 327.

27. Hyland C. Kirk, *Heavy Guns and Light: A History of the 4th New York Heavy Artillery* (New York: C. T. Dillingham, 1890), p. 111.

28. Brown to the Adjutant-General, July 20, 1863, Records of the A.G.O.'s Office, Register of Letters Received by the A.G.O., 1812–1889, R.G. 94, N.A.

29. Wool to Horatio Seymour, July 20, 1863, Fairchild Collection, Seymour Papers, N.Y.H.S.; *New York Herald*, July 30, 1863; Lieutenant T. P. McElrath to Brown, July 28, 1863, printed in Headley, *Great Riots*, p. 330.

30. Historical Report of Henry P. West, Capt., and P.M., 5th District, May 31, 1865, Records of the P.M.G.'s Bureau, R.G. 110, N.A.; Claim of Stephen Abbott, RC, 1:310–18; Claim of Louis Raphael, RC, 2:372–76; Claim of Thomas Connelly, RC, 2:437–38.

31. Meyer Berger, *The Story of the New York Times, 1851–1951* (New York: Simon and Schuster, 1951), pp. 24–25; Elmer Davis, *History of the New York Times, 1851–1921* (New York: New York Times, 1921), p. 60.

32. Gilmore, *Recollections*, pp. 170–85; Horace Greeley to Mrs. Louisa Rowe, August 24, 1863, Greeley Papers, N.Y.P.L.; *New York Dispatch*, August 2, 1863; *New York Evening Post*, August 12, 1863; *New York Commercial Advertiser*, August 12, 1863; Case of James H. Whitten, Indictments, August 1863, CCB; Case of George Burrows, Indictments, October 1863, CCB; George Smalley, *Anglo-American Memories* (New York: G. P. Putnam's Sons, 1911), pp. 161–62; Berger, *Times*, pp. 24–25. Some reports give Carpenter's words as "Up, Guards, and at 'em," but it is doubtful if Carpenter admired Wellington that much. Gilmore, *Recollections*, pp. 185–89.

33. Claim of Abram Wakeman, RC, 1:648–73; Claim of William Hanlon, RC, 2:559–60.

34. Claim of Nathaniel M. Freeman, RC, 1:126–28; Claim of Thomas J. Crombie, RC, 1:72–73; Claim of Hugh Crombie, RC, 1:73–74; Claim of James M. Boyd, RC, 1:370–71; *New York Daily Transcript*, October 7, 1863.

35. Leonard, *Three Days,* pp. 4–5; Torrey to Asa Gray, July 13, 1863, Historic Letter File, Torrey, J., 1851–1873, Gray Herbarium Library, Harvard University.

36. Claim of Theodore Keeler, RC, 1:186–87.

37. Mitchell, *Memoirs*, pp. 61–62.

38. *New York Sunday Dispatch*, August 9, 1863.

39. Cases of Richard Lynch and Nicholas Duffy, Indictments, August 1863, CCB; Claims of Mrs. Sarah Ely, for New York Magdalen Asylum, RC, 1: 1175–77.

40. Claim of John Turner, RC, 1:96–97; Claim of Mettler and Demarest, RC, 1:860–73; Claim of Robert Lennox, RC, 1:835–39; Claim of John Kelly, RC, 2:321–22; Claim of Stephen O'Hara, RC, 2:572–75; Claim of John B. Miller, RC, 2:677–81.

41. Cases of Charles Smith, Patrick Golding, Henry Fellbein, Mary Fuchs, Wesley Adams, Patrick Sheron, and John Hagan, Indictments, August 1863, CCB; Case of John O'Hara, Indictments, August 1863, CCB; Claim of Ellen Washington, RC, 1:125–26.

42. Claim of Clara B. Giebert, RC, 1:286–88.

43. Claim of Abraham G. Crasto, Comptroller's Records; *New York Times*, October 21, 1863.

44. Torrey to Asa Gray, July 13, 15, 1863, Historic Letter File, Torrey, J., 1853–1873, Gray Herbarium Library, Harvard University; Journal of Alfred Goldsborough Jones, July 13, 1863, N.Y.P.L.; Erhardt to P.M.G., July 14, 1863, OR, Series 1, vol. 27, pt. 3, p. 904.

45. Jay, Strong, Gibbs and Wadsworth to Lincoln, July 13, 1863, Abraham Lincoln Papers, L.C.; Diary of George Templeton Strong, July 13, 1863, Columbia.

46. His name was really spelled Albohm.

47. Case of John Piper, Indictments, November 1863, CCB.

*Chapter 5*

1. Quoted in Herbert Asbury, *The Gangs of New York: An Informal History of the Underworld* (New York: Alfred A. Knopf, 1928), p. 237. Except where noted, the following account is based on *Volcano under the City,* passim; Barnes, *Draft Riots,* passim; *New York Times,* July 15, 1863; *New York Daily News,* July 15, 1863; *New York Sun,* July 15, 1863; *New York World,* July 15, 1863; *New York Journal of Commerce,* July 15, 1863; *New York Evening Post,* July 14, 23, 1863; *New York Commercial Advertiser,* July 15, 1863; *New York Caucasian,* July 18, 1863; *New York Herald,* July 15, 1863; *New York Tribune,* July 15, 1863.

2. Cases of John McAllister, William Butney, Edward Canfield and James Lamb, Indictments, October 1863, CCB; The People vs. John McAllister, October 8–9, 1863, CCB. The autopsy on Williams includes mention of "a gunshot wound traversing the anterior fleshy portion of left arm at about its middle," although no witness testified that a gun was fired. The surgeon who did the

autopsy, Frank T. Foster, when giving evidence at McAllister's trial, said that the gunshot would not have caused death by itself. It seems likely that Butney and Williams had got into a fight on board the *Belvidere*, that Butney had shot Williams, and that the latter had gone ashore to buy some bandage or medication.

3. Claim of Thomas Mann, RC, 1:112–15; Claim of Rebecca S. Johnston, RC, 1:137–38; Claim of William Taylor, RC, 1:144–46; Claim of Anna Maria Dickerson, RC, 1:171–73; Claim of Emily Giles, RC, 1:175–76; Claim of John Peter Liverpool, RC, 1:176–77; Claim of Deborah S. Davis, RC, 1:184–85; Claim of Clarissa Jefferson, RC, 1:188–90; Claim of William H. McKinney, RC, 1:217–18; Claim of Temperance Clift, RC, 1:288–90; Claim of Eliza Frisbee, RC, 1:303–4; Claim of William Giles, RC, 1:305–7; Claim of Don Joseph P. Fleary, RC, 1:393–97; Claim of Joshua Smith, RC, 1:589–90; Claim of Alice Green, RC, 1:707–8; Claim of Sarah Cohn, RC, 1:758–60; Claim of E. M. Atwater, RC, 1:1082–92; Claim of Georgianna Anderson, RC, 2:70–72; Claim of Burris Stedwell, RC, 2:76–77; Claim of John A. Fisher, RC, 2:89–90; Claim of Jane Richardson, RC, 2:113–14; Claim of Hannah Sears, RC, 2:144–45; Claim of John G. Powell, RC, 2:257–61; Claim of Silas Blanchard and Wife, RC, 2:271–74; Claim of James Anderson, RC, 2:280–81; Claim of Rachael Martin, RC, 2:305–6; Claim of A. J. and Susan R. Dudley, RC, 2:323–25; Claim of Thomas Lewis, RC, 2:378–81; Claim of Hester Scott, RC, 2:393–95; Claim of Josephine Ludlow, RC, 2:423–24; Claim of L. F. Ludlow, RC, 2:441–43; Claim of Hannah Argall, RC, 2:503–4; Claim of Margaret Corbett, RC, 2:561; Claim of Elizabeth Gordon, RC, 2:645–50; Claim of Martha Garner, RC, 2:711–12; Claim of William P. Powers, RC, 2:751–52; Claim of Hecker Brothers, RC, 2:762–63; Claim of Susan Robinson, RC, 2:766–69; Claim of Charles Parker, RC, 2:778–80; Claim of Thomas M. McLean, RC, 2:790–92; Claim of Theodore Martine, RC, 2:844–45; Cases of James McGuire and Patrick Rooney, Indictments, August 1863, CCB; Case of Charles Donaldson, Grand Jury Dismissals, September 1863, CCB; *New York Evening Post*, August 3, 1863; *Report of the Merchants' Committee*, pp. 22–24; *New York World*, July 25, 1863.

4. Dorothy Clarke Wilson, *Lone Woman: The Story of Elizabeth Blackwell, the First Woman Doctor* (Boston: Little, Brown, 1970), p. 392.

5. *New York Journal of Commerce*, July 23, 1863; *Boston Morning Journal*, July 24, 1863; *New York Weekly Day Book and Caucasian*, October 17, 1863; *The Albion: A British Colonial and Foreign Weekly Gazette* (New York), July 25, 1863; *New York Times*, July 21, 22, 1863.

6. Maria Lydig Daly, *Diary of a Union Lady, 1861–1865*, ed. Harold E. Hammond (New York: Funk & Wagnalls, 1962), p. 249.

7. The incident that gave it the name of "The Little Church Around the Corner" did not take place until 1870.

8. George MacAdam, *The Little Church Around the Corner* (New York: G. P. Putnam's Sons, 1925), pp. 72–74; Reminiscences of Charles C. Burlingham, p. 1, Oral History Project, Columbia University.

9. Claim of Elizabeth Roberts, RC, 1:202–6.

10. Claim of John R. Adkins, RC, 2:955–56; John J. Sturtevant, "Recollections," p. 73, N.Y.P.L.

11. The famous "Fire Zouaves."

12. Coroner's Journal, July 15, 1863, H.R.; *New York Tribune*, July 17, 20,

1863; Franklin to Brown, July 23, 1863, printed in Headley, *Great Riots*, pp. 314–15.

13. Claim of Robert Taylor, Comptroller's Records; Cases of Francis Cusick and Henry Wade, Grand July Dismissals, August 1863, CCB; Cases of Martin Beach and James McDonald, Indictments, October 1863, CCB; *New York World*, July 28, 1863.

14. The dead were Patrick Boylan, John Gaffney, Patrick Garvey, Thomas Gibson, Philip O'Reilly, William Stevens, William Henry Thompson, and Jeremiah Tracy. Garvey was 14, Stevens was 13, and Thompson was 10. Boylan and Stevens, shot in the back, must have been running away. The wounded were Michael Hewitt, Michael Hughes, Joseph McMullen, and William Kelly, aged 14. Coroner's Journal, July 15, 20, 24, August 2, 1863, H.R.; *New York Tribune*, July 16, 17, 18, 20, 21, 24, August 3, 1863.

15. Lieutenant Thomas O. Wood to Brown, July 20, 1863, printed in Headley, *Great Riots*, pp. 322–23; *New York Sunday Mercury*, July 26, 1863; Case of John Hussey, Grand Jury Dismissals, July 1863, CCB.

16. Case of Bridget Barrett, Grand Jury Dismissals, July 1863, CCB; Cases of Catherine Delaney and Mary Hall, Grand Jury Dismissals, November 1863, CCB.

17. Wall, *Seymour*, pp. 97–99; Mitchell, *Memoirs*, pp. 323–29; Saul W. Benedict to Mrs. Charles S. Fairchild, October 30, 1890, Uncatalogued Material, Fairchild Collection, Seymour Papers, N.Y.H.S.

18. Case of James H. Whitten, Indictments, August 1863, CCB.

19. Seymour to Hughes, July 14, 1863, Box A18, Hughes Papers, Cardinal James Francis McIntyre Reading Room, Archbishop Corrigan Memorial Library, St. Joseph's Seminary, Yonkers, N.Y. [hereafter cited as St. Joseph's].

20. Proclamation, July 14, 1863, Mayor's Letterbooks, Box 5335, MARC; Mary L. Booth, *History of the City of New York* (New York: E. P. Dutton, 1880), p. 829; Richard Lowitt, *A Merchant Prince of the Nineteenth Century: William E. Dodge* (New York: Columbia University Press, 1954), p. 220; William O. Stoddard, Jr., ed., *Lincoln's Third Secretary: The Memoirs of William O. Stoddard* (New York: Exposition Press, 1955), p. 184.

21. Kirk, *Heavy Guns*, p. 112; *New York Times*, July 14, 1871; John Torrey to Asa Gray, July 15, 1863, Historic Letter File–Torrey, J., 1851–1873, Gray Herbarium Library, Harvard University; Charles S. Barths to P.M.G., July 16, 1863, Letters Received, Box 3, Records of the P.M.G.'s Bureau, R.G. 110, N.A.; Monthly Return, August 31, 1863, 13th Company, 1st Battalion, U.S. Invalid Corps, Box 5065, Office of the Adjutant-General, Volunteer Organizations, Civil War, Veterans Reserve Corps, 10th, R.G. 94, N.A.; Major C. S. Christensen to Major R. A. Wainwright, July 14, 1863 (six); Christensen to Assistant Surgeon Joseph L. Smith, July 14, 1863; Christensen to Major Stewart Van Vliet, July 14, 1863 (three); Christensen to O. C., White Street Arsenal, July 14, 1863; Christensen to Supervisor Blunt, July 14, 1863; Christensen to Colonel Ladue, July 14, 1863–all in Department of the East, Letters Sent, January 1863–February 1864, 6/20/95, R.G. 393, N.A.; Special Order No. 110, July 14, 1863, Special Orders, January 1863–December 1864, 46/143, Department of the East, R.G. 393, N.A.; Christensen to Captain Sluyter, July 14, 1863, Department of the East, Letters Sent, January 1863–February 1864, 6/20/95, R.G. 393, N.A.

22. Gilmore, *Recollections*, pp. 190–92; Assistant Surgeon Joseph L. Smith to

Brown, July 21, 1863, printed in Headley, *Great Riots*, pp. 320–21; John Crawford Brown, "Early Days of the Department Stores," *Valentine's Manual of Old New York* 5 (1921):145; J. Henry Harper, *The House of Harper: A Century of Publishing in Franklin Square* (New York: Harper & Brothers, 1912), p. 189.

23. *New York Herald*, April 21, 1857; *New York Journal of Commerce*, August 4, 1857; Claim of Clara B. Giebert, RC, 1:286–88; Claim of Emily A. Bucknor, RC, 2:607–9; *New York Evening Post*, July 24, 1863; Daly, *Union Lady*, p. xliii; Case of Thomas Fitzsimmons, Grand Jury Dismissals, August 1863, CCB; Diary of John Ward, January 8, 1864, N.Y.H.S. Other firemen, of course, continued to riot. Diary of George Templeton Strong, September 26, 1863, Columbia; *New York Evening Post*, July 16, 1863.

24. Perry, *Letters*, p. 62; *New York World*, July 23, 1863.

25. Among all the battle orders, there were two more personal messages: Tuesday, 1:12 P.M., Central Office to the 5th Precinct. "Send to Dr. Purple, 183, Hudson Street, to go as soon as possible to Inspector Leonard's house. Baby very sick." Tuesday, 1:19 P.M., Inspector Carpenter to the 20th Precinct. "Notify Mrs. Carpenter I am all right."

26. *New York Sunday Dispatch*, July 19, 1863; *Banquet . . . of the Union League Club*, pp. 42–43; *New York Journal of Commerce*, July 24, 1863; Claim of Daniel Walker, Comptroller's Records.

27. Telegram from Halleck to General D. N. Couch, July 14, 1863; telegram from Halleck to General Robert C. Schenck and Colonel Ed. Schriver, July 14, 1863; telegram from Edwin M. Stanton to Hon. F. B. Cutting, July 14, 1863, OR, Series 1, vol. 27, pt. 2, pp. 914–15; telegram from State Adjutant-General John T. Sprague to Seymour, July 14, 1863, Letters Received by the Secretary of War, Irregular Series, 1861–1866, R.G. 107, Microfilm-492, Roll 32, N.A.

28. Halleck to Seymour, July 14, 1863, OR, Series 1, vol. 27, pt. 2, p. 915.

29. Cases of James McDade and William Patten, Indictments, August 1863, CCB; Cases of Fergus Brennan and Patrick Monahan, Indictments, August 1863, CCB.

30. Case of William Stanton, Indictments, August 1863, CCB; Case of Patrick Carney, Grand Jury Dismissals, August 1863, CCB; *New York Sun*, August 1, 1863; Claim of Jane Stroube, RC, 2:413–16; Claim of Edward Corfield, RC, 2:718–25; Cases of John O'Keefe and Daniel Vaughan, Indictments, October 1863, CCB.

31. Case of James Fingleton, Grand Jury Dismissals, September 1863, CCB; Claim of Frederick Zschocke, RC, 1:90–91; Claim of Margaret Manning, RC, 1:101–2; Claim of Henry Panning, RC, 1:281–83; Claim of Thomas Egan, RC, 1:737–42; Claim of Miller and Shawman, RC, 1:805–9; Claim of Herman Schauss, RC, 1:1060–62; Claim of Ebenezer Wilson, RC, 2:249–50; Claim of Louis Bermann, RC, 2:266–68; Claim of Henry Montz, RC, 2:352–53; Claim of John Farrell, RC, 2:367–68; Claim of Catharine Schuele, RC, 2:601–2; Claim of William Lipman, RC, 2:621–25; Claim of John Heller, RC, 2:761; Claim of Philip Bick, Comptroller's Records; Case of John Piper, Indictments, November 1863, CCB; *Banquet . . . of the Union League Club*, p. 43; Case of Andrew Smith, Grand Jury Dismissals, August 1863; Case of Miles Garrity, Grand Jury Dismissals, October 1863, CCB; Frank Moss, *The American Metropolis, From Knickerbocker Days to the Present Time. New York City Life in All its Various Phases* (New York: Peter Fenelon Collier, 1897), 3:242, 246; *New York Daily News*, July 21, 1863; Claim of Royal Houghton, RC, 1:765–67.

32. One of the witnesses who supported Hexter's claim for compensation implied that he was a police informer: "Adolph Fischel, sworn: . . . I heard his neighbors say the mob would attack his store because he talked too much." Claim of Aaron Hexter, RC, 1:646–48.

33. Cases of Adam Chairman and Caspar Henry, Indictments, August 1863, CCB; Cases of Adam Chairman, Frederick Smith, and John Stepphan, Grand Jury Dismissals, [July?] 1863, CCB; Claim of Goldschmidt & Solinger, RC, 1:721–25.

34. *New York Evening Post*, August 5, 1863.

35. During the war, the price of silver skyrocketed, and many people hoarded small silver coins. Ordinary postage stamps were used as fractional currency until August 1, 1862, when the Treasury issued paper money in small denominations. Although these notes were finely engraved, printed on thick paper, and had no gum on the back, they were also called postal currency. *New York Herald*, July 23, 1862.

36. Case of William Watson, Indictments, August 1863, CCB; The People vs. William Watson, August 5, 1863, CCB.

37. Apparently Byrnes was boasting about the battles he had been in with the police and troops when he said this. He lived at 1390 Third Avenue. Case of Patrick H. Byrnes, Grand Jury Dismissals, August 1862, CCB; *New York Evening Post*, August, 31, 1863.

*Chapter 6*

1. Leonard, *Three Days*, p. 6. Except where noted, the following account is based on *Volcano under the City*, passim; Barnes, *Draft Riots*, passim; *New York Times*, July 15, 1863; *New York Daily News*, July 15, 1863; *New York Caucasian*, July 18, 1863; *New York Sun*, July 15, 1863; *New York Evening Post*, July 14, 15, 23, 1863; *New York World*, July 15, 1863; *New York Journal of Commerce*, July 15, 1863; *New York Commercial Advertiser*, July 15, 1863; *New York Tribune*, July 15, 1863; *New York Herald*, July 15, 1863.

2. Claim of William C. Holmes, RC, 1:1080; Leonard, *Three Days*, p. 7; Case of Michael Cronin, Indictments, August 1863, CCB; Franklin to Brown, July 23, 1863, printed in Headley, *Great Riots*, pp. 315–16.

3. Claim of Charles Plath, RC, 1:1041–59; Claim of Robert Faber, RC, 1:304–5; Claim of John Wagner, RC, 1:419–22; Claim of R. and D. Postill, RC, 1:621–36; Claim of John Gaynor, RC, 1:815–18; Claim of Alexander Dodin, RC, 2:401–2; Claim of Mrs. William Callen, Comptroller's Records; Case of John William Joyce, Grand Jury Dismissals, August 1863, CCB.

4. Claim of R. H. Lievesley, RC, 1:87–89.

5. *New York Tribune*, July 17, 20, 1863; *New York Daily Transcript*, August, 22, 1863; Memoir of William E. Annin, copy in possession of Mrs. William S. Annin, Richmond, Mass.; Carl Sandburg, *Abraham Lincoln: The War Years* (New York: Harcourt, Brace, 1939), 2:364; *New York Times*, October 18, 1863.

6. Claim of Mrs. Colonel H. F. O'Brien, RC, 1:69–70.

7. Cases of Patrick Keegan and Patrick O'Brien, Indictments, November 1863, CCB; Case of Henry Tilton, Grand Jury Dismissals, August 1863, CCB; Claim of Andrew J. Hatch, RC, 2:364–65; Claim of Catherine Gill, RC, 2:418–19; Claim of Margaret Stiles, RC, 2:421–22; Claim of Conrad Rose, RC, 2:881–84; Claim

of Bernard Metzger, RC, 2:884–88; Claim of Henry M. Wilson, Comptroller's Records; C. S. Christensen to Surgeon C. McDougall, July 16, 1863, Department of the East, Letters Sent, January 1863–February 1864, 6/20/95, R.G. 393, N.A.; John Talbot Smith, *The Catholic Church in New York: A History of the New York Diocese from Its Establishment in 1808 to the Present Time* (New York: Hall & Locke, 1905), 1:270.

8. Captain John D. Wilkins to McElrath, July 21, 1863, printed in Headley, *Great Riots*, p. 318; Journal of Alfred Goldsborough Jones, July 14, 1863, N.Y.P.L.

9. Case of Thomas Cooney, Indictments, August 1863, CCB.

10. Not without some sarcasm. After doing all he could to avoid addressing a request to Brown by directing his messages to Colonel Nugent, Sandford sent one headed "Police Commissioners, 300, Mulberry Street, under Brig. Gen. Brown."

11. Walling, *Recollections*, pp. 80–81; Captain H. R. Putnam to Lieutenant McElrath, July 21, 1863, printed in Headley, *Great Riots*, pp. 307–8; Jews' Hospital, N.Y.C. Records, Class: Reg. No. 369, Sick & Wounded; N.Y. Register 411, (Civil) Hospitals in New York, 1861 to 1865, R.G. 94, N.A.; Case of Fergus Brennan, Indictments, August 1863, CCB.

12. Ayres, *Muhlenberg*, pp. 349–51; "Muhlenberg and the American Fabric," *The Journal of St. Luke's Hospital Center, New York*, March 1970, p. 16; Entry No. 553, Ladies' Home, Record of General Hospitals, R.G. 94, N.A. This hospital had 247 patients on July 11 and 348 on July 18.

13. Claim of the Colored Home, RC, 2:785–86.

14. Claim of Amelia O'Bryon, RC, 2:823–28; Claim of John McGrady, RC, 2:769–71; Claim of Mary L. Martine, RC, 1:371–72.

15. Claim of Thomas Crawford, RC, 2:960–61.

16. *Banquet . . . of the Union League Club*, p. 43.

17. Coroner's Journal, July 21, 1863, H.R.; *New York Sun*, July 16, 1863; *New York Tribune*, July 21, 1863; *New York Daily News*, July 27, 1863.

18. Cases of Thomas Conner, Mary Kennedy, Michael Leary, and Dennis Walsh, Indictments, August 1863, CCB; Case of Michael Kebrick, Grand Jury Dismissals, July 1863, CCB; Case of John Corrigan, Grand Jury Dismissals, August 1863, CCB; Claim of John Hopper, RC, 2:830–33; Claim of Abby H. Gibbons, RC, 2:870–75; Joseph H. Choate to his mother, July 15, 1863, printed in Martin, *Choate*, pp. 256–57; *New York Sunday Dispatch*, July 19, 1863; *New York World*, August 3, 1863; *New York Evening Post*, July 25, November 18, 1863; Franklin to Brown, July 23, 1863, printed in Headley, *Great Riots*, p. 316.

19. Cases of John Fitzherbert and Michael O'Brien, Indictments, October 1863, CCB.

20. Claim of Clinton W. Conger, RC, 1:727–30.

21. *New York Daily News*, July 30, 1863; Walling, *Recollections*, pp. 81–84.

22. Claim of John Callahan, RC, 2:653–54.

23. Walling, *Recollections*, p. 84.

24. Claim of Charles Diem, RC, 2:524–26; Diary of George Templeton Strong, July 14, 1863, Columbia; Leonard, *Three Days*, pp. 8–9.

25. Claim of Robert Marshall, RC, 1:1002–5; *New York Journal of Commerce*, March 24, 1863; *Boston Morning Journal*, July 17, 1863; James A. Rawley, *Edwin D. Morgan, 1811–1883* (New York: Columbia University Press, 1955), p. 154.

26. Claim of Brooks Brothers, RC, 2:963–1044; Cases of Patrick Coleman and William McCarthy, Indictments, August 1863, CCB. The firm claimed $71,552.22 for damage done to its building and the clothes stolen or spoiled, but the Riot Claims Commission awarded them $51,907.58; *New York Commercial Advertiser*, August 1, 1863; Riot Damages Checks, Records Room, Office of the Comptroller, City of New York, Old Vault, Municipal Building.

27. Claim of Albert Irving, RC, 2:698–700; Claim of Nathan Abrahams, RC, 2:424–31; Claim of Demas Strong, RC, 1:1095–98; Claim of Elias Silberstein, RC, 2:431–33; Claim of E. Silberstein and Co., RC, 1:859–65; Claim of Bernhard Stern, RC, 1:640–45; Claim of John Weschusen, RC, 1:333–40; Claim of Laura Smith, RC, 1:361–64; Claim of Duncan S. Fowler, RC, 1:556–59; Cases of William Carroll, Robert Mitchell, and John Ryder, Indictments, August 1863, CCB.

28. Case of John Martin, Grand Jury Dismissals, August 1863, CCB; Claim of Maria Casey, RC, 1:222–24.

29. Claim of Frederick Lewer, RC, 1:459–62; Claim of Harriet B. Douglas, RC, 1:1130–32; Claim of Moses Lowenstein, RC, 2:370–72; Claim of Henry Fischer, RC, 2:675–76; Claim of John Henry Kramer, RC, 2:754–59; Claim of Francis Rust, RC, 2:775–76; Claim of Julius Sander, RC, 2:787–88; Case of Theodore Osterstock, Indictments, August 1863, CCB; The People vs. Theodore Osterstock, August 7, 1863, CCB; Coroner's Journal, July 15, 1863, H.R.; *New York Sunday Mercury*, July 26, 1863; *New York Daily News*, July 27, 1863; Claim of Jacob Lachenbruch, RC, 1:109–11; Claim of Joseph Pannes, RC, 1: 833–34; Claim of E. B. A. Schierman, RC, 1:873–76; Claim of Magdalena Keisele, RC, 1:1023–30; Claim of John Reiss, RC, 2:308–10; Claim of T. A. Gill, RC, 2:841–42.

30. Claim of Jacob Crowthal, RC, 1:210–11; Claim of Margaret McGinnis, RC, 1:220–22; Claim of Michael Devoy, RC, 1:424–25; Claim of George Allen, RC, 1:612–13; Claim of Robert H. Imlay, RC, 1:714–17; Claim of Samuel Sulken, RC, 1:755–57; Claim of George Gruminger, RC, 2:82–83; Claim of Erastus Titus, RC, 2:250–52; Claim of J. H. Robinson, RC, 2:515–16; Claim of William Conroy, RC, 2:539; Claim of Charles Saenger, RC, 2:747–49; Claim of Henry A. Linderman, RC, 2:805–7; Claim of Mrs. E. de Cockerville, RC, 2:807–9; Claim of Jacob Warner, RC, 2:821–22; Cases of Peter McGeough and James Lee, Indictments, August 1863, CCB; Cases of John McMahon and George Bauer, Indictments, October 1863, CCB; Historical Report of F. C. Wagner, Captain and Provost Marshal, September 1, 1865, Records of the P.M.G.'s Bureau, R.G. 110, N.A.; Harlow, *Bowery*, p. 534; Telegram from Lovett to Eckert, July 14, 1863, OR, Series 1, vol. 27, pt. 2, p. 917; General George W. Wingate, *History of the Twenty-Second Regiment of the National Guard of the State of New York from Its Organization to 1895* (New York: Edwin W. Dayton, 1896), pp. 334–39.

31. Daly, *Union Lady*, p. 249.

32. *New York Times*, October 21, 1863; Claim of Mary Johnston, RC, 2:154–66; Edward N. Crapsey, *The Nether Side of New York* (New York: Sheldon, 1872), pp. 155–56; Case of William Rigby, Indictments, October 1863, CCB; Claim of Anna Bailey, RC, 1:201–2.

33. Cases of John Leary, Sr., and John Leary, Jr., Indictments, October 1863, CCB; Claim of Jeremiah G. Hamilton, RC, 1:293–94; Mrs. William H. Leonard to Robert W. Leonard, July 23, 1863, Robert W. Leonard Papers, N.Y.H.S.

34. It would be interesting to know why the court reporter left out the name here, but the implication is plain that these were white prostitutes and that Cruise objected to them associating with the Negro.

35. Where they were quickly chased off.

36. Coroner's Journal, August 21, 1863, H.R.; Cases of William Cruise, James Best, Michael Bannin, and Charles Tooker, Indictments, October 1863, CCB; The People vs. William Cruise, December 21–23, 1863, CCB; *New York Times*, December 22, 1863.

*Chapter 7*

1. [James Dawson Burn], *Three Years among the Working Classes in the United States during the War* (London: Smith, Elder, 1865), p. xiv. Except where noted, the following account is based on *Volcano under the City*, pp. 217–58; Barnes, *Draft Riots*, passim; *New York Times*, July 16, 1863; *New York Daily News*, July 16, 1863; *Brooklyn Daily Eagle*, July 15, 16, 1863; *New York Sun*, July 16, 1863; *New York World*, July 16, 1863; *New York Journal of Commerce*, July 16, 1863; *New York Evening Post*, July 15, 16, 23, 1863; *New York Commercial Advertiser*, July 15, 16, 1863; *New York Weekly Caucasian*, July 18, 1863.

2. *New York Times*, October 21, 1863; Cases of Thomas Fitzgerald, Patrick Henrady, Thomas Cumiskie, and Daniel McGovern, Indictments, August 1863, CCB; Case of Cornelius Callaghan, Grand Jury Dismissals, September 1863, CCB; Claim of Hiram B. Gray, RC, 1:852–60; Diary of Caroline Dunstan, July 15, 1863, N.Y.P.L.; Diary of George Templeton Strong, July 15, 1863, Columbia.

3. Mealy, who lived in West 32nd Street, near the Seventh Avenue, was also a shoemaker, and it is possible he recognized Costello as a business competitor.

4. He died on July 25.

5. Coroner's Journal, July 27, 1863, H.R.; *New York Tribune*, July 17, 20, 27, 29, October 10, 1863; Case of Matthew Zweick, Indictments, August, October 1863, CCB; Case of Jacob Long, Indictments, August 1863, CCB; Claim of Julia Danforth, RC, 1:845–49; *Report of the Merchants' Committee*, pp. 17–18; John Torrey to Asa Gray, July 15, 1863, Historic Letter File, Torrey, J., 1851–1873, Gray Herbarium Library, Harvard University.

6. Claim of Lila Johnson, RC, 1:91–93; Claim of Christopher R. Brown, RC, 1:102–3; Claim of Julia Jones and Son, RC, 1:104–5; Claim of Sarah Ann Wynkoop, RC, 1:128–29; Claim of William W. Wilson, RC, 1:129–30; Claim of Sarah Jane Eato, RC, 1:131–32; Claim of Eunice Brine, RC, 1:146–48; Claim of Abraham Stevens, RC, 1:148–49; Claim of Amelia Bagwell, RC, 1:159–61; Claim of Anna E. Addison, RC, 1:182–84; Claim of Sarah Jane Baker, RC, 1:194–95; Claim of Angelina Thompson, RC, 1:197–98; Claim of Lyna M. Robertson, RC, 1:198–99; Claim of Elizabeth Brown, RC, 1:214–16; Claim of Emily Augustus, RC, 1:278–79; Claim of John Henry Hall, RC, 1:307–9; Claim of Mary A. Brown, RC, 1:418; Claim of William C. Payne, RC, 1:571–73; Claim of Anna E. Whiley, RC, 1:581–83; Claim of Charles Weldon, RC, 1:730–33; Claim of Harriet Wilson, RC, 1:814–15; Claim of Elizabeth Jones, RC, 2:75–76; Claim of Anne Frances Hartwell, RC, 2:91–92; Claim of Jane Franklin, RC, 2:92–94; Claim of Elizabeth Durling, RC, 2:98–99; Claim of Henry Thomas, RC,

2:112–13; Claim of Eliza Jane Francisco, RC, 2:132–34; Claim of Mary Wilson, RC, 2:242–44; Claim of Robert Hazzard, RC, 2:274–76; Claim of Rebecca Stedwell, RC, 2:285–88; Claim of Mary Bailey, RC, 2:330; Claim of Elizabeth Monroe, RC, 2:506–8; Claim of John Lane and Wife, RC, 2:521–22; Claim of Abbey A. Halsey, RC, 2:551–53; Claim of Diana Ringold, RC, 2:567; Claim of Rebecca R. Lockwood, RC, 2:660–63; Claim of Mary Costello, RC, 2:837–38; Claim of Sarah Francis, RC, 2:850–51; Claim of William Yeandle, RC, 2:852–53; Claim of Amanda P. Kendall, RC, 2:853–54; Claims of Margaret Van Cleef, Gertrude Taylor, William C. Rogers, and Rebecca Hazzard, Comptroller's Records.

7. Claim of Harriet L. Sandford, RC, 1:143–44.

8. Cases of Frank A., James and Anne Shandley, and James Cassidy, Indictments, October 1863, CCB; Claim of John Alexander, RC, 1:122–24. (Mrs. Alexander was a white woman, married to a Negro.) Claim of Cornelius Conkright, RC, 2:616–19.

9. Cases of Peter and Sarah Pine and Painter Springstein, Indictments, August 1863, CCB; Case of Maria Carrol, Grand Jury Dismissals, July 1863, CCB; Claim of Charles Link, RC, 2:733–34; Claim of Margaret Robinson, RC, 1:591.

10. 28th Independent Battery, New York Light Artillery, Records of the A.G.O., Compiled Records showing service of Military Units in Volunteer Union Organizations, microcopy 594, reel 113, R.G. 94, N.A.; Lieutenant B. Franklin Ryer to Lieutenant Col. B. Frothingham, July 20, 1863; and Captain Richard L. Shelley to General Brown, July 29, 1863, printed in Headley, *Great Riots*, pp. 323–24, 332; Henry and James Hall, *Cayuga in the Field, A Record of the 19th New York Volunteers, All the Batteries of the 3d New York Artillery, and 75th New York Volunteers, Comprising an Account of their Organization, Camp Life, Marches, Battles, Losses, Toils and Triumphs in the War for the Union, With Complete Rolls of Their Members* (Auburn, N.Y.: privately published, 1873), pp. 167–69; *Report of the Merchants' Committee*, pp. 14–15; *New York Daily News*, July 27, 30, 1863; Coroner's Journal, July 25, 1863, H.R.

11. Cases of Mark J. Silva, Dennis Carey, and Patrick Butler, Indictments, August 1863, CCB; Case of George Glass, Grand Jury Dismissals, July 1863, CCB; Claim of John Kennedy, RC, 1:328–30.

12. The People vs. Joseph Marshall, Court of General Sessions, August 5, 1863, CCB; Case of Joseph Marshall, Indictments, August 1863, CCB.

13. Cases of John Fitzpatrick, Patrick Henrady, Thomas Cumiskie, and Daniel McGovern, Indictments, August 1863, CCB; Claim of Gregory Alvis, RC, 1:115–16; Claim of Jacob Wright, RC, 1:190–91; Claim of Jemima Belchizer, RC, 2:316–21; Claim of Cyrus Evings, RC, 2:99–100; Case of Daniel Brown, Indictments, August 1863, CCB; Case of Edward Murphy, Grand Jury Dismissals, August 1863, CCB; Case of Matthew P. Sennott, Indictments, October 1863, CCB; Claim of Kaiser and Petrie, RC, 1:381–85; Claim of Henry Brien, RC, 1:433–35; Claim of Conrad F. Weltyen, RC, 1:684–86; Claim of Louis Schlamp, RC, 2:615–16; Claim of Margaretta Bauman, RC, 2:406; Claim of Cherry L. Plet, RC, 2:153; Claim of Michael Newman, RC, 2:434–36; Claim of William Fetterich, RC, 2:815–16; Claim of Gustave Neubauer, RC, 2:845–47; Case of Edward Smith, Grand Jury Dismissals, August 1863, CCB; Case of John F. Wells, Indictments, August 1863, CCB.

14. Cases of John Halligan, Martin Hart, Adam Schlosshauer, and Michael

McCabe, Indictments, August 1863, CCB; The People vs. Michael McCabe. The People vs. Martin Hart, Court of General Sessions, CCB; Cases of Charles Dowd, Ellen Doyle, John Larkin, Thomas Lyons, Patrick Henrady, and Daniel McGovern, Grand Jury Dismissals, July 1863, CCB.

15. Mayor Opdyke to District Attorney A. Oakey Hall, August 25, 1863; Depositions of Ellen and Josiah Porter, August 10, 1863, Mayor's Letterbooks, Box 5335, MARC; Cases of Matthew Powers, Patrick Kiernan, Bernard Clark, Frederick Hammers, Bernard Fagin, and Patrick O'Neill, Indictments, August and October 1863, CCB.

16. Claim of Charles Tracy (St. George's Church), RC, 1:950–51; Claim of Joseph Hecht, RC, 1:583–85; Claim of John G. Petrie, RC, 1:566–70; Case of Patrick Carroll, Indictments, November 1863, CCB.

17. Claim of Michael Mayer, RC, 1:324–27.

18. Franklin to General Brown, July 23, 1863, printed in Headley, *Great Riots*, p. 316; Kirk, *Heavy Guns*, p. 114.

19. Putnam to McElrath, July 21, 1863, printed in Headley, *Great Riots*, pp. 308–9.

20. Proclamation, July 15, 1863, Mayor's Letterbooks, Box 5335, MARC.

21. Diary of George Templeton Strong, July 15, 1863, Columbia.

22. Telegrams from Fry to Nugent, July 14, 15, 1863; Nugent to Fry, July 16, 1863, OR, Series 1, vol. 27, pt. 2, pp. 895, 901–2; Nugent to Fry, July 16, 1863, Records of the P.M.G.'s Bureau, Letters Received, Box 35, R.G. 110, N.A.

23. Proceedings of the Board of Aldermen, Special Session, July 15, 1863, vol. 150, MARC.

24. Ryer to Frothingham, July 20, 1863, printed in Headley, *Great Riots*, pp. 324–26; 28th Independent Battery, New York Light Artillery, Records of the A.G.O., Compiled Records showing service of Military Units in Volunteer Union Organizations, microcopy 594, reel 113, R.G. 94, N.A.; Case of Barney MacKay, Grand Jury Dismissals, July 1863, CCB.

25. Only 168 patrolmen for a population of 266,674.

26. *New York World*, July 14, 1863; *New York Journal of Commerce*, July 15, 1863; *New York Daily News*, July 15, 1863; H. B. Duryea, Major-General Commanding 2nd Division N.Y.S.M., to Adjutant-General Sprague, December 20, 1863, printed in State of New York, *Annual Report of the Adjutant General of the State of New York, Transmitted to the Legislature, February 1, 1864*, Assembly Doc. No. 80, I, pp. 315–16. Admiral Paulding to Commander R. W. Meade, commanding Receiving ship, July 13, 1863; Paulding to Lieutenant Commander E. Barrett, commanding U.S.S. *Savannah*, July 13, 1863; Paulding to Act. Master G. B. Livingston, Act. Ensign S. G. Sluyter, Lt. Commander Jonathan Young, and Acting Vice-Lieutenant E. N. Stodder, July 13, 1863; Paulding to Acting Vice-Lieutenant E. N. Stodder, July 14, 1863, Comdt., New York Yard to Officers, March 7, 1863–November 13, 1863,–all in Navy Department Records, R.G. 45, N.A.

27. Costello, "The New York City Labor Movement," pp. 51–52.

28. Diary of George Templeton Strong, July 15, 1863, Columbia.

29. Leonard, *Three Days*, pp. 10–35; Alfred Davenport, *Camp and Field Life of the Fifth New York Volunteer Infantry (Duryea Zouaves)* (New York: Dick and Fitzgerald, 1879), pp. 464–66; Claim of Dr. Simon Hirsch, Comptroller's Records; Putnam to McElrath, July 21, 1863; Shelley to Brown, July 29,

1863, printed in Headley, *Great Riots*, pp. 309–10, 333–34; Matthew J. Graham, *The Ninth Regiment New York Volunteers (Hawkins' Zouaves) being a History of the Regiment and Veteran Association from 1860 to 1900* (New York: n.p., 1900); Claim of Alvah Blaisdell, M.D., RC, 1:76–77; Claim of Francis Rooney, RC, 2:889–90; *New York Times*, July 30, 1863.

30. William F. Berens, Col. commanding 65th Regt. N.Y.S.N.G., to General John T. Sprague, January 30, 1864, printed in *State Adjutant-General's Report*, pp. 359–60; William Swinton, *History of the Seventh Regiment, National Guard, State of New York, During the War of the Rebellion: With a Preliminary Chapter on the Origin and Early History of the Regiment, a Summary of its History since the War, and a Roll of Honor, Comprising Brief Sketches rendered by members of the Regiment in the Army and Navy of the United States* (New York: Fields, Osgood, 1870), pp. 350–52; Marshall Lefferts, Col. commanding 7th Regiment N.Y.S.N.G., to Sprague, October 1863, printed in *State Adjutant-General's Report*, pp. 355–56.

*Chapter 8*

1. *Battle Pieces and Aspects of the War*, a facsimile reproduction with an introduction by Sidney Kaplan (Gainesville, Fla.: Scholars' Facsimiles and Reprints, 1960), pp. 86–87. Except where noted, the following account is based on: *Volcano under the City*, passim; Barnes, *Draft Riots*, passim; *New York Daily News*, July 17, 18, 1863; *New York Sun*, July 17, 18, 1863; *New York World*, July 17, 18, 1863; *New York Journal of Commerce*, July 17, 18, 1863; *New York Evening Post*, July 16, 17, 18, 1863; *New York Commercial Advertiser*, July 17, 18, 1863; *New York Express*, July 17, 18, 1863; *New York Times*, July 17, 18, 1863; *New York Tribune*, July 17, 18, 1863; *New York Herald*, July 17, 18, 1863.

2. 74th N.Y.N.G., Compiled Records showing service of Military Units in Volunteer Union Organizations, Records of the A.G.O., microcopy 594, reel 113, R.G. 94, N.A.; Mayor Opdyke to Stanton, July 16, 1863, Mayor's Letterbooks, Box 5335, MARC. The turnips were hollowed out and the candles placed inside – like pumpkins at Halloween.

3. Journal of Alfred Goldsborough Jones, July 15, 16, 1863, N.Y.P.L.; Putnam to McElrath, July 21, 1863, printed in Headley, *Great Riots*, p. 310.

4. Patrick Oatis, the ex-policeman with a taste for chewing off people's ears, got into a fight on Seventh Avenue with a white man named Michael McCann and bit off his whole left ear and a piece of his right ear too; Case of Patrick Oatis, Grand Jury Dismissals, October 1863, CCB.

5. E. S. Sanford to Stanton, July 16, 1863, OR, Series 1, vol. 27, pt. 2, p. 891.

6. Torrey to Gray, Thursday [July 16], 1863, Historic Letter File, Torrey, J., 1851–1873, Gray Herbarium Library, Harvard University.

7. Case of James Purdy, Grand Jury Dismissals, September 1863, CCB.

8. Diary of Edward N. Tailer, Jr., July 16, 1863, N.Y.H.S.; Minutes of the Stuyvesant Square Home Guard, July 16, 1863, N.Y.H.S.; Francis Lieber to Halleck, August 2, 1863, printed in Thomas Sergeant Perry, ed., *The Life and Letters of Francis Lieber* (Boston: James R. Osgood, 1882), p. 336; Recollections of Charles L. Chapin, pp. 95–101, N.Y.H.S. Although Chapin undoubtedly exag-

gerates the importance of his role in the Yorkville home guard, these pages seem to be authentic–unlike the rest of his "recollections" of the riots, which are copied from the pages of Joel Tyler Headley.

9. Claim of Ann Frances Hartwell, RC, 2:91–92.

10. The story was put about that Andrews had deserted his wife and four children to go and live with a Negro prostitute. But this hardly seems likely, especially as Andrews's obituary records that he was married for the first time in 1870; *New York Times*, December 8, 1883.

11. Paulding to Seymour, July 16, 1863; Paulding to Act. Vol. Lieutenant E. Conroy, July 16, 1863, New York Yard to Officers, March 7, 1863–November 13, 1863, Navy Department Records, R.G. 45, N.A.

12. Wool to Brown, July 15, 1863, Department of the East, Letters Sent, January 1863–February 1864, 6/20/95, R.G. 393, N.A.; William F. Berens, Col. commanding 65th Regiment, N.Y.S.N.G., to Sprague, January 30, 1864, printed in *State Adjutant-General's Report*, pp. 360–61.

13. Both were reinstated the next day, since Brown was a federal officer and had only temporary control of the state forces like the 65th. The state military authorities did not see fit to bring charges against either officer.

14. Shelley to Brown, July 29, 1863, printed in Headley, *Great Riots*, pp. 334–35.

15. By implication, the police too, since Acton and Brown had adopted a policy of sending out mixed forces when they expected opposition.

16. This is an argument often heard during civil disturbances today, and one that has a certain amount of validity–if the riot area is small, if the riot has not been going on for more than four hours, and if the people who are rioting have a strong sense of community. But on two occasions during recent years, the withdrawal of police from a riot area has led to disaster. One was during the Los Angeles riot of 1965; the other (and here it is not clear if the withdrawal was the result of a conscious decision or due to a failure of communications) was at the very start of the 1967 riots in Detroit, when police left the 12th Street area after raiding a blind pig in the early hours of a Sunday morning.

17. *Banquet . . . of the Union League Club*, pp. 43–44. Earlier that day a politician named D. C. Birdsall had come to headquarters and told Commissioner Acton that there was no need to use troops anywhere on the East Side. Acton showed him the door and told him not to come back.

18. Diary of George Templeton Strong, July 16, 1863.

19. Acton did, in fact, make a special request to Stanton for Putnam's promotion; see Sanford to Stanton, July 17, 1863, OR, Series 1, vol. 27, pt. 2, p. 892; Putnam to McElrath, July 21, 1863, printed in Headley, *Great Riots*, pp. 310–13; 28th Independent Battery, New York Light Artillery, Records of the A.G.O., Compiled Records showing service of Military Units in Volunteer Union Organizations, microcopy 594, reel 113, R.G. 94, N.A.

20. Remarks for the Month of July 1863, Morning Reports, Cos. G,H,K,L,M, Regimental Headquarters Records, 13th New York Cavalry (Civil War), R.G. 94, N.A. Both Dalemetta and Davids are mistakenly listed as killed on Wednesday. Precisely what Dalemetta was doing so far uptown when his unit was stationed in Gramercy Park is not clear. Most likely, he was paying a quick visit to his home. Lefferts to Sprague, October 1863, printed in *State Adjutant-General's Report*, pp. 356–57; Emmons Clark, *History of the Seventh Regiment of New*

*York, 1806–1889* (New York: published by the Seventh Regiment, 1890), 2: 112–13; Lefferts to Brown, July 17, 1863, U.S. Army Commands, Department of the East, H.Q., U.S. Troops, New York City and Harbor, Letters Received, August 1863–September 1863, 17, 5th A.C., R.G. 393, N.A. On Thursday morning, Superintendent Kennedy, his face badly cut and discolored, put in an appearance at police headquarters for the first time since he was attacked.

21. Proclamation, July 17, 1863, Mayor's Letterbooks, Box 5335, MARC.

22. Estimates of the number varied. Hughes himself thought his audience numbered 6,000 or 7,000; Hughes to the Reverend Dr. William McCloskey, July 22, 1863, St. Joseph's. The *Daily News,* and the *Sun* both said 5,000; the *Times* and the *Tribune* estimated 3,000–4,000. Major E. S. Sanford agreed with their figure; Sanford to Stanton, July 17, 1863, printed in OR, Series 1, vol. 27, pt. 2, p. 893.

23. Hughes to McCloskey, July 22, 1863, St. Joseph's; General Order No. 3, July 17, 1863, Department of the East, U.S. Troops, New York City and Harbor, General Orders, July 1863–July 1865, v. 79/207, R.G. 393, N.A.

24. General Halleck wrote to the adjutant-general recommending that Wool and Brown be placed on the retired list on July 15, which means that the decision was taken at a time when only the barest details of the riot were known in Washington. Yet the administration did nothing to thank or honor Brown later, when the full story was known; Halleck to the Adjutant General, July 15, 1863, Register of Letters Received by the A.G.O., 1812–1889, Records of the A.G.O., Microcopy 711, reel 38, R.G. 94, N.A. Brown came to believe that his retirement and relief were due to the enmity of General Wool and former Governor Edwin D. Morgan, but this seems to have been a misapprehension. Brown to Morgan, July 22, 1863, Morgan Papers, N.Y.S.L.

25. 8th U.S. Infantry, Returns from Regular Army Infantry Regiments, Records of the A.G.O., Microcopy 665, reel 92, R.G. 94, N.A.; Joseph H. Choate to his mother, July 17, 1863, printed in Martin, *Choate,* p. 259.

26. Congdon to his father, Friday morning, July 17, [1863], Henry Martyn Congdon Papers, N.Y.H.S.

27. Mott to Canby, July 17, 1863, 14th New York Cavalry, Volunteer Organizations of the Civil War, A.G.O., Muster Rolls, Returns, Regimental Papers, R.G. 94, N.A.

*Chapter 9*

1. *How the Other Half Lives: Studies among the Tenements of New York,* American Century Series (New York: Hill & Wang, 1957), p. 226.

2. Charles C. Jenkins, Captain and P.M., 9th District, New York, to P.M.G., July 21, 1863, Letters Received, Box 26, Records of the P.M.G.'s Bureau, R.G. 110, N.A.

3. William H. Armstrong, Mayor's Private Secretary, to the Police Commissioners, July 18 (two), 20, 21 (two), 22, 23, 29, 1863, Mayor's Letterbooks, Box 5335, MARC; John Duffy to P.M.G., August 5, 20, 1863, Letters Received, Box 12, Records of the P.M.G.'s Bureau, R.G. 110, N.A.; Opdyke to Sidney D. Roberts, July 28, 1863; W. H. Armstrong to Messrs. Cathcart, Needham & Co., July 21, 1863 – both in Mayor's Letterbooks, Box 5335, MARC.

4. *New York Journal of Commerce*, July 20, 21, 1863.

5. Mott to Captain A. T. Fiske, A.A. Gen., July 21, 1863, Department of the East, 1st Brigade, U.S. Troops, New York City and Harbor, 17, 5th A.C., Letters Received, August–September 1863, R.G. 393, N.A.; *New York Evening Post*, July 21, 1863.

6. Much to the relief of many officers, who found their men deserting at an alarming rate when confronted with New York's opportunities for enjoying life and the high bounties offered for enlistment in new regiments. H.Q. 8th Infantry to Christensen, August 16, 1863, 8th U.S. Infantry, Letters Sent, R.G. 391, N.A. Special Orders No. 1, July 17; No. 2, July 18; No. 3, July 19; No. 4, July 20; No. 8, July 25, 1863, Department of the East, U.S. Troops, New York City and Harbor, Special Orders, July–August, 1863, v. 78/205, R.G., 393, N. A. Sandford to Canby, July 21, 1863; General Orders No. 7, July 23, 1863, N.Y. Militia, 1st Division, N.Y.P.L. Lt. Commander Richard W. Meade, U.S.N., to Canby, July 18, 1863, Department of the East, 1st Brigade, U.S. Troops, New York City and Harbor, 17. 5th A.C., Letters Received, August–September 1863, R.G. 393, N.A.; *New York Herald*, July 19–23, 1863.

7. *New York Daily News*, July 15, 1863; *New York Sun*, July 16, 1863; *New York Journal of Commerce*, July 16, 1863; *New York Commercial Advertiser*, July 15, 16, 1863; *New York Evening Post*, July 16, 1863; William Frederic Reekstin, "The Draft Riots of July, 1863, on Staten Island," *Staten Island Historian* 19 (October–December 1958):27–30; *New York Evening Post*, July 21, 1863.

8. Telegram from Canby to Halleck, July 19, 1863, Department of the East, U.S. Troops, New York City and Harbor, Letters Sent, July 1863–July 1865, 74/201/200, R.G. 393, N.A.

9. Some veteran volunteers of Wilson's Zouaves had been sent to pacify the island on Wednesday, July 15, and they preserved calm. Later they were relieved by several companies of Fire Zouaves. On Monday, July 20, some of the Zouaves got drunk and blundered into a fight in which two soldiers and one civilian were killed. The islanders were rabid at the behavior of the troops, and Dickson's expedition was intended to help quiet them; *New York Herald*, July 16, 21, 22, 1863; Barnes, *Draft Riots*, pp. 89, 92–93; Col. Walter A. Fox, 74th N.Y.N.G., to Major-General Nelson Randall, comanding 8th Division, September 10, 1863, printed in *State Adjutant-General's Report*, p. 398; Special Orders No. 40, 41, July 21, 1863, N.Y. Militia, 1st Division, N.Y.P.L.

10. General Orders No. 8, First Division, New York National Guard, July 25, 1863, Department of the East, 1st Brigade, U.S. Troops, New York City and Harbor, 17. 5th A.C., Letters Received, August 1863–September 1863, R.G. 393, N.A.

11. *New York Evening Post*, July 25, 1863; *New York World*, July 30, 1863; Opdyke et al. to Stanton, July 22, 1863, Letters Received by the Secretary of War, Irregular Series, 1861–66, Microcopy 492, reel 32, R.G. 107, N.A.

12. Friday, July 31, 1863. Three days earlier, Tuesday, July 28, the paper printed a gushing encomium about the Black Joke's vigilante activity in the Twenty-second Ward.

13. Butler, of course, bulked much larger in 1863 than in later years, after his resounding failures at Bermuda Hundred and Fort Fisher. Although Lincoln thought Butler was "as full of poison gas as a dead dog," he was prepared to

take him as vice president in 1864. Few federal generals had been very successful during the first years of the war, and the South's anguished howls of indignation over Butler's administration of New Orleans had endeared him to the northern public.

14. *New York Dispatch*, July 19, 1863; Fry, *New York and the Conscription of 1863*, p. 68; William A. Hall to Montgomery Blair, July 15, 1863; Robert A. Maxwell to Lincoln, July 15, 1863; telegram from Jay, Strong, Gibbs and Wadsworth to Lincoln, July 13, 1863; telegram from David Dudley Field to Lincoln, July 15, 1863–all in Lincoln Papers, L.C. Charles Gould to Salmon P. Chase, July 16, 1863; John T. Hugeboom to Chase, July 18, 1863, Chase Papers, L.C. Charles S. Barths to P.M.G., Letters Received, Box 3; Nugent to P.M.G., July 18, 1863, Letters Received, Box 35, Records of the P.M.G.'s Bureau, R.G. 110, N.A. William L. Halfenstein to Stanton, July 14, 1863, Letters Received by the Secretary of War, Irregular Series, 1861–1866, Microcopy 492, roll 29, R.G. 94, N.A. *Diary of Gideon Welles, Secretary of the Navy under Lincoln and Johnson*, ed. Howard K. Beale and Alan W. Brownsword (New York: W. W. Norton, 1960), 1:373, July 16, 1863.

15. *New York Commercial Advertiser*, August 25, 1863. Stanton to Dix, August 15, 1863, Dix Papers, Columbia. Opdyke to Sanford, n.d., Mayor's Letterbooks, Box 5335, MARC. Dix to Major S. Van Vliet, August 17, 1863, Department of the East, Letters Sent, January 1863–February 1864, 6/20/95, R.G. 393, N.A. Halleck to Dix, August 14, 1863, Letters Sent, Headquarters of the Army, V. 13A, February 9, 1862–October 2, 1863, No. 329, R.G. 108, N.A.

16. Though Lincoln refused Seymour's request to suspend the draft in New York State until it became clear how well volunteer enlistments were proceeding. He was, however, willing to facilitate the submission of the Draft Act to the Supreme Court for a decision on its constitutionality–a risky step. Chief Justice Taney actually prepared an opinion ruling the act unconstitutional, though he was never given the chance to deliver it. Horatio Seymour to Dix, August 7, 15, 1863, Dix Papers, Columbia. Randall, *Lincoln the President: Midstream*, pp. 298–311. Lincoln to Seymour, August 7, 1863, Fairchild Collection, Seymour Papers, N.Y.H.S. Seymour to J. B. Fry, August 1, 1863; Telegram from Seymour to Lincoln, August 3, 1863, Lincoln Papers, L.C.; Nugent to P.M.G., August 13, 1863, Letters Received, Box 35, Records of the P.M.G.'s Bureau, R.G. 110, N.A.

17. Proceedings of the Board of Aldermen, Special Session, July 27, 1863, vol. 150, MARC.

18. First of all, the Common Council returned to the charge, voting $3 million for similar purposes. On the day the draft began, the mayor announced he would sign it if some amendments were accepted. Later he changed his mind and vetoed it. Finally the New York County Board of Supervisors authorized the "Two Million Act." *New York Herald*, August 16, 19, 25, 29, 1863.

19. *Report of the Merchants' Committee*, pp. 1–13, 30; *New York Evening Post*, July 28, 1863; *New York Journal of Commerce*, December 1, 1864. "Arrangements for the relief of colored sufferers, through the ward missionaries, etc." July 25, 1863, Archives of the Community Service Society, New York.

20. Examples are scattered throughout RC, but see, for example, Claim of Thomas Mann, RC, 1:112–15; Claim of Lila Johnson, RC, 1:91–93; Claim of Christopher R. Brown, RC, 1:102–3; Claim of Sarah Berry, RC, 1:679–80; Claim of Josephine Ludlow, RC, 2:423–24; Claim of Mary Johnston, RC, 2:154–66;

Claims of Margaret Van Cleef and Gertrude Taylor, Comptroller's Records.

21. *Report of the Merchants' Committee*, p. 11; *New York Commercial Advertiser*, August 3, 1863; *New York Evening Post*, July 22, 1863; *New York Journal of Commerce*, February 15, December 1, 1864.

22. Gompers, *Seventy Years*, p. 53; *Banquet . . . of the Union League Club*, p. 37.

23. Sir Frederick Bruce to Lord Russell, May 22, 1865, 30: 22: 38, Russell, Papers, Public Record Office, London, England. Diary of A.W. Tower, 56th New York State National Guard, July 19, 1863, N.Y.P.L.; Brace, *Dangerous Classes*, p. 214.

24. New York State Census of 1875, p. 151, quoted in Seth M. Scheiner, *Negro Mecca: A History of the Negro in New York City, 1865–1920* ([New York]: New York University Press, 1965), p. 221. Brooklyn's Negro population dropped slightly over the same period, from 4,999 to 4,861. The tale that many Negro refugees from New York migrated to Brooklyn after the riots is not true. It seems to have been started by W. E. B. Du Bois in an article entitled "The Black North" which he wrote for the *New York Times*, November 17, 1901. *New York Evening Post*, July 18, 1863.

25. Supervisor Elijah Purdy, head of the committee, noted that "it is worthy of remark that we find most of the claimants for clothing–and this applies as well to other articles–have invariably lost property of the most valuable character. What is remarkable is, that the clothing is all new. It would seem as though they must have drained the clothing stores. . . some of the bills presented are very extravagant, which has led to the remark that there is not in all cases as much difference between the consciences of claimants and the rioters as there ought to be." *New York Daily Transcript*, August 27, 1863; Claim of Anna C. Kane, RC, 2:142–43; Claim of Aaron Hexter, RC, 1:646–48.

26. This sum includes the salaries of the examiners and clerks of the Riot Committee, payments for advertising the bond issue, fees of counsel retained in court cases, the wages of militia on duty during the riots, and the cost of feeding the police and troops. Claims of $1,122,805.49 were paid out; RC, passim. Mitchell, *Seymour*, p. 334. Riot Damages Checks, Records Room, Office of the Comptroller of the City of New York.

27. Lefferts to Sprague, October 1863, printed in the *State Adjutant-General's Report*, p. 355; Swinton, *Seventh Regiment*, p. 358; *New York Journal of Commerce*, July 21, 1863; *New York Tribune*, July 25, 1863; Walling, *Recollections*, p. 85.

28. *New York Herald*, July 19, 1863; Case of George Bauer, Indictments, October 1863, CCB; Case of Michael McCabe, Indictments, August 1863, CCB.

29. Mayor Opdyke to the Police Commissioners, August 11, 1863, Mayor's Letterbooks, Box 5335, MARC; *New York Times*, October 8, 1863.

30. Harjes went to the police the day after Larkin and Lyons paid their call on him, and both were arrested. Larkin agreed to enlist, and the charges against him were dropped. Since the case against him was bound up with the case against Lyons, the latter was freed, too.

Cronin was indicted for assault and battery with intent to kill, and spent a while in the Tombs until he could raise bail, but the case was dismissed by Justice Kelly on October 9. Apparently Cronin's brand of persuasion was effective, for Rafferty never did reveal what he knew about Cronin's activities during the riots.

Cases of John Larkin and Thomas Lyons, Grand Jury Dismissals, July 1863, CCB; Case of Michael Cronin, Indictments, August 1863, CCB; Minute Book, 1863, Court of General Sessions, CCB.

31. Statement of Charles Swift, Case of Dennis Carey, Indictments, August 1863, CCB.

32. Mayor Opdyke to District Attorney A. Oakey Hall, July 22, 1863; Proclamation, July 22, 1863, Mayor's Letterbooks, Box 5335, MARC.

33. Six of these men–John William Joyce, John Larkin, Edward Murphy, Patrick Oatis, Joseph Stehel, and Henry Wade–had not been indicted at the time they enlisted. Patrick Coleman, Henry Fellbein, John Fitzpatrick, Charles Smith, John F. Wells, and Matthew Powers had all been indicted. James Lee had been indicted and tried, but the jury failed to agree on a verdict. Indictments and Grand Jury Dismissals, July, August, October 1863, CCB.

34. Powers to Brennan, August 31, December 25, 1863, in Cases of Matthew Powers, Frederick Hammers, Patrick Kiernan, Bernard Fagan, and Bernard Clark, Indictments, August 1863, CCB.

35. Thomas Lyons and Sebastian Stehel.

36. Nine of them were juveniles who were sent to the House of Refuge, a reformatory where they might be kept for several years, depending on their age and degree of incorrigibility.

37. John Tracey was found guilty in a Brooklyn police court, and John U. Andrews in federal court.

38. Daniel Brown, John Conway, William Cruise, Michael Doyle, John Hagan, Joseph Marshall, Theodore Osterstock, Rogers, Patrick Sherron, George Smith, Patrick Sweeney, William Watson, James H. Whitten. See Appendix 3.

39. Theodore Arnold, James Best, Patrick Butler, Adam Chairman, Thomas Conners, Thomas Cooney, Thomas Cumiskie, Mary Fox, John Gleason, John Halligan, Martin Hart, Daniel McGovern, James McGuire, Patrick Monahan, Patrick Murphy, Ellen O'Beirne, John O'Hara, John Hart, Adam Schlosshauer, William Stanton, Catharine Stapleton, and John Ward. See Appendix 3.

40. Indictments, August, October 1863, CCB.

41. Indictments, August, October 1863, CCB.

42. Their robbery was accompanied by violence–though far less than that used by rioters who lynched Negroes–and they were described in the press as notorious Philadelphia thieves. Indictments, August 1863, CCB.

43. Indictments, August 1863, CCB; *New York Commercial Advertiser*, August 7, 1863.

44. Indictments, August, October 1863; Minute Book, Court of General Sessions, 1863, CCB.

45. A case of life anticipating art–or, at least, Cayatte's *La Glaive et le balance*–by a century.

46. The People vs. John McAllister, CCB.

47. *New York Commercial Advertiser*, October 9, 1863.

48. *New York Evening Post*, August 8, 1863.

49. For example, James Fingleton, George Bauer, James W. Collier, and Thomas Sutherland. Indictments, August, October 1863; Grand Jury Dismissals, September 1863; *New York Daily News*, July 31, 1863; *New York Herald*, October 9, 1863.

50. "The test case on this failed in riot trial week," reads a notation on one file. Case of James Fingleton, Grand Jury Dismissals, September 1863, CCB.

51. On the first day of the riot trials, when William Watson's court-appointed counsel wanted to put in a plea of guilty, with a view to mitigation of punishment, District Attorney Hall announced that he would refuse to make any compromises in these cases. He was, however, quite willing to make them a little later. *New York Commercial Advertiser*, August 5, 1863.

52. The People vs. William Cruise, CCB.

53. A careful examination of the testimony before the grand jury, at the inquest, and at the trials of McAllister and Butney leaves no doubt that Canfield, Lamb, and Butney were guilty.

54. Indictments, October 1863; Minute Books, 1863, 1864, Court of Oyer and Terminer, CCB; *New York Tribune*, December 12, 1863.

55. It is by no means impossible that an officer on a large transport would not take enough notice of a mere fireman to recognize him nine months later.

56. Statement by the District Attorney, April 28, 1864; S.R.H., Col. and Chief Q.M., Dept. of the Gulf, to Robert C. Hutchings, Assistant D.A., New York City, January 21, 1864, in Case of William Butney, Indictments, October 1863, CCB.

57. *New York Times*, November 22, December 4, 1863. The second story did say that Hall was ready to try Andrews "for the violation of the State laws in exciting a riot, whenever the prisoner shall be placed in the custody of the City authorities, accompanied by sufficient evidence on which to base a prosecution," once the federal proceedings were over. But, in fact, he never made any move to do so.

58. A third witness said: "When he finished [his speech] the crowd took him on their shoulders, and carried him a little way; then they let him down; he was only down a few minutes before the picket-fences were pulled to pieces, and the crowd armed themselves with clubs and followed Andrews; they turned down Lexington-avenue; after they passed they turned back and attacked two houses; Andrews stood and looked at them." This has the ring of truth, but all the information available forces the conclusion that the other two witnesses perjured themselves.

59. Since Andrews was a lawyer, it is not clear why he did not defend himself; he could hardly have done worse. Since his legal practice had not been of the most exalted kind, it is possible that he did not feel competent to handle a federal case. Or, perhaps he agreed with the adage that the defendant who acts as his own lawyer has a fool for a client.

60. One witness, Marvin R. Brewer, recalled that Andrews said "he congratulated the crowd upon what they had already accomplished; that they had done a work worthy of freemen; the draft was intended only to operate and oppress the poor; that it was illegal and unjust; that the people owed it to themselves to put a stop to it, and, in order to stop it, they must arm themselves; that they must seize the arsenals, destroy the Provost-Marshals' offices, the enrollment books and papers, the ballots, the wheels and every paper connected with the enrollment; they should destroy the Customhouse, the telegraph wires and police, and that if they had no one to lead them he himself would do it." A second witness, Samuel R. Buck, testified that Andrews said "the crowd had done well, and had yet more to do; the draft would take the poor man from his wife and children, and if they had no leader he would lead them." According to Calvin Papper, Andrews "said that when the people heard of their uprising they would

rise all over this country, and this tyrannical Government would be destroyed; he said they must march in a solid body and keep together in Broadway, and that he would lead them." Compare the newspaper accounts, above, pp. 60–61, 286 n44. Burke's, and even Pepper's, testimony can be reconciled with the newspaper stories, but it is not so easy to accept Brewer's account, which goes beyond even the unsupported version published in the *New York Caucasian*, July 18, 1863.

61. *New York Times*, May 25, 1864. Criminal Docket, Volume 1, pp. 362–64, Records of the U.S. Circuit Court, Southern District of New York; Box 4, Criminal Case Files, 1853–1875, U.S. Circuit Court, S.D.N.Y., R.G. 21, N.A., Annex, Suitland, Md. Telegram from E. Delafield Smith to Attorney-General Bates, May 24, 1864, Attorney-General's Papers, Letters Received, Southern District of New York, (U.S. Attorney), 1862–1864, R.G. 60, N.A. General Register of Prisoners, August 1861–December 1865, Selected Records of the War Department relating to Confederate Prisoners of War, 1861–1865, War Department Collection of Confederate Records, microcopy 598, roll 144, R.G. 109, N.A. Andrews served out his sentence in Sing Sing and then returned to New York in 1870. He married Miss Esmeralda West and continued to eke out a living practicing law until his death of diabetes on Friday, November 30, 1883, at his house at 59th Street and Avenue A (now York Avenue). *New York Times*, December 8, 1883.

62. *New York Evening Post*, August 5, 1863; *New York Commercial Advertiser*, August 5, 1863. McCunn had busied himself issuing writs of habeas corpus for the release of arrested rioters, until the state supreme court ruled that the City Judge had no power to issue such writs. *New York Times*, July 24, 1863; *New York World*, July 21, August 4, 1863; *New York Evening Post*, August 7, 1863.

63. John B. Jones, *A Rebel War Clerk's Diary at the Confederate States Capital*, ed. Howard Swiggett (New York: Old Hickory Bookshop, 1935), 1:382, July 18, 1863; *Daily Richmond Enquirer*, July 18, 20, August 4, 1863.

64. *Richmond Daily Dispatch,* July 18, 1863; *Montgomery Daily Advertiser*, July 21, 1863; *Mobile Daily Advertiser and Register*, July 24, August 5, 1863.

65. *New York Evangelist*, August 20, 1863; *New York Herald*, August 10, 12, 15, 1863; *New York Tribune*, August 14, 1863; *New York Daily Transcript*, August 11, 1863.

66. Diary of John Bigelow, July 27, 1863, N.Y.P.L.; *New York Commercial Advertiser*, August 11, 1863.

67. *Report of the Police Commissioners*, January 22, 1864, p. 10; William W. Turner, *The Police Establishment* (New York: G. P. Putnam's Sons, 1968), p. 41.

68. *New York Journal of Commerce*, July 22, 1863; *New York Irish-American*, July 25, 1863; Diary of George Templeton Strong, July 19, 20, 1863, Columbia.

69. See, for example, the effusions of *Plunkitt of Tammany Hall*, passim.

70. Costello, *Our Firemen*, pp. 779–815; Limpus, *New York Fire Department*, pp. 241–50; *New York Times*, March 23, 1865.

71. As claimed in Duffy, *Public Health in New York City*, pp. 552–53.

72. One cartoon, entitled "Matched," contrasted Grant receiving the surrender of Vicksburg in 1863 with Seymour temporizing with the rioters. "This is

a White Man's Government" showed the Democratic National Chairman, August Belmont, a member of Forrest's cavalry and an Irish Five Points thug clasping hands and trampling on a prostrate Negro soldier carrying the Stars and Stripes. Behind the Neanderthal figure of the Irishman could be seen the body of a Negro hanging from a lamppost and the burning Colored Orphan Asylum. The same scene appeared in the background of "Patience on a Monument": Patience was a Negro, and the monument was inscribed with all his wrongs, in which the Draft Riots figured prominently. In another, Seymour, with his hair drawn to give an impression of satyr's horns, was depicted as Lady Macbeth, trying to wash the blood of the Draft Riots off his hands. *Harper's Weekly*, August 8, 22, October 24, 1863; September 5, October 3, 10, 24, 31, 1868; Albert Bigelow Paine, *Th. Nast: His Period and His Pictures* (New York: Macmillan, 1904), pp. 126–30; J. Chal Vinson, *Thomas Nast: Political Cartoonist* (Athens: University of Georgia Press, 1967), p. 13, illustration no. 33; Mitchell, *Seymour*, pp. 353, 453; Charles H. Coleman, *The Election of 1868: The Democratic Effort to Regain Control*, Columbia University Studies in History, Economics and Public Law, no. 392 (New York: Columbia University Press, 1933), pp. 255–56; *New York Times*, October 31, 1863; Diary of George Templeton Strong, August 26, September 12, 1863, Columbia.

## Chapter 10

1. Diary of George Templeton Strong, August 1, 1865, Columbia.

2. *New York Daily Transcript*, October 13, 1863; Mitchell, *Seymour*, p. 333; *Volcano under the City*, p. 293. Of all the contemporary estimates, Archbishop Hughes's came the closest. He gave the figure as "nearly 200" killed. Hughes to McCloskey, July 22, 1863, St. Joseph's.

3. Six Negroes lost their lives in the riots: James Costello, Abraham Franklin, William Jones, William Williams, Samuel Johnson, and Alexander Stewart. Perhaps William Johnson, Jeremiah Robinson, Joseph Thompson, Lydia Vanthorn, and Charles Watson should be added to this number. Fifteen of the dead were minors: Jane Barry, Charles Fisbeck, Jr., Mary Ann Carmody, and Patrick Casey, all ten years old; William Conway, aged fourteen; John Costello, aged twelve; Peter Farrell, aged thirteen; Patrick Garvey, aged fourteen; Ellen Kirke, aged two; Elizabeth Marshall, aged six; Honora Murphy, aged eleven; William Stevens, aged thirteen; William Henry Thompson, aged ten; and Catharine Waters, aged twelve. One of the unidentified bodies was that of a young boy about thirteen years old. Eight soldiers were killed; Ukell, Brown, O'Brien, Carpenter, Davids, Dalemetta, Kearney, and McKinna. Possibly Proctor's name should be added to this list. Two policemen, Dipple and McIntyre lost their lives; Van Buren and a volunteer special, Starkey, died later. See Appendix 1.

4. Such tales are common after every riot. During the disturbances of May 1968 in Paris, it was rumored that the Compagnies Républicaines de Sécurité had killed hundreds of students and thrown their bodies into the Seine.

5. Besides that, many of the areas in which rioters were supposedly buried have been extensively excavated and rebuilt since 1863, some more than once. No skeletons have been unearthed.

6. Much the easiest way to dispose of an unwanted corpse in Manhattan

would have been to weight it and throw it in the Hudson or the East River. Oddly, no newspaper ever suggested that dead rioters were finding a watery grave. *New York Journal of Commerce*, July 29, 1863; *New York Evening Post*, July 20, 1863.

7. The others were Bridget Barrett, Maria Carroll, Ellen Clyne, Mary Corcoran, Maria De Lamastany, Ellen Doyle, Mary Fox, Julia Hennessey, Mary Kennedy, Mary McGovern, Ellen Perkinson, Sarah Pine, Ann Shandley, Ann Farrell, Maria Pilkin, and Mary Ann Driscoll. See Appendix 4.

8. The figures, ward by ward: Eighteenth, 31; Twentieth, 24; Twenty-first, 18; Twenty-second, 16; Nineteenth, 12; Twelfth, 11; Seventeenth, 8; Seventh, 7; Eleventh, 6; Thirteenth, 6; Sixteenth, 5; Ninth, 5; Fourth, 4; Fifth, 3; Fifteenth, 2; Eighth, 2; Sixth, 2; First, 2; Third, 2. See Appendix 4.

9. John Torrey to Hamilton Fish, October 6, 1863, Fish Papers, Columbia.

10. And baker, harness maker, coach maker, machinist, tinsmith, butcher, pianoforte maker, painter, and basket maker.

11. And blacksmith's helper, butcher's boy, stage driver, teamster, drugstore clerk, sailor, junk dealer, tobacconist, hack driver, mattress maker, longshoreman, and storekeeper. In one or two cases, there is contradictory information about rioters' occupations. Henry Tilton described himself as a gardener, but a witness in his case said that he kept a small grocery store at 152 East 32nd Street. Theodore Osterstock called himself a circus rider, but he had apparently been unable to find any employer for his peculiar talents, and at the time of the riots he was proprietor of a lager beer saloon in Greenwich Street.

12. This includes James Shandley, who answered "work in fish market" when asked his occupation; Painter Springstein, who replied "anything I can get to do"; Patrick Merry, who was a cellar-digger, and Daniel Vaughan, a mason's laborer. The last two jobs might conceivably require some skill—the latter more than the former.

13. Dentist, 1; professor, 1; contractor, 1; merchant, 1; real estate agent, 1; lawyer, 1; actor, 1; tinsmith, 1; barber, 1; storekeeper, 2; longshoreman, 3; basketmaker, 1; carman, 5; housewife, 4; domestic, 3; sailor, 6; mattress maker, 1; drug store clerk, 1; butcher, 1; plumber, 3; harness-maker, 1; coach-maker, 1; shoemaker, 5; baker, 2; boilermaker, 5; blacksmith, 4; painter, 3; cabinet maker, 2; physician, 1; glass-cutter, 1; brass finisher, 1; tailor, 3; rope maker, 1; barkeeper, 3; peddler, 5; driver, 1; grocer, 3; street paver, 1; tobacconist, 1; junk dealer, 1; hack driver, 1; hostler, 3; washerwoman, 2; stage driver, 1; teamster, 1; milkman, 1; gardener, 1; bricklayer, 3; gunsmith, 1; unemployed, 1; carpenter, 4; piano maker, 1; machinist, 1; stonemason, 1; butcher's boy, 2; cartman, 3; blacksmith's boy, 1.

14. The number of Irish among the rioters was actually even higher. At least eleven of those born in the United States had Irish parents or distinctively Irish names. The latter is also true of thirty-one of those whose birthplaces cannot be discovered.

15. *New York Commercial Advertiser*, July 16, 1863; *Boston Post*, July 20, 1863.

16. Mayor's veto message, July 25, 1863, in Proceedings of the Board of Aldermen, Special Session, July 27, 1863, vol. 150, MARC.

17. See RC, 1:87–89, 210–11, 304–5, 419–22, 424–25, 579–80, 591, 612–13, 730–33, 737–42, 805–9, 852–60; 2:82–83, 250–52, 330–40, 361–64, 367–68,

401–2, 503–4, 567, 601–2, 621–25, 785–86, 807–9. Case of John William Joyce, Grand Jury Dismissals, August 1863, CCB. It is by no means easy to find reliable testimony on the size of the mob, since many people were too scared to take any interest in how many rioters there were, and others used "hundreds" to mean "quite a few." I have relied on witnesses who show elsewhere in their evidence that they were level-headed and accurate observers of detail. Diary of George Templeton Strong, July 13, 1863, Columbia; Claim of Lewis Ward, RC, 1:618–21; Claim of Michael Newman, RC, 2:434–36; Claim of Joseph Hecht, RC, 1:583–85; see also Cases of John. Leary, Sr., and John Leary, Jr., Indictments, October 1863, CCB; RC, 1:101–2, 192–94, 214–16, 303–4, 310–18; 581–83, 684–86, 755–57, 765–67; 2:112–13, 257–61, 761, 845–47; Case of James Fingleton, Grand Jury Dismissals, September 1863, CCB. RC, 1:242–43, 357–66, 381–85, 562–64, 714–17; 2:148–50, 252–53, 278–79, 352–53, 413–16, 815–16, 884–88; Claim of Philip Bick, Comptroller's Records.

18. Tuesday, July 21, 1863.

19. One good thing about television coverage of recent riots is that people stay home and watch the disorders, instead of going out into the streets to get in the way of the police and troops.

20. Unknown [probably Caleb Lyon of Lyonsdale] to Charles Sumner, August 1, 1863, Sumner Papers, Houghton Library, Harvard University; Thomas Addis Emmet, *Incidents of My Life. Professional-Literary-Social. With Services in the Cause of Ireland* (New York: G. P. Putnam's Sons, 1911), p. 184.

21. C. B. Conant in the *New York Evening Post*, July 16, 1863; *Volcano under the City*, p. 47; *New York Evening Post*, July 14, 1863; Carl Benson, in the *New York Times*, July 25, 1863; Gilmore, *Recollections*, p. 172.

22. Case of Theodore Arnold, Indictments, August 1863, CCB.

23. *New York Evening Post*, August 5, 1863; Claim of John Weschusen, RC, 2:333–40.

24. Thus, William Cruise knew Alfred Derrickson before the riots; William Butney and William Williams served on the same ship; Henrady, McGovern, and Cumiskie knew the Martins. Maria Pilkin and Mary Ann Driscoll, accused of looting Dr. William Powell's house at 2 Dover Street, lived nearby in Water Street. The Pines and Painter Springstein, arrested for looting in West 32nd Street, all lived in West 30th Street; Maria Carroll, charged with the same offense, lived in West 33rd Street. All the murderers of Abraham Franklin lived within a few blocks of the victim. "This house was attacked by the rioters, who mostly resided in the neighborhood," reported the examiner on the claim of Hannah Sears, RC, 2:144–45. Many of the white victims, of course, were also known to their attackers before the riots; Maria Lydig Daly, *Union Lady*, p. 251.

25. Cases of Frank A., Ann and James Shandley and James Cassidy, Indictments, October 1863, CCB.

26. *New York Daily Transcript*, October 7, 1863; The People vs. Martin Hart, Court of General Sessions, Affidavits, August 1863, CCB.

27. Whose name was really spelled Cumiskie.

28. Cases of Patrick Henrady, Thomas Cumiskie, and Daniel McGovern, Indictments, August 1863, CCB.

29. Ibid.

30. There were also sexual undertones in the indignities to which Negroes were subjected by the rioters, such as being stripped naked. When Patrick Butler

pulled Abraham Franklin's body up and down the street, he grabbed hold of the dead man's genitals.

31. See David Brion Davis, *The Slave Power Conspiracy and the Paranoid Style*, The Walter Lynwood Fleming Lectures in Southern History (Baton Rouge: Louisiana State University Press, 1970); George F. E. Rude, " 'Mother Gin' and the London Riots of 1736," *The Guildhall Miscellany* 10 (1959):61–63; "The Gordon Riots: A Study of the Rioters and their Victims," *Transactions of the Royal Historical Society*, 5th series, no. 6 (1956):101; J. P. De Castro, *The Gordon Riots* (London: Oxford University Press, 1926), pp. 217–25; Hibbert, *King Mob*, pp. 122, 169, 171–72.

32. Welles to Sumner, July 20, 1863, Sumner Papers, Houghton Library, Harvard University; also Sydney Howard Gay to Abraham Lincoln, July 26, 1863, Lincoln Papers, L.C.; Charles Gould to Salmon P. Chase, July 16, 1863, J. W. Alden to Chase, July 24, 1863, Chase Papers, L.C.; Diary of George Templeton Strong, July 16, 27, August 12, 1863, Columbia; John Bigelow to Isaac Henderson, August 6, 1863, Bryant-Godwin Collection, N.Y.P.L.; *New York Times*, July 21, 1863; *Wilkes' Spirit of the Times*, quoted in the *New York Times*, July 23, 1863; Adam Gurowski, *Diary, from November 18, 1862, to October 18, 1863* (New York: Carleton, 1864), p. 268; Orestes A. Brownson, "Catholics and the Anti-Draft Riots," *Brownson's Quarterly Review*, 3rd N.Y. Series, 4 (October 1863):386; *Speeches, Correspondence, etc., of the Late Daniel S. Dickinson of New York*, ed. John R. Dickinson (New York: G. P. Putnam's Sons, 1867), 2:260–65; Nicholas B. Wainwright, ed., *A Philadelphia Perspective: The Diary of Sidney George Fisher Covering the Years, 1834–1871* (Philadelphia: Historical Society of Pennsylvania, 1967), pp. 457–58; John Jay to Stanton, July 18, 1863, Letters Received, Box 26, Records of the P.M.G.'s Bureau, R.G. 110, N.A.; *New York Evangelist*, July 23, 1863.

33. James R. Gilmore to Lincoln, July 17, 1863, Lincoln Papers, L.C. "Most, if not all, of the Democratic politicians are at the bottom of this riot." Nugent to P.M.G., July 18, 1863, Letters Received, Box 35, Records of the P.M.G.'s Bureau, R.G. 110, N.A.; *New York National Anti-Slavery Standard*, July 25, 1863.

34. Albon P. Man, Jr., "The Church and the New York Draft Riots of 1863," *Records of the American Catholic Historical Society of Philadelphia* 62 (March 1951):33–50; John R. G. Hassard, *The Life of . . . John Hughes* (New York: Appleton, 1866), pp. 42–44, 435, 437, 438; Carl Wittke, *The Irish in America* (Baton Rouge: Louisiana State University Press, 1956), pp. 129, 132–33, 145; Benjamin J. Blied, *Catholics and the Civil War* (Milwaukee: [n.p.], 1945), pp. 20–21; Claim of Henry Brien, RC, 1:433–35; *New York Commercial Advertiser*, July 20, 1863.

35. According to the *New York Daily News*, July 23, 1863, white longshoremen beat Johnson, but this cannot be corroborated from any other source. Since the *News* was constantly trying to incite white labor against black, it cannot be considered thoroughly reliable on this matter.

36. Claim of Silas Blanchard and Wife, RC, 2:271–74; Claim of Robert Hazzard, RC, 2:274–76; Claim of Charles Parker, RC, 2:778–80.

37. The sole possible exception is the threatened assault on Crook's restaurant on Monday. But all the evidence indicates that the rioters menaced the restaurant merely because the waiters were Negroes, not because they wanted their jobs.

One reporter for the *Herald* heard a rumor that a sugar house and some foundries in the 29th Ward were to be burned because they employed Negroes, but they were not, in fact, attacked. *New York Herald*, July 15, 1863.

38. Quoted in Charles H. Wesley, *Negro Labor in the United States, 1850–1925: A Study in American Economic History* (New York: Vanguard Press, 1927), pp. 61–62, 101; Albon P. Man, Jr., "Labor Competition and the New York Draft Riots of 1863," *Journal of Negro History* 36 (October 1951):376–77; Scheiner, *Negro Mecca*, pp. 45–47; William Chambers, *Things as They Are in America* (London: William and Robert Chambers, 1857), p. 189.

39. *Harper's Weekly*, December 21, 1861; Man, "Labor Competition," pp. 377–83.

40. Only two incidents can be adduced to show that white workers were worried about possible competition from cheap black labor. One is Edward Canfield's drunken warning to people, after the murder of William Williams, "not to put niggers to work." The other is the cry from the crowd reported in some newspapers' accounts of Archbishop Hughes's speech: "Let the niggers stay in the South."

Just two of those who commented on the riots thought that white fear of black labor competition caused the trouble, and neither was in close touch with New York's working classes. Archbishop Hughes had been gravely ill and was beginning to slide into senility. Hamilton Fish had been living the life of a wealthy rentier ever since he retired from the Senate in 1857. Fish to Chase, July 18, 1863, Chase Papers, L.C. Hughes to William H. Seward, July 19, 1863, Hughes Papers, St. Joseph's.

41. This was after the riots proper.

42. *New York Sunday Mercury*, August 2, 9, 16, 23, 1863. An officer named Harson was also charged, but no details are available about this case. The *Tribune* carried a story that a few officers had resigned rather than be brought to trial on charges of cowardice during the riots, but this cannot be corroborated; August 7, 1863.

43. As a matter of fact, they did not go back immediately: Inspector Carpenter commandeered them for his expedition down to the *Tribune* building.

44. Juvenal, *An Englishman in New York* (London: Stephen Swift, 1901), p. 249.

45. See Reports of Captains—Gangs and Loafers, Police, 1888, Mayor's Papers, Boxes 378, 379, MARC. Captain Thomas M. Ryan, 21st Precinct, to Superintendent William Murray, May 25, 1888, Box 378, and "A Gentleman" to Mayor Abram S. Hewitt, June 29, 1888, Box 379, are typical examples.

46. Alfred H. Lewis, *The Boss: And How He Came to Rule New York* (New York: A. S. Barnes, 1903), pp. 168–69, 221.

# Bibliographical Essay

The most valuable source for this study was the huge collection of Indictments and Grand Jury Dismissals in the Records Room of the New York County Supreme Court at the Criminal Courts Building in downtown Manhattan. Besides the testimony of the witnesses, victims, arresting officers, and the accused, the files usually contain the records of the police examination (which were extremely useful in compiling a statistical profile of the rioters) and sometimes include memoranda from the staff of the District Attorney's Office, requests for pardon, and details of the prisoner's fate. My pleasure on discovering this Comstock Lode of material for social history was only equaled by my surprise that no other historian had previously exploited it. Some transcripts of trials and the Minute Books of the Court of General Sessions and the Court of Oyer and Terminer are also in the Records Room.

Another very important source were the claims for damage done by the rioters of July 1863, which are held by the Office of the Comptroller of the City of New York. Many of them can be found conveniently printed in Document No. 13 of the New York County Board of Supervisors, 1868, *Communication of the Comptroller . . . on account of the damage by riots of 1863*. The canceled checks that were paid to the successful claimants are in the Comptroller's Office. Information about civil disorders, police practices, and municipal problems is scattered throughout the massive bulk of Mayor's Papers; City Clerk, Filed Papers; City Clerk Documents, Approved; and the Proceedings of the Board of Aldermen in the New York Municipal Archives and Record Center. The New York County Coroner's Journal in the Hall of Records and the Index of Inquisitions from the King's County Coroner's Office, in the Municipal Archives, helped to establish the death toll in the Draft Riots.

The National Archives in Washington, D.C., hold many records relevant to the Draft Riots. The trouble that the federal authorities experienced across the country in carrying out the first draft in American history fill the Letterbooks and Letters Received, Records of the Provost-Marshal-General's Bureau, R.G. 110. Correspondence and orders in Letters Received by the Secretary of War, Main Series, 1801–1870; Irregular Series, 1861–1866, Records of the Office of the Secretary of War, R.G. 107, and Letters Sent, Headquarters of the Army, R.G. 108, show how the Lincoln administration and the high command reacted to the emergency in New York City. The part that federal soldiers and sailors played in putting down the riots is detailed in three groups of records: in Letters of the Commandant, New York (Brooklyn) Navy Yard, Navy Department Records, R.G. 45; in Hospital Records, Regimental Returns, Records of Volunteer Organizations, Register of Letters Received by the Adjutant-General's Office, 1812–1889, Letters Received by the A.G.O. (Main Series), 1861–1870, Records of the A.G.O., R.G. 94; and in General Orders, Special Orders, Letters Sent and Letters Received, U.S. Troops, New York City and Harbor, Letters Sent and Special Orders, Department of the East, U.S. Army Commands, R.G. 393.

Two great diaries, Philip Hone's (in the New-York Historical Society) and George Templeton Strong's (in the Special Collections, Butler Library, Columbia University), give a magnificent picture of the splendors and miseries of life in nineteenth-century New York. Other, less copious personal journals were also useful: the diaries of Caroline Dunstan, Andrew Lester, Henry A. Patterson, Edwin N. Tailer, Jr., Charles J. Tracy, and John Ward, all in the New-York Historical Society, which holds the interesting 1834 Riot Papers, too. The personal correspondence of the politicians of the period proved most unrewarding.

Allowing for the confusion of the "bloody week," the physical dangers that journalists for Republican newspapers ran, and for obvious bias, I found the press a tremendous help: the *Caucasian, Commercial Advertiser, Sunday Dispatch, Evening Express, Herald, Journal of Commerce, Leader, Sunday Mercury, Daily News, Evening Post, Standard, Sun, Times, Tribune,* and *World* were the papers I consulted most frequently. I profited, too, from a number of public documents, especially the New York State Assembly *Report of the Select Committee appointed to examine into the condition of Tenement Houses in New York and Brooklyn* (Assembly Doc. No. 127, March 2, 1857); the *Annual Reports* of the Metropolitan Police Board Commissioners; the 1864 *Report of the Adjutant-General of the State of New York* (Assembly Document No. 80, February 1, 1864); the *Report of the Council of Hygiene and Public Health of the Citizens' Association of New York upon the Sanitary Condition of the City* (New York, 1865); and the *Report of the Committee of Merchants for the Relief of Colored People, suffering from the Late Riots in the City of New York* (New York, 1863).

*The Volcano under the City* (New York, 1887) by "A Volunteer Special" (actually President Lincoln's third secretary, William O. Stoddard) was indispensable. Stoddard was given access to Police Department records when writing his book, and he printed verbatim large numbers of police orders and messages, all of which have since disappeared. I learned more about the role of the police in the riots from David M. Barnes, *The Draft Riots in New York, July, 1863. The Metropolitan Police: Their Services During Riot Week, Their Honorable Record* (New York, 1863). Commissioner Acton gave his recollections of the riots at the *Banquet given by the members of the Union League Club of 1863 and 1864, to commemorate the departure for the seat of war of the 20th regiment of United States Colored Troops, Raised by the Club* (New York, 1886), and George W. Walling, a captain in 1863, told his story in *Recollections of a New York Chief of Police* (Denver, Colo., 1890). Vivid reminiscences of the riots were supplied by Ellen Leonard in her article "Three Days of Terror, or the July Riots in 1863," published in *Harper's Magazine* for January 1867.

I supplemented the diaries of Hone and Strong with the classic works of George G. Foster: *Fifteen Minutes Around New York* (New York, 1854); *New York Naked* (N.p., n.d.); *New York in Slices, by an Experienced Carver* (New York, 1849); and *New York by Gas-light; with Here and There a Streak of Sunshine* (New York, 1850), as well as Solon Robinson's *Hot Corn. Life Scenes in New York Illustrated* (New York, 1854).

Among secondary works, I found Robert Ernst's *Immigrant Life in New York City, 1825–1863* (New York, 1949); John Duffy, *A History of Public Health in New York City (1625–1866)* (New York, 1968); and Robert G. Albion, with the collaboration of Jennie Barnes Pope, *The Rise of New York Port* (New York, 1939), most useful. Regrettably, there is nothing comparable to Roger Lane's superlative *Policing the City. Boston, 1822–1885* in New York historiography. I learned a great deal both about riots and the way to study them from the works of George Rudé and E. J. Hobsbawm and from two excellent doctoral dissertations: Richard D. Lambert, *Hindu-Moslem Riots* (University of Pennsylvania, 1951), and Allen D. Grimshaw, *A Study in Social Violence: Urban Race Riots in the United States* (University of Pennsylvania, 1959).

# Index

Acton, Commissioner Thomas C., 42, 59, 140, 166; asks Sandford for help, 102, 103; assessment of his performance during the riots, 207–8; campaigns for a paid Fire Department, 189; congratulates Captain Putnam, 164; deals with feeding and quartering police and refugees, 109; orders all police to the Central office, 67; orders all precincts to take in refugees, 159; orders Captain Petty to West 16th Street, 103; orders Captain Walling to clear the Ninth Avenue barricades, 127; orders Captain Walling to the Twentieth and Twenty-second wards, 120; orders Inspector Carpenter to Broadway, 74; orders Inspector Carpenter to Second Avenue, 100; orders Inspector Dilks to the Union Steam Works, 101; orders the Broadway Squad to the Armory, 68–69; orders the police to Gramercy Park, 163; orders the police to the Thirteenth Precinct, 103; receives "Black Hand" letter, 167; refuses to give police muskets, 152; rejects proposal by Connolly and Bradley, 162; takes over command of the police, 66; urges Eighteenth Precinct Police to hold on, 104

Anderson, Joshua R., 24

Andrews, John U., 159, 285 n. 43, 286 n. 44, 308 n. 58–60; addresses the mob, 60–61; trial of, 184–87

Annin, Joseph, 117–18

anti-abolitionist riots, 21, 24

*Anticipations of the Future to Serve as Lessons for the Present Time* (Ruffin), xi

Arch, The, 134, 154

Armory, Second Avenue and 21st Street, 68, 69–70, 115

Association for Improving the Condition of the Poor, 174, 175

Astor Place Riot, 25–27

Atlantic Dock, attack on grain elevators at, 151

Baker, Lew, 21

Barnard, Judge George G., 73, 182

barricades, 126–27

Berens, Colonel, 160–61

Bergen, Commissioner John G., 67

Best, James, 135–36, 179, 180

Black Joke Engine Company No. 33, 30, 57, 108; starts the Draft Riots, 56

Bogart, Captain James Z., 125

Boole, City Inspector Francis I. A., 33

Boston, draft riot in, 139

Bowery Boys Gang, 29, 33, 41

Bowery Theatre, 24

Brace, Charles Loring, 14, 76

Broadway railroad syndicate, 35

Broadway Squad, 68–70, 125

Brooklyn, 67, 90; during the Draft

THE ARMIES OF THE STREETS *has been set in Times New Roman, which Stanley Morison designed expressly for* THE TIMES *of London in 1931.*

*Composition and printing by Heritage Printers, Inc.*

*Binding by The Delmar Companies*

*Design by Katie Bullard*